Photoshop Elements 11

JEFF CARLSON

Peachpit Press

Photoshop Elements 11: Visual QuickStart Guide
Jeff Carlson

Peachpit Press
1249 Eighth Street
Berkeley, CA 94710

Find us on the Web at: www.peachpit.com
To report errors, please send a note to errata@peachpit.com
Peachpit Press is a division of Pearson Education.

Project Editor: Susan Rimerman
Production Editor: Myrna Vladic
Copyeditor: Liz Welch
Indexer: Karin Arrigoni
Composition: Jeff Carlson
Cover Design: RHDG / Riezebos Holzbaur Design Group, Peachpit Press
Interior Design: Peachpit Press
Logo Design: MINE™ www.minesf.com

Notice of Rights

Notice of Liability

Trademarks

ISBN-13: 978-0-321-88515-9
ISBN-10: 0-321-88515-5

9 8 7 6 5 4 3 2 1

Printed and bound in the United States of America

Dedication:

For Bob

And always for Eliana, who waited.

Special Thanks to:

Susan Rimerman, Liz Welch, Karin Arrigoni, and Myrna Vladic made everything smooth in the editing, indexing, and production of this edition of the book. They jumped in when they were most needed and waited patiently when some sections took longer than I anticipated.

Thank you to Roman Skuratovskiy at Edelman, and Roma Dhall, Neha Tyagi, and Bob Gager at Adobe for their assistance in providing the software and information I needed.

The content in these pages also owes a great debt to Glenn Fleishman, Agen G. N. Schmitz, Jeff Tolbert, and Laurence Chen, who assisted with an earlier edition just before the birth of my daughter. Agen also pitched in this time around by capturing a bunch of screenshots on short notice.

I also want to thank Craig Hoeschen for providing great material to work with: the editions prior to version 5.

My gratitude also extends to Parie Hines, Cindy Dorsey, Steve Horn, Jill Thompson, Lynn Christenot, and Scott and Lisa Johnson for their permissions to use photos either of them or their adorable kids.

Lastly, I want to extend my appreciation and love to Kim and Ellie for making me a happy husband and father.

Contents at a Glance

Table of Contents

Introduction

Welcome to Photoshop Elements, Adobe's powerful, easy-to-use, image-editing software. Photoshop Elements gives hobbyists, professional photographers, and artists many of the same tools and features found in Adobe Photoshop (long the industry standard), but packaged in a more accessible, intuitive workspace.

Photoshop Elements' friendly user interface, combined with its bargain-basement price, has made it an instant hit with the new wave of amateur digital photographers lured by the recent proliferation of sophisticated, low-cost digital cameras.

Photoshop Elements makes it easy to retouch your digital photos; apply special effects, filters, and styles; prepare images for the Web; and even create wide-screen panoramas from a series of individual photos. And Photoshop Elements provides several features geared specifically to the beginning user. Of particular note are the Quick and Guided photo editing controls that make complex image corrections easy to apply.

In the next few pages, I'll cover some of Photoshop Elements' key features (both old and new) and share a few thoughts to help you get the most from this book. Then you can be on your way to mastering Photoshop Elements' simple, fun, and sophisticated image-editing tools.

What's New in Photoshop Elements 11

For most of its existence, Elements has been "Photoshop Light," a scaled-back version of Adobe's image-editing behemoth. Over time, Adobe has retooled Elements to be a powerful asset for digital photographers.

Photoshop Elements 11 continues Adobe's quest to make an image editing application that responds to people's real-world needs. With this revision, the company has dramatically overhauled the entire application. Over the years, Elements has taken the basic Photoshop structure and bolted features and interfaces onto its frame. Now, items are placed in more natural locations—beginners won't be intimidated by lots of floating palettes, for example (but experienced editors can bring them back).

After all, there's a lot of power in being able to apply adjustment layers and clipping masks and filters, but that isn't always helpful when your goal is to just improve the exposure in a too-dark photo—and you don't have the time to learn all the science behind the tools.

The Organizer is the Elements component that lets you manage your photo library—a library that, if yours is like mine, grows larger every year. To help you locate photos, the Organizer now includes an advanced search mode that lets you winnow results based on keywords, people, places, and events. The Map mode, which disappeared in Photoshop Elements 10 due to technical issues, is back as the Places view, and is much improved (and also now available on the Mac for the first time).

Adobe is also in the process of phasing out its Photoshop.com service, which no longer appears in the Organizer, in favor of Revel, a way to share photos among computers and mobile devices like the iPad and iPhone.

The Editor, the component of Elements where you do the actual editing, gains the new interface and new guided edits like a Vignette Edit and Tilt-Shift Edit. A ton of little details and performance improvements have been worked into the corners, too, such as operations that a previewed in real time (instead of requiring that you remember to select a Preview checkbox), Exposure and Vibrance adjustment controls in the Quick edit mode, and a way to run Photoshop actions without digging deep into your computer's folder structure, as in the past.

Overall, Photoshop Elements has received not only a refreshed interface geared toward helping all levels of users, but also benefited from quite a bit of internal work that should make photo organizing and editing smoother and faster.

How to Use This Book

This Visual QuickStart Guide, like others in the series, is a task-based reference. Each chapter focuses on a specific area of the application and presents it in a series of concise, illustrated steps. I encourage you to follow along using your own images. I've also made 20 sample images available for download at **peachpit.com/elements11vqs**. After you complete the process for registering your book, look for the "Access Bonus Content" text next to the book title in the Registered Products tab. I believe the best way to learn is by doing, and this Visual QuickStart Guide is the perfect vehicle for that style of learning.

This book is meant to be a reference work, and although it's not expected that you'll read through it in sequence from front to back, I've made an attempt to order the chapters in a logical fashion.

The first chapter speeds through five steps to import, edit, and share your digital photos. The next chapter takes you on a tour of the work area to make sure we're all on the same page. From there you dive into importing pictures and managing your photo library using the Organizer. Then you explore cropping and straightening, making selections, working with layers, adjusting lighting and color, retouching and correcting images, applying effects, painting, and adding text. Next, you move along to learn a variety of techniques for saving, printing, and sharing images, including special formatting options for distributing images over the Web.

This book is suitable for the beginner just starting in digital photography and image creation, as well as hobbyists, photo enthusiasts, intermediate-level photographers, illustrators, and designers.

Sharing Space with Windows and Mac OS X

Photoshop Elements is almost exactly the same on Windows as it is under Mac OS X, which is why this book covers both platforms. In the few places where a feature is found in one environment but not the other, or if the steps are different for each, I make it clear which version is being discussed.

You'll also see that the screenshots are a mix of Windows and Mac—but despite obvious cosmetic differences such as title bars and menu bars, everything pretty much tracks the same within the user interface itself.

I also frequently mention keyboard shortcuts, which are faster methods of accessing commands compared to choosing items from menus. Keyboard shortcuts are great time-savers and prevent you from having to constantly refocus your energy and attention as you jump from image window to menu bar and back again.

When this book introduces a command, the keyboard shortcut is frequently also listed, with the Windows version appearing first and the Mac version trailing after a forward-slash. For example, the keyboard shortcut for the Copy command is displayed as "Ctrl+C/Command-C."

You'll find a complete list of Photoshop Elements' keyboard shortcuts in the appendices.

Editing Photos in 5 Easy Steps

You're going to encounter a lot of powerful, in-depth information about how to use Photoshop Elements in this book's 400-plus pages. But who wants to sit and devour the whole thing while a memory card full of photos is waiting to be explored?

If you're anxious to get started with Elements, the steps outlined in this short chapter will improve nearly all of your digital photos. Then, when you're ready to fiddle with settings sliders and really take advantage of what Elements has to offer, continue exploring the rest of the book.

In This Chapter

1. Import and Open Images

Photoshop Elements is really made up of two programs that work together—the Organizer and the Editor—and as a result, you can open a photo for editing in two ways. The Organizer stores your entire photo library and lets you apply metadata such as keyword tags. When you want to make adjustments to an image, you send it to the Editor. If you want to edit a photo independently of the Organizer, you can open the file directly from within the Editor.

Make sure your camera is connected to your computer, or the camera's memory card is plugged into a card reader.

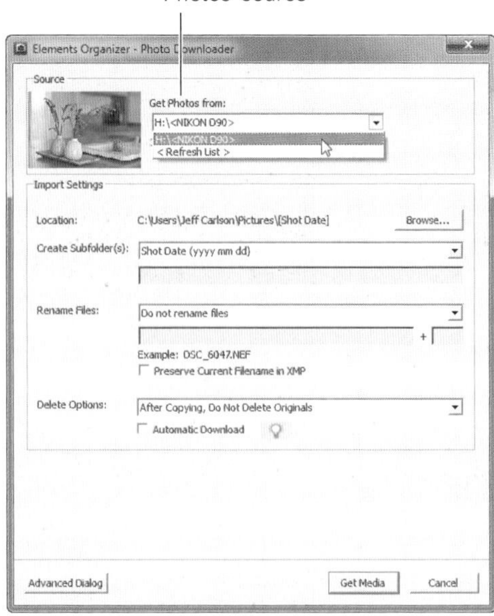

A Use the Photo Downloader to import pictures into the Elements Organizer.

To import into the Organizer:

1. Open Photoshop Elements and, in the Welcome screen, click the Organize button to open the Organizer.
2. Click the Import button at the top left of the window and choose From Camera or Card Reader (or press Ctrl+G/Command-G). The Photo Downloader application launches.
3. Choose your camera or memory card from the Get Photos from drop-down menu (if it's not already selected) **A**.
4. Click the Get Media button to download the selected images to your computer.
5. After the images have been imported, click the one you want to edit and then open it in the Editor by right-clicking and choosing Edit with Photoshop Elements Editor; or, in the task bar, click the Editor button **B**.

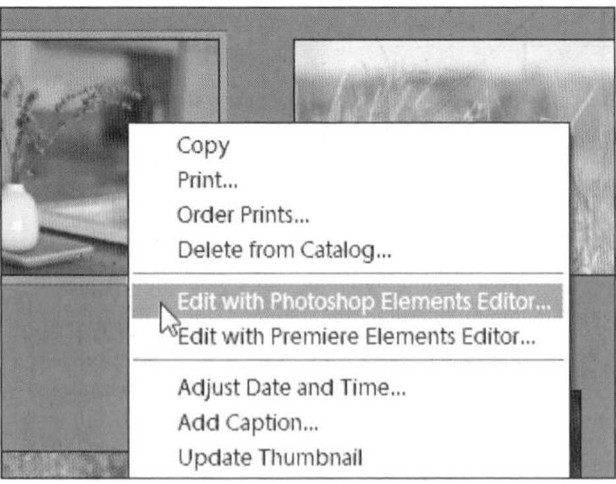

B Open the image in the Editor using the contextual menu (top) or the task bar (bottom).

TIP **See Chapter 3 for details on importing photos into the Organizer.**

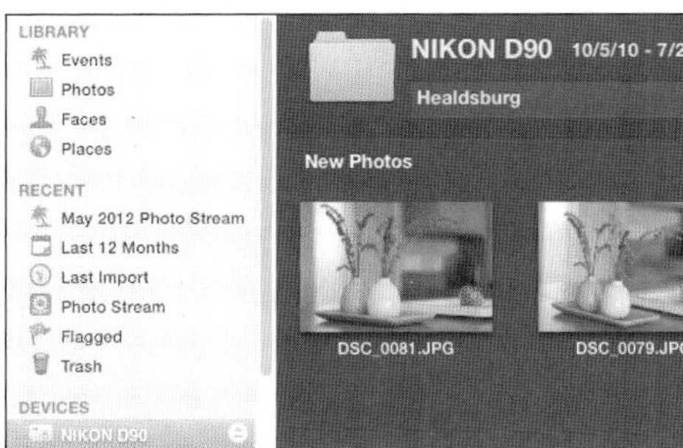

C Select a device and type an Event Name in iPhoto on the Mac.

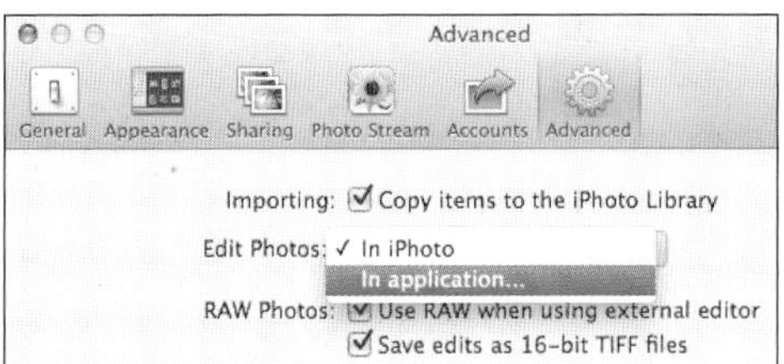

D iPhoto can hand off editing duties to an external application like Elements.

E Choose to edit in Elements instead of using iPhoto's editing tools.

To open a photo directly in the Editor:

1. Open Photoshop Elements and, in the Welcome screen, click the Edit button to open the Editor.
2. Choose File > Open.
3. In the Open dialog, navigate to the image file you wish to edit and select it.
4. Click the Open button to open the file.

To import into iPhoto (Mac):

1. If you use iPhoto on the Mac to organize your photo library, launch iPhoto.
2. Click the camera or memory card name in the sidebar, listed under Devices.
3. Type a name in the Event Name field **C**; one way iPhoto organizes the library is by grouping images into Events based on when the photos were imported.
4. Click the Import All button, or select the photos you want and click the Import Selected button.
5. When the import process is finished, click the Keep Photos button in the dialog that asks if you wish to remove or keep the pictures you just imported.
6. To be able to edit photos in Elements instead of using iPhoto's editing tools, you need to do this step just once: Go to iPhoto > Preferences, click the Advanced button, and in the drop-down menu for Edit Photos, choose In application **D**. Locate Elements on your disk and click Open.
7. Select a photo to edit and then either click the Edit button or right-click and choose Edit in External Editor **E**.

TIP Photos shot in raw format first open in Adobe Camera Raw before reaching the Editor. See Chapter 10 to learn more about working with raw photos.

2. Crop and Rotate

The composition of a photo is often just as important as what appears within the frame. If you're not happy with the image's original framing, or you want to excise distracting elements like tree branches from the edges, recompose the shot using the Crop tool.

Another common correction is to adjust a photo's rotation. Unless you set up the shot on a sturdy tripod, it's not uncommon to get shots that are slightly tilted. Don't worry, Elements offers easy fixes.

To crop a photo:

1. With the image open in the Editor, choose the Crop tool **A** (or press the C key).
2. Click and drag across the image to define a selection representing the boundaries of the visible area **B**. Don't worry about being precise at first.
3. Instead of drawing a freeform rectangle, you can constrain the selection to match preset aspect ratios, such as common photo sizes or the photo's original dimensions. Choose an option from the Aspect Ratio drop-down menu in the Tool Options bar **C**.
4. Click the Commit button **D** or press Enter or Return to apply the crop.

TIP You can also enter specific sizes for the width and height of the crop, as well as the image's pixel resolution. See Chapter 4 to learn more.

A The Crop tool

B Drag to define the image's new dimensions after cropping.

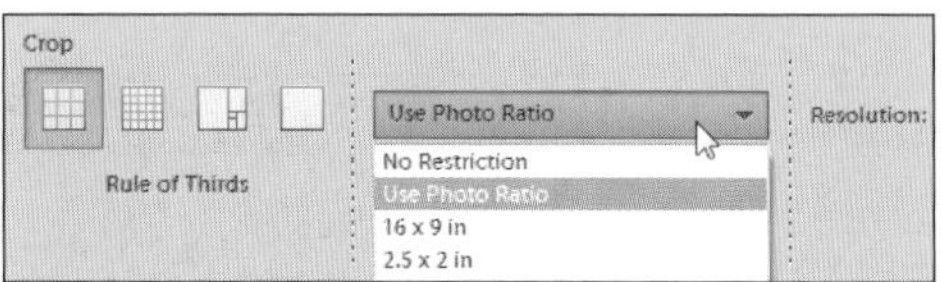

C Set a crop ratio using the controls in the Tool Options bar.

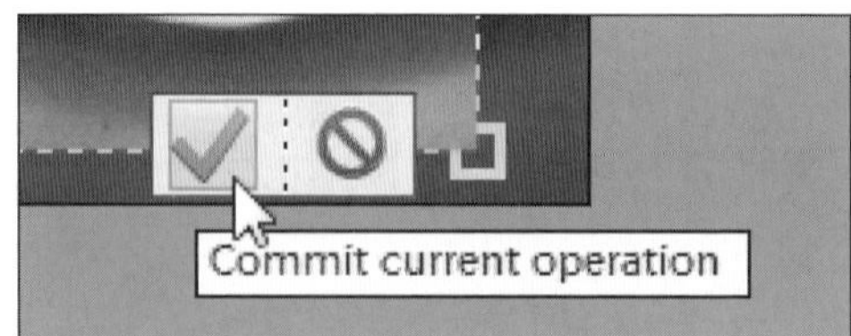

D The Commit button appears at the bottom of the crop area.

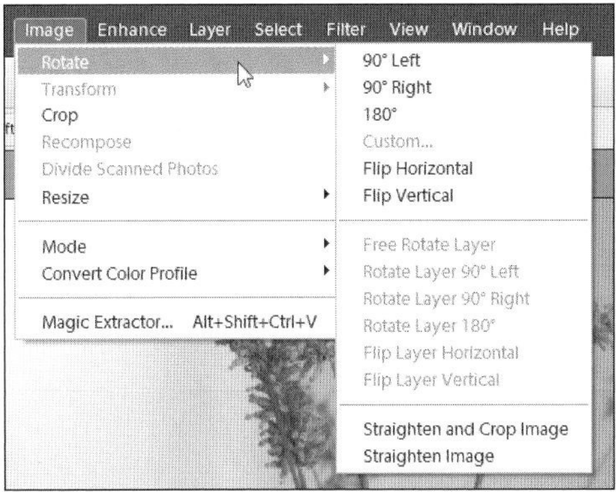

E Elements' rotation options

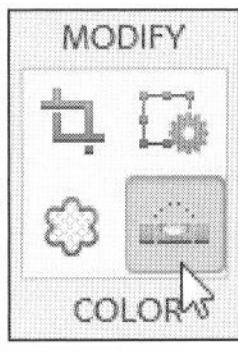

F The Straighten tool

G Drag as if you're defining a "horizon line."

To rotate a photo:

In the Quick Edit mode, click the Rotate button on the task bar to turn the entire image counter-clockwise in 90-degree increments. Click and hold the tool to reveal a clockwise tool.

In the Expert edit mode, choose Image > Rotate and choose from the following options E.

- Choose one of the first three items in the list to turn the entire image in 90-degree increments, such as when you shot a photo in portrait (tall) orientation but the image file was imported with a landscape (wide) orientation.
- To rotate just the active layer, choose one of the layer options further down the menu.

To straighten a photo:

There are a few ways to nudge the rotation and straighten an image, but the easiest is to use the Straighten tool:

1. Click the Straighten tool in the Tools panel F.
2. In the Tool Options bar, choose how the straightened image will appear. The default is Grow or Shrink Canvas to Fit, but I prefer to use Remove Background for a cleaner result.
3. Drag a horizontal line that compensates for the amount the picture is rotated. This approach is easier if you have a well-defined horizon line, but in this example, I'm drawing the line perpendicular to the vertical wall corners in the background G. The image straightens.

TIP The Straighten and Crop and Straighten options in the Image > Rotate menu direct Elements to do the straightening for you. My experience with this command is mixed, so I prefer to do the straightening myself.

TIP If you're cropping the image, save time and straighten it before you apply the crop. Drag just outside a corner of the selection to rotate the image and then commit the change.

3. Adjust Lighting and Color

Almost every photo needs a little lighting and color adjustment, whether it's lightening shadows or punching up the saturation slightly to make colors pop. Elements is awash in color and lighting adjustment choices, but this is where I start.

Quick Fixes

One of the appeals of Photoshop Elements is its Quick Fix adjustments. You don't need to be a digital imaging expert—you may just want to correct a few shots with the least amount of fuss. See Chapter 5 for more information.

To apply quick fixes:

1. Open a photo in the Editor.
2. Click the Quick heading **A** to reveal the Quick Edit options (if it's not already selected).
3. Click an attribute (such as Smart Fix) and drag the slider to make the adjustment. Or, click a preset from the grid; positioning your mouse pointer over a thumbnail previews the change, and clicking it applies the adjustment **B**.

   You can also drag within a preset in the grid to make incremental adjustments.
4. If you don't like the effect, click the thumbnail that contains the reset icon to return to the original state.

A The Quick Fix edits handle many common corrections.

Reset to original

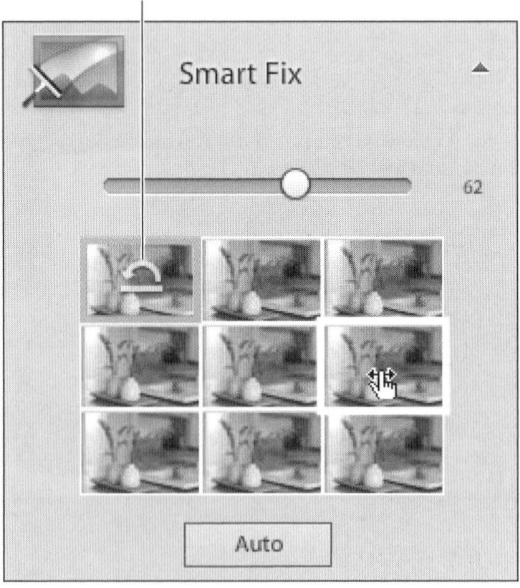

B Reveal a grid of settings presets and see how they affect the image.

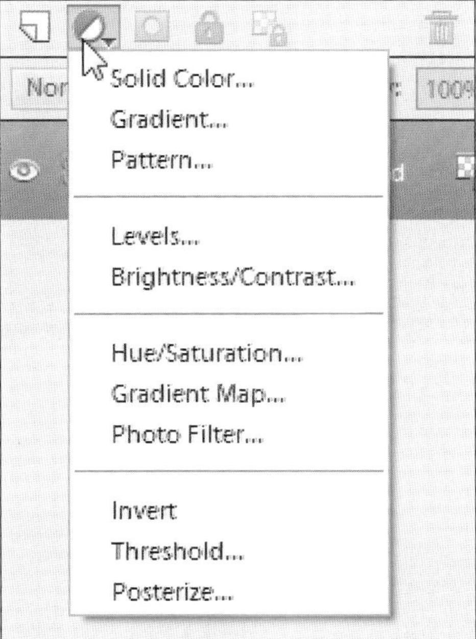

C Add an adjustment layer to make edits that don't interfere with the image's original pixels.

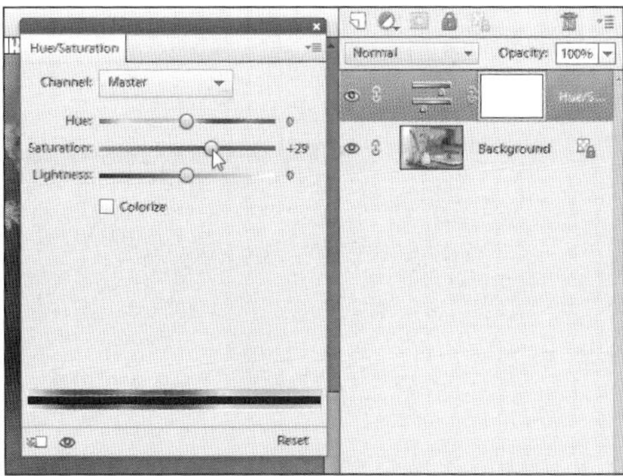

D The Adjustments panel includes settings specific to the adjustment layer you're on.

Manual Adjustments

If you'd rather handle the details yourself, turn to manual corrections. I prefer to use adjustment layers in the Expert environment, which let you apply corrections without changing any of the original pixels in your image. Other controls, such as those found in the Enhance menu, are less flexible.

To apply an adjustment layer:

1. Click the Expert button to switch to that editor.
2. Click the Layers button in the task bar to reveal the Layers panel.
3. In the Layers panel, click the Create New Fill or Adjustment Layer button **C** and choose one of the options. A new adjustment layer is created, and a panel containing options appears.
4. Manipulate the controls in the panel to alter the look of the image **D**.

For example, to increase the saturation of a flat image, add a Hue/Saturation adjustment layer and, in the Hue/Saturation panel, increase the value of the Saturation slider.

TIP Chapter 8 contains much more information about adjusting lighting and color.

4. Apply Corrections

In many cases, you'll probably be finished editing a photo after the previous step. Sometimes, though, you'll want to perform a little correction to remove dust spots, crumbs, or other distracting blemishes. The Spot Healing Brush smartly fixes areas like that without any fuss.

Of course, Elements includes an arsenal of correcting tools, enabling you to not only repair small areas but to also take the best parts of several photos and merge them together, or even remove people or objects from a scene entirely. Chapter 9 covers all of those options.

To repair areas using the Spot Healing Brush:

1. In either the Quick or Expert edit environment, choose the Spot Healing Brush from the Tools panel, or press J.
2. In the Tool Options bar, specify a brush size for the tool **A** that roughly matches the area you want to repair.
3. Click once on the area to apply the brush's healing properties **B**.
4. If the area wasn't repaired to your satisfaction, try clicking it one more time. Elements examines nearby pixels to determine how best to fill the area you're fixing, and sometimes the first pass may not be exactly what you're looking for.

TIP For finer detail work and more control, you may want to break out the Stamp tool for making repairs. See Chapter 9.

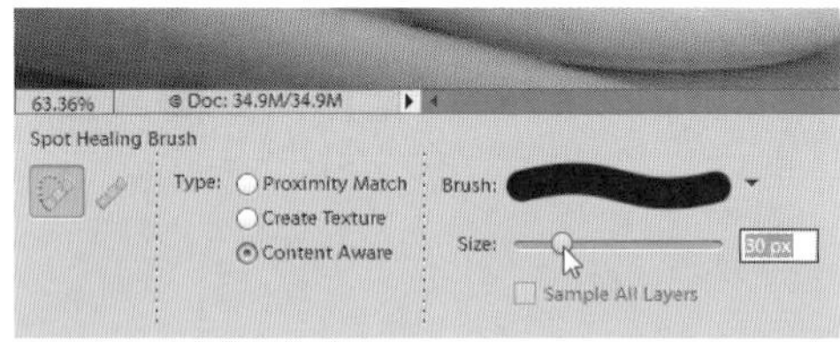

A Adjust the Size slider of the Spot Healing Brush to define how large an area to correct.

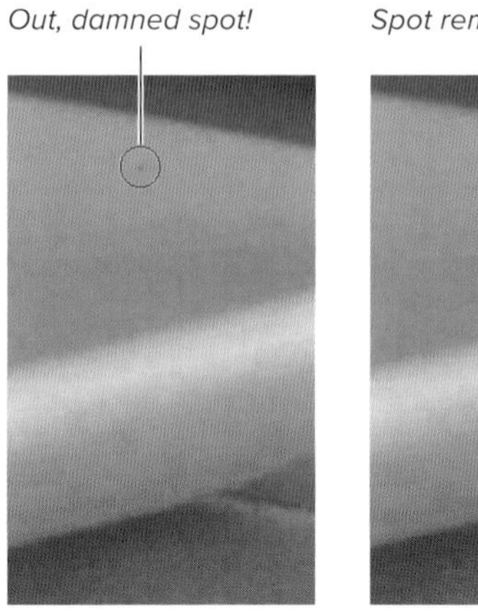

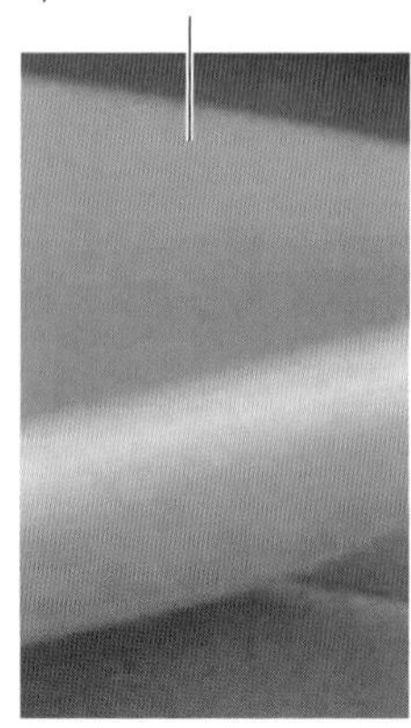

B The Spot Healing Brush really does fix blemishes with one click.

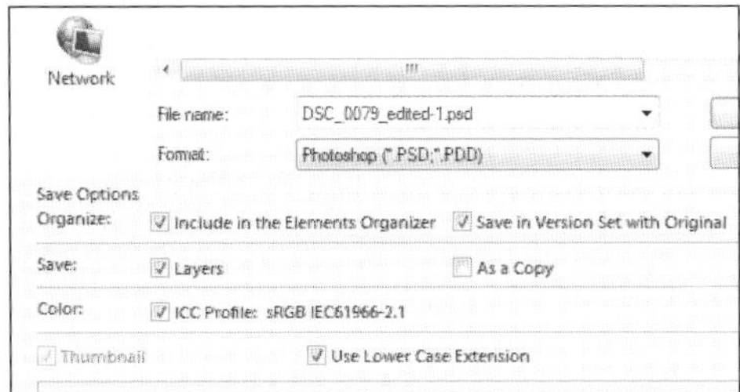

Ⓐ Save the file so you can edit it later.

5. Save the Photo

Now the photo looks more like what you had in mind when you were shooting it. When you're finished making adjustments, save the image back to the Organizer or to a location on your hard disk.

To save the photo:

1. Choose File > Save or press Ctrl+S/Command-S. Or, choose File > Save As (Ctrl+Shift+S/Command-Shift-S) to save a new copy of the file.
2. In the Save dialog that appears, select a location on your hard disk (if you want to move it to a new location) Ⓐ.
3. Type a name for the file in the File name field (or the Save As field, on the Mac).
4. Choose a file format from the Format drop-down menu; use the native Photoshop format (PSD) to retain any layers you applied.
5. Enable the Include in the Elements Organizer checkbox to make the edited file appear in the Organizer.

   To group the edited version with the original, mark the Save in Version Set with Original box.
6. Click the Save button.

TIP See Chapter 15 for more details on saving files, including other file formats.

TIP To share the photo to an online photo service, as a slideshow, or via email, see Chapter 16.

2

The Basics

Before you start really working in Photoshop Elements, it's good to take a look around the work area to familiarize yourself with the program's tools and menus.

If you're new to the software, this chapter will orient you to the work area, which includes the document window, where you'll view your images, along with many of the tools, menus, and panels you'll use as you get better acquainted with the program.

If you're upgrading from an earlier version of Photoshop Elements, take a spin to get comfortable with Adobe's redesign of your favorite photo editor.

In This Chapter

Understanding the Work Area

The Photoshop Elements work area is designed like a well-organized workbench, making it easy to find and use menus, panels, and tools.

The Welcome screen

When you first start Photoshop Elements, the Welcome screen automatically appears. Click Organizer to open the Adobe Elements 11 Organizer application, or click Photo Editor to open the Adobe Photoshop Elements Editor application. (You can bypass the Welcome screen by opening either of those apps by themselves.)

The Organizer and the Editor

Photoshop Elements is made up of two separate components: the Organizer and the Editor, which can be (and often are) open simultaneously. The conventions in this chapter primarily apply to the Editor; the Organizer's unique interface items are covered in Chapter 3.

TIP Click the Settings button (the gear icon) at the upper-right corner of the Welcome screen to set how Elements starts up Ⓐ.

Menus, panels, and tools

The **menu bar** offers drop-down menus for performing common tasks, editing images, and organizing your work area. Each menu is organized by topic Ⓑ.

The **Tool Options bar**, running above the work area, provides unique settings and options for each tool in the Tools panel. For instance, when you're using the Marquee selection tool, you can choose to add to or subtract from the current selection Ⓒ.

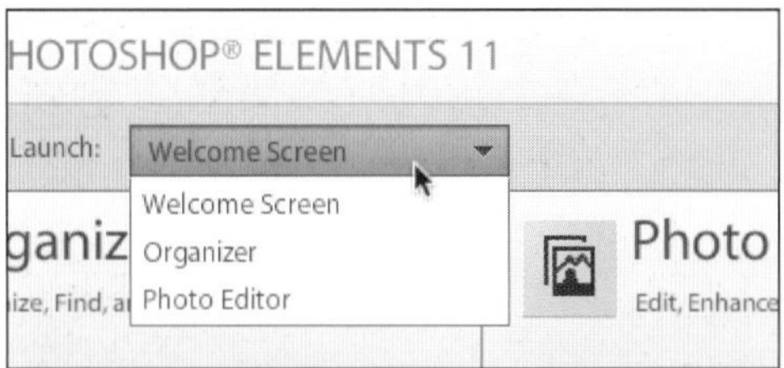

Ⓐ Choose which parts of Photoshop Elements should launch at startup.

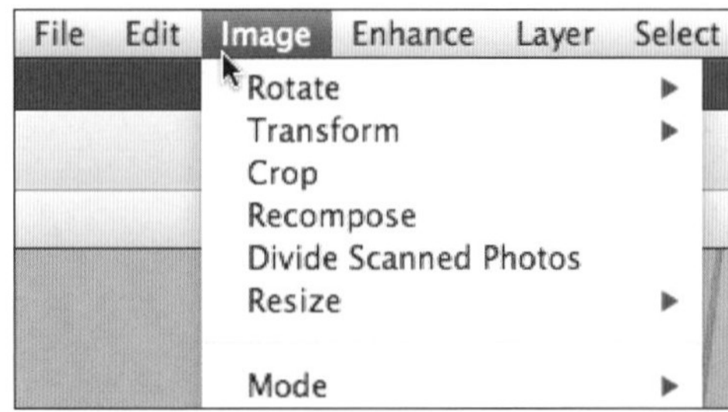

Ⓑ The menu bar offers myriad drop-down menus, with commands you choose to help perform tasks.

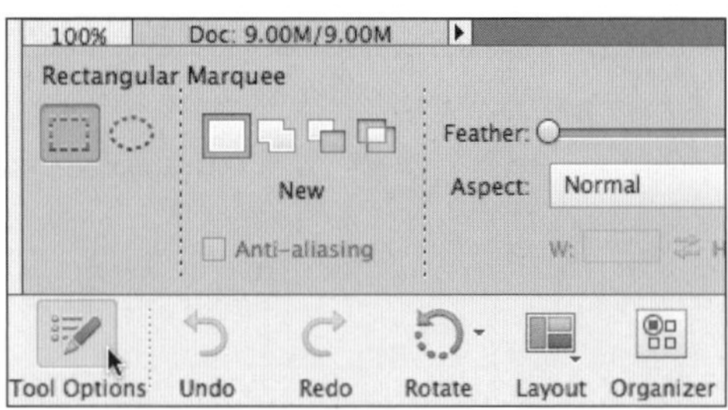

Ⓒ The Tool Options bar changes its display depending on the tool you select in the Tools panel.

The Editor and the Mac App Store

If you purchase the Photoshop Elements Editor application from Apple's Mac App Store on your Mac, the Organizer is not included in the download. Adobe has made only the Editor available. If you want to use the Organizer, you'll need to buy Photoshop Elements as a disc or as a download from Adobe.

D The Photo Bin is a holding area where you can access all of your open images.

E The Panel Bin holds controls for the Quick (shown here) and Guided edit modes, and items such as layers and effects in the Expert mode.

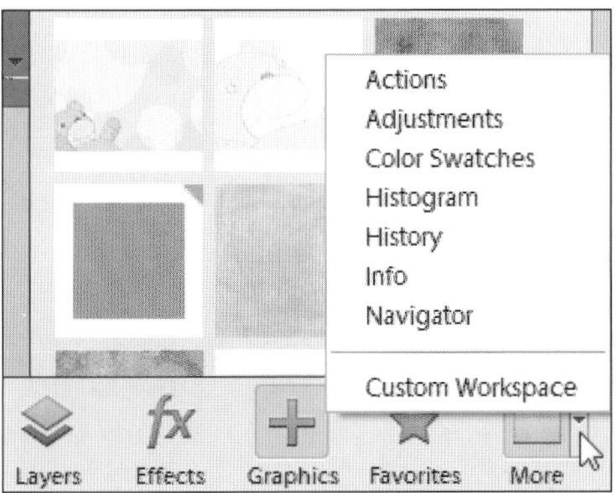

F Reveal other panels in the Expert edit mode by clicking the drop-down portion of the More button.

The **Photo Bin**, located at the bottom of the work area, serves as a convenient holding area for all of your open images D. In addition to providing a visual reference for any open image files, the bin allows you to perform several basic editing functions. Click to select any photo thumbnail in the Project Bin, and right-click to display a pop-up menu. From the thumbnail menu you can get file information, minimize or close the file, duplicate it, and rotate it in 90-degree increments.

The **Panel Bin** (also referred to as the **Task Pane** in the Organizer) groups common tasks and controls into the right edge of the window E. Clicking a heading displays the panels for editing, creating, and sharing. To temporarily hide this area and make more room for working, click the Hide Panel button (Quick edit mode) or choose Window > Panel Bin.

When you're in the Expert edit interface, the Panel Bin contains the Layers, Effects, Graphics, and Favorites panels. The More button reveals a host of other panels that float outside the Panel Bin F.

TIP The Panel Bin's default arrangement is known as the Basic workspace, but you can customize it (which makes it act a bit more like earlier versions of Photoshop Elements). From the More drop-down menu, choose Custom Workspace. Instead of buttons, the four main panels are arranged as tabs, which you can manipulate in several ways. See "Working with Panels," three pages ahead.

Selecting Tools

The **Tools** panel contains all the tools you need for editing and creating your images. You can use them to make selections, paint, draw, and easily perform sophisticated photo retouching operations. To view information about a tool, rest the pointer over it until a tool tip appears showing the name and keyboard shortcut (if any) for that tool.

To use a tool, first select it from the Tools panel **A**. Some tools hide additional tools.

To select a hidden tool:

Do one of the following:

- Hold Alt/Option and click any tool that displays a small triangle in the corner of the tool icon. The next tool is enabled.
- With a tool selected, go to the Tool Options bar and click an alternate **B**.

TIP For easier access to tools, just use keyboard shortcuts. You'll find them in tool tips and in the online help. For example, press T on your keyboard to activate the Type tool. (Note that when you press a letter to select a tool with a hidden tool group, Elements selects the tool from the group that was used most recently.)

TIP To cycle through hidden tools, repeatedly press the tool's shortcut key.

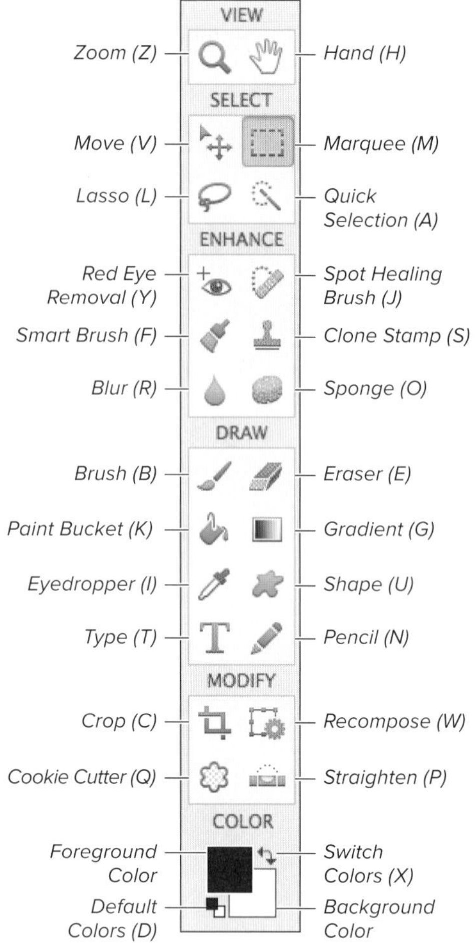

A The Tools panel contains the tools to edit your images.

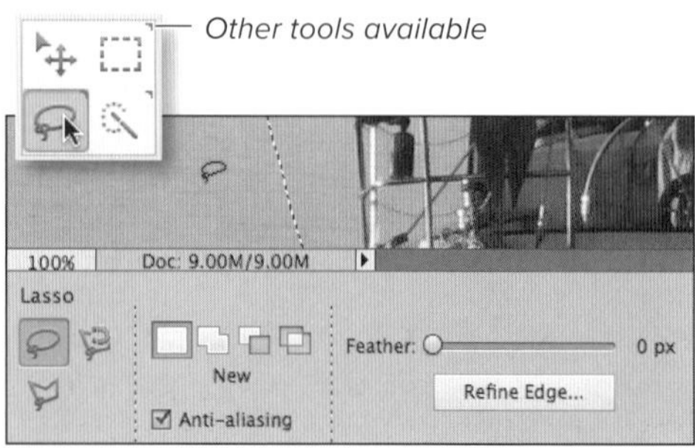

B Hidden tools, indicated by a triangle in the Tools panel, are available in the Tool Options bar.

Windows

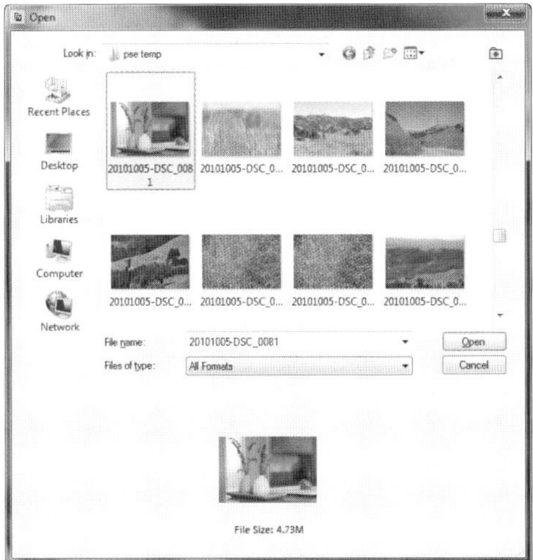

Mac

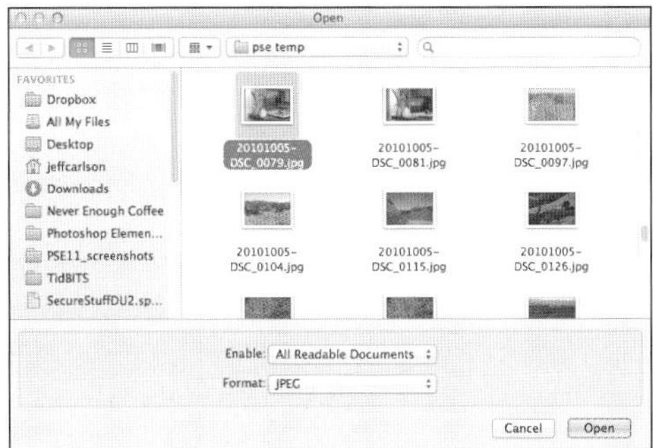

A The Open dialog displays all files that match formats Elements understands.

TIP If several files are open, you can close them all at once by choosing Close All from the File menu or by pressing Ctrl+Alt+W/ Command-Option-W.

Opening and Closing Files

It's easy to open photos, depending on whether you're working in the Organizer or the Editor. (If you need to import photos into the Organizer, see Chapter 3.)

To edit a file from the Organizer:

- Select a thumbnail and choose Edit > Edit with Photoshop Elements Editor; the image opens in the Editor. You can also right-click an image and choose the same item from the contextual menu, or press Ctrl+I/Command-I.
- With a thumbnail selected, click the Editor button in the task bar at the bottom of the screen.

To open a file in the Editor:

1. To find and open a file, choose Open from the File menu, click the Open button above the Tools panel, or press Ctrl+O/Command-O. The Open dialog appears **A**.
2. Browse to the folder that contains your images.
3. To open the file you want, do one of the following:
   - Double-click the file.
   - Select the file and click the Open button.

   The image opens in its own document window.

To close a file in the Editor:

- Click the close button on the title bar for the active window.
- From the File menu, choose Close, or press Ctrl+W/Command-W.

Working with Panels

The Editor is designed so it doesn't overwhelm you with options. The Quick and Guided edit modes feature just the one Panel Bin that includes editing tools. The Expert edit mode, as you would expect, offers many more options, including the ability to arrange panels outside the bin.

The following options apply to the Expert edit mode. As mentioned a few pages back, you can also switch to the Custom Workspace, which groups panels in the Panel Bin as a group of tabs.

To display a panel:

Do one of the following:

- Click the respective button in the lower-right corner to view the Layers, Effects, Graphics, or Favorites panel.
- Click the More button to display a floating tab group that contains most of the other panels **A**. (The Adjustments panel is a little snooty and prefers to appear in its own window.)
- From the Window menu, choose any panel to display it.

To switch to the Custom Workspace:

Click the drop-down menu attached to the More button and choose Custom Workspace. The panels appear as tabs at the top of the Panel Bin **B**.

To move a panel into its own window:

1. Click the tab of the panel that you want to liberate.
2. Drag the tab until the panel is in the desired location in your work area **C**. This action also works for tabs in the Panel Bin under the Custom Workspace.

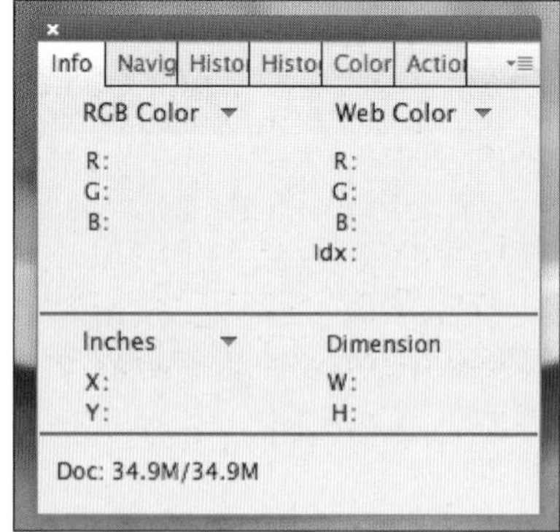

A A floating tab group appears when you click the More button.

Basic Workspace

Custom Workspace

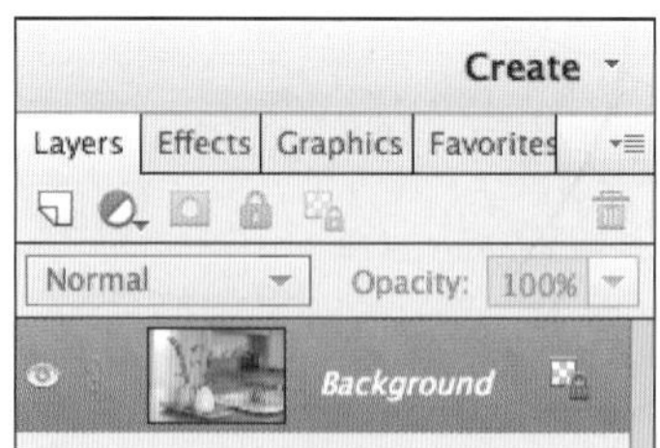

B When the Custom Workspace is enabled, panels appear as tabs in the Panel Bin.

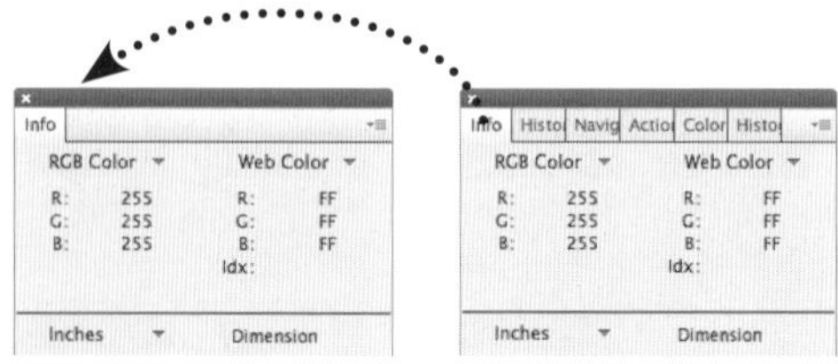

C To move a panel into its own window, drag the tab outside the group.

Close box (Mac) *Panel options menu*

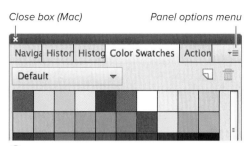

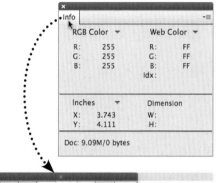

Ⓓ The panel options menu includes more actions. To close a panel, click the close icon on the title bar (at left on the Mac, at right in Windows).

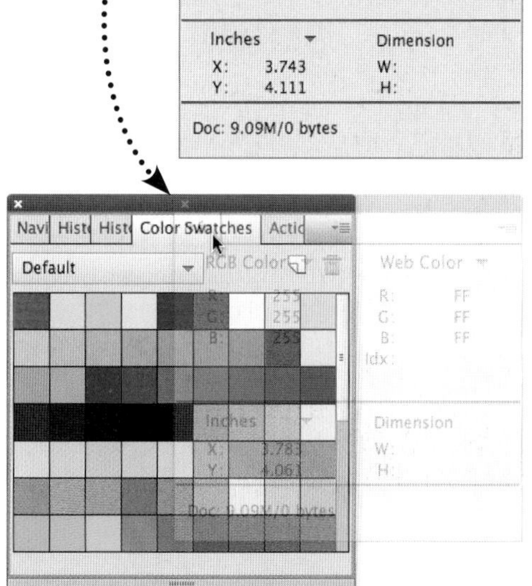

Ⓔ Drag a panel tab into another tab group to return it to the group, or to create a new tab group.

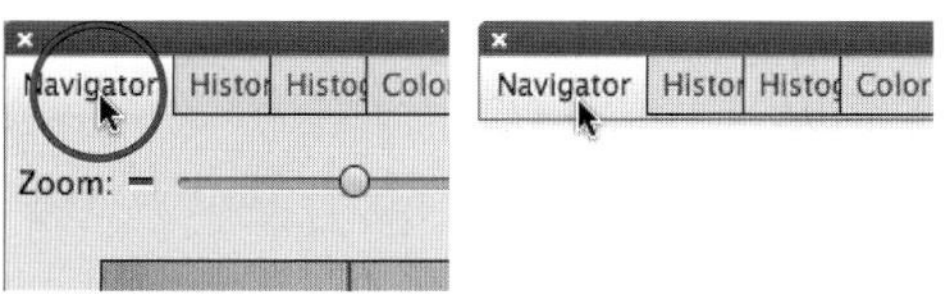

Ⓕ Double-click the panel tab to collapse a panel or panel group.

To use panel options menus:

Click the panel options menu in the upper-right corner of any panel to access settings specific to the panel Ⓓ.

To close a panel:

Do one of the following:

- From the Window menu, choose any open panel; open panels are indicated by a check mark.
- If the panel is open in your work area (outside the Panel Bin), click the close box on the panel title bar. In Windows, it's on the right side; on the Mac, it's on the left side.

To return a panel to a tab group:

Click the panel tab and drag the panel back into the Panel Bin. A horizontal blue line appears in the bin to indicate where the panel will end up when you drop it Ⓔ.

You can also use this technique to create your own custom tab groups

To collapse panels to titles:

Double-click the panel tab or title bar Ⓕ. Double-click again to reveal the panel.

TIP If you choose to close a single panel residing in a panel group, the entire panel group will close. However, making one panel in the group visible using the Window menu makes the entire group visible again.

To dock panels:

Drag any panel's tab to the bottom of any panel outside the Panel Bin. Drag the panel by its title bar to successfully dock it to the top or bottom of another panel; a horizontal blue line indicates a connection **G**.

To undock a panel, click on one panel's tab and drag it away from the other panel.

To return panels to their default positions:

Click the Reset Panels button at the top of the Photoshop Elements window; or, from the Window menu, choose Reset Panels.

To hide the Panel Bin entirely:

From the Window menu, choose Panel Bin (so its checkbox goes away) to gain the most screen space for your image.

To do the same thing in the Organizer, choose Window > Hide Task Pane.

TIP Pay attention to the blue line that appears when adding panels to the Panel Bin. A horizontal line indicates that the panel will be stacked with the rest. An outline means the panel will be added to a panel group.

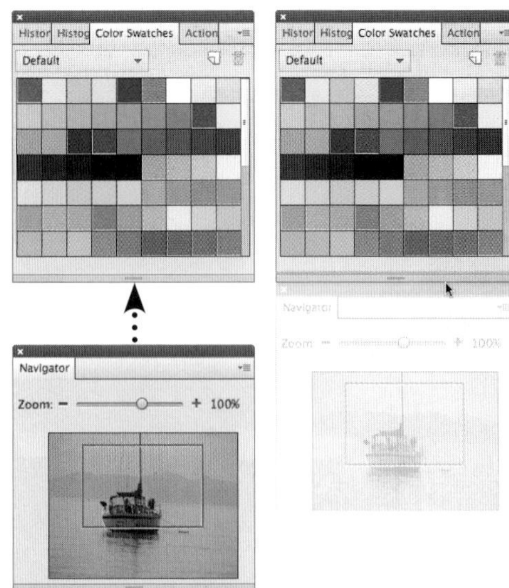

G Docking one panel below another can help remove clutter in your work area.

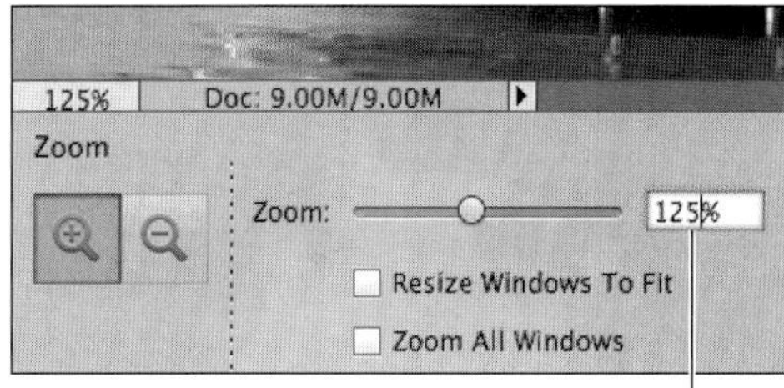

A With the Zoom tool selected, adjust the magnification level using the Tool Options bar.

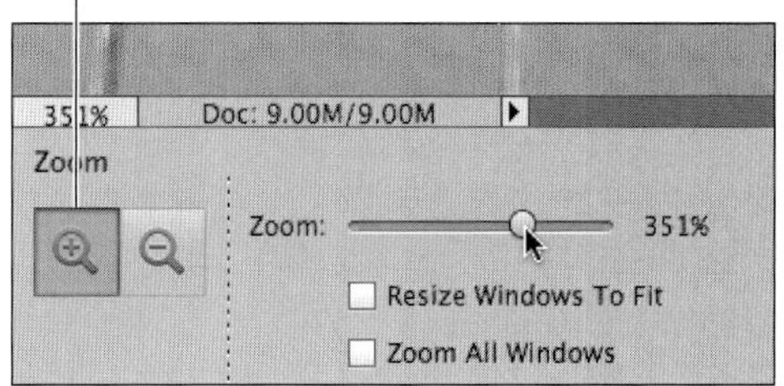

B To zoom in on an image, check that the Zoom In button is selected in the Tool Options bar.

Using the Zoom Tool

You'll never want to view your images at just one magnification level—editing out dust, for example, requires a close-up view. The Zoom tool magnifies and reduces your view, which you can control using a variety of methods.

The current level of magnification is shown in the document status bar at the lower-left corner, and, when the Zoom tool is selected, in the Tool Options bar. You can adjust the magnification either with the Zoom slider or by entering a value in the Zoom text field **A**.

To zoom in:

1. In the Tools panel, select the Zoom tool, or press Z on the keyboard. The pointer changes to a magnifying glass when you move it into the document window.
2. Be sure that a plus sign appears in the center of the magnifying glass. If you see a minus sign (–), click the Zoom In button in the Tool Options bar **B**.
3. Click the area of the image you want to magnify.

   With a starting magnification of 100 percent, each click with the Zoom In tool increases the magnification in 100 percent increments up to 800 percent. From there, the magnification levels jump to 1200 percent, then 1600 percent, and finally to 3200 percent!

TIP If you turned on the "Allow Floating Documents in Expert Mode" setting in the Elements preferences, you can automatically resize the document window to fit the image when zooming in or out (see "Arranging Windows," later in the chapter). With the Zoom tool selected, click the Resize Windows to Fit checkbox in the Tool Options bar. To maintain a constant window size, deselect the option.

To zoom out:

1. In the Tools panel, select the Zoom tool, or press Z on the keyboard.
2. Click the Zoom Out button in the Tool Options bar, and then click in the area of the image that you want to zoom out from.

   With a starting magnification of 100 percent, each click with the Zoom Out tool reduces the magnification as follows: 66.7 percent; 50 percent; 33.3 percent; 25 percent; 16.7 percent; and so on, down to 1 percent.

To zoom in on a specific area:

1. In the Tools panel, select the Zoom tool; if necessary, click the Zoom In button in the Tool Options bar to display the Zoom tool with a plus sign.
2. Drag over the area of the image that you want to zoom in on.

   A selection marquee appears around the selected area C. When you release the mouse button, the selected area is magnified and centered in the image window.
3. To move the view to a different area of the image, hold the spacebar until the hand pointer appears. Then drag to reveal the area you want to see. For more information on navigating through the document window, see "Moving Around in an Image" two pages ahead.

TIP You can also change the magnification level from the zoom-percentage text field in the lower-left corner of the document window. Double-click the text field to select the zoom value, and then type in the new value.

C Drag with the Zoom tool to zoom in on a specific area of an image.

D Clicking the 1:1 button in the Tool Options bar returns the image view to 100 percent.

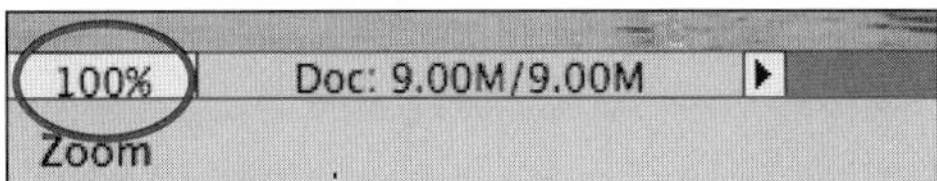

E Entering 100 in the status bar also changes the image view to 100 percent.

To display an image at 100 percent:

To display an image at 100 percent (also referred to as displaying actual pixels), do one of the following:

- In the Tools panel, double-click the Zoom tool.
- In the Tools panel, select either the Zoom or Hand tool, and then click the 1:1 button in the Tool Options bar **D**.
- From the View menu, choose Actual Pixels, or press Ctrl+Alt+0/Command-Option-0 (that's a zero, not an O). I use this method more than any other zoom technique.
- Enter **100** in the Zoom text field in the Tool Options bar, and then press Enter.
- Enter **100** in the status bar at the bottom of the document window, and then press Enter **E**.

TIP With any other tool selected in the toolbar, you can toggle to the Zoom tool. Hold down Ctrl+spacebar/Command-spacebar to zoom in or Alt+spacebar to zoom out.

TIP To change the magnification of the entire image, press Ctrl++/Command-+ (Ctrl or Command and the plus sign) to zoom in or Ctrl+–/Command-– (Ctrl or Command and the minus sign) to zoom out.

TIP Toggle the Zoom tool between zoom in and zoom out by holding down the Alt/Option key before you click.

TIP You can automatically resize the document window to fit the image (as much as possible) when zooming in or out. With the Zoom tool selected, click the Resize Windows to Fit checkbox in the Tool Options bar. To maintain a constant window size, deselect the Resize Windows to Fit option.

Moving Around in an Image

When working in Photoshop Elements, you'll often want to move your image to make a different area visible in the document window. This can happen when you're zoomed in on one part of an image or when an image is just too large to be completely visible within the document window.

To view a different area of an image:

Do one of the following:

- From the Tools panel, select the Hand tool and drag to move the image around in the document window **A**.
- Use the scroll arrows at the bottom and right side of the document window to scroll to the left or right and up or down. You can also drag the scroll bars to adjust the view.

To change the view using the Navigator panel:

1. Choose Window > Navigator to open the Navigator panel.
2. Drag the view box in the image thumbnail **B**.

   The view in the document window changes accordingly.

TIP With any other tool selected in the toolbar, press the spacebar to give you temporary access to the Hand tool.

TIP Drag the slider in the Navigator panel to adjust the magnification level in the document window.

Drag with the Hand tool...

...to move the image.

A To view a different area of the same image, drag with the Hand tool.

B You can also use the Navigator panel to view a different area of the same image.

Ⓐ Open documents occupy the main workspace and are only visible one at a time. Click a tab to bring a document to the front.

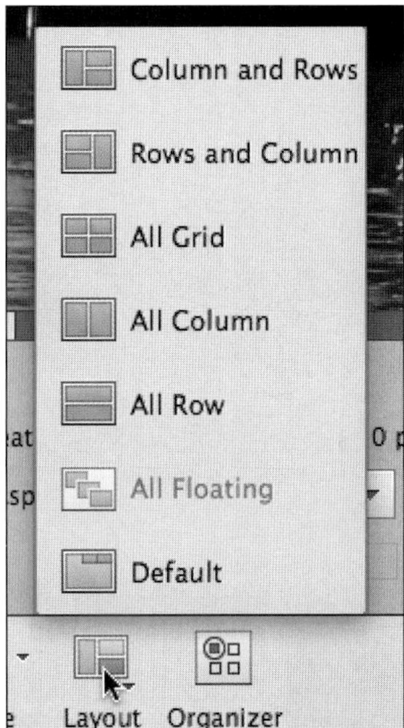

Ⓑ Click the Arrange Documents button to set how multiple files appear in the Editor.

Arranging Windows

Photoshop Elements takes a different approach to arranging open file windows than many applications. Instead of windows floating on top of each other, they occupy the entire work area, with tabs that indicate open files Ⓐ.

If you prefer overlapping windows, a preference enables them to float like traditional windows in Expert edit mode.

To arrange multiple windows:

1. Click the Layout button in the task bar.
2. From the menu that appears, click a preset layout icon Ⓑ.

To enable floating windows:

Go to Edit > Preferences > General and enable the option titled Allow Floating Documents in Expert Mode. (On the Mac, access the Preferences menu from the Adobe Photoshop Elements Editor menu.)

With that active, you can drag a window's title bar away from the workspace edge to make it appear as a free-floating window.

The options in the next section assume you've enabled floating windows; otherwise, many of those options are not available.

Arranging Multiple Views

You can open multiple windows with different images, or, if you prefer, you can open multiple views of the same image. This is a handy way to work on a detailed area of your image while viewing the full-sized version of the image at the same time. It's especially useful when you're doing touch-up work, such as correcting red eye or erasing a blemish in a photo.

To open multiple views of an image:

From the Arrange Documents menu, choose New Window. The window appears as a new tab or, if you enabled the Allow Floating Documents in Expert Mode preference, as a new floating window. You can also look in the Photo Bin to see the new view.

To arrange multiple views:

Do one of the following:

- To create cascading, overlapping windows, choose Float All in Windows.
- If the windows are floating, position them by dragging their title bars, or use the commands under Window > Images to tile or cascade them (A).

To close multiple view windows:

Do one of the following:

- To close a single window, click the close button on that window's title bar.
- To close all document windows, from the File menu choose Close All or press Ctrl+Alt+W/Command-Option-W.

(A) Multiple image views let you work on a detailed area (left) while at the same time allowing you to see how the changes affect the overall image (right).

TIP To quickly switch from one open window to another, press Ctrl+~/Command-~ (tilde).

TIP You can set different levels of magnification for each window to see both details and the big picture at the same time.

TIP When you're working on a zoomed-in image, it's easy to get lost. Choose Window > Images > Match Zoom to set all open windows to the same zoom level. Or, choose Match Location to make the same visible pixels appear in all windows. That's a quicker option than scrolling around looking for a match or using the Navigator panel.

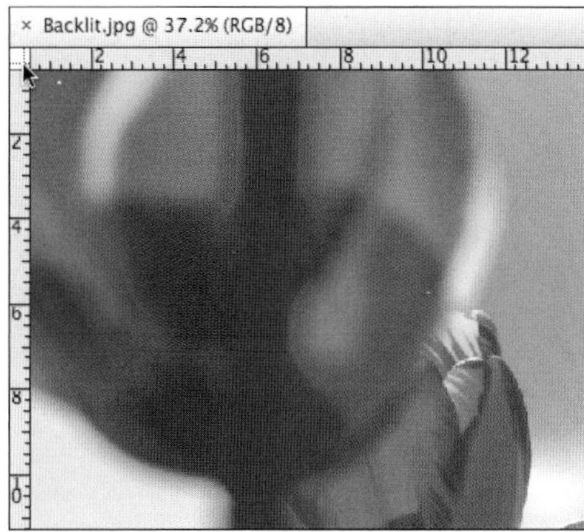

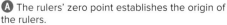

A The rulers' zero point establishes the origin of the rulers.

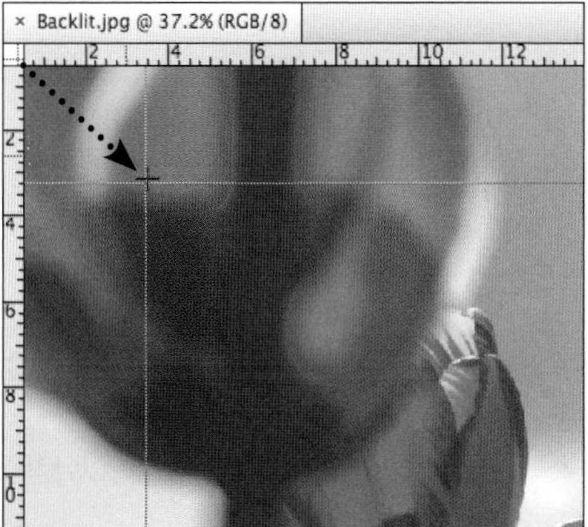

B Drag the zero point to a new location anywhere in the document window.

Using Rulers

Customizable rulers, along the top and left sides of the document window, can help you scale and position graphics and selections. The rulers are helpful if you are combining photos with text (in a greeting card, for example) and want to be precise in placing and aligning the various elements. Interactive tick marks in both rulers provide constant feedback, displaying the position of any tool or pointer as you move it through the window. You can also change the ruler origin, also known as the *zero point*, to measure different parts of your image.

To show or hide the rulers:

From the View menu, choose Rulers to turn the rulers on and off, or press Ctrl+Shift+R/Command-Shift-R.

To change the zero point:

1. Place the pointer over the zero point crosshairs in the upper-left corner of the document window **A**.
2. Drag the zero point to a new position in the document window.

   As you drag, a set of crosshairs appears, indicating the new position of the zero point **B**.
3. Release the mouse button to set the new zero point.

To change the units of measure:

Right-click on either ruler. A contextual menu appears, from which you can choose a new measurement unit.

TIP **To reset the zero point to its original location, double-click the crosshairs in the upper-left corner of the document window.**

Setting Up the Grid

A nonprinting, customizable grid appears as an overlay across the entire document window. As with the rulers, it can be used for scaling and positioning, but it can be especially helpful for maintaining symmetry in your layout and design, or for occasions when you'd like objects to snap to specific points in the window.

To show or hide the grid:

From the View menu, choose Grid to turn the grid on and off.

To change the grid settings:

1. From the Edit menu (or, on the Mac, the Adobe Photoshop Elements Editor menu), choose Preferences > Guides & Grid to open the Guides & Grid Preferences.
2. From the Color drop-down menu, choose a preset grid color, or choose Custom **A**.

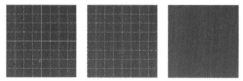

   Choosing Custom displays the Color Picker, where you can select a custom grid color.
3. From the Style drop-down menu, choose a line style for the major grid lines **B**.
4. In the Gridline every drop-down menu, choose a unit of measure; then enter a number in the accompanying field to define the spacing of the major grid lines.
5. In the Subdivisions field, enter a number to define the frequency of minor grid lines **C**.
6. Click OK.

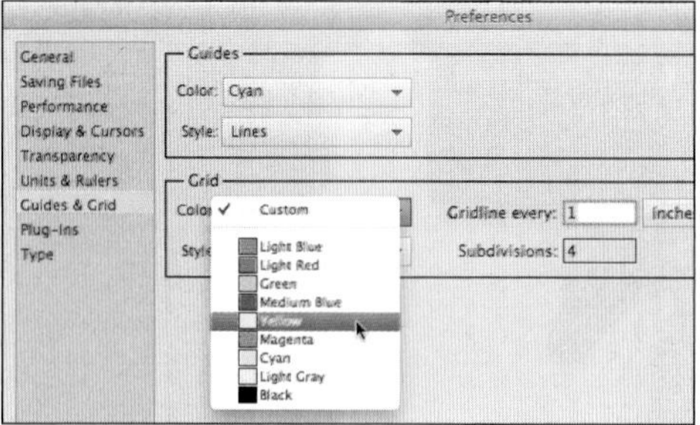

A Choose a grid color from the list of preset colors or create a custom color.

B Examples of grid line styles.

C This figure shows a document grid with major grid lines set every inch, subdivided by four minor grid lines.

Getting Information about Your Image

The Info panel displays measurement and color information as you move a tool over an image. In addition, you can customize the status bar at the bottom of the Info panel to display different file and image information.

To use the Info panel:

1. From the Window menu, choose Info to view the Info panel.
2. Select a tool and then move the pointer over the image. Depending on the tool you are using, the following information appears:
   - The numeric values for the color beneath the pointer. You can view any two sets of color modes at the same time **A**. Choose which modes to display by clicking the drop-down lists **B**.
   - The x and y coordinates of the pointer, and the starting x and y coordinates of a selection or layer, along with the change in distance as you move the pointer over your image **C**.
   - The width and height of a selection or shape and the values relating to transformations, such as the percentage of scale, angle of rotation, and skew (which distorts a selection along the horizontal or vertical axis) **D**.

TIP It's usually quicker to change units of measure using the Info panel rather than by going into the Elements preferences.

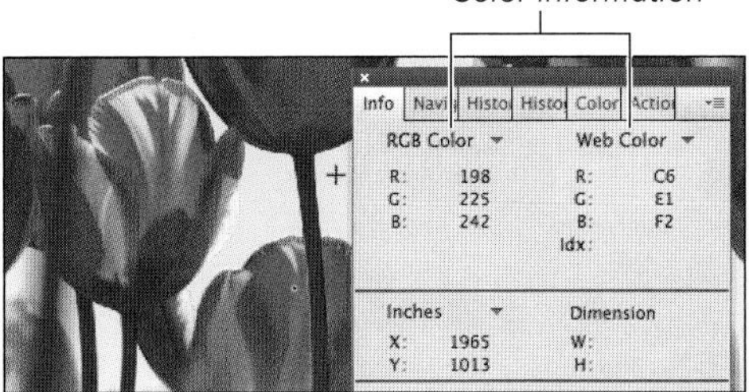

A Any two sets of color information (RGB, HSB, Web Color, or Grayscale) can be viewed at once.

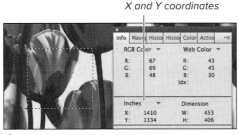

B Color modes (and other settings) can be changed from drop-down lists in the panel.

C The x and y coordinates of the pointer are shown in the Info panel.

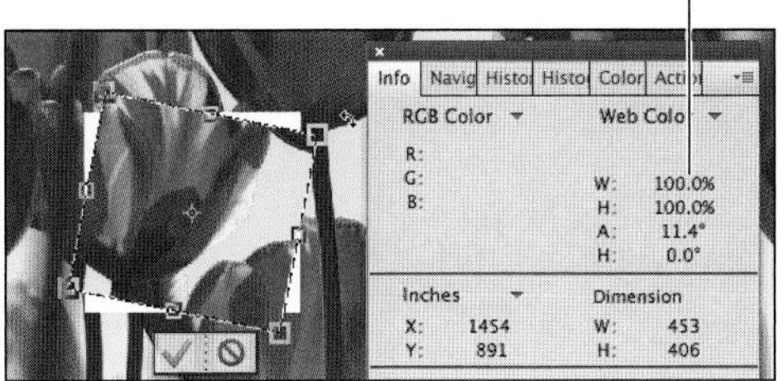

D Any change in the scale or transformation of a selection or layer is visible in the Info panel.

Using the History Panel

The History panel lets you move backward and forward through a work session, allowing you to make multiple undos to any editing changes you've made to your image. Photoshop Elements records every change and then lists each as a separate entry, or state, on the panel. With one click, you can navigate to any state and then choose to work forward from there, return to the previous state, or select a different state from which to work forward.

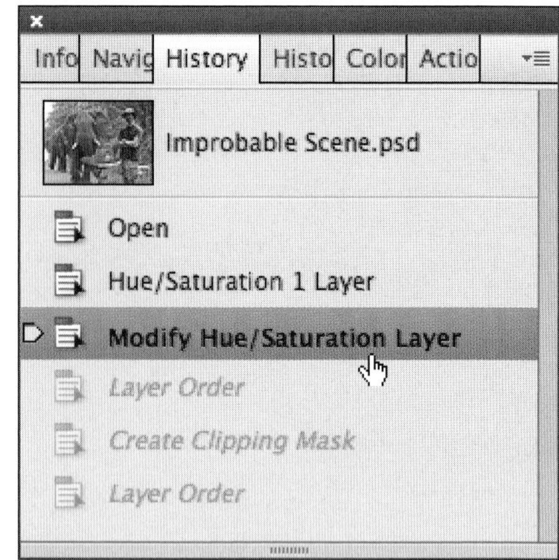

Ⓐ Move to virtually any point in time in the creation of your project using the History panel.

To navigate through the History panel:

1. To open the History panel, choose History from the Window menu.
2. To move to a different state in the History panel, do one of the following:
   - Click the name of any state Ⓐ.
   - Drag the panel slider up or down to a different state.

TIP The default number of states that the History panel saves is 50. After 50, the first state is cleared from the list, and the panel continues to list only the 50 most recent states. The good news is you can bump the number of saved states up to 1000, provided that your computer has enough memory. In the Photoshop Elements preferences, choose Performance. In the History & Cache box enter a larger number in the History States field.

TIP If memory is at a premium (and you'd rather Photoshop Elements not clog up your precious RAM by remembering your last 50 selections, brushstrokes, and filter effects), set the number in the History States field to 1. You can still undo and redo your last action as you work along, but for all practical purposes, the History panel is turned off.

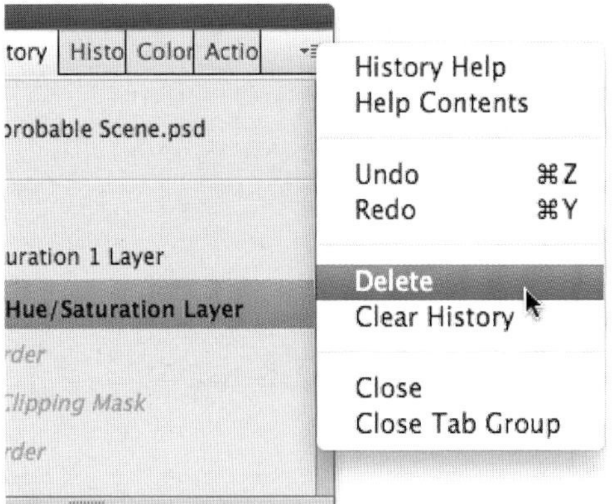

B Delete any state by selecting it and choosing Delete from the panel menu.

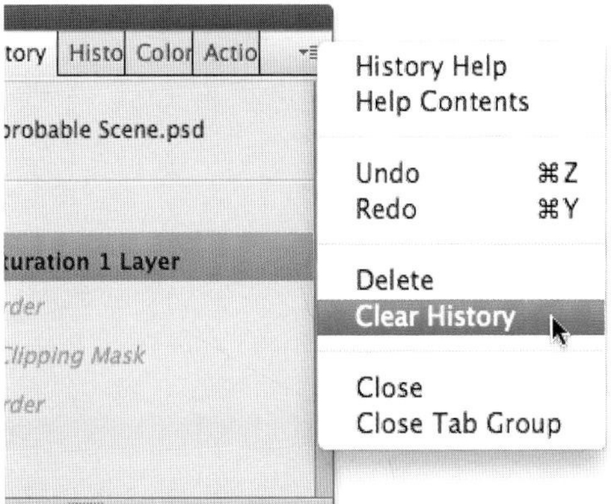

C If system memory is a concern, you can periodically clear the panel of all states.

To delete a state:

Click the name of any state, then choose Delete from the panel menu B.

The selected state and all states following it are deleted.

To clear the History panel:

Do one of the following:

- From the panel menu, choose Clear History C.

  This action can be undone, but it doesn't reduce the amount of memory used by Photoshop Elements.

- Hold down the Alt/Option key, then choose Clear History from the panel menu.

  This action cannot be undone, but it does purge the list of states from the memory buffer. This can come in handy if a message appears telling you that Photoshop Elements is low on memory.

TIP Deletion of a state *can* be undone, but only if no changes are applied to the image in the interim. If you make a change to the image that creates a new state on the panel, all deleted states are permanently lost.

TIP Sometimes—when you're working on an especially complex piece, for instance—the History panel may become filled with states that you no longer need to manage or return to, or that begin to take their toll on your system's memory. At any time, you can clear the panel's list of states without changing the image.

Using Multitouch Gestures

If you own a device that accepts touch input—such as a laptop's trackpad or a touch-sensitive screen—Photoshop Elements supports multitouch gestures that let you work in a more hands-on manner.

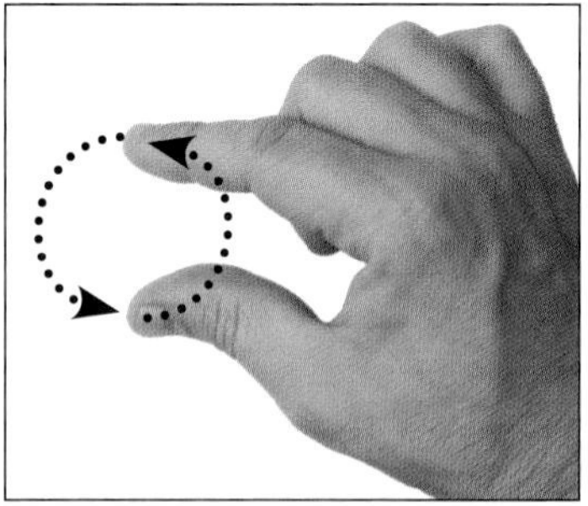

Ⓐ Rotate your hand to turn an image 90 degrees.

To rotate an image:

1. Place two fingers on the multitouch surface.
2. Turn your fingers clockwise or counter-clockwise, like you're turning a physical knob, to rotate the image 90 degrees in that direction Ⓐ.

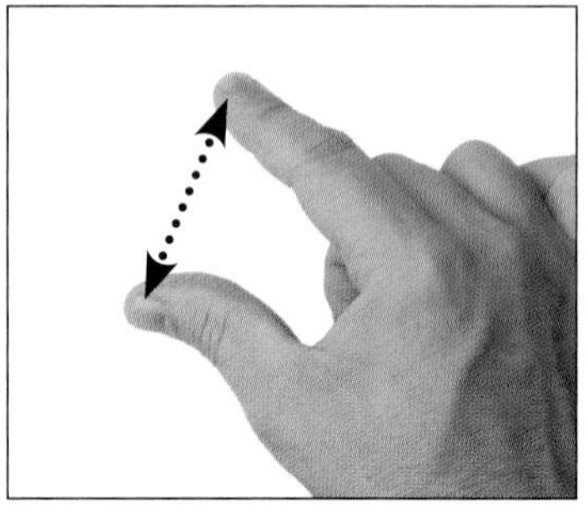

Ⓑ Pinch out to zoom.

To zoom:

1. Place two fingers on the surface.
2. Pinch outward to enlarge the image (zoom in), or pinch inward to reduce the image (zoom out) Ⓑ.

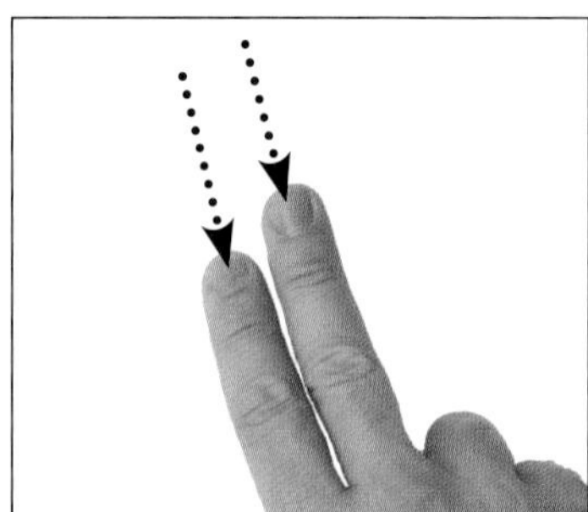

Ⓒ Drag two fingers to scroll.

To scroll in an image:

1. Place two fingers on the surface.
2. Drag in the direction you wish to move the visible portion of the image Ⓒ.

TIP Adobe calls the scrolling gesture a "flick," because the image continues to move after you've lifted your fingers, depending on how you made the gesture. The movement approximates physics and quickly comes to a smooth stop.

Managing Photos in the Organizer

Digital photography can be a double-edged sword. Ironically, its greatest advantage to the amateur photographer—the ability to quickly and easily capture a large number of images, and then instantly download them to a computer—can also be its greatest source of frustration. Once hundreds of images have been downloaded, photographers find themselves faced with the daunting task of sorting through myriad files, with incomprehensible file names, to find those dozen or so "keepers" to assemble into an album or post to the Web for friends.

The Organizer workspace comes to the rescue with a relatively simple and wonderfully visual set of tools and functions to help you locate, identify, and organize your photos. And once your photos are organized, you can import categories and collections of images that you assemble directly into projects like slide shows, calendars, flipbooks, and online albums.

Because we need some source material to work with, this chapter jumps right into importing photos from a digital camera and opening images already on your hard disk.

In This Chapter

Importing Images

Digital cameras have revolutionized photography and are a main force driving the need for products like Photoshop Elements. Typically, these cameras come with their own software to help you browse and manage photos—but don't bother breaking the seal on the disc's envelope. You can access your camera from within Elements and then download your images, or download photos from the camera to your hard drive and then open them in Elements.

Ⓐ Choose From Camera or Card Reader to download photos from your digital camera.

To import images from a digital camera (Standard dialog):

1. Connect your digital camera to your computer using the instructions provided by the camera manufacturer.

   If the Photo Downloader launches automatically, skip to step 3. If you don't see the Photo Downloader dialog, continue to step 2.

2. If you're in the Editor, click the Organizer button to launch the Organizer.

   If you're in the Organizer already, click the Import button and choose From Camera or Card Reader Ⓐ. You can also go to File > Get Photos and Videos, or press Ctrl+G/Command-G.

   The Photo Downloader dialog opens in its Standard mode Ⓑ. For more importing options, see "To import images from a digital camera (Advanced dialog)," just ahead in this chapter.

3. Your camera will likely be selected in the Get Photos from drop-down menu, but if not, choose your camera.

   Listed below the menu are the number of pictures, and their combined size.

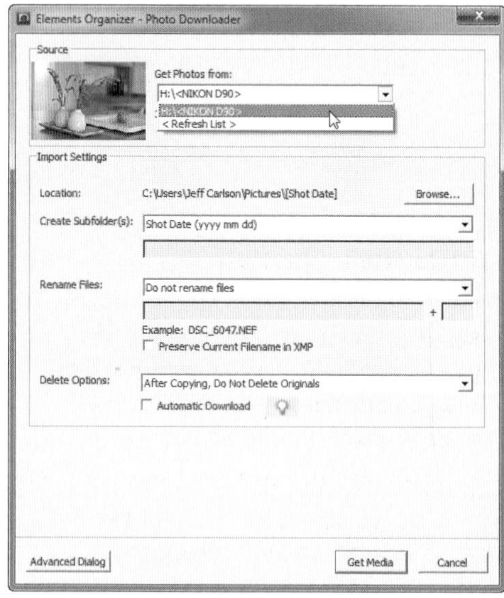

Ⓑ The Photo Downloader's Standard dialog makes it easy to import all photos in one fell swoop.

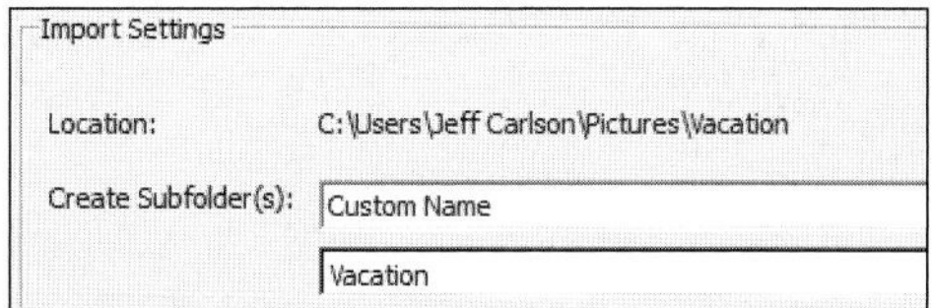

C To make it easier to find images on disk later, specify a custom name for subfolders.

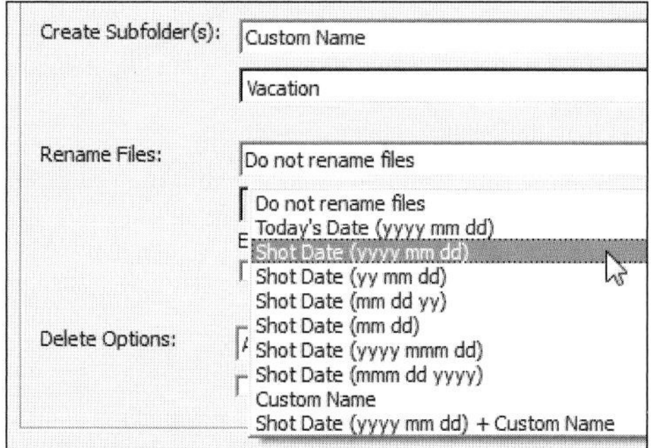

D Choose a date format for naming subfolders with the images' shot dates.

Open the Organizer Automatically (Mac)

Is iPhoto automatically launching when you connect a camera or card reader? You can change that behavior in Apple's Image Capture application.

1. Launch the Image Capture app.
2. Connect your camera or card and select it in the Devices list.
3. Open the Device settings box at the bottom of the sidebar by clicking the button at the lower-left corner of the window (if the box isn't already visible).
4. From the "Connecting this camera opens" drop-down menu, choose Other.
5. Locate the Adobe Elements 11 Organizer application and click Choose.
6. Quit Image Capture.

4. By default, images are saved to your Pictures folder; hold your mouse pointer over the truncated path listed next to Location to view the full destination.

   If you want to save the files to a different location, click the Browse (Windows)/ Choose (Mac) button and select a folder or create a new one. Then click OK.

5. The Photo Downloader dialog is set to create new subfolders to store each batch of imported images, named according to the shot dates. From the Create Subfolder(s) drop-down menu, you can customize this behavior by choosing one of the following options:

   - None saves the files in the folder specified by Location, normally your My Pictures folder.
   - Custom Name creates a folder with a name that you enter **C**.
   - Today's Date automatically creates a folder named with the current date.
   - Shot Date creates folders with the date the images were captured; choose your preferred date format from one of the options **D**.

6. The Rename Files drop-down menu gives you the option of automatically naming the imported files something more descriptive than what your camera assigns. Choose an option from the drop-down menu.

   For example, your camera's default naming scheme is probably something like "IMG_1031.JPG." With a Rename Files option selected, you can name and number a set of photos "Vacation," for instance. Then your photos will be saved and named "Vacation001.jpg," "Vacation002.jpg," and so on.

continues on next page

7. In the Delete Options area, choose what happens to the files on the memory card. Just to be safe, I like to leave the option set to After Copying, Do Not Delete Originals, and then erase the card in-camera later.

   Under Windows, the Automatic Download option is useful if you want to offload pictures onto the computer without going through the Photo Downloader. Images download automatically when a camera or other device is attached. You can turn it off later in the program's preferences.

8. Click the Get Media button to download the selected images to your computer.

   Your downloaded photos first appear in their own Organizer window. Click the Back button (which sometimes reads All Media, depending on context) to return to the main Organizer window **E**.

To view your entire photo library, click the Back button.

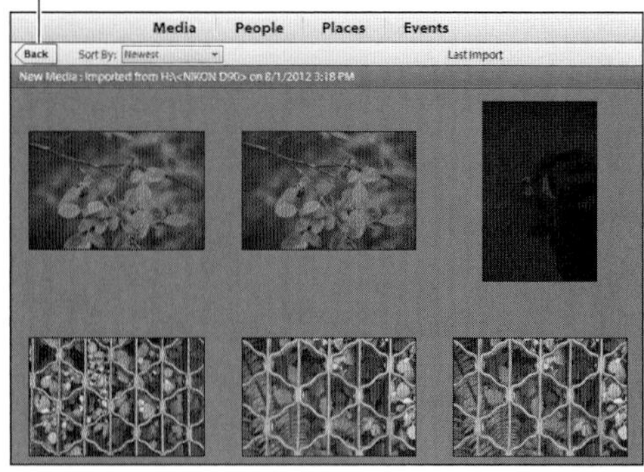

E Photos downloaded from the camera or memory card appear in the Organizer.

To import images from a digital camera (Advanced dialog):

1. Follow steps 1 through 8 in the previous sequence, but click the Advanced Dialog button in step 2 to view the Advanced options **F**.

2. Click to deselect the checkbox under any photos you do not want to download.

   By default, Elements assumes you want to download every image.

3. In the Advanced Options area, choose to enable or disable the following **G**:

   - Automatically Fix Red Eyes attempts to correct red eye problems in your photos as they're downloaded.

   - Automatically Suggest Photo Stacks groups similar photos together for easy organization and review later (see "Using Stacks to Organize Similar Photos," later in this chapter).

F Preview all photos on your camera before importing them in the Advanced dialog (left side of window shown here).

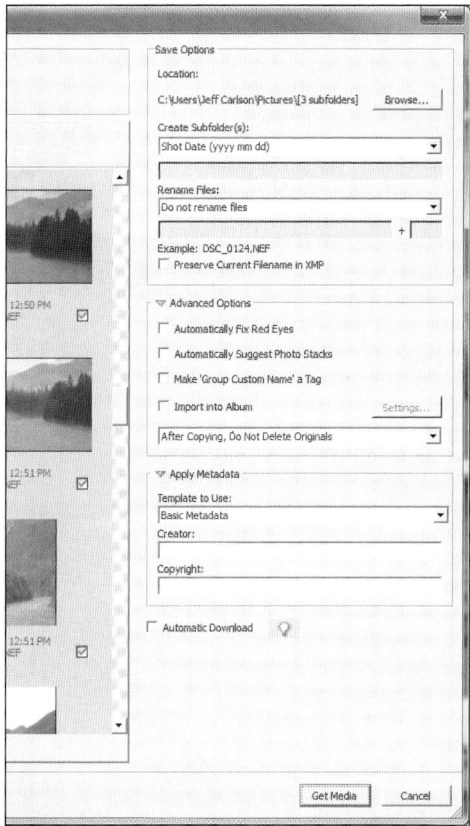

G Further customize the importing process in the Advanced dialog (right side of window here).

Rotate buttons

H Rotate images during import so you won't have to do it later.

- Make 'Group Custom Name' a Tag takes the name you specified in step 5 two pages back and creates a keyword tag (see "Creating Keyword Tags," later in this chapter).
- Import into Album assigns the photos to a photo album you've previously set up (see "Using Albums to Arrange and Group Photos," later in this chapter).

4. Type your name (or the name of whoever took the photos) and a copyright notice in the Apply Metadata fields. This text is embedded with the image files.
5. If you want to rotate an image as it's imported, select it and click the Rotate Left or Rotate Right button at the lower-left corner **H**. You can also press Control and the left or right arrow key.

TIP For a fast way to select just a few photos for import, first click the UnCheck All button, and then click on the photos you want—don't worry about clicking their individual checkboxes. With the images selected, click just one checkbox to enable the boxes of your selections.

TIP Photoshop Elements can import photos stored in Camera RAW formats, which are the unprocessed versions of the captured images. RAW enables more adjustment possibilities than JPEG (which is processed and compressed in the camera). Elements brings RAW files into the Organizer without editing the image information. When you edit the photo, Elements first brings up the Camera Raw dialog to set initial edits before opening the image in the Editor. For more information, see Chapter 9.

TIP The contents of the Creator and Copyright metadata fields are applied to all photos imported in that batch. If you want different authors for the pictures, for example, either import them in several batches or edit the metadata after they've been added to the catalog.

To import images from files or folders:

1. In the Organizer, go to the File menu, highlight Get Photos, and choose From Files and Folders.

   Under Windows, If you insert media that contains photos, such as a CD, you may be asked what action you'd like to take (if you haven't specified it already). Click the icon labeled Organize and Edit using Adobe Photoshop Elements 11.0, which opens a dialog to locate files.

2. Select the files you want to import **I**; Shift-click to select a consecutive range of files, or Ctrl-click/Command-click to select noncontiguous files.

3. If the images are stored on removable media and you want to import only low-resolution versions, disable the Copy Files on Import option and enable the Generate Previews option (see the sidebar for more information).

4. As in the Advanced dialog mentioned on the previous pages, select from the processing options below the preview.

5. Click the Get Media button to import the photos. If the photos already include keyword tags, you have the option to import them.

TIP Now that we've gotten those steps out of the way and you understand what's going on, here's a much quicker method: Simply drag image files from a folder on your hard disk to the Organizer's window. Elements imports them without fuss.

TIP If you know some photos exist on your hard disk but can't find them, let Elements hunt for them instead. Under the Get Photos submenu of the File menu, choose By Searching, enter criteria about the files, and click the Search button.

I Import images from other areas of your hard disk or from removable media such as CDs.

Working with Offline Images

With removable media, you have the option of importing just a low-resolution file to the hard disk. This feature can save hard disk space, especially if lots of files are stored on a shared network drive or on several CDs or DVDs. Importing them as offline images allows you to view and track your entire media catalog.

Offline images are designated with an icon in the upper-left corner of the image in the Organizer **J**. You can apply tags, build collections, and perform other tasks. However, if you want to edit the image, Elements asks you to insert the original media. If it's not available, you can still edit the low-res proxy, but the results won't look good. Once you make the original available again, Elements copies the source image to your catalog as an online image.

J Offline images are denoted by a corner icon.

Ⓚ Elements can keep an eye on one or more folders and import photos when they're added.

To import images using Watch Folders (Windows only):

1. You can specify one or more folders that Elements watches in the background for new files. In the Organizer, choose Watch Folders from the File menu.
2. Click the Add button and navigate to the folder you wish to watch Ⓚ. Repeat for as many folders as you'd like.
3. Select an action under When New Files are Found in Watched Folders; Elements can notify you when files are found, or add them to the Organizer automatically.
4. Click OK when you're done.
5. When you add photos to your watched folder, Elements asks if you want to import them (if you opted to be notified in step 3). Click Yes to add the photos, which are moved from the watched folder to the directory where Elements stores your catalog.

To scan an image into the Organizer (Windows only):

1. Connect the scanner to your computer using the instructions provided by the scanner manufacturer.
2. In the Organizer, click the Import button and choose From Scanner. Or, you can choose File > Get Photos and Videos > From Scanner (or press Ctrl+U).
3. Select your scanner software from the Scanner pop-up menu.
4. Choose an image format and quality level.

continues on next page

5. Click the OK button. Elements hands off the actual scanning duties to the scanner's software for you to complete the scan.
6. When you complete the scan and exit the scanner's software, Elements imports the image to your catalog.

TIP If you're planning to use only part of an image, you'll save a lot of time by using your scanning software to crop your image *before* importing it into Photoshop Elements.

TIP On the off chance that you want to scan an image in black and white (not grayscale), well, don't. Elements doesn't recognize bitmap images.

Importing photos from iPhoto (Mac only)

Elements offers a feature to move your iPhoto library into the Organizer. This is a one-way operation, which attempts to import *all* of your iPhoto photos; there's no way to specify just a few photos or albums. If you want to completely switch from iPhoto to the Organizer, here are the steps.

To import photos from iPhoto (Mac only):

From the File menu, choose Get Photos and Videos > From iPhoto.

Elements copies the media to its catalog. Depending on the size of your iPhoto library, the process could take a while.

L The Frame From Video dialog enables you to snag shots from video footage you captured.

M I grabbed three frames from the video clip, which appear in the Editor as three separate image files.

Importing Video Files

The Organizer accepts video files as well as still images, a necessity now that most still cameras shoot decent video. Double-clicking a video file's thumbnail lets you play the movie and assign keyword tags; press Esc to exit the player window.

To capture frames from video footage:

1. In the Editor, go to the File menu and choose Import > Frame From Video. (This feature appears only in the Editor, not the Organizer.)

   The Frame From Video dialog appears.

2. Click the Browse button to locate the file you want, and then click Open to see the video footage.

   The video clip appears in the dialog **L**.

3. To view your footage, click the Play button. When you see the frame you want, click the Grab Frame button or press the spacebar.

   To grab the frame you want, you can also use the Pause button to stop the video at the desired frame. Another useful option is to simply move the slider to the correct frame in the video.

4. Grab as many video frames as you want, one by one, and then click Done.

   As you click the Grab Frame button, the images appear as new files in the Editor **M**.

5. Once you've captured the frames, you can save and edit them just like other images.

TIP Use the left and right arrow keys to view frames in the video one at a time.

TIP You'll likely encounter a greater variety of exposure problems with video frames than with the still shots you take with a digital camera. You can easily fix contrast and tonal problems with a few of Photoshop Elements' correction tools, which you'll explore more in Chapter 8.

Understanding the Organizer Work Area

The Organizer is dominated by the Media Browser, which is used to find and view thumbnail representations of your photos. It's flanked by two panels that you use to group and organize your image files **A**, which can be hidden to make room for more photos.

A The Organizer workspace makes it easy to browse your entire photo collection.

The Media Browser

At the core of the Organizer is the Media Browser. Every digital photo or video downloaded into Photoshop Elements is automatically added there. Resizable thumbnails in the Media Browser window make it easy to scan through even a large number of images.

Media is typically organized according to the dates the photos or videos were captured, but you can also view images grouped by the people in them, by places where they've occurred (using geotagging information embedded in the files or locations you've specified on a map), or by time-based events. I cover each mode in this chapter.

The Folders List

The pane at left displays albums you create to organize your media, as well as a Folders List that reveals where the files are stored on disk. Click a folder name to view its contents **B**.

You can also click the Show Folder Hierarchy button to expose your drive's structure. This approach is more comfortable for people who like to keep track of where their files are, but is also useful for organizing. For example, in this view you can move images between drives so the Organizer properly keeps track of them.

Show Folder Hierarchy

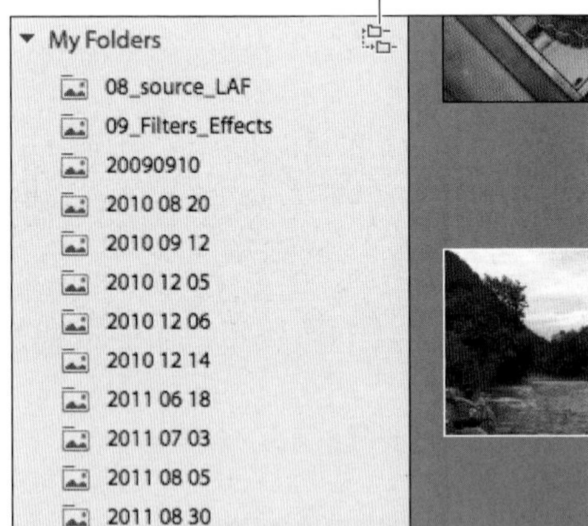

B The Folders List reveals directories where your photos are located.

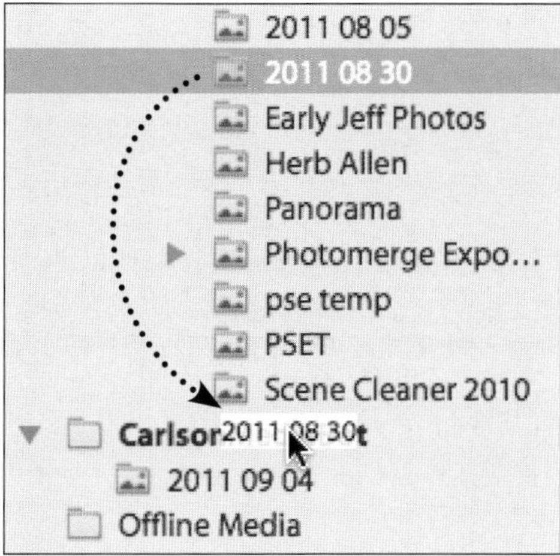

Ⓒ Move photos or folders using the Folder Hierarchy List.

Ⓓ Click a month marker in the Organizer timeline to view that month's photos on the Media Browser.

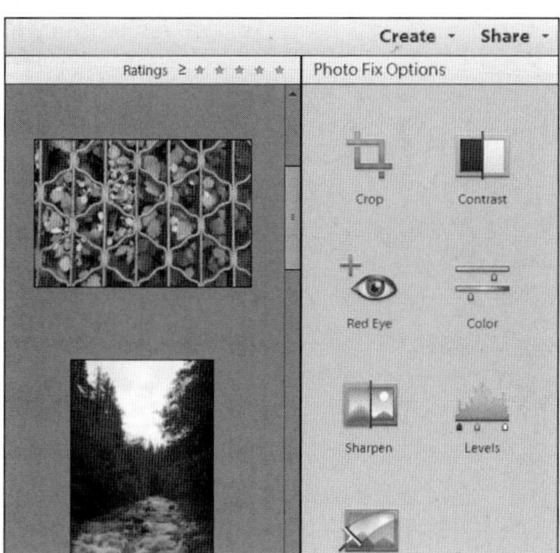

Ⓔ Make quick fixes in the Organizer.

To move files in the Folder List:

1. Click the Show Folder Hierarchy button.
2. Drag a folder to a new location Ⓒ; or, select images in the Media Browser and drag them to a folder.

The timeline

An optional, but helpful, way to quickly navigate your photos by date is the timeline, located just above the Media Browser. Choose Timeline from the Window menu, or press Ctrl+L/Command-L. For example, when a Date viewing option is selected in the Browser window, the timeline uses date and time information embedded in each image to construct bars (month markers) to represent sets of photos taken within specific months and years. When a month marker is selected in the timeline, that month's photos are displayed at the top of the Media Browser Ⓓ.

Instant Fix and information

The pane at right includes either a collection of Instant Fix operations—such as Crop, Red Eye, and Smart Fix Ⓔ—or keyword tags and general information about selected images.

Working in the Media Browser

The centerpiece of the Organizer is the Media Browser, a flexible workspace that provides a number of options for customizing the way you manage and view your image files. Throughout this chapter I'll cover a variety of ways to work in the Media Browser to label, identify, and organize your photos. But first it's important to know how best to select, sort, and display the image thumbnails.

To select photo thumbnails:

Do one of the following:

- Click to select a thumbnail in the Media Browser. The frame around it becomes light blue, indicating that the thumbnail is selected **A**.
- Ctrl-click/Command-click to select non-adjacent thumbnails at once **B**.
- Shift-click to select a group of thumbnails in sequence **C**.
- From the Edit menu, choose Select All, or press Ctrl+A/Command-A to select every thumbnail in the Media Browser.

To deselect photo thumbnails:

Do one of the following:

- Ctrl-click/Command-click to deselect a single thumbnail.
- From the Edit menu, choose Deselect, or press Ctrl+Shift+A/Command-Shift-A to deselect every thumbnail in the Media Browser.

TIP You can tweak the appearance of the Media Browser. From the View menu, choose to display details such as grid lines, file names, ratings, timestamps, and people recognition.

A A selected thumbnail appears with a light blue frame around it.

B Ctrl-click/Command-click to select thumbnails that are not consecutive.

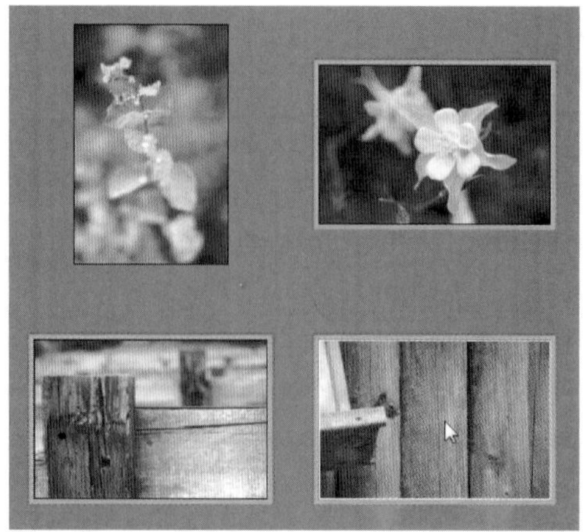

C Shift-click to select thumbnails that are consecutive.

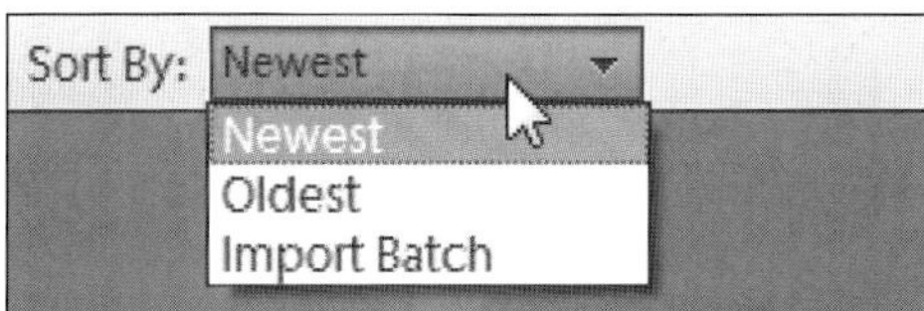

D Select an option to sort thumbnails in the Media Browser.

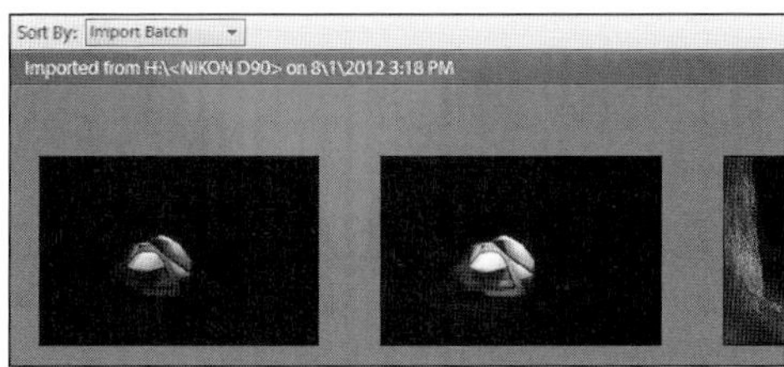

E When you select the Import Batch option, thumbnails in the Media Browser are displayed in grouped batch sets.

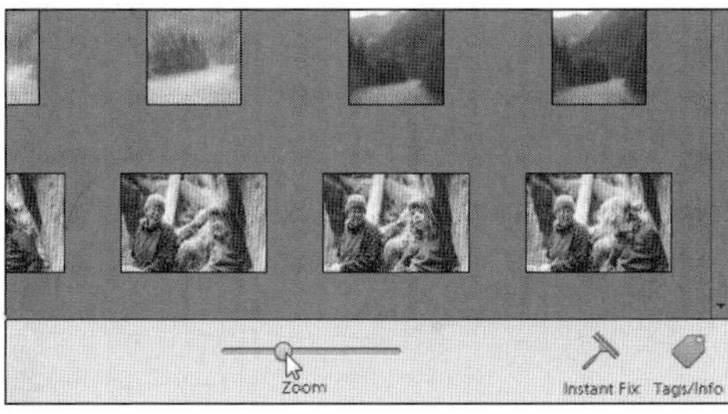

F When you drag the thumbnail slider to the right, the thumbnails grow larger (top). When you drag the slider to the left, they become smaller (bottom).

To sort photo thumbnails:

- From the Sort By drop-down menu above the Media Browser, choose a sorting option D:
  - Newest displays the most recent photos at the top, judged by the images' creation dates.
  - Oldest displays photos in order, with the oldest at the top.
  - Import Batch groups photos into the batches they were imported in E.

To resize photo thumbnails:

- Below the Media Browser, drag the Zoom slider to the right to increase the size of the thumbnails, or to the left to make them smaller F.
- Click the far left of the Zoom slider to display the thumbnails at their smallest possible size.
- Click the far right of the Zoom slider to display just one large photo thumbnail at a time (also known as Single Photo View).

TIP Double-click on any thumbnail to change to Single Photo View. Double-click the image to return to your most recent multiple thumbnail view settings.

Displaying and Changing Information for Your Photos

Images you import carry embedded file information—everything from the date and time a photo was shot or scanned to whether or not the camera's flash fired. The Organizer uses that date and time information to determine the display order of the photo thumbnails in the Media Browser.

If your camera's clock wasn't set properly before shooting (a problem especially if the batteries die), the Adjust Date and Time dialog lets you substitute a new date and time for any image file. You can also easily adjust for time zone differences by shifting the time a set number of hours.

To adjust the date and time:

1. From the View menu, check that the Details option is enabled to display date and file name information below the image thumbnails **A**.
2. In the Media Browser, click to select the thumbnails whose date and time you would like to change.
3. From the Edit menu, choose Adjust Date and Time (or Adjust Date and Time of Selected Items if more than one thumbnail is selected), or press Ctrl+J/ Command-J.
4. In the dialog that appears, choose one of the options and click OK **B**:
   - **Change to a specified date and time** opens the Set Date and Time dialog where you can set a specific year, month, day, and time **C**.

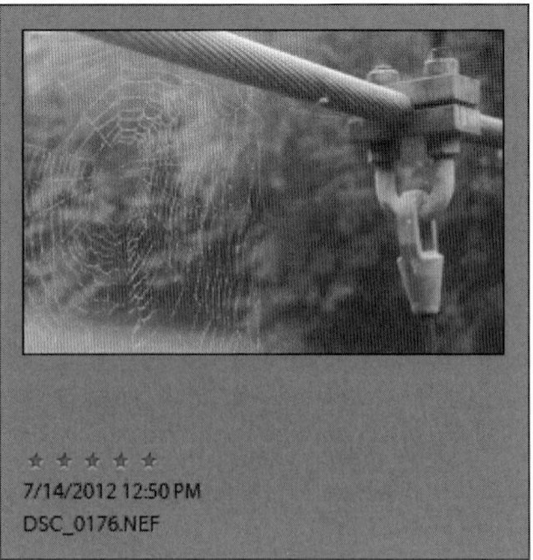

A The Details option displays title and date information in the Media Browser.

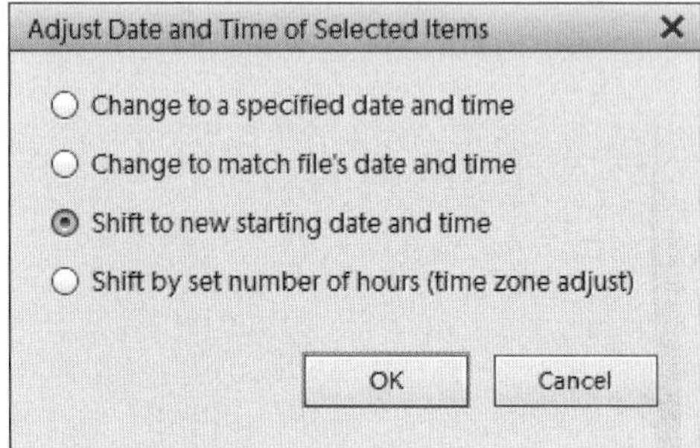

B The Adjust Date and Time dialog offers different options for changing an image's date and time information.

C The Set Date and Time dialog.

Marking Photos as Hidden

If you have some photos you feel are cluttering up the Media Browser, use the Hidden attribute to keep them out of sight until you need them. Select a photo and choose Edit > Visibility > Mark as Hidden (or press Alt+F2) to make the image disappear from view.

To view hidden photos, choose View > Visibility and choose either Show All Files or Show Only Hidden Files. An eye icon with a strikethrough mark appears on the face of each photo thumbnail **D**. You can hide them again by choosing View > Visibility > Hide Hidden Files. To make a photo permanently visible, choose Edit > Visibility > Mark as Visible, which removes the Hidden attribute.

D Hidden files display an eye icon when viewed.

- **Change to match file's date and time** reverts the date and time information to what is embedded in the original image file.

  Remember, date and time changes you enter here are only for sorting and organizing your images within the Photo Organizer.

- **Shift to new starting date and time** appears only when multiple files are selected, and maintains their relative time information, offset from what you enter.

- **Shift by set number of hours (time zone adjust)** adjusts the time of selected images forward or backward by the number of hours you specify.

TIP A preference enables you to open the Adjust Date and Time dialog by simply clicking on the date in the Media Browser. From the Edit menu, choose Preferences > General, and then select the Adjust Date and Time by Clicking on Thumbnail Dates option.

TIP You can view file names in addition to dates. From the View menu, choose Show File Names.

To rate a photo:

1. If you have Details enabled in the Media Browser, position your mouse pointer over the gray star icons **E**.

   Otherwise, click the Tags/Info button in the Task bar to bring up the Information pane.

2. Click to select the rating you wish to apply: One star typically denotes a low-quality photo, while five stars is excellent. (You can choose your own values, of course; this feature provides an easy way to separate good from bad photos, as you'll see later in "Finding Photos.")

E Apply a rating to quickly identify your higher-quality photos.

To add a caption to a photo:

1. Click to select an image thumbnail.
2. Click the Tags/Info button in the Task bar to view the Information pane.

   (You can also choose Edit > Add Caption, or press Ctrl+Shift+T/Command-Shift-T, to bring up the Add Caption dialog. But I despise single-purpose dialogs like that, especially now that the Information pane is available.)

3. In the Caption field, type a caption for your image **F**. Although captions don't display with images in the Media Browser, they do appear along with your photos when you share the photos online.

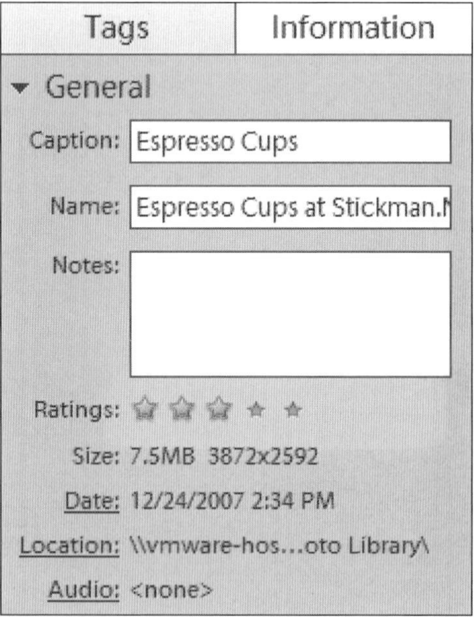

F Add a caption in the Information pane.

TIP **You can also add and edit captions in Single Photo View. In Single Photo View, click the Click here to add caption text. The text changes to a text field where you can type a new caption. If you've previously entered a caption, click on the text to edit or delete it.**

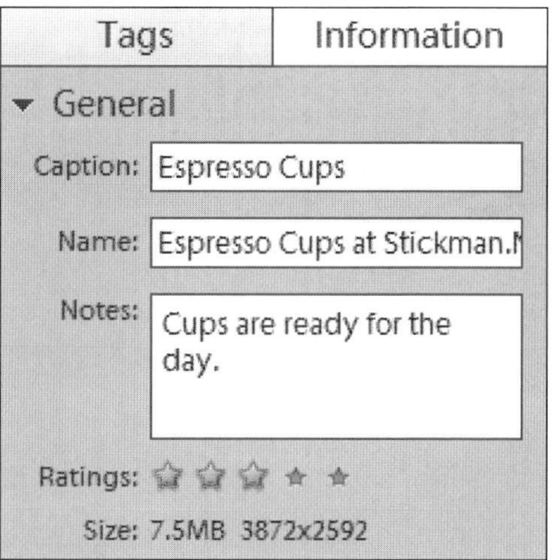

G Notes entered for images are accessible only in the Information pane.

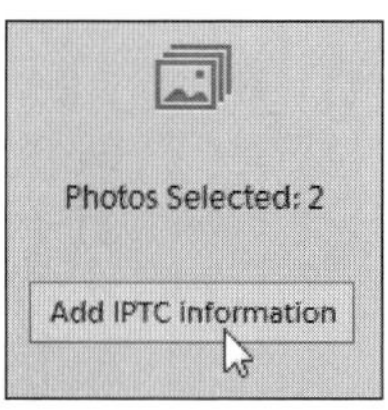

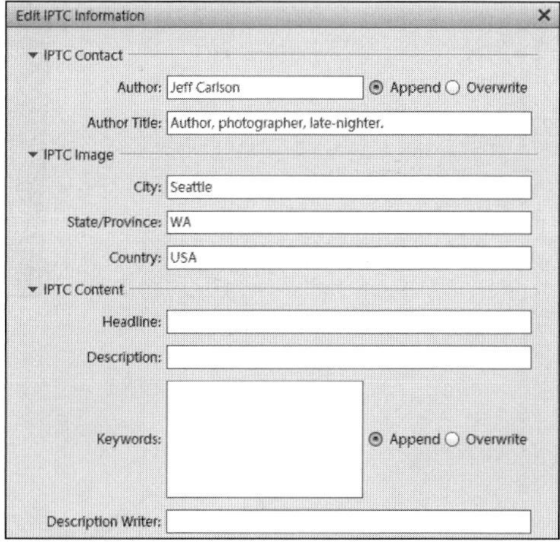

H Enter IPTC information to include even more data about the photo.

To rename a photo:

1. In the Media Browser, click to select an image thumbnail.
2. Click the Tags/Info button in the Task bar to reveal the Information pane.
3. Enter a new name for your image file in the Name field.

To add a note to a photo:

1. Select an image thumbnail.
2. Click the Tags/Info button in the Task bar to reveal the Information pane (if it's not already visible).
3. In the Notes field, enter the text you want to include with your photo G.

To add IPTC information to images:

1. To embed IPTC data (metadata for identifying and categorizing photos), first select two or more images in the Media Browser.
2. Click the Tags/Info button to reveal the Information pane.
3. Click the Add IPTC information button that appears H.
4. Enter any information you choose into the Edit IPTC Information dialog, and then click Save.

TIP You can add the same caption to multiple images at the same time. Select a group of images in the Media Browser, and then from the Edit menu choose Add Caption to Selected Items. The caption you enter in the Add Caption to Selected Items dialog is applied to the selected images.

Creating Keyword Tags

The humble little tag serves as the foundation for the Organizer's sorting and filing system. You can create a tag from scratch or create one based on a set of photos grouped within a folder. Click the Tags/Info button to reveal the panel along the right side of the screen, and then click the Keyword Tags tab.

To create a new keyword tag:

1. Click the New button (the plus sign) at the top of the Tags pane **A**, or press Ctrl+N/Command-N to bring up the Create Keyword Tag dialog.
2. From the Category menu, choose the category or sub-category in which you want to place your new tag **B**. (I go into more depth about categories a few pages ahead.)
3. In the Name text field, enter a name for your tag.
4. In the Note text field, enter information relevant to the photos that will have the tag applied.
5. Click OK to close the dialog.

   Your new tag appears in the Tags pane within the category you chose **C**.

TIP The first photo to which you attach a new tag automatically becomes the icon for that tag. This is an easy and convenient way to assign tag icons, so I'll ignore the Edit Icon button for now.

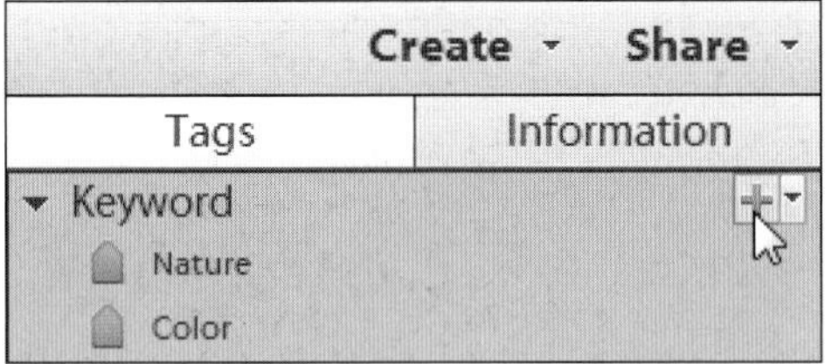

A Click the New button at the top of the Tags pane to create a new tag.

B All tags reside in categories. Define a category for your new tag in the Create Keyword Tag dialog.

C Tags appear nested below their categories in the pane.

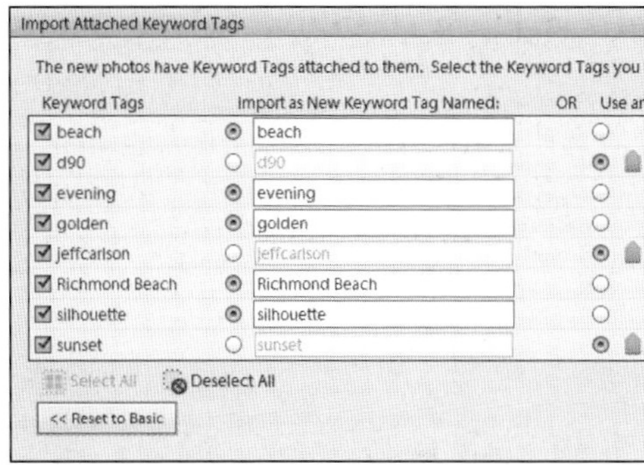

D When you import photos that already contain keyword tags, you can opt to add them to the list in the Tags pane.

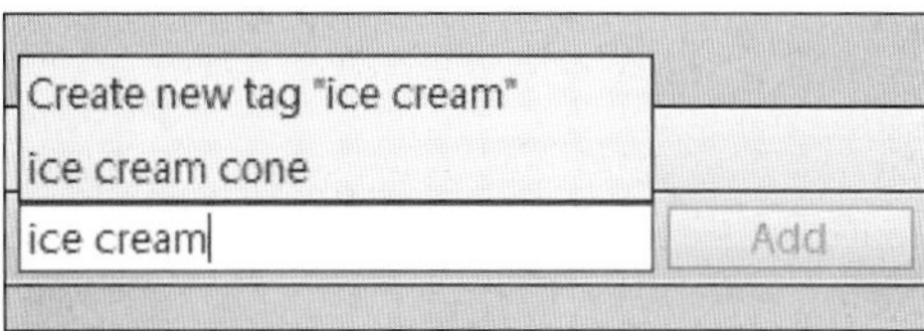

E Type a word into the Add Custom Keywords field to create a new tag for it.

To import tags from other images:

1. Using the steps outlined earlier, import photos from your hard disk that may already contain keywords (for example, if someone sent you the images or you used another program to assign tags).
2. In the Import Attached Keyword Tags dialog, choose which tags you want to add to your list. Click OK. The tags can be applied to any photos in your library.

TIP Click the Advanced button to access more options such as renaming the tags before they're imported D.

To create a tag using the Image Keywords field:

1. Select one or more images in your library.
2. Type a keyword in the Add Custom Keywords field **E**.

   Better yet, type *several* keywords, separated by commas, to create and apply them together.
3. Press Enter or click Add. The new tag is created and applied to the selected image(s).

TIP I'm happy to detail the different methods of creating and applying keyword tags in this chapter, but for me, the capability to do it from the Tag selected media field trumps the other methods. It's quick and promises to make keyword tagging much less of a chore than in the past.

To change a tag's properties:

1. In the Tags pane, select the tag you want to edit.
2. Click the drop-down menu attached to the New button (the plus sign) and choose Edit **F**.

Or

1. In the Tags pane, right-click the tag whose properties you would like to change.
2. From the tag contextual menu, choose Edit.
3. In the Edit Keyword Tag dialog, make the desired changes and click OK.

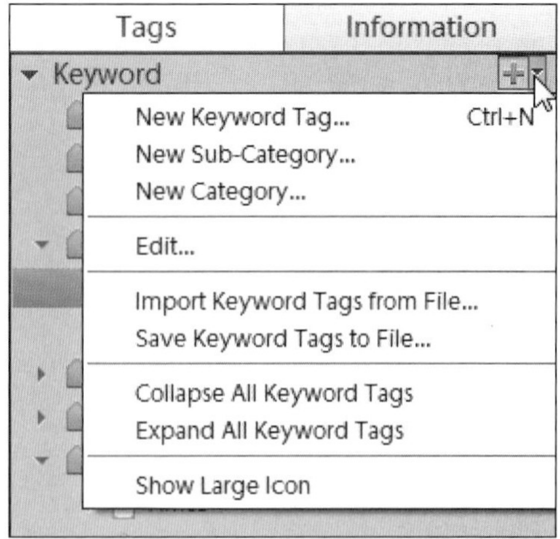

F Edit a tag's properties.

To delete a tag:

In the Tags pane, select the tag you want to delete and press the Delete key.

Or

1. In the Tags pane, right-click on the tag you would like to delete.
2. From the tag contextual menu, choose Delete **G**.
3. In the Confirm Keyword Tag Deletion warning box, click OK.

   The tag is removed from the Tags pane, from any photos tagged in the Media Browser, and any saved searches that use it.

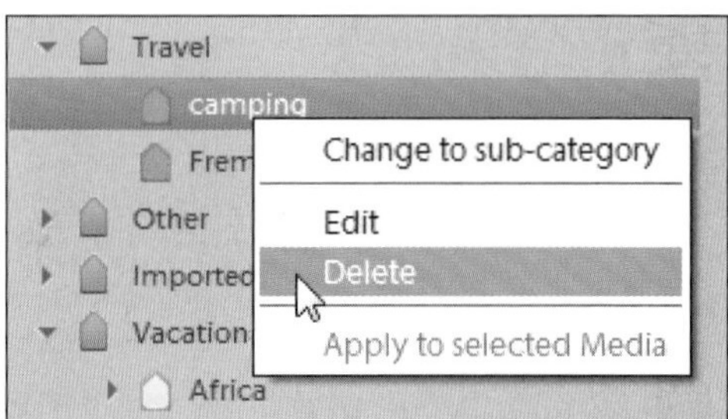

G Delete a keyword tag you don't want to use.

To merge tags:

1. Select tags with similar terms (or other criteria you want to simplify).
2. Right-click on the tags and choose Merge Keyword Tags.
3. In the dialog that appears, choose one tag to keep **H**; the others are deleted and the photos get the chosen tag.

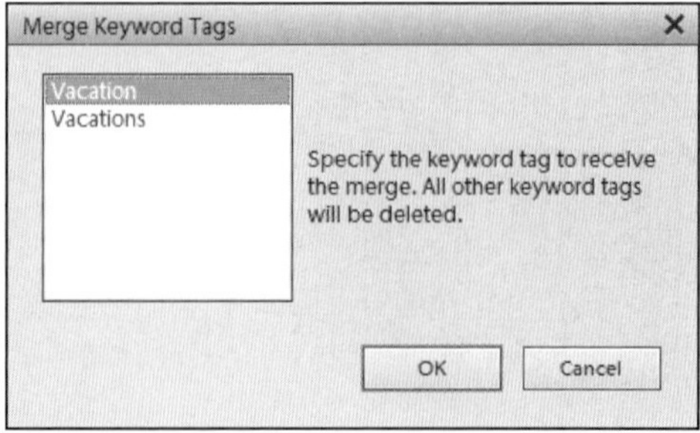

H Merge tags to remove duplicate terms.

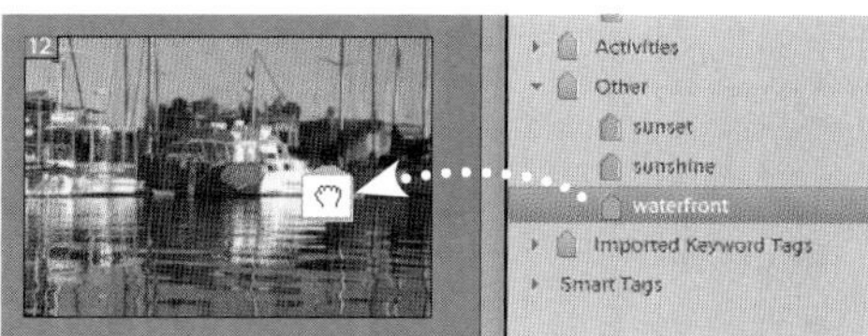

A To attach a tag to a photo, drag it from the Tags pane to a thumbnail image in the Media Browser.

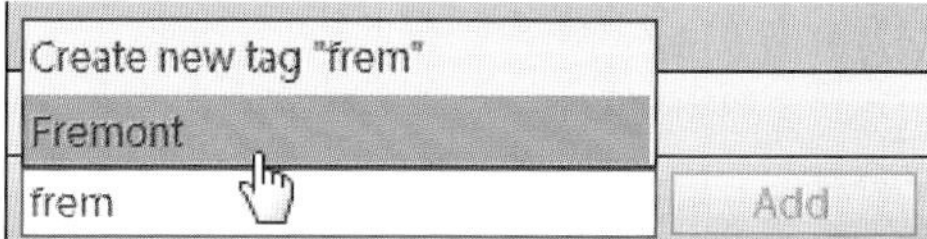

B Existing tags appear as you type into the Image Keywords field.

C You can select multiple photos, and then tag them all by dragging a tag icon over just one.

D When you use a tag for the first time, the photo you attach it to is used for the tag's icon.

Using Keyword Tags to Sort and Identify Photos

Tags operate independent of where photos are located on your computer, which means you can attach a tag to photos in different folders—even on different hard drives—and then use that tag to quickly find and view those photos all at once.

To attach a tag to a single photo:

- Drag a tag from the Tags pane onto any photo in the Media Browser **A**.
- Type a term into the Add Custom Keywords field; if the tag already exists, click it from the pop-up list that appears **B**.

A category icon appears below the photo to indicate that it has been tagged.

To attach a tag to multiple photos:

1. In the Media Browser, Ctrl-click/Command-click to select any number of photos.
2. From the Tags pane, drag a tag onto any one of the selected photos **C**.

   A category icon appears below all of the selected photos in the Browser window to indicate that they have been tagged.

TIP You can also drag a photo to a tag in the Tags pane to attach it.

TIP Hover the mouse pointer over a photo's tag icon to view which tags are applied.

TIP Tags normally appear with a generic blue icon, but they can also display a photo thumbnail for its tag icon D. With a tag selected, click the the Add (+) drop-down menu, and choose Show Large Icon.

To view a set of tagged photos:

In the Tags pane, position your mouse pointer over a tag and click the angle-bracket (>) button that appears E.

That activates the Organizer's Advanced search mode with the keyword selected and results displayed F. You can click other keywords to expand the selection if you choose. (See "Finding Photos" later in this chapter for more details.)

To view all photos again, click the Back button, or click the X button in the Advanced search pane to collapse the search criteria.

To remove a tag from a photo:

Select a photo thumbnail in the Media Browser, and then do one of the following:

- Right-click a photo thumbnail; then, from the contextual menu, choose Remove Keyword Tag > (name of tag).
- Right-click on the category icon below the photo thumbnail and select Remove (name of tag) Keyword Tag from the contextual menu G.

TIP If you're viewing photos by import batch (choose Import Batch from the Sort By drop-down menu), click the batch's heading to select all of its photos, then apply tags to them all at once.

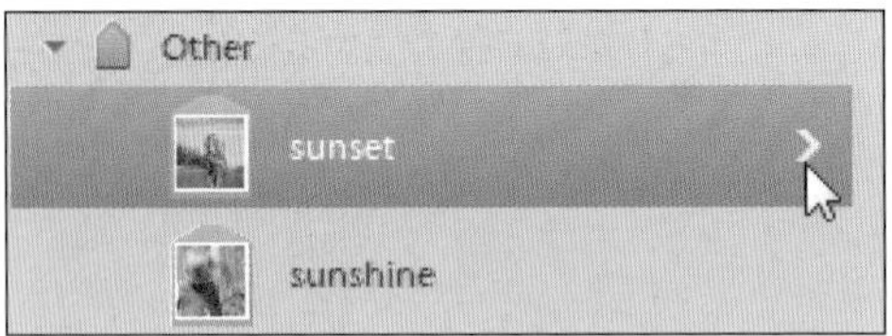

E When the binoculars icon is visible next to a tag in the Tags pane, only that tag's photos appear in the Media Browser.

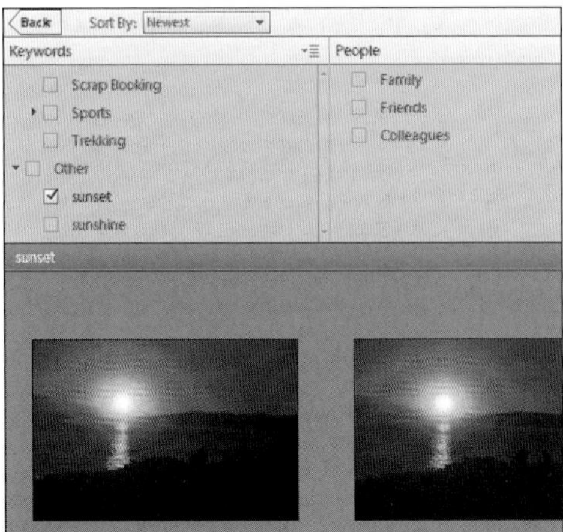

F When a tag is selected in the Advanced search pane, only that tag's photos appear.

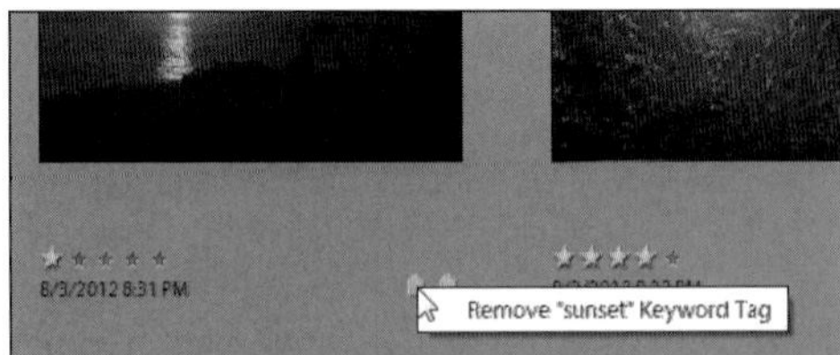

G Remove a tag from a photo by right-clicking on the category icon below the thumbnail in the Media Browser.

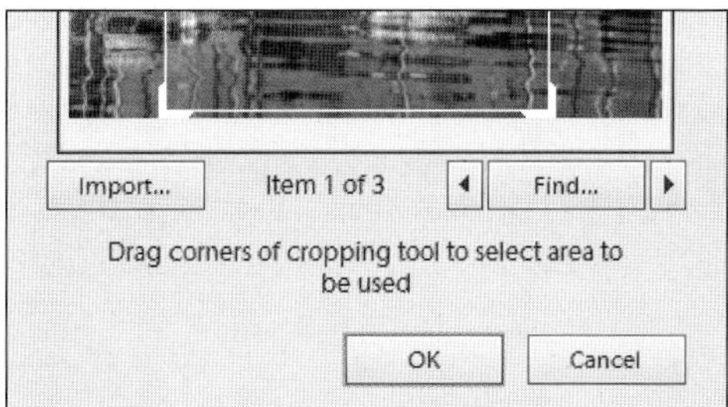

H Click the Find button in the Edit Tag Icon dialog to browse for a new photo to use as the source for your tag icon.

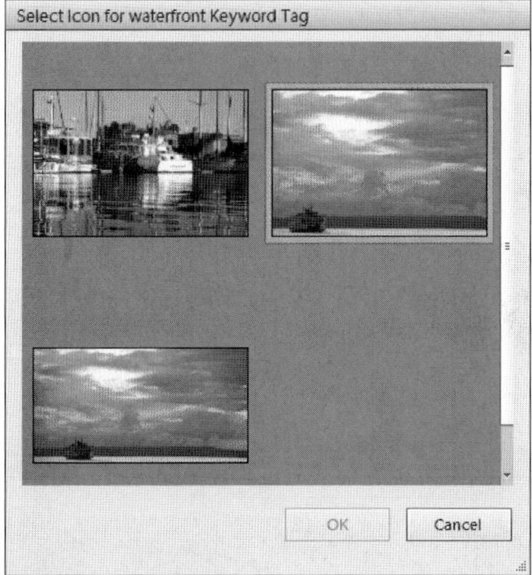

I The Select Icon dialog.

J Resize the selection rectangle in the Edit Tag Icon dialog to choose the visible area of the icon.

K Drag the selection rectangle to choose a different area of a photo to use for the tag icon.

To change a tag's icon:

1. In the Tags pane, right-click on the tag you would like to change.
2. From the tag drop-down menu, choose Edit.
3. In the Edit Keyword Tag dialog, click the Edit Icon button.

   To assign a new icon image in the Edit Tag Icon dialog, you can select from any of the photos to which the tag has been applied, or you can import a completely new photo.
4. To select a different tagged photo, click the Find button H.
5. In the Select Icon for (name of tag) Keyword Tag dialog, click to select a photo thumbnail and click OK I.

   The new image appears in the preview window of the Edit Tag Icon dialog.
6. To crop the area of the photo that will appear on the tag icon, click and drag any of the four cropping handles in the image preview J.
7. To select a different cropped area of the photo to appear on the tag icon, click inside the crop box and drag it in the preview window K.
8. When you're satisfied with the look of your icon, click OK to close the Edit Tag Icon dialog, and then click OK again to close the Edit Keyword Tag dialog. The new icon appears on the tag in the Tags pane.

TIP If you don't want to use any of your tagged photos for a particular keyword icon, click the Import button in the Edit Tag Icon dialog to browse your computer and select a different image.

Using Categories to Organize Tagged Photos

All tags must reside in either a category or sub-category. The Organizer starts you off with a few ready-made categories, but you can create as many new categories and subcategories as you want. Tags can be easily moved from one category to another and also converted to a sub-category that contains its own set of tags.

Ⓐ Use the New menu in the Tags pane to open the Create Category dialog.

To create a new category:

1. Click the drop-down menu accompanying the New button at the top of the Tags pane Ⓐ.
2. Choose New Category to open the Create Category dialog.
3. In the Create Category dialog, enter a name in the Category Name text field.
4. In the Category Icon area of the dialog, optionally click to select a category icon that appears when icons are visible Ⓑ.
5. Also optional, but if you'd like to color-code your categories, click the Choose Color button to open the Color Picker. Colors are applied to sub-category and tag icons within the category.
6. Click to select the color and then click OK Ⓒ.
7. If you're satisfied with your other category settings, click OK to close the dialog. Your new category appears in the panel.

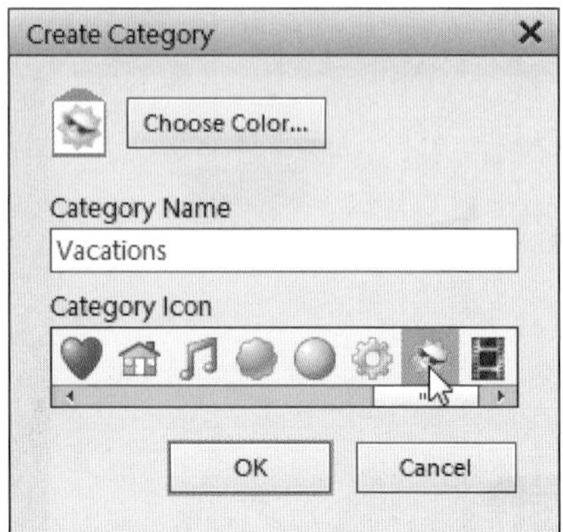

Ⓑ The Create Category dialog includes a variety of icons you can use to represent your new category.

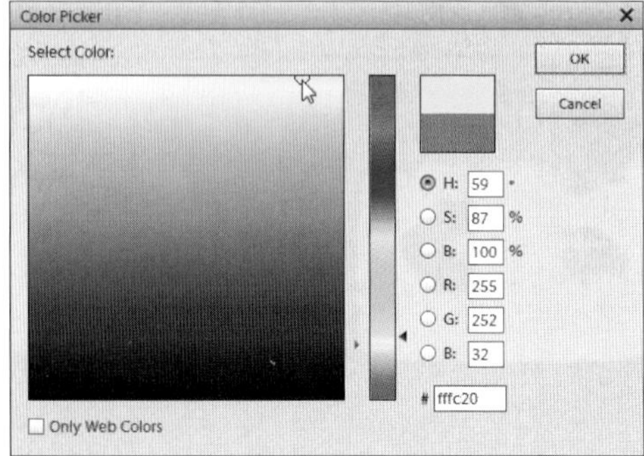

Ⓒ The color you choose in the Color Picker appears on the icons for tags in your new category.

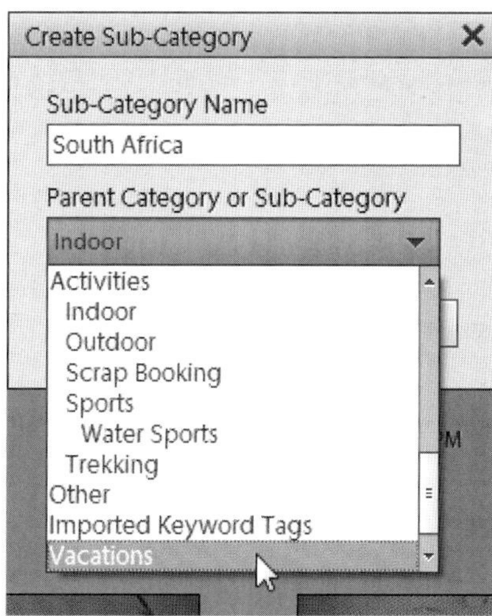

D Sub-categories can be nested within categories or other sub-categories.

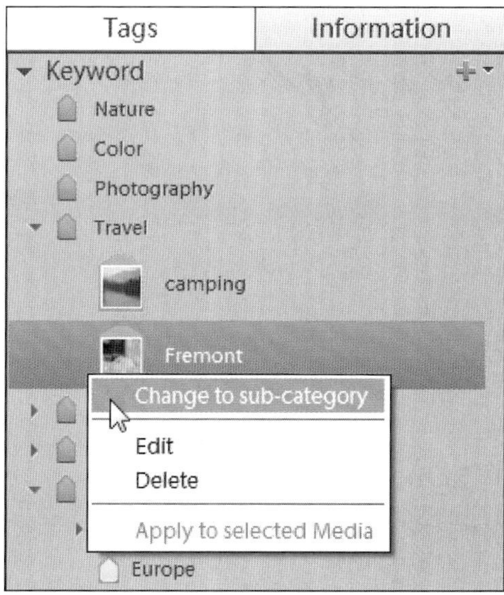

E Convert a tag to a sub-category from the tag contextual menu in the Tags pane.

To create a new sub-category:

1. From the New drop-down menu, choose New Sub-Category to open the Create Sub-Category dialog.
2. In the Create Sub-Category dialog, enter a name in the Sub-Category Name text field.
3. From the Parent Category or Sub-Category drop-down menu, choose a location in which to place your new sub-category **D**.
4. Click OK to close the dialog.
5. Your new sub-category appears in the Tags pane, within the category or sub-category you selected.

To convert a tag to a sub-category:

1. In the Tags pane, right-click on the tag you want to convert.
2. From the tag contextual menu, choose Change to sub-category **E**. The tag icon changes to a sub-category icon.

TIP If you decide you'd like to convert a sub-category (that was formerly a tag) back to a tag, go to the Sub-Category contextual menu and choose the Change sub-category to a tag option. All the tag's properties, including its icon, are retained.

To assign a tag to a new category or sub-category:

1. In the Tags pane, right-click the tag you want to place and choose Edit.
2. From the Category menu in the Edit Keyword Tag dialog, choose the category or sub-category in which you want to place the tag **F**.
3. Click OK to close the Edit Keyword Tag dialog. In the Tags pane, the tag appears within the category and sub-category you defined **G**.

   If you've already applied the tag to a photo or photos in the Media Browser, the category icons below the photo thumbnails will automatically update to display the icon of the new category.

TIP You can also move tags into new categories or sub-categories right in the Tags pane. With both the tag and the category or sub-category visible, simply click to select a tag and then drag it onto a category or sub-category icon. The tag will nest beneath the category or sub-category you choose. The disadvantage of this method (as compared to the one outlined in the procedure) is that you must be able to see the tag and category or sub-category in the Tags pane. Since the Tags pane can get filled with categories quickly, it may require that you do quite a bit of scrolling and searching, whereas the Category menu in the Edit Keyword Tag dialog gives you a list of every category and sub-category in one convenient place.

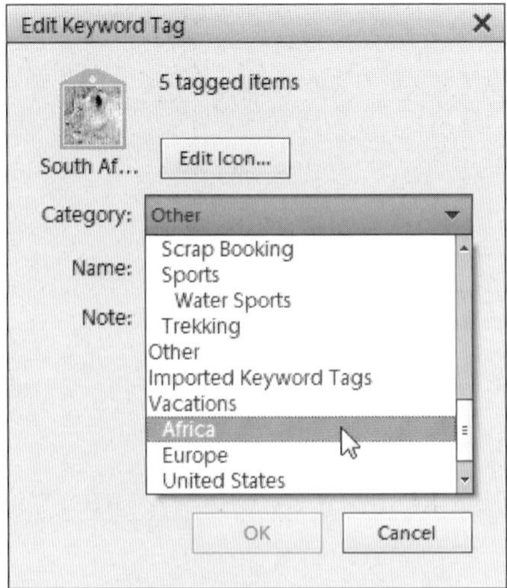

F You can easily move a tag from one category to another using the Edit Keyword Tag dialog.

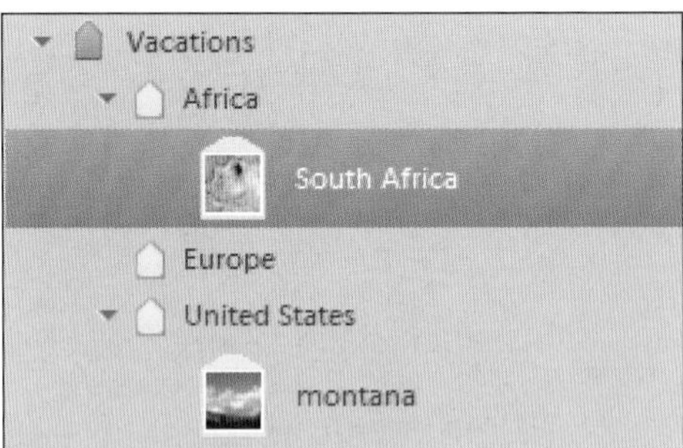

G Changes you make to a tag's placement in the Edit Keyword Tag dialog appear instantly in the Tags pane.

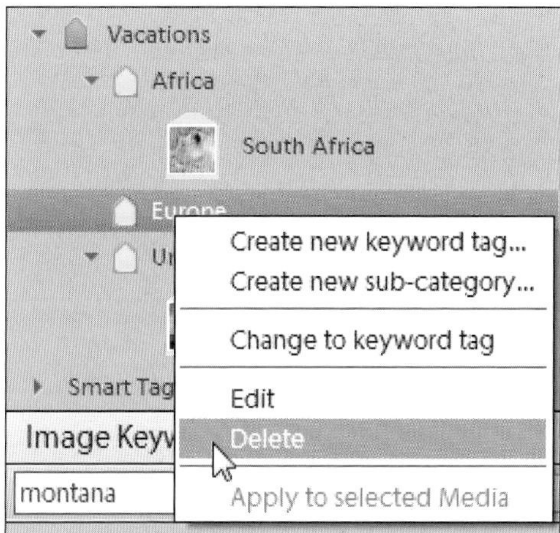

H Delete a category or tag from the Tags pane by clicking the Delete button.

To view photos belonging to a category or sub-category:

In the Tags pane, position your mouse pointer over a category or sub-category and click the angle-bracket (>) button that appears to activate the Advanced search mode. All tags in that category appear.

To view all photos again, click the Back button, or click the X button in the Advanced search pane to collapse the search criteria.

To delete a category or sub-category:

In the Tags pane, click a category or sub-category, and then right-click and select Delete **H**.

However, before you delete a category or sub-category, bear in mind that you will also delete all related sub-categories and tags and will remove those tags from all tagged photos. In some circumstances, a better alternative may be to change a category or sub-category's properties to better match the content or theme of related tagged photos.

TIP Deleting a category does not delete the photos that belong to the category.

Auto-Analyzing Photos

The Organizer's Auto-Analyzer feature scans your library and applies Smart Tags for characteristics such as High Contrast, Blurred, and more. You can then locate images matching those criteria using keyword tags.

To analyze selected photos:

1. Select one or more photos in the library.
2. Choose File > Run Auto-Analyzer, or right-click on a photo and choose Run Auto-Analyzer from the contextual menu.
3. After the Organizer analyzes the files, click OK.

The photos gain a Smart Tag icon; hold your pointer over the icon or right-click to reveal which tags were applied **A**.

To analyze photos automatically:

1. Go to Edit > Preferences > Media-Analysis to view controls for the feature.
2. Enable the Analyze Media for Smart Tags Automatically option **B**.

   You can also choose which filters to apply; disabling the Brightness and Contrast filter, for example, won't point out pictures that are too dark. Click OK.

TIP Hover over the Auto-Analyzer status icon to check or pause the analysis C.

TIP If you've installed only Photoshop Elements, just three filters are available in the preferences: Blur, Brightness & Contrast, and Face. With Premiere Elements also installed, additional filters appear.

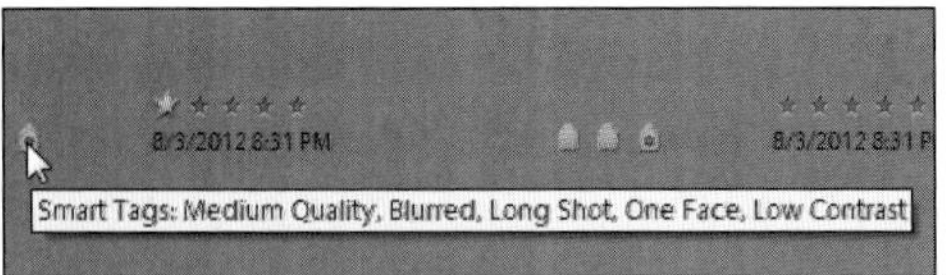

A The Organizer can apply tags based on its analysis of an image.

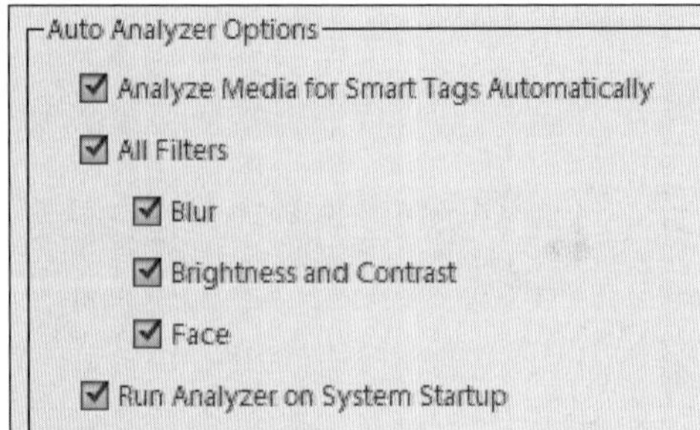

B Choose which attributes are considered in the image analysis.

C Auto-Analyze can take a while, but you can check its status.

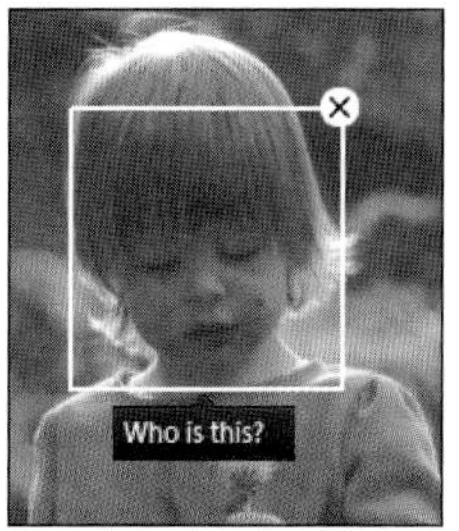

Ⓐ When the Organizer asks, click and enter a name in the "Who is this?" field.

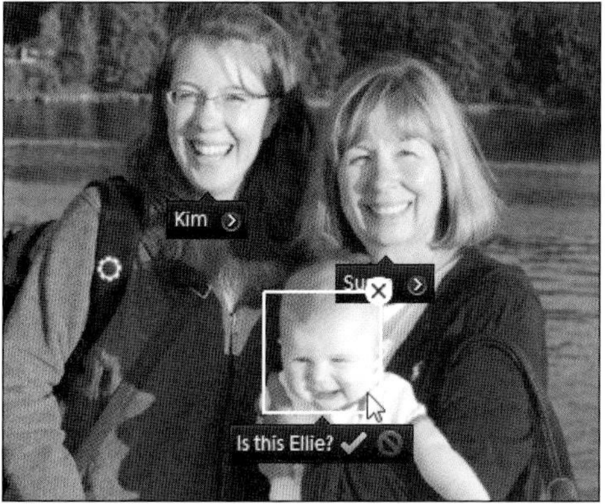

Ⓑ As the database of recognized photos builds, the Organizer attempts matches.

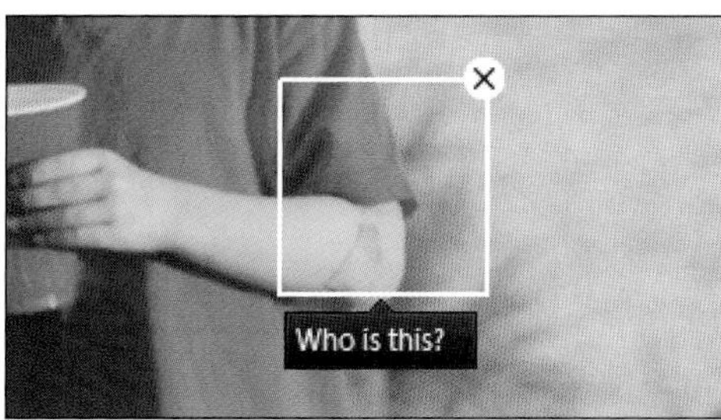

Ⓒ Well, no one ever said computers were perfect.

Identifying and Locating People

The People feature offers an easy way to sort, identify, and tag photos based on the people in them.

Identifying people

The Organizer does a good job finding areas of photos that resemble faces. With your help, it can also determine who those people are.

To identify one person:

1. Double-click a photo containing a person to view it full-size.
2. When the Organizer displays a "Who is this?" field, click it and do one of the following:
   - Type a name Ⓐ. If it's a new person, a new keyword tag is created under the People category and applied to the photo.
   - Click the name of an existing tag that appears below the field.
   - The Organizer will start to make suggestions as the database of faces grows Ⓑ. Click the green check mark button if the suggestion is correct; click the red button to enter a different name.
   - If the Organizer suggests an area that isn't a face, click the Close button (X) to dismiss it Ⓒ.
3. If a person is in the picture but wasn't identified, click the Mark Face button in the Task bar, draw a box around their face, and then enter the person's name.

To identify several people:

1. Click the People button at the top of the screen.
2. In the Task bar, click the Add People button. The Organizer scans your library for photos it has previously identified as containing people.
3. In the Label People dialog, type the names of people who are identified **D**.
4. In the next dialog, the Organizer attempts to match other photos with the one you identified. If a face doesn't match, click the drop-down menu that appears when you position the mouse pointer over the thumbnail and choose Not [name] **E**. You don't need to identify thumbnails that are positive matches.

   If it's helpful, choose Show in Full Size View to see the person in context.
5. Click the Save button to view more potential matches.
6. When you're finished, click the Cancel button.

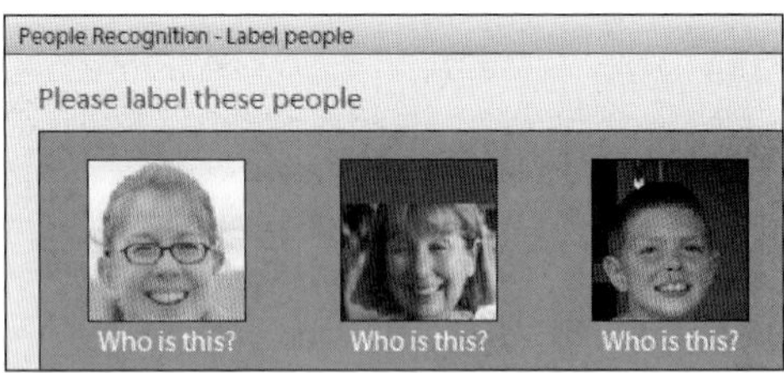

D The Organizer find faces but needs your help identifying them.

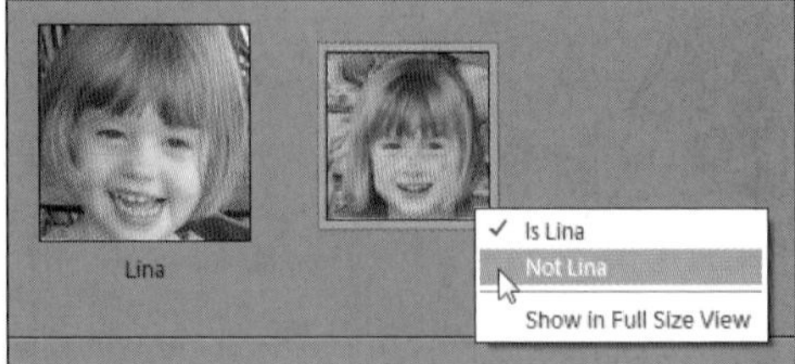

E Exclude photos that don't match the person.

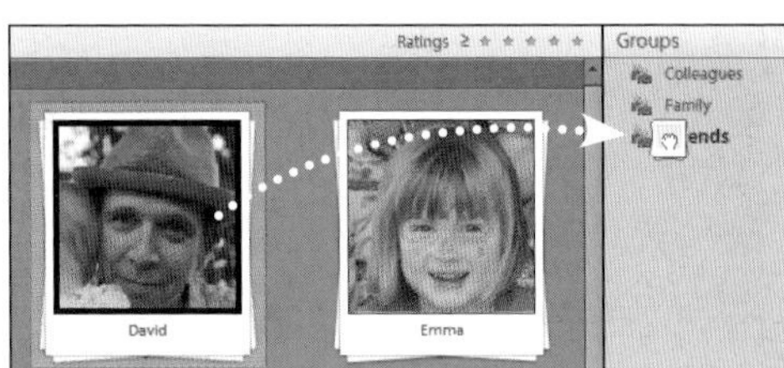

F To better locate people, add them to groups.

To assign people to groups:

1. In the People view, click the Group toggle switch to reveal the Groups pane.
2. Three suggested groups already exist (Colleagues, Family, and Friends), but if you want to create your own, click the New (+) button. In the Add Group dialog, enter a name for the group and click OK.
3. Drag one or more people to a group name **F**.

TIP In the Label People dialog, speed through the selections by pressing Tab to advance to the next person.

TIP The Organizer can bring in some extra help identifying people, if you want. In the Label People dialog, click the Download/ Update Facebook Friends' List to Name People button. After you authorize Elements to use information from Facebook, people from your Friends' list show up as options when you type a person's name.

Ⓖ Find people easily in the People view.

Ⓗ Sometimes it's not helpful to view just a closeup of someone's face. Switch to the Photos view to see the entire picture.

To remove people:

1. Switch to the People view.
2. Select a person you wish to remove from the People feature. This action disassociates a name from the photos it's been tagged with; the images themselves are not deleted.
3. Click the Remove button in the Task bar.
4. Confirm that you want to remove the person by clicking Yes in the dialog that appears.

Locating people

Once the Organizer identifies people, use the People view to quickly locate photos in which they appear.

To locate people:

1. Switch to the People view.
2. Double-click a person's stack to view the photos tagged with their name Ⓖ.
3. To toggle between thumbnails of the faces and full images, click the Faces/Photos switch Ⓗ.

TIP For a quick preview of which photos are marked with each person, move your mouse pointer horizontally across their thumbnail.

TIP Is it time to show off photos of kids or friends? Select one or more names in the People view, click the Slide Show button, sit back, and enjoy.

Using Albums to Arrange and Group Photos

Although photos have gone digital, we don't have to discard our analog thinking. Just as you store Polaroids and prints in a photo album, you can collect your digital photos in Elements albums.

An album can be composed of photos from several different tags or categories. Plus, the photos within albums can be sorted and reordered, independent of their date or folder structure.

To create a new album:

1. Click the New button at the top of the Albums list.
2. From the New drop-down menu, choose New Album Ⓐ. The Add New Album pane appears along the right side of the Media Browser Ⓑ.
3. Leave the Category menu set to None (Top Level). You'll learn more about album categories later in this section.
4. In the Name field, enter a name for your album.
5. Drag the photos you want to add to the album to the Items field Ⓒ.
6. Click OK to close the pane. Your new album appears in the Albums pane at the left side of the Media Browser. By default, albums are sorted in alphabetical order.

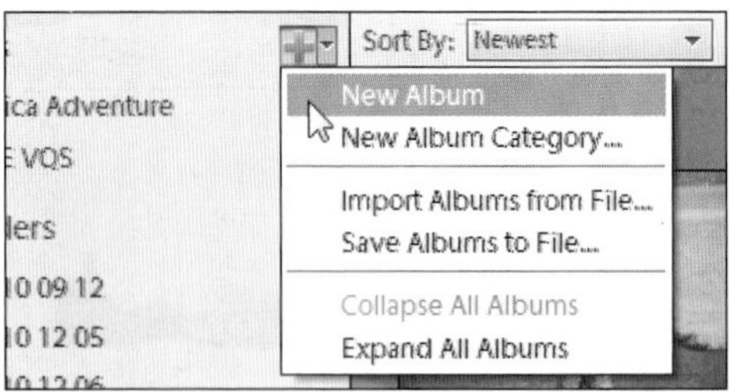

Ⓐ Use the New menu in the Albums list to open the Create Album dialog.

Ⓑ Give the album a descriptive name.

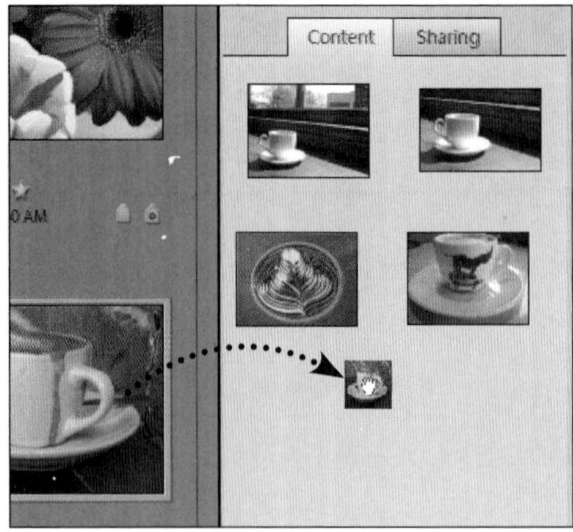

Ⓒ Populate the album by dragging photos to it or by selecting them and clicking the Add button.

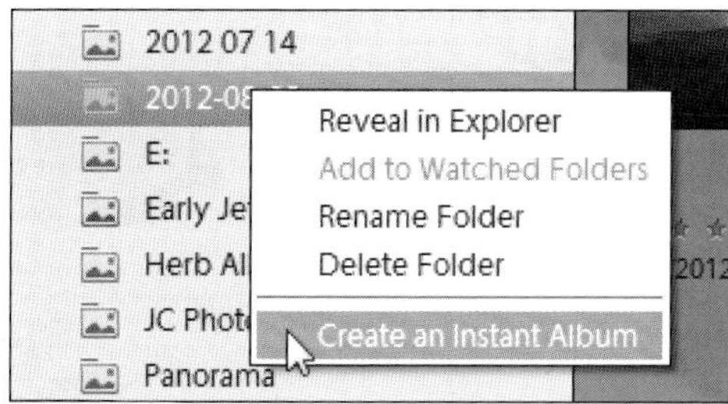

D Every folder group in the Media Browser has its own Create an Instant Album button.

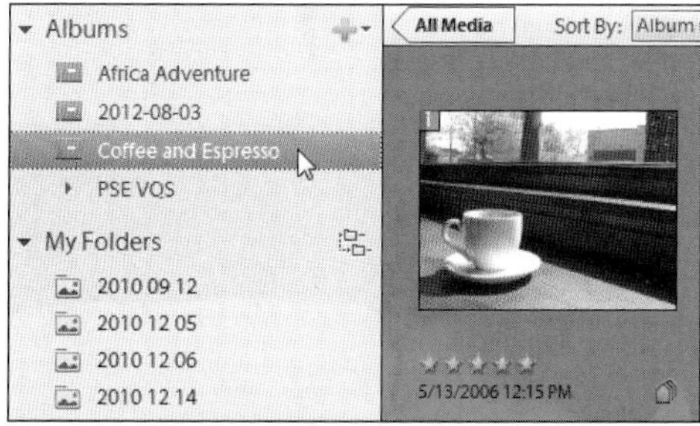

E Click an album name to view only its photos.

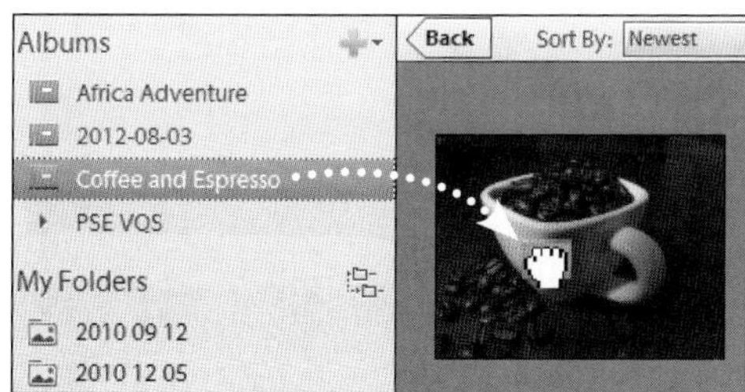

F One way to populate an album is to drag its icon from the Albums list to one or more photos.

To create an album from a folder:

1. Right-click a folder in the Folders List.
2. Choose Create an Instant Album **D**. The album is created with the name of the folder.

To view a photo album:

Click an album name in the Albums list. The Media Browser displays only the photos in that album **E**.

To view your entire catalog, click the Show All button.

To add more photos to an album:

Do one of the following:

- From the Media Browser, drag one or more photos onto the appropriate album in the Albums list.
- From the Albums list, drag an album onto a photo thumbnail in the Media Browser **F**. An album icon appears below the photo in the Browser window to indicate it is part of an album.
- Select one or more photos, and choose Add Selected Media to Album from the contextual menu.

Or

1. In the Edit Album pane, select an album and choose Edit from the contextual menu.
2. Drag photos to the Content area of the pane.
3. Click OK.

To rename an album:

1. In the Albums list, select an album and choose Rename from the contextual menu.
2. Enter a new name in the dialog that appears and click OK.

Or

1. In the Albums list, choose Edit from the contextual menu.
2. Change the text in the Name field and click OK.

To arrange photos within an album:

1. In the Albums list, click an album name.
2. In the Media Browser, click to select a photo, and then drag it to a new location **G**.

Or

1. In the Albums list, select an album choose Edit from the contextual menu.
2. Drag to rearrange the photos in the Edit Album pane and click OK.

To remove photos from an album:

With an album displayed in the Media Browser, select a photo thumbnail and then do one of the following:

- Right-click on the album icon below the photo thumbnail and select Remove from (name of album) Album **H**.
- Right-click inside a photo thumbnail, and then choose Remove from Album > (name of album).

Or

1. In the Albums list, select an album and click the Edit icon.
2. Select one or more photos and click the Remove (–) button.

G To reorder photos within an album, drag a thumbnail to a new location in the Media Browser. The numbers on the thumbnails indicate their order.

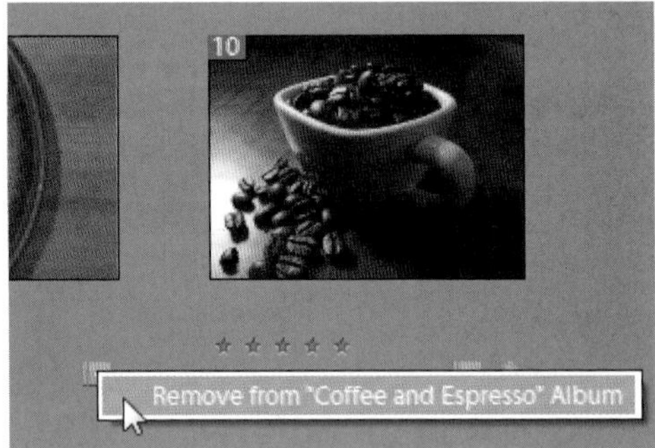

H Right-click a photo's album icon to remove it from the album.

I The Create Album Category dialog.

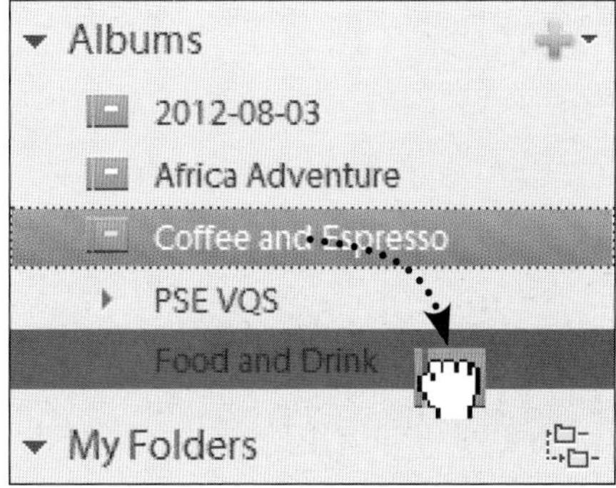

J Once you've created an album category, you can add albums to it from the Albums list.

TIP It's possible to group one album category within another when creating a category. If you've already created an album category, its name appears in the Parent Album Category menu of the Create Album Category dialog. You then have the option of nesting your new album category within the existing one.

TIP You can't drag an album out of an album category to take it back to the top level. Instead, click the Edit Album button, and then choose None (Top Level) from the Album Category drop-down menu.

To create an album category:

1. Click the New button at the top of the Albums list and choose New Album Category to open the Create Album Category dialog.
2. In the Album Category Name text field, enter a name **I**.
3. Leave the Parent Album Category option set to None (Top Level).
4. Click OK to close the Create Album Category dialog. The category appears at the bottom of the list.

To add an album to a category:

In the Albums list, drag an album icon onto the name of the album category **J**.

Or

1. In the Albums list, right-click the album you want to include.
2. From the album contextual menu, choose Edit.
3. In the Edit Album pane, click the Category drop-down manu and choose an existing category.
4. Click OK.

To delete an album:

1. In the Albums list, right-click the album you would like to delete.
2. From the contextual menu, choose Delete.
3. In the Confirm Album Deletion warning box, click OK. The album is removed from the Albums list, but the images within the album remain untouched.

Using Events

A photo by itself is a momentary slice of time, but a collection of photos cover many spans of time. Unless you're the type to capture just a single shot every few hours, your images are probably grouped according to events—a birthday party, an afternoon cruise, or even just breakfast.

Rather than scroll through all thumbnails, you may find it easier to locate images based on events you create, or events the Organizer suggests based on the photos' time information (called Smart Events).

Create a new event

The Organizer initially opts to let you create your own custom events. Did you spend two weeks on vacation? That's an ideal event. Here's how to create it.

To create a new event:

1. In the Events view, click the Add Event button in the Task bar. The right pane of the Media Browser becomes the Add New Event pane.

   Or, in the Media view, select a range of photos and click the Add Event button.
2. Type a title for the event in the Name field.
3. Drag photos for the event from the Media Browser to the pane **A**.
4. Click Done. The event appears as a new stack **B**.

TIP When you create an event from the Media view, the Organizer updates the start and end dates automatically. If you start from the Events view, those fields show only the current date—you need to update them manually by clicking the calendar buttons to the right of each field.

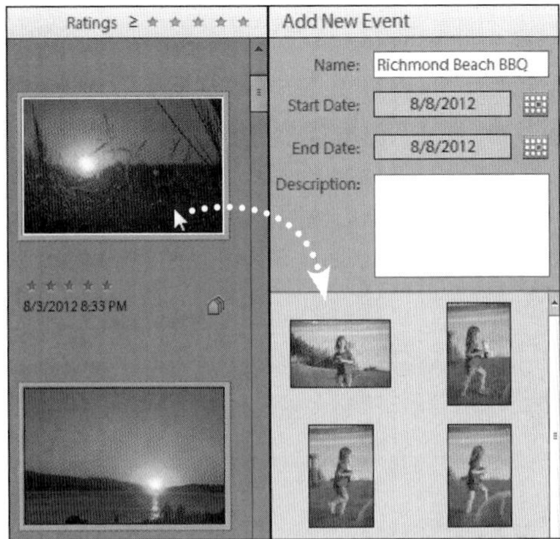

A Drag photos to the Add New Event pane to populate the event you just created.

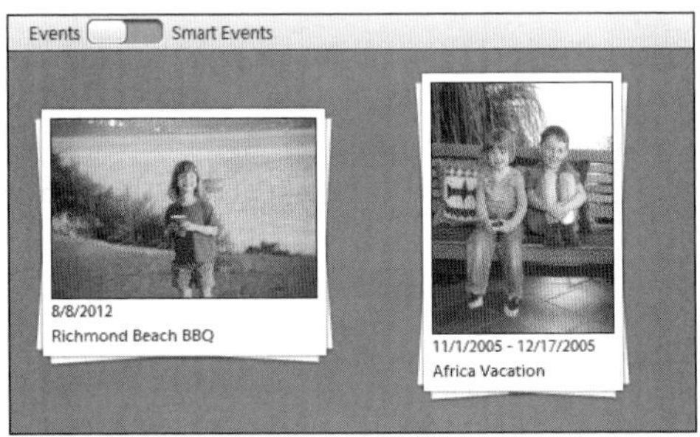

B The new event appears in the Events view.

Calendar Clear
2012

Jan	Feb	Mar
Apr	May	Jun
July	Aug	Sep

S	M	T	W	T	F	S
1	2	3	4	5	6	7
8	9	10	11	12	13	14
15	16	17	18	19	20	21
22	23	24	25	26	27	28
29	30	31				

Oct	Nov	Dec

C Months and dates that contain photos appear highlighted.

D Choose which photo appears as the cover.

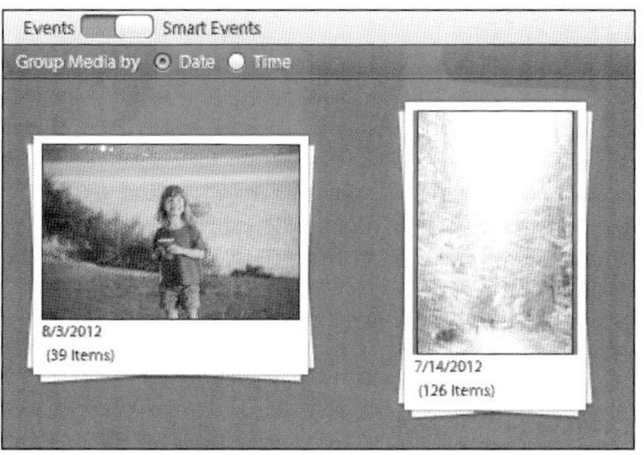

E Smart Events are grouped by date.

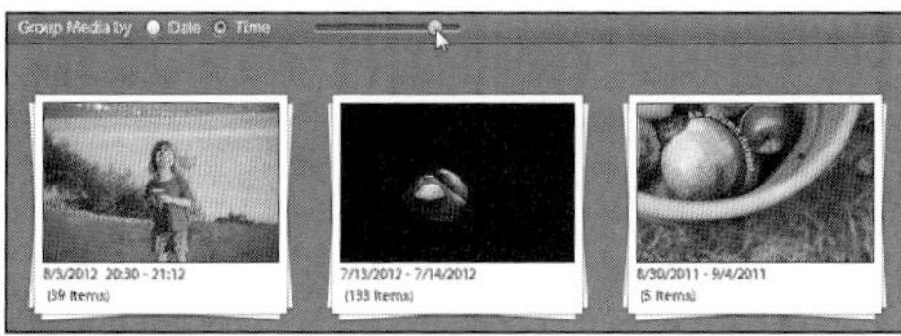

F The Time slider lets you view fewer (top) or more (bottom) events; note the dates for each event.

To view an event's photos:

- Double-click an event.
- Click the Calendar button in the Task bar (if the Calendar isn't visible) and then choose a year, month, and day **C**.

To change an event's cover image:

1. Double-click an event to view its photos. Or, better yet, move the mouse pointer over the event to preview its contents.
2. When you find the photo you want to use as the thumbnail, right-click and choose Set As Cover **D**.

Use Smart Events

The advantage of creating your own events is the ability to specify any time range you like. But I find that's sometimes too much work—let the computer figure it out instead. Click the Events toggle to switch it to Smart Events, and the Organizer displays photos in stacks based on the date they were captured **E**.

There's also a more clever method. Change the Group Media By option from Date to Time, and use the slider to view fewer events (move to the left) or more events (move to the right) **F**.

TIP Clicking an album, folder, or ratings in the Events view narrows the visible matches to events that include only those criteria.

TIP Smart Events appear as dates, but you can give them custom names, too. Select an event, click the Name Event(s) button in the Task bar, and enter a name. The name doesn't appear in the Events view, but will come up when you perform a search for the text.

Reviewing Photos Full Screen

When you're looking over a set of photos, you want to see the photos, not everything else around them. The full-screen reviewing option lets you see just your images, with a minimal set of controls for ranking and sorting, and even for applying basic edits.

To review photos full screen:

1. Choose View > Full Screen, or press Ctrl+F11/Command-F11. If you have a photo selected, it fills the screen; if not, the first item in your library appears **A**.
2. Use the navigation controls at the bottom of the screen to switch between files, play a slideshow, or hide or show the Quick Organize and Quick Edit panels **B**.
3. Use the Quick Organize panel to apply keyword tags and create new tags: click tag names in the Keyword Tags field to apply them.

   You can also use the Quick Edit panel to make basic adjustments if you're in a hurry.
4. Press Esc or click the Exit button to leave full-screen mode when you're finished reviewing.

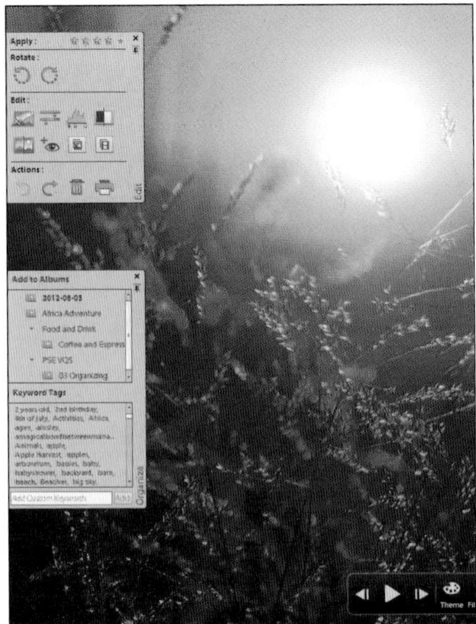

A The full-screen review includes panels that automatically hide when not being used.

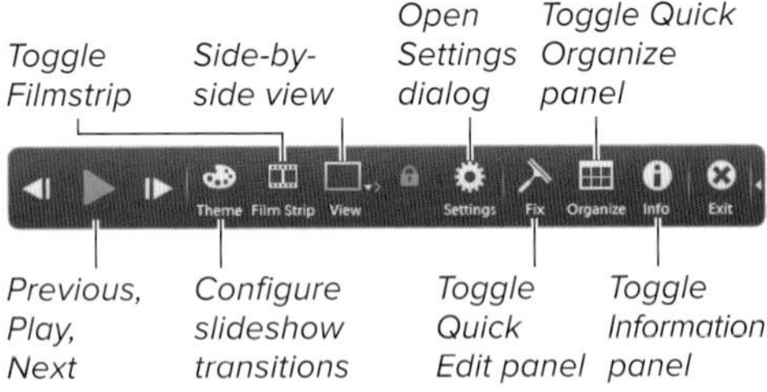

B The full-screen control bar.

TIP **If you apply a QuickEdit to a RAW image, you're asked to save the edited version in a different file format, such as JPEG.**

TIP **Click the tiny pushpin icon on the panels to toggle between remaining visible and automatically retracting to the edge of the screen.**

TIP **To sort and rate your photos quickly, forget the panels and just type the keys 1-5 to apply ratings.**

Full-Screen Slideshows

The full-screen review feature is good even if you're not reviewing. Use it to play quick slideshows, including background music and transitions. Click the Play button in the control bar (or press the spacebar) to start; adjust the settings by clicking the Settings button; and choose a transition by clicking the Theme button.

Finding Photos

In addition to locating photos using keyword tags and albums, the Organizer offers a host of other options for finding and viewing photos in your catalog. I'll touch on just a few of the more popular methods here for locating photos by their embedded date information. For example, the text search capability takes advantage of the keyword tags you applied earlier.

To find photos using a text search:

- Type a term in the Search field. The Media Browser searches the photos' metadata and displays matches (including keywords) as you type **A**.
- The Organizer is smart enough to understand the operators AND, OR, and NOT, which allow you to quickly narrow your search **B**.
- For more specific searching, enter any of the following search tags into the field. For example, typing `make:canon` (note the lack of a space after the colon) finds all photos in my library shot using a Canon camera. You can also group tags to narrow the results **C**.
    - `tag:`
    - `filename:`
    - `caption:`
    - `make:`
    - `model:`
    - `author:`
    - `notes:`
    - `date:##/##` (month/day, depending on date preferences in Organizer)
    - `date:####` (year)
    - `date:`(`today`, `yesterday`, `lastweek`, `thisyear`, or `lastyear`)

A Type a word in the Search field to view photos that include that term.

B You can omit terms by specifying NOT in the Search field.

C Here I've used two terms to define a more specific search (photos shot with a Canon camera sometime in 2006).

To find photos using Advanced Search:

1. Click the Search field's drop-down menu and choose Advanced Search **D**, or choose Find > Advanced Search.

   If you're viewing the Tags pane, you can also click the search button (>) that appears to the right of a tag when your mouse pointer is over it.

2. In the Advanced Search pane that opens above the Media Browser, select specific keywords, people, places, and events to narrow the search results **E**.

3. If the results don't pull up what you were expecting, click the Options drop-down menu and choose Show close match results **F**.

4. To hide the pane temporarily, click the collapse button (^) **G**.

   You can also click the Clear button above the results to reset the Advanced Search choices and start fresh.

5. Click the close button (X) to exit the Advanced Search pane.

TIP **Advanced searches are inclusive, meaning the Organizer looks for items that contain each item you select (an AND search). You can also exclude items, as in the text example on the previous page: Right-click a criterion, such as a tag, and choose Exclude. That returns results that specifically do not include the tag.**

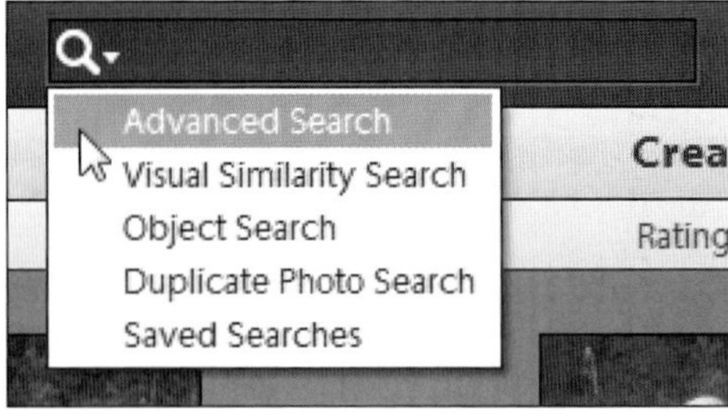

D Access the Advanced Search pane from the Search field.

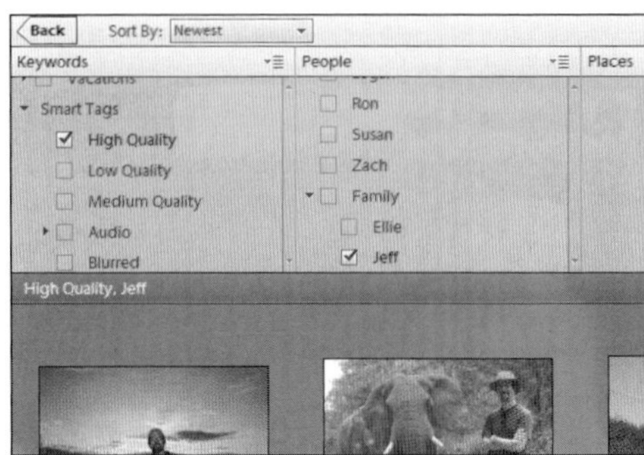

E Specify multiple criteria to locate photos.

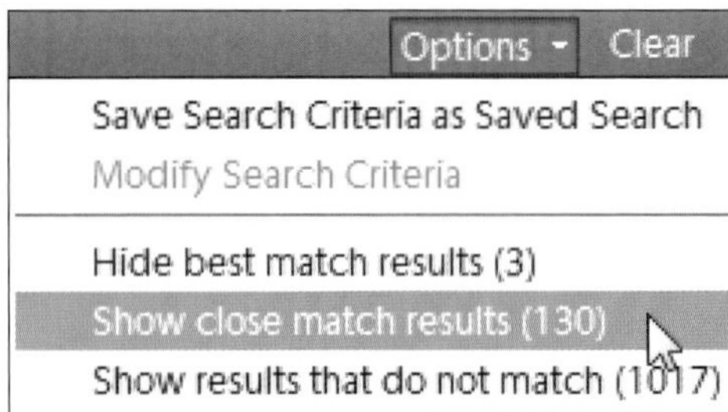

F It's okay to be close when searching.

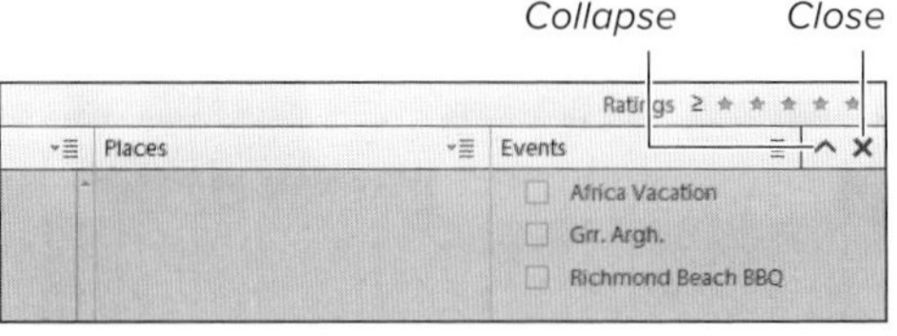

G The Advanced Search pane's minimalist collapse and close buttons.

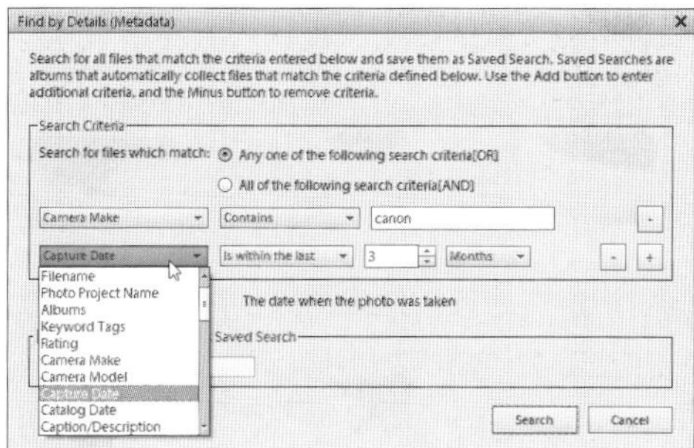

H Find files using more specific metadata.

I Bars (month markers) in the timeline represent sets of images shot or acquired in specific months. Click a timeline marker to view its photos.

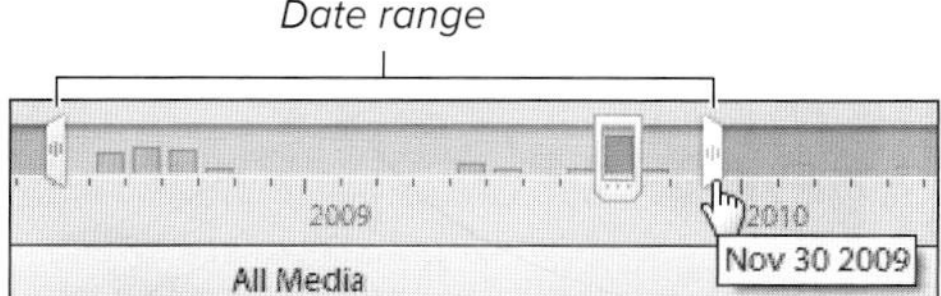

J After you set a date range, only those photos that fall within the specified range are visible.

TIP From the Find menu, you can search photos by a number of different criteria. Some that you'll probably use most often are by caption or note; by file name; by history (imported on date, and printed on date, among others); and by media type (photos, video, audio, and creations). Just choose an option and then fill in its dialog (when applicable) to refine your search.

To find photos by details (metadata):

1. Choose Find > By Details (Metadata).
2. In the Search Criteria section of the dialog, choose an attribute from the first drop-down menu and specify details (such as "Camera Make Contains canon").
3. Click the Add button (+) to add more criteria (such as Capture Date) **H**. Repeat this step until you've added all the attributes you want.
4. Using the "Search for files which match" buttons, choose whether results should include any or all of the criteria.
5. Click Search to display results.

To find photos using the timeline:

1. If the timeline isn't visible, choose Window > Timeline (Ctrl+L/Command-L).
2. In the timeline, click on a bar that corresponds to a specific month and year **I**. The Media Browser automatically scrolls to display the photos for the month you selected.

To display photos within a date range:

1. From the Find menu, choose Set Date Range, or press Ctrl+Alt+F/Command-Option-F.
2. In the Set Date Range dialog, use the text fields and drop-down menus to enter your dates.
3. The timeline highlights just the range of dates you selected **J**.

TIP You can also move the date range markers on the timeline to view photos within that range.

Finding photos using visual information

A text search doesn't help if your photos don't include any keyword tags or file names that point to their contents. When you want to locate a photo that looks a lot like another one—whether the similiarity is in color scheme or objects that appear—turn to a trio of Organizer features.

To find visually similar photos:

1. Select a photo that you want to use as a starting point.
2. Choose Find > By Visual Searches > Visually similar photos and videos. Or, click the drop-down menu in the Search field and choose Visual Similarity Search.

   The Media Browser displays photos that are like the one you selected, with a percentage badge indicating how similar it thinks the photo is **K**.
3. Drag the Refine Search slider to display more photos that match the original in terms of color or shape **L**.
4. Another way to refine the search is to add more photos for the Organizer to compare: Drag an image to the placeholder that appears next to the first photo **M**.

   You can remove a photo from the search criteria by double-clicking it in the Find bar. (Or, right-click it and choose Remove from search.)

TIP You don't need to select a photo first. You can also start by choosing Visual Similarity Search from the Search drop-down menu and then add a photo to the Find bar.

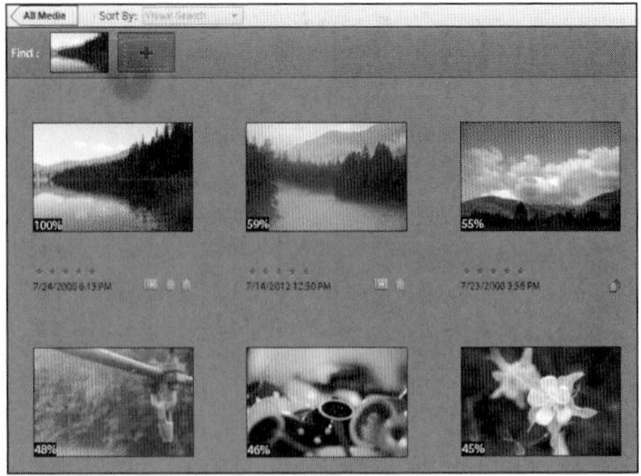

K Visual search brings up related photos.

L Moving the slider toward Color locates photos with similar colors to the reference image.

M Add photos to the Find bar to bring up more visually similar results.

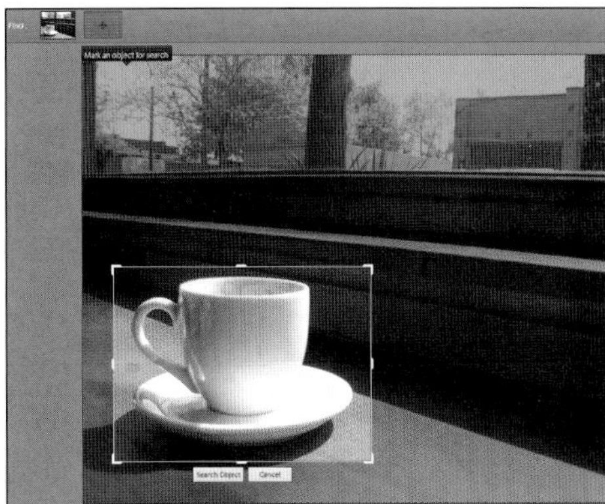

N Select an object to locate photos containing similar-looking objects.

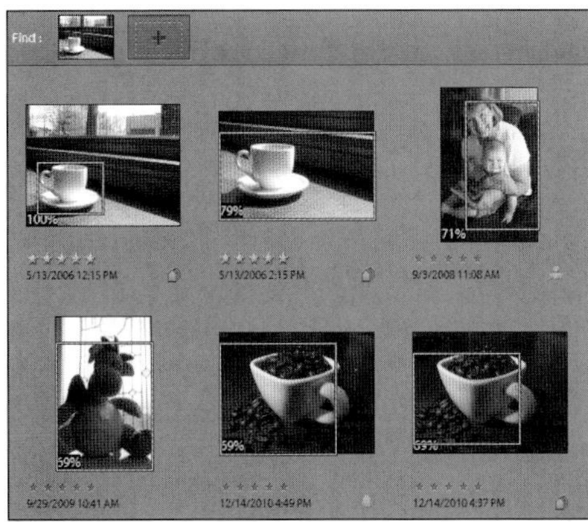

O The Organizer identifies photos and areas that (roughly) match your source object.

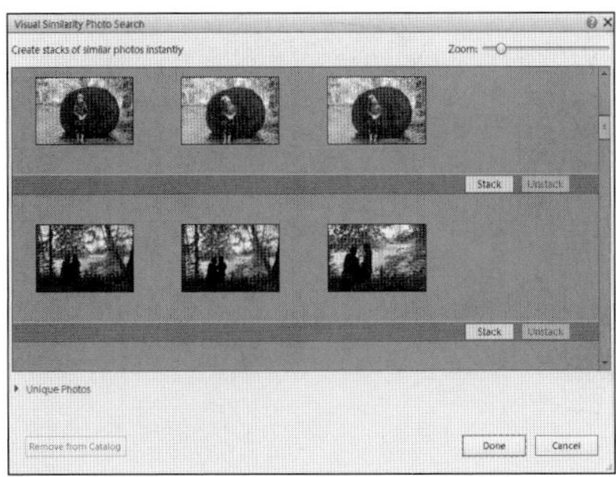

P Find duplicates—or photos that are visually very similar—and put them into stacks.

To find similar objects in photos:

1. Select a photo that contains an object you want to locate.
2. Choose Find > By Visual Searches > Objects within photos.

   The Media Browser adds a selection box to the photo.
3. Click the center of the box, drag it to an object in the photo, and resize the box as needed **N**.
4. Click the Search Object button to view the results.
5. If necessary, drag the Refine Search slider to prioritize the hunt between color or shape **O**.

To find duplicate images:

1. Choose Find > By Visual Searches > Duplicate photos. Elements searches your entire collection and brings up the Visually Similarity Photo Search dialog, which arranges the images in rows **P**.
2. To remove a duplicate photo, select it and click the Remove from Catalog button, and then confirm the deletion.

   To group a row of photos, click the Stack button. (See "Using Stacks to Organize Similar Photos," later in this chapter.)
3. Click Done when you're finished.

TIP Make sure no photo is selected before you look for duplicates; otherwise you get an error message.

Find photos using Saved Searches

One of my grandmother's cupboards was filled with photo albums, organized roughly chronologically, along with a bunch of envelopes and stacks of free-floating pictures that weren't in any order. The problem with lots of photos is that there's only so much time you can spend sorting them.

But what if you had an assistant who could do the organizing for you? Not just once, but ongoing, changing the albums based on new photos or keyword tags or other criteria? Saved Searches operate just like that (and they don't mind the workload).

To create a Saved Search:

1. Click the Search drop-down list and choose Saved Searches.
2. Click the New Search Query button.
3. Type a descriptive title in the Name field.
4. Specify photo attributes using the drop-down menus in the Search Criteria section **Q**.

   The other drop-down menu and field change depending on the criteria. For example, choosing Keyword Tags presents a list of tags.
5. To add more criteria, click the plus button **R** and specify the attributes.
6. By default, the search picks up photos containing any of the criteria you specify. To view only photos that match every attribute, choose the radio button labeled All of the following search criteria [AND] **S**.
7. Click OK. Only the images matching the criteria are displayed **T**.

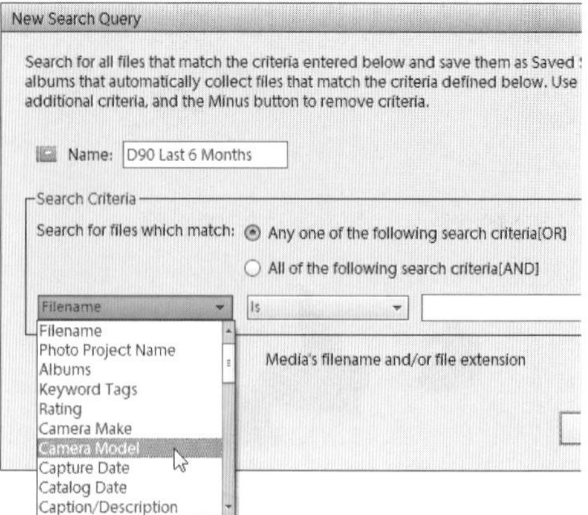

Q Choose from several attributes to start building the saved search.

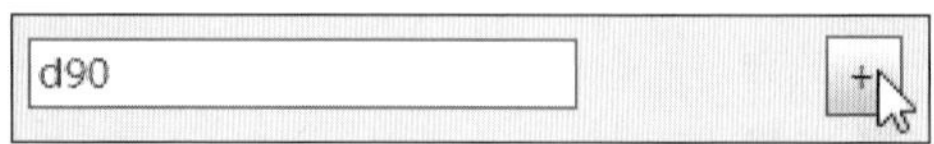

R Click here to add additional criteria.

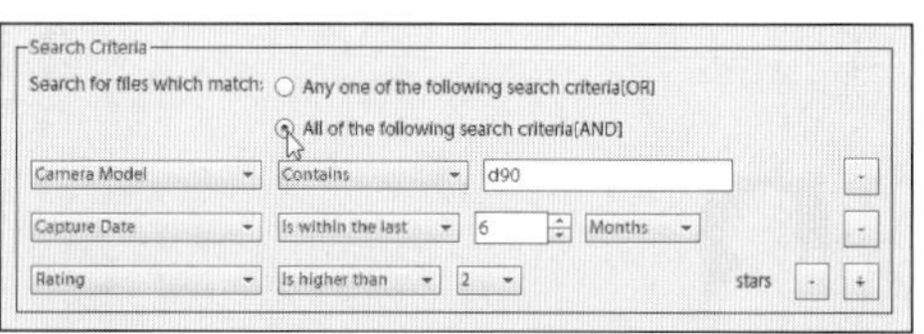

S This Saved Search will display only photos shot with a Nikon D90 within the last six months and having a rating of 3, 4, or 5 stars.

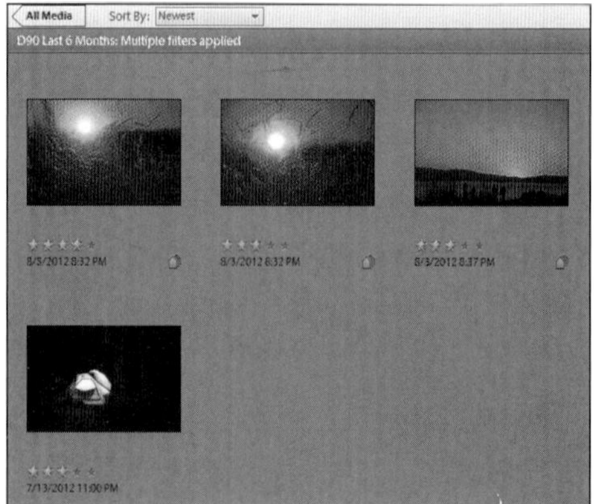

T After the Saved Search is created, the pictures that match its criteria are displayed.

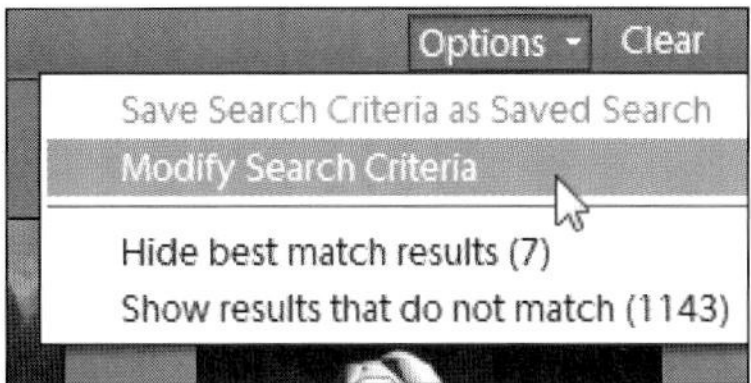

Ⓤ Choose Modify Search Criteria when you're viewing the contents of a Saved Search.

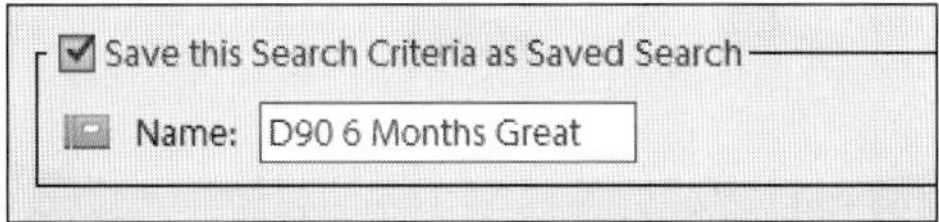

Ⓥ Make sure you mark the criteria as a Saved Search, or Elements will modify the search for that instance only.

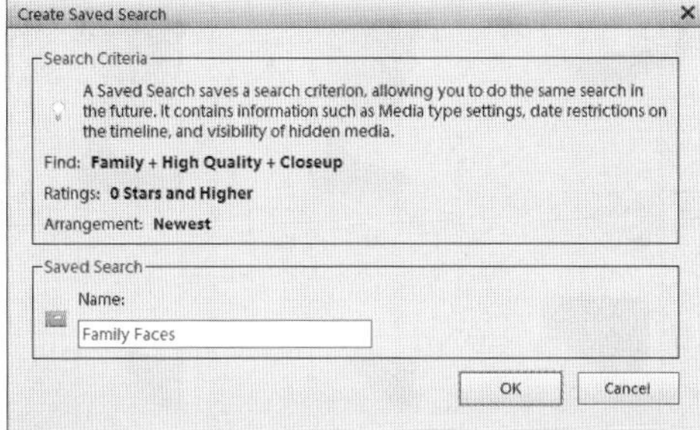

Ⓦ A Saved Search can be built using the criteria of a regular album.

Where Are My Smart Albums?

If you've upgraded to Photoshop Elements 11 from an earlier version, you probably noticed that the Organizer no longer includes Smart Albums. Or rather, the "Smart Album" name is gone. Saved Searches perform the same task, and in fact, aside from being pushed out of sight into the Search box, are almost the same as the Smart Albums of old. If you had created Smart Albums in Elements 10 or earlier, they now appear in the list of Saved Searches.

To modify a Saved Search:

1. Select a search in the Saved Searches and click Open to view its contents.
2. From the Options drop-down menu, choose Modify Search Criteria Ⓤ.
3. In the Find by Details (Metadata) dialog that appears, edit the attributes you set up originally.
4. To keep the new criteria, mark the checkbox labeled Save this Search Criteria as Saved Search Ⓥ.
5. Enter a name for the search (and see the tip below).
6. Click Search to save the settings. The images in the Media Browser reflect the new criteria.

To create a Saved Search from search results:

1. Perform a search using any of the techniques described on the preceding pages.
2. From the Options drop-down menu, choose Save Search Criteria as Saved Search.
3. In the Create Saved Search dialog, give the search a name and click OK Ⓦ.

TIP If you give a modified Saved Search the same title as the original album you're editing, Elements creates a brand-new search instead of replacing the old one.

TIP To easily view all photos *except* those in the Saved Search, go to the Options drop-down menu and choose Show results that do not match.

Using Stacks to Organize Similar Photos

You've spent a day on the valley floor of Yosemite shooting picture after picture, and when you return home in the evening and download all of those photos to your Media Browser, you realize you have about a dozen shots of the same waterfall: some lit a little differently than others; some with different zoom settings; but all similar.

Stacks serve as a convenient way to group those related photos together. They not only save valuable space in the Media Browser, they also make assigning tags much faster, because tagging a stack automatically tags every photo in the stack. When you're ready to take a careful look at all of those waterfalls and weed out the greats from the not-so-greats, you simply expand the stack to view all of the stacked photos at once.

To create a stack:

1. In the Media Browser, Ctrl-click/Command-click to select the photos you want to include in a stack **A**.
2. Choose Edit > Stack > Stack Selected Photos, or press Ctrl+Alt+S/Command-Option-S.

   The photos are stacked together, indicated by a Stack icon in the upper-right corner of the top photo in the stack **B**.

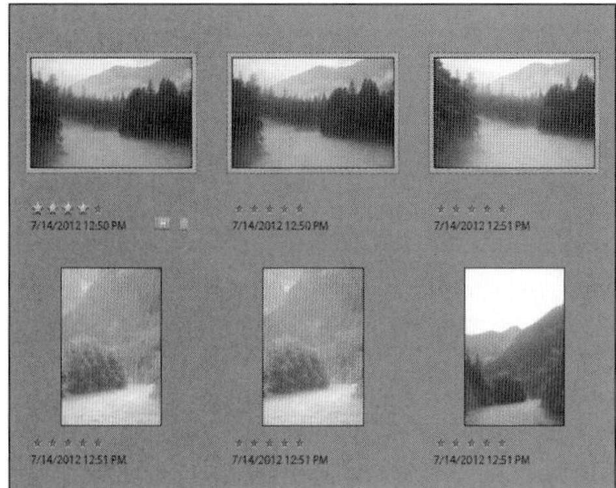

A Select similar photos to organize them into a stack.

B When stacked, the photos occupy just one thumbnail, and are indicated by the Stack icon.

C An expanded stack reveals the photos that have been grouped together.

D A warning box reminds you that you are about to delete all but the top photo in your stack.

To view all photos in a stack:

In the Media Browser, click the arrow icon at the right of the stack. Or, choose Edit > Stack > Expand Photos in Stack (press Ctrl+Alt+R/Command-Option-R). The photos in the stack appear **C**.

To unstack photos in a stack:

Choose Edit > Stack > Unstack Photos.

The stacked photos return to their original locations in the Media Browser window.

To flatten a stack:

1. If you're certain you don't want any photo in a stack except for the top one, you can "flatten" the stack and delete the others. Choose Edit > Stack > Flatten Stack.
2. In the warning dialog that appears, click OK to delete all of the photos except for the top photo in the stack **D**.

   You can also choose to delete the associated image files from your hard disk.

TIP **While you're viewing the expanded stack, you can also remove specific photos from a stack, or designate a new photo to be the top photo (the photo that appears at the top of the stack in the Media Browser). Just right-click on any stacked photo and then, from the thumbnail contextual menu, select an option from the Stack submenu.**

Locating Photos Using Places

Sometimes where you took a photo is as important as what's in the image. The Places feature lets you associate locations with your photos, or pull geographic data from photos whose cameras embed it.

Ⓐ The Places view lets you plot photos anywhere on the globe.

To view photos on a map:

1. Click the Places button. All photos that have been tagged with geolocation information appear in the Media Browser Ⓐ.
2. Select one or more photos to locate them on the map.

   Or, click a pin and then click the Show Media button that appears Ⓑ.

   You can also type a destination into the Search the Map field to see if any images are tagged with that location.
3. Use the map controls to zoom in, if needed. Click and drag to reposition the map, or use the navigation controls.

Or

1. In the Places view, click the List button.
2. Select a location from the list to view all photos assigned to that place Ⓒ.

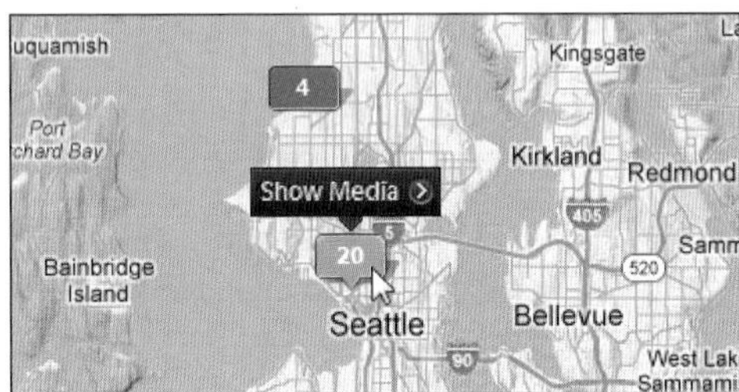

Ⓑ Select a pin to display the photos at its location.

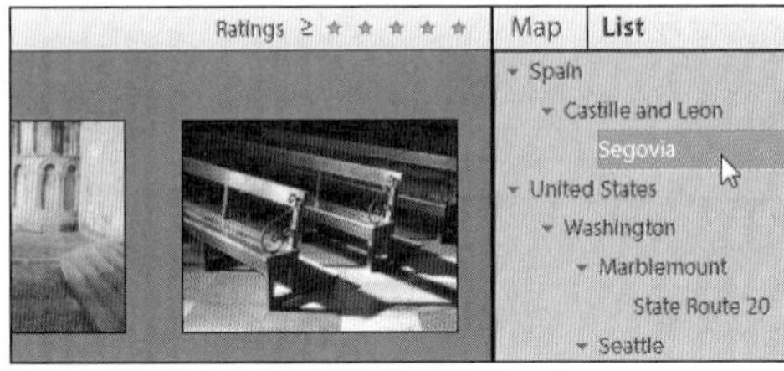

Ⓒ You may find the List view to be a quicker way to locate photos.

To place photos on the map:

1. Select one or more photos in the Media Browser.
2. Click Add Places on the Task bar. The Organizer opens the Add Places dialog.
3. Type an address in the Search the Map field and click Search; or, if a possible result is found, select it from the list that appears Ⓓ. The location is highlighted.

   You can also drag photos from the filmstrip directly onto the map.

D Type a location to pull up Google Maps results.

E Confirm that you want to the photos' Place information to be that location.

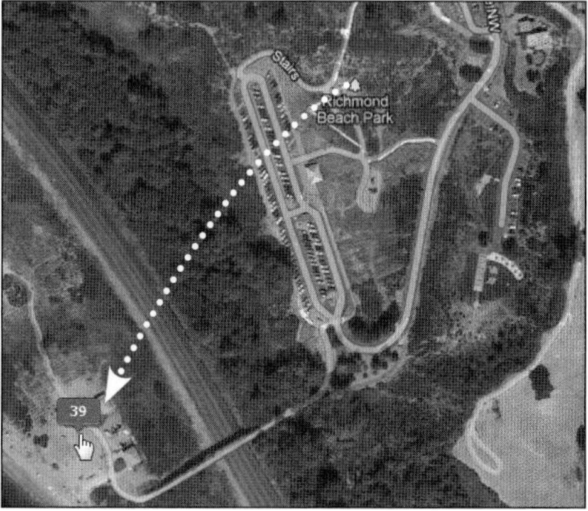

F Drag the pin to a new location to refine the Place information.

4. When asked, "Place Media Here?" click the Accept button (the green check mark) to assign that location to the selected photos E.
5. If you want to refine the location, drag the placeholder to a new spot and then confirm you want to use it F.
6. Click Done to exit the dialog. You can then click the Places button to see the photos in the Places view.

To remove Place information from a photo:

1. In the Places view, select the photo(s) you want to remove.
2. Click the Remove button in the Task bar.
3. Click OK in the dialog that appears to confirm that you want to remove the Place information from the photo.

TIP Select the "Limit search to map area" checkbox to view photos that appear only in the current visible portion of the map.

TIP The View pop-up menu at the upper-right corner of the Map pane lets you display the map with different appearances, such as a Hybrid combination of satellite imagery and street names.

TIP You can also start in the Places view to specify new Places, but that can be confusing at first because the only photos you see are ones that already have location information applied. Click the Add Places button in the Task bar, and then choose the photos you want to assign in the filmstrip. But be careful—if you don't choose photos before finding a location, the Organizer will want to assign every image in your catalog to that place!

Using Catalogs to Store Your Photos

Catalogs are the behind-the-scenes backbone of the Organizer workspace, where all the information for tags and categories and albums are stored. When you install Elements, the program sets up a default catalog (called My Catalog) for you. That might be enough to work with, but you can also create additional catalogs—for example, if more than one person is using the same computer. Or, you may want discrete catalogs for each person's photos: Bob's Catalog, Sara's Catalog, and so on.

To create a new catalog:

1. From the File menu choose Catalog, or press Ctrl+Shift+C/Command-Shift-C.
2. In the Catalog Manager dialog, click a radio button to specify whether the catalog is available to all user accounts on the computer, just the current user, or saved to a custom location **A**.
3. Click the New button.
4. In the File name text field, enter a name for your new catalog **B**.

   At the bottom of the naming dialog is the Import free music into this catalog checkbox. Leave this option selected so the music files you received with Elements (to use as background tracks for PDF slide shows and other creations) will be available in the new catalog.
5. Click OK to create your new catalog.

To switch to a different catalog:

1. From the File menu choose Catalog, or press Ctrl+Shift+C/Command-Shift-C.

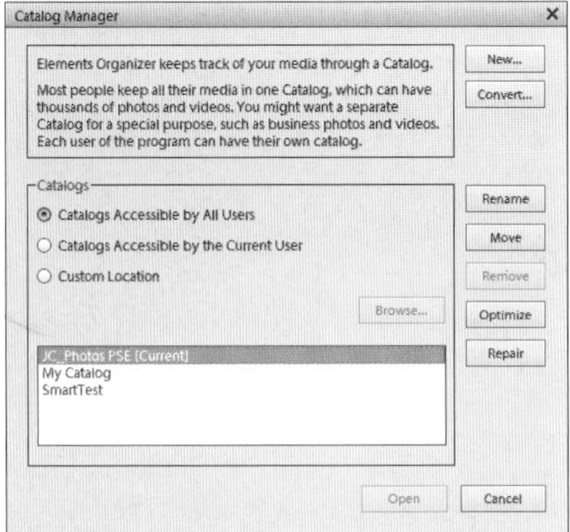

A Choose which users can access the catalogs, as well as the catalogs' locations.

B Make sure your new catalog name is different from any existing catalog names.

Repair and Optimize Catalogs

If your library seems out of sorts—maybe not all thumbnails are appearing, for example—turn to the Catalog Manager for help. Select a catalog name and click the Repair button to scan for problems and fix them.

Clicking the Optimize button pares the catalog size and can also improve performance if the Organizer seems sluggish.

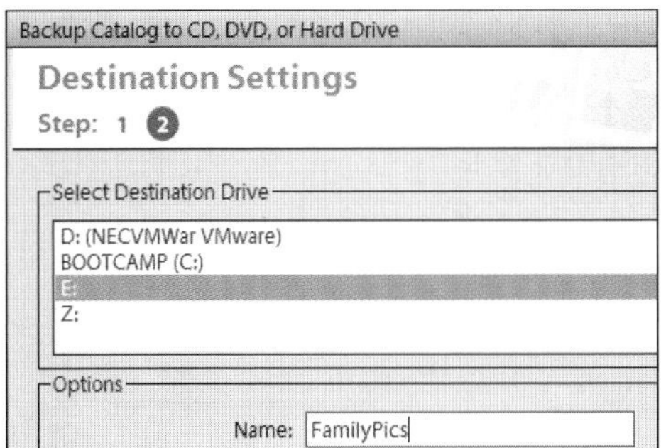

Ⓒ Specify where your backup files are to be copied.

Ⓓ If you need to reconstruct a catalog from your backup, use the Restore Catalog command.

2. Select the name of the saved catalog you want to open.
3. Click the Open button.

To make a backup of a catalog:

1. Since you obviously don't want to lose your photos, choose File > Backup Catalog.
2. In the Backup dialog, choose Full Backup to make a complete copy of the catalog. On subsequent backups, you can choose Incremental Backup to copy only new and changed image files.
3. Click Next.
4. Select a destination drive Ⓒ, and optionally specify a location by clicking the Browse button for Backup Path.
5. Click Save Backup when you're ready. Elements copies the image files and catalog information to the drive.

To restore a catalog from backup:

1. In the unfortunate event that your catalog becomes unreadable, choose File > Restore Catalog from Hard Drive.
2. In the Restore dialog, choose the media on which the backup is stored Ⓓ; click the Browse button to locate the `.tly` file that accompanies the backup.
3. Choose where to copy the restored files: the catalog's original location or another location.
4. Click Restore.

TIP The downside to the Organizer's catalog backup scheme is that making an incremental backup creates a new file. So, to restore your catalog, you must have the original backup and all of the incremental ones at hand. Make sure you have another backup of your data as well, using commercial backup software (which is a fantastic idea anyway).

Cropping and Straightening Images

Have you ever captured a photo, then looked at it later and realized it would be much better if only you had gotten a little closer to your subject, or if a person was to the left of the frame instead of the center? Or maybe the shot is great except for a trash can peeking into the edge of the frame. The ability to crop an image can instantly improve the composition of a photo or remove unwanted elements at its borders.

Another common annoyance is a photo that's just a bit off-kilter. Using Elements' straightening tools, you can bend that horizon back into line (or skew it further for a dramatic effect).

In This Chapter

Cropping an Image

Professional photographers almost always use cropping techniques to achieve perfect composition. In spite of all the advances in film and digital cameras, rarely is a picture taken with its subjects perfectly composed or its horizon line set at just the proper level. More often than not, subjects are off-center, and unwanted objects intrude into the edge of the picture frame. Photoshop Elements offers two simple and quick methods for cropping your images.

To crop an image using the Crop tool:

1. Select the Crop tool from the toolbox (or press C) **A**.
2. In the image window, drag to define the area of the image you want to keep **B**.

   The image outside the selected area is dimmed to indicate the portions that will be deleted.
3. If you want to modify your selection, move the pointer over one of the eight handles on the edges of the selection; then drag the handle to resize it **C**.
4. When you're satisfied with your crop area, double-click within the selection, press Enter, or click the Commit button on the lower corner of the selection **D**.

   The image is cropped to the area you selected **E**.

   If you're not satisfied with your selection and want to start over, click the Cancel button.

TIP A Crop selection includes an overlay splitting the area into thirds to help you compose the shot B. In the Tool Options bar, choose other guides from the Overlay drop-down menu.

A The Crop tool.

B Elements highlights the image that will be preserved and dims the portions to be deleted.

C Easily move and resize the area you choose to crop by dragging the handles around the perimeter of the cropping selection.

D The Commit and Cancel buttons appear on the lower edge of the crop selection.

TIP You can define color and opacity options for the Crop tool shield (the dimmed area that surrounds your cropped selection) in the Display and Cursors area of the Preferences dialog. The default color is black, and the default opacity is 75 percent.

E The final, cropped image.

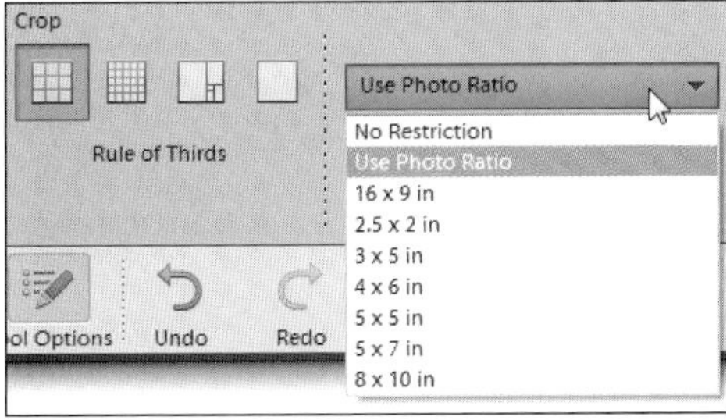

F Use the Aspect Ratio drop-down menu to choose common photo dimensions.

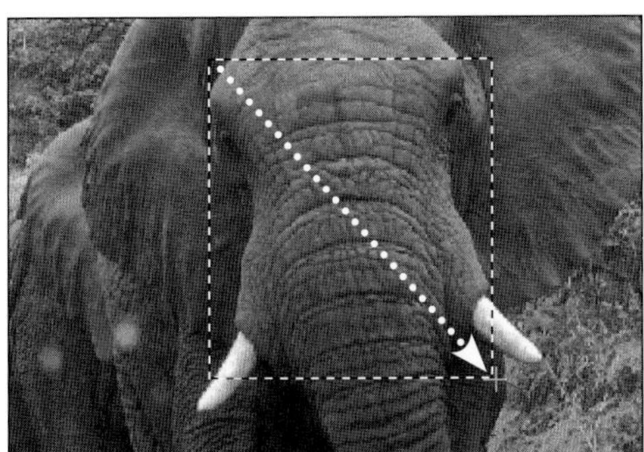

G Drag with the Rectangular Marquee tool to define the part of the image you want to crop.

To resize an image to specific dimensions using the Crop tool:

1. Follow steps 1–3 on the previous page to specify an area to crop.
2. In the Tool Options bar, choose a common photo size from the Aspect Ratio drop-down menu F.

   Or, enter a size in the Width and Height fields. The double-arrow button between the fields swaps values, making it easy to turn a horizontal crop area into a vertical one, and vice versa.
3. If you need to change the image's resolution, edit the Resolution field; you can define it in pixels per inch or pixels per centimeter using the associated drop-down menu. However, see the sidebar on the next page, "The Crop Tool Size and Resolution Options," for important information.
4. Double-click within the selection, press Enter, or click the Commit button to crop the photo.

To crop an image using the Rectangular Marquee tool:

1. Select the Rectangular Marquee tool from the toolbox, or press M.
2. In the image window, drag to define the area of the image you want to keep G.
3. From the Image menu, choose Crop. The image is cropped to the area you selected.

TIP If you're planning to print your photos using a commercial print service, be sure to crop your images to a standard size first. The images that digital cameras create don't match standard photo aspect ratios, which can lead to prints with black bars around the edges.

The Crop Tool Size and Resolution Options

Every digital photo is made up of millions of *pixels*, colored squares that you typically never see unless you're zoomed in; the more pixels, the higher the resolution, and in general the more detail you're able to see.

If you're cropping the edges of your photo slightly, you don't need to worry about resolution. However, if you make dramatic cuts, like keeping just one corner of a photo, you could significantly reduce the quality of the image if you print it later.

Using the Crop tool's Aspect Ratio and Resolution options can lead you down a slippery slope, introducing unexpected image quality problems—foremost among them, unwanted resolution upsampling, which creates a fuzzy, ghosted, and generally out-of-focus effect. For more information on upsampling, see the "Downsampling vs. Upsampling" sidebar in Chapter 14.

As an example, let's say you have a 4 x 5-inch image with a resolution of 150 pixels per inch. Select the Crop tool, choose "4 x 6 in" from the Aspect Ratio drop-down menu, and enter 150 in the Resolution field. Define the area you want to crop (which by definition will be a smaller area than the original 4 x 5 image), and then crop.

H Be cautious when using the Crop tool's size and resolution options. Here, an image was cropped with a final size defined that was larger than the original image (top). During cropping, the image was *upsampled,* sacrificing image quality (bottom). Both detail boxes are shown at 100 percent.

The area you crop from the original image, no matter the selected size, will be forced up to 4 x 6, and will introduce upsampling **H**.

You can use the Aspect Ratio drop-down menu to control the Width and Height ratios of your cropping selection; just leave the Resolution text field blank, and use the Image Size dialog (after you crop) to set the image resolution (described in Chapter 14).

Straightening a Crooked Photo

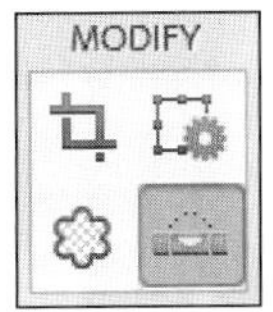

Ⓐ The Straighten tool.

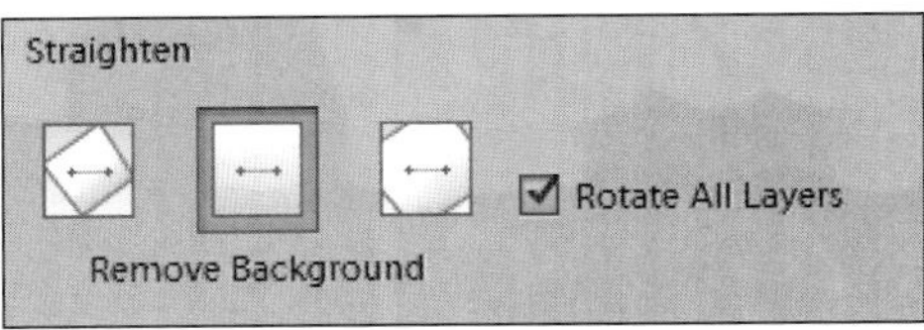

Ⓑ Choose how the Organizer handles extra space caused by the rotation.

Grow or Shrink

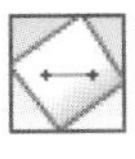

Remove Background

Original Size

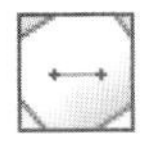

Ⓒ With the Straighten tool, you simply click and drag within a tilted photo (top) to align it perfectly.

Sometimes even your most carefully composed photos may be just a little off angle, with a not-quite-level horizon line or tilted portrait subjects. The nifty Straighten tool makes short work out of getting your crooked photos back into alignment.

Or, perhaps you've scanned an image that shifted when you closed the scanner cover. Elements can automatically straighten it, with the option of cropping it to a clean rectangle.

To use the Straighten tool:

1. Select the Straighten tool from the toolbox, or press P Ⓐ.
2. In the Tool Options bar, choose how the image will be cropped after you straighten it Ⓑ.
3. Using a horizon line or other subject as a point of reference, click and drag from one side of the photo to the other Ⓒ.

   When you release the mouse button, your image rotates and aligns along the new horizontal plane you defined.

To let the Editor straighten a photo:

Choose one of the following:

- Image > Rotate > Straighten and Crop Image.
- Image > Rotate > Straighten Image.

  The Straighten and Crop Image command will do its best to both straighten the image and delete the extra background surrounding the image. The Straighten Image command simply straightens without cropping.

continues on next page

Both methods have their own sets of limitations. Rotate and Straighten works best if there is a space of at least 50 extra pixels or so surrounding the image. If this surrounding border is much smaller, Elements can have a difficult time distinguishing the actual photograph from the border and may not do a clean job of cropping.

Although you'll still need to manually crop your image after using the Straighten Image command, this method is probably a better choice, because you avoid the risk of Elements indiscriminately cropping out areas of your image you may want to keep.

For the surest control, however, straighten your images using the Crop tool as described in the next procedure.

To straighten an image using the Crop tool:

1. Select the Crop tool from the Tools pane.
2. In the image window, drag to select the area of the image you want to crop and straighten.
3. Move the pointer outside the edge of the selection area until it changes to a rotation pointer D.
4. Drag outside of the selection until its edges are aligned with the image border.
5. Drag the selection handles, as necessary, to fine-tune the positioning; then press Enter E.

   The image is cropped and automatically straightened.

D After you define a preliminary cropping selection (top), rotate the selection so it aligns with your image border (bottom).

E Make final adjustments to your cropping selection (top) before Elements automatically crops and straightens the image.

5

Quick Edits

As you'll discover in the rest of the book, Photoshop Elements is a sophisticated image editor, enabling anyone to make photo corrections that would have been absurdly difficult years ago. But sometimes you don't want to be an image expert. Let the computer do the work for you, analyzing photos and correcting them automatically.

When you don't want to mess with the particulars, or when you know that a photo needs just a bit of tweaking but you want a bit more control over the adjustments, turn to the Quick edit features. You can experiment on your photo—ranging from slight tonal changes to radical tints and lighting adjustments—and then undo those changes if they seemed better in your mind's eye than they look on the screen.

The concepts behind the tools in the Quick edit mode, such as adjusting levels and sharpening, are dealt with later in the book. Use this chapter as a jumping-off point.

In This Chapter

Making Quick Edits

When you want Elements to take over and make corrections according to its analysis of a photo, the speediest method is directly in the Quick edit pane.

Using the Quick editor

The Quick edit component of the workspace gives you a bit more control than the buttons in the Organizer's Instant Fix pane.

To edit photos in the Quick editor:

Open a file in Elements and then click the Quick button. The Quick edit workspace opens **A**.

To set view options:

- From the View menu located below the photo, choose whether you want to see the end result (After Only), the original (Before Only), or a comparison layout (both the Before & After options) **B**.
- Use the Zoom field and slider to specify how zoomed-in you want to be **C**. In the Before and After views, the zoom level applies to both versions.

  When the Zoom or Hand tool is active, you can also click the Actual Pixels, Fit Screen, or Print Size buttons in the Tool Options bar to switch to those zoom levels.
- If Elements did not rotate your image correctly during import, click the Rotate buttons to turn it clockwise or counterclockwise in 90-degree increments.

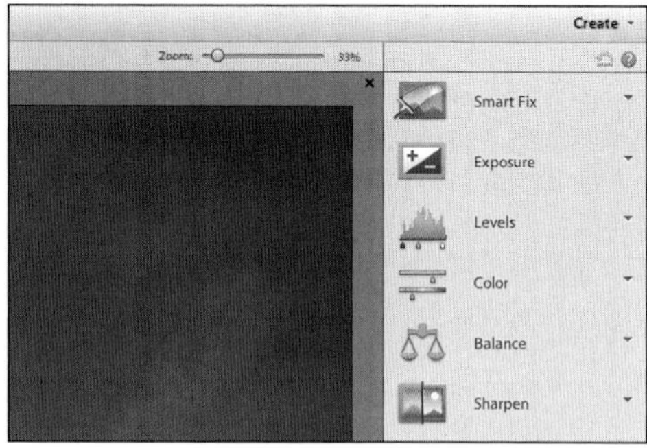

A The Quick edit workspace includes your image and a set of common photo manipulations.

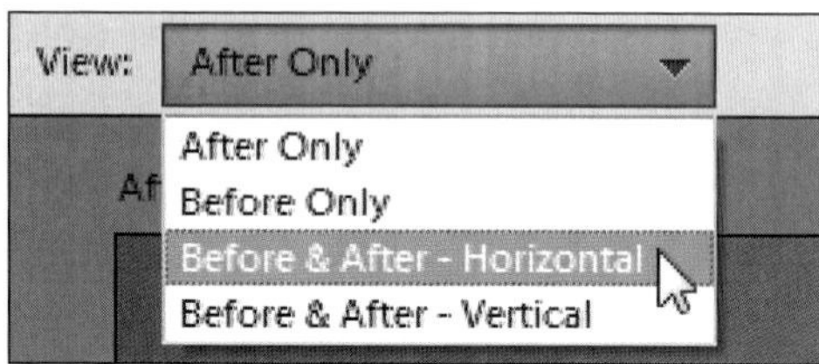

B The Before & After options offer split-screen views of how fixes are affecting the photo.

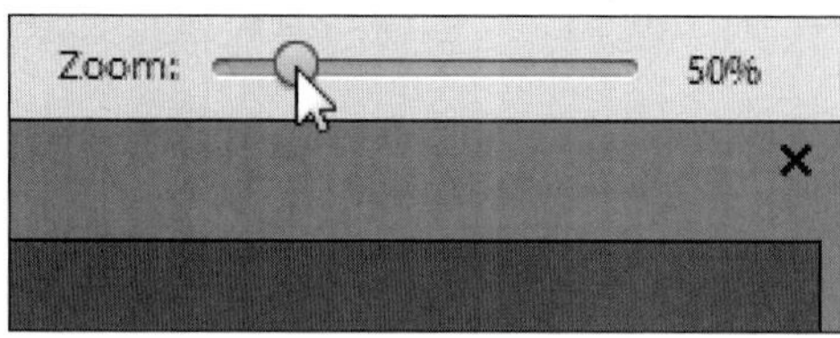

C Use the Zoom field or slider to view the photo close-up.

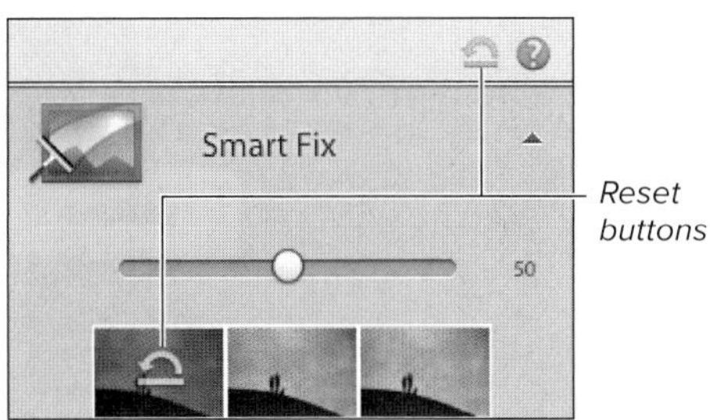

Ⓓ Clicking the Cancel button restores the image to the state before you made the adjustment(s).

Ⓔ Drawing with the Quick Selection tool creates a selection based on that area.

Ⓕ Use the sliders associated with each type of fix to adjust the After image.

Applying Quick edits

The following tools perform common image correction tasks, but we want to start with the most important command first: Reset.

To reset and undo changes:

- After making an adjustment, click the Reset button that appears in the tool's thumbnails Ⓓ.
- Click the Undo button, or choose Edit > Undo to undo the previous command.
- If you've made several edits and want to revert to the original image, click the Reset button above the pane. This removes any Quick edit adjustments.

To select areas for applying edits:

1. Select the Quick Selection tool from the toolbar.
2. Draw within the area that you want to select. Elements makes a selection based on the colors of the pixels you drew upon Ⓔ.

To apply edits:

1. To apply fixes to a specific area of the image, use the Quick Selection tool to select an active area. Otherwise, skip to the next step.
2. Click a type of edit (Smart Fix, Exposure, Levels, etc.) to reveal its controls.
3. If an Auto button is available, click that to first see what Elements suggests.
4. Drag the sliders for specific adjustments to fine-tune the settings Ⓕ.

To apply fixes using previews:

1. Click the triangle icon to the right of an adjustment slider to reveal thumbnails of the range of that fix's settings.
2. Move your pointer over a thumbnail to preview the edit G.

   The slider is still available for fine-tuning, but there's a better way. Click and drag left or right within the thumbnail to make smaller adjustments.
3. Click the thumbnail to apply the setting.

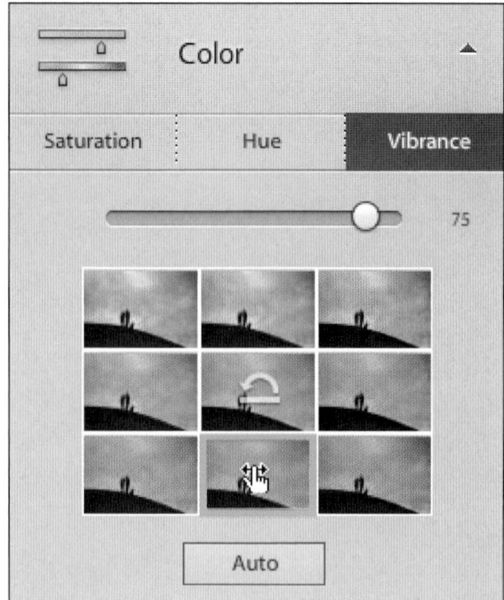

G The preview grid gives you an immediate sense of how the adjustment will appear.

To crop the image:

1. Select the Crop tool from the toolbar.
2. In the image's After version, drag to select the area you wish to keep H.
3. Click the Commit button (the check mark) that appears outside the selection to apply the crop.

H Drag a selection using the Crop tool to keep only that area and discard the rest of the image.

To apply all edits:

1. Choose File > Close, or click the close button in the upper-right corner of the workspace.
2. When prompted, save your changes.

TIP See Chapter 8 for details on the settings offered by each tool.

TIP It never hurts to play with the Smart Fix slider. Smart Fix adjusts lighting, color, and sharpening based on its algorithms. In some cases, this may be the only edit you need.

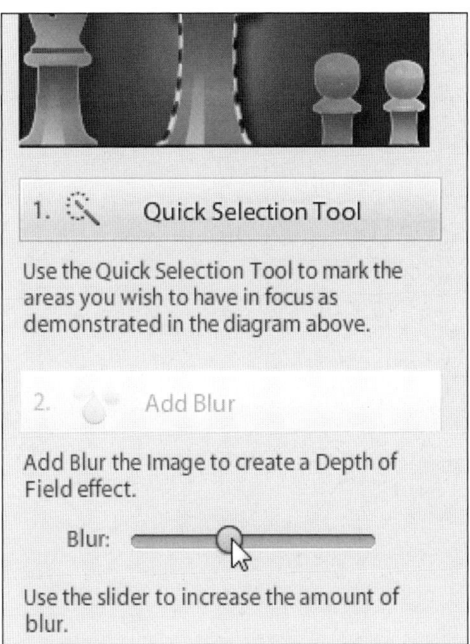
1. Quick Selection Tool
Use the Quick Selection Tool to mark the areas you wish to have in focus as demonstrated in the diagram above.
2. Add Blur
Add Blur the Image to create a Depth of Field effect.
Blur:
Use the slider to increase the amount of blur.

Ⓐ The Guided Edit interface.

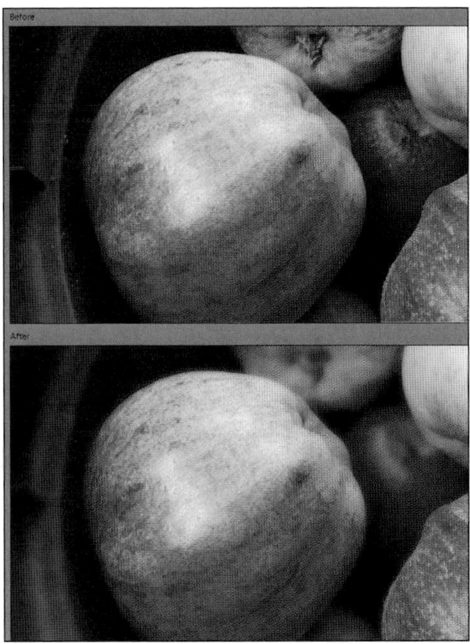
Before
After

Ⓑ The Depth Of Field guided edit separates the foreground from background using a blur effect.

Walking Through Adjustments Using Guided Edit Mode

If you want to start with a little more hand-holding than what's offered by the Quick edits, try the Guided edit mode; access it by clicking the Guided button.

Clicking a task in this mode provides step-by-step instruction on performing editing tasks Ⓐ.

When you've accomplished each step, click the Done button to apply the changes, or click Cancel to discard them. You can also click the Reset button that appears in each category to go back to the state before you applied those particular edits if you want to try a different setting.

Some Guided Edit options include:

- Basic adjustments such as Brightness and Contrast and Enhance Colors.
- Photomerge tools such as Scene Cleaner and Style Match (see Chapter 8 for more information).
- Photographic effects such as Depth Of Field Ⓑ, Old Fashioned Photo, and Tilt-Shift.
- Fun Edits such as adding a reflection or making part of the photo pop out from the rest of the image.
- Effects that replicate cameras or lenses, such as Lomo Camera Effect or Orton Effect.

6

Making Selections

One of the advantages of using Photoshop Elements to edit photos is the ability to apply corrections and enhancements to selected areas in an image. Most photo-editing programs instead apply fixes to the entire image.

You can also use selections to create a protective mask for specific portions of an image. It's easy to select one area of an image, apply a change to the rest, and keep the selected area untouched.

In this chapter, you'll learn about all of the selection tools and when to choose one tool over another. You'll also learn how to use these tools in tandem to make the quickest and most accurate selections, depending on your specific needs.

In This Chapter

About the Selection Tools

Often, you'll want to change and adjust only a portion of an image. For example, you may want to eliminate a distracting element in your photo, change the color of a specific item, or adjust the brightness of the background. Photoshop Elements gives you a wide variety of selection tools from which to choose.

The selection tools are all grouped near one another at the top of the toolbar **A**. You make rectangular and elliptical selections using the marquee tools. When you select one of the marquee tools, the selection area is indicated by a row of moving dots, like the sign outside an old-style movie theater—hence the name **B**.

You select free-form, or irregularly shaped, areas using the lasso tools **C**. These include the regular Lasso tool; the Polygonal Lasso, which is great for selecting areas that include straight sections; and the Magnetic Lasso, which can select the edge of an area based on its color or tonal values.

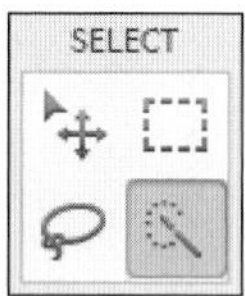

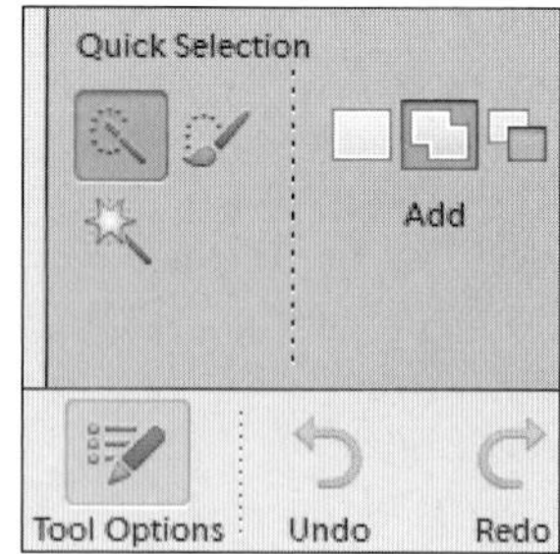

A Access additional related tools in the Tool Options bar.

B A selection border is represented by a row of moving dots, called a marquee.

C Each lasso tool works best in a particular situation.

The Magic Wand lets you select areas with the same (or similar) color or tonal value. This tool is probably the most difficult to master, but with a little practice it allows you to make selections that would be difficult to make with any of the marquee or lasso tools D. For example, if your photo displays a field of yellow poppies, you can select them all at once, rather than having to select each flower individually.

D The Magic Wand lets you select areas based on color.

The selection tools work well on their own, but often the area you want to edit includes all sorts of angles and edges. In these situations, you can use the tools in combination to expand and change the selection area.

You can also expand or contract a selection area using the same tool with different settings. For example, the Magic Wand allows you to alter the range of your selection by adjusting the tolerance using the Tool Options bar before making a selection E.

E The Magic Wand also lets you set the tolerance, or range of colors selected.

When a photo includes an object surrounded by a large background area, it's often easier to select the background and then invert the selection to select the object. Once the selection is made, you can copy and paste it into another composition or make any other changes F.

F Here, the black background was selected with the Magic Wand, and then the selection was inverted to capture the buttons.

continues on next page

Once you've selected an area, you can add to or subtract from it. Using one tool to make your initial selection and then editing the selection area using another selection tool is often easier than trying to make a perfect selection with a single tool all at once G.

The Selection Brush allows you to make selections simply by dragging across any area or object in an image. Like the lasso tools, it works especially well for selecting irregular areas. Unlike the other selection tools, you actually "paint on" the selection using any of the brush shapes available in Elements' vast collection of brush sets H. This method of selection affords you great control and flexibility, although you need quite a bit of dexterity.

The Quick Selection tool works in much the same way as the Magic Wand tool—selecting areas based on similar color and tonal values. What distinguishes the Quick Selection tool from the other selection tools is the method you use to make the selections. By painting a series of scribbles and dots on the image, Photoshop Elements creates a selection area based on the color or tonal values below the painted marks I. Selections are additive: As you paint, the selection grows larger; use other selection tools to shrink the area.

G Here, the Elliptical Marquee tool was used to select the ladybug's main body, and then the Magic Wand tool was used to add the legs and head.

H The Selection Brush can be used in either Selection or Mask mode, selectable from the Mode menu in the Tool Options bar.

I When you "paint" through an area with the Quick Selection tool (a small area painted at left, and a larger area at right), any pixels similar in color or tonal value to those you brush over will be selected.

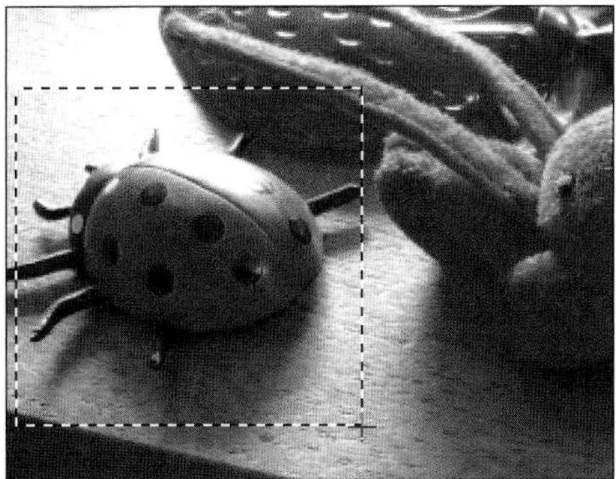

Ⓐ After grabbing one of the marquee tools, just click and drag to make a selection.

Ⓑ To select a perfect square or circle, hold down the Shift key while dragging.

Ⓒ To draw a selection outward from the center, hold the Alt/Option key as you drag.

Using the Marquee Tools

The Rectangular and Elliptical Marquee tools are the easiest and most straightforward selection tools to use. You'll often want to move a selection area to align the area perfectly, and Photoshop Elements offers a couple of quick and simple ways to make these kinds of adjustments.

To make a rectangular or elliptical selection:

1. From the toolbar, select the Marquee tool, and choose either the Rectangular Marquee or Elliptical Marquee in the Tool Options bar.

   The default setting creates a new selection. See "Adjusting Selections," later in this chapter, for more information on other options when creating selections.

2. Click and drag to choose the selection area Ⓐ.

TIP You can create a perfect circle or square selection using the marquee tools by holding down the Shift key as you drag Ⓑ.

TIP You can draw the marquee from the center outward by holding down the Alt/Option key Ⓒ.

TIP To toggle between marquee tools, press the M key. In fact, this works for any tool with hidden tools—simply press the keyboard shortcut key repeatedly to toggle through all of the choices.

TIP To select all pixels on a layer, press Ctrl+A/Command-A. This creates a selection around the entire image window, and is useful when you want to make universal color corrections or add special effects to your image. (See Chapter 7 for more on working with layers.)

To reposition a selection border:

1. Once you've made a selection, with the New selection icon active, position the pointer anywhere in the selection area.

   The pointer becomes an arrow with a small selection icon next to it **D**. Note that if either the Add to, Subtract from, or Intersect with icon is active, the pointer indicates that choice and the selection can't be moved.

2. Click and drag to reposition the selection area.

   The pointer arrow changes to solid black as you move the selection **E**.

To reposition a selection border while making a selection:

1. Click and drag to create the selection area.
2. While keeping the mouse button pressed, press the spacebar. (The pointer arrow shows a set of cross-hairs whether or not the spacebar is pressed.)
3. Move the selection area to the desired location and release the spacebar and mouse button **F**.

TIP You can use the arrow keys on your keyboard to move a selection in 1-pixel increments. Holding the Shift key at the same time moves the selection in 10-pixel increments.

D To move the selection area, position the pointer within the selection boundary.

E Drag the selection border to a new location.

F To move the marquee during a selection, just press the spacebar while holding down the mouse button and adjust the border's location.

Ⓐ Select any area by tracing around it with the Lasso tool.

Ⓑ When you release the mouse button, the ends of the selection automatically join together.

Selecting Areas Using the Lasso Tools

Use the lasso tools to select areas with irregular shapes. The standard Lasso tool lets you draw or trace around an object or area freehand, much as you would draw with a pencil. This method takes patience, but with practice you can use the Lasso tool to make accurate selections.

The Polygonal Lasso tool is useful for selecting areas that include straight edges; you can toggle between the freehand and straight-edge modes when your object includes both irregular and straight edges.

As you trace around an area using the Magnetic Lasso tool, it automatically "snaps" the selection border to edges based on differences in color and tonal values in adjoining pixels. For this reason, the tool usually works best on high-contrast images. Experiment with the settings in the Tool Options bar to get the best results.

To select with the Lasso tool:

1. From the toolbar, choose the Lasso tool (or press L).
2. Keeping the mouse button pressed, drag all the way around an object or area in your image Ⓐ.

   When you release the mouse button, the open ends of the selection automatically join together Ⓑ.

TIP Use the Alt/Option key to switch between the Polygonal Lasso and regular Lasso tools.

TIP Making lasso selections is much easier with a pressure-sensitive drawing tablet.

To select with the Polygonal Lasso:

1. From the toolbar, choose the Polygonal Lasso tool.
2. Click points along the edge of the object to create straight-line segments for your selection **C**.
3. Click back at the original starting point to join the open ends of the selection.

   You can also Ctrl/Command-click or double-click anywhere to close the selection.

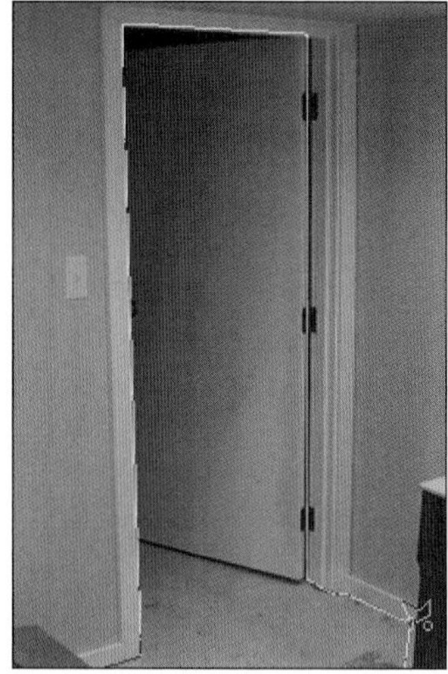

C The Polygonal Lasso tool creates a border of straight-line segments.

To select with the Magnetic Lasso:

1. From the toolbar, choose the Magnetic Lasso tool.
2. Click on or very close to the edge of the area you want to trace to establish the first fastening point **D**.
3. Move the pointer along the edge you want to trace. The Magnetic Lasso tool traces along the selection border to the best of its ability and places additional fastening points along the way **E**.
4. If the selection line jumps to the edge of the wrong object, place the pointer over the correct edge and click the mouse button to establish an accurate fastening point **F**.
5. To close the selection line, click the starting point. You can also Ctrl/Command-click, double-click anywhere on the image, or press Enter.

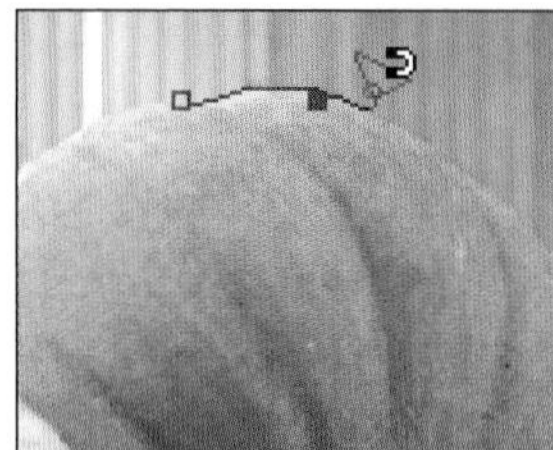

D To start a selection border with the Magnetic Lasso tool, click the edge of the area you want to trace to create the first fastening point.

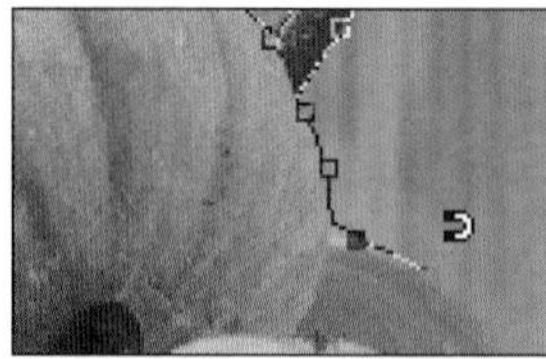

E As you trace with the Magnetic Lasso tool, it places additional fastening points along the selection edge.

TIP Be warned: The Polygonal Lasso tool can sometimes slip out of your control, creating line segments where you don't want them to appear. If you make a mistake or change your mind, you can erase line-segment selections as long as you haven't closed the selection. Just press the Backspace or Delete key, and one by one the segments will be removed, starting with the most recent one.

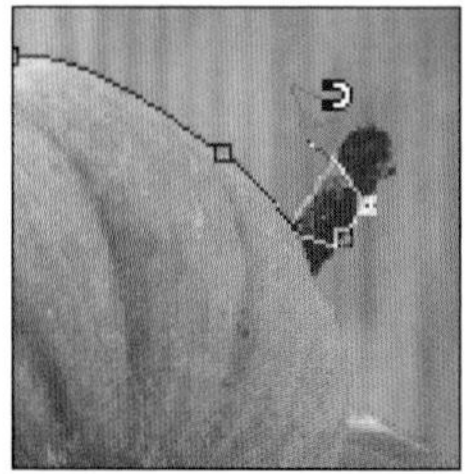

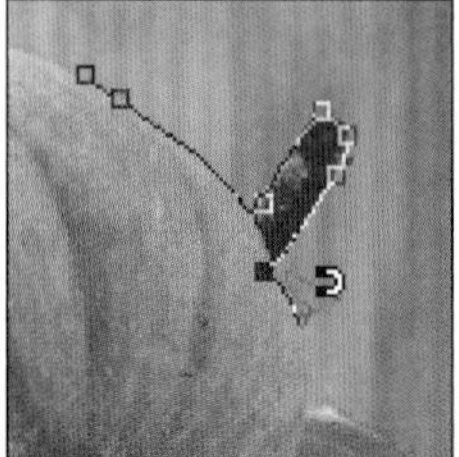

F Sometimes the Magnetic Lasso tool jumps to another edge (left). To correct the path, just click the correct edge to bring the border back to the right location (right).

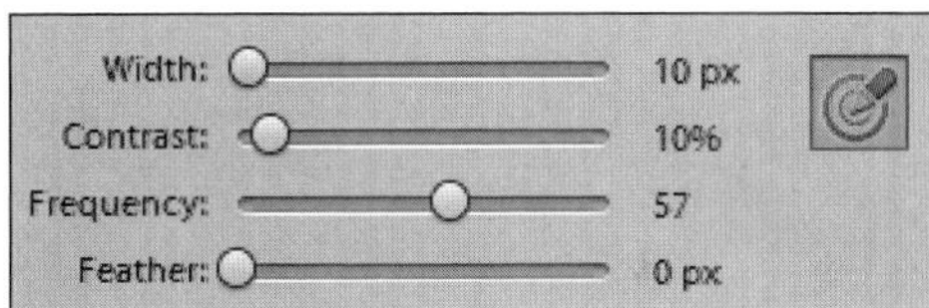

G Control how magnetic the Magnetic Lasso tool acts using controls in the Tool Options bar.

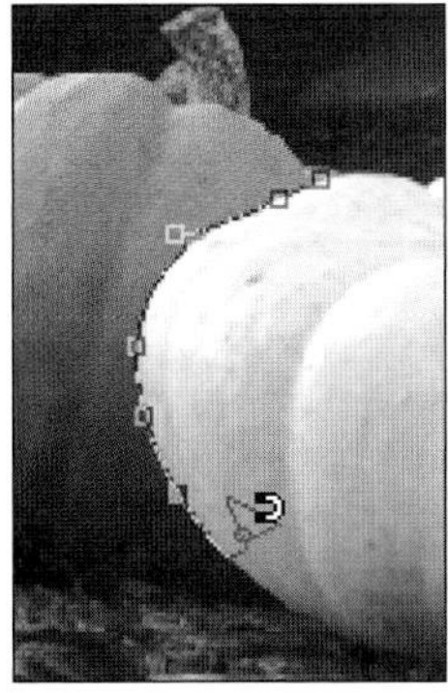

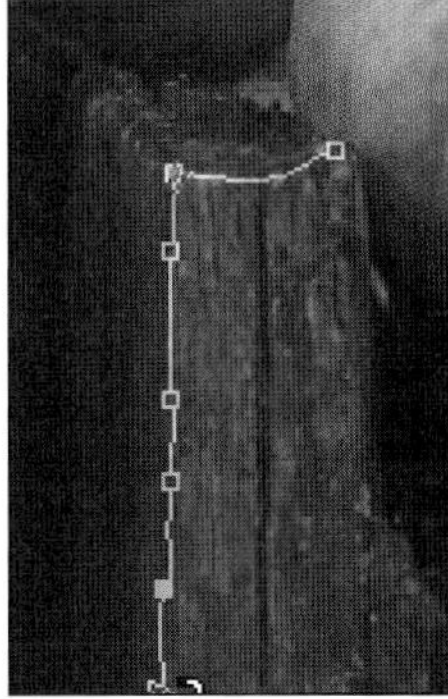

H The Edge Contrast setting makes it easy to find an edge in high contrast areas (left, set to 80 percent) and low contrast areas (right, set to 5 percent).

I The Frequency option lets you determine how closely the fastening points are spaced. Top is set to 7. Bottom is set to 70.

To set Magnetic Lasso tool options:

1. Select the Magnetic Lasso tool.
2. Set any of the options visible in the Tool Options bar G.
   - Width sets the size of the area the tool scans as it traces the selection line.

     Wide widths work well for images with high contrast, and narrow widths work well for images with subtle contrast and small shapes that are close to each other.
   - Contrast sets the amount of contrast between shapes required for an edge to be recognized and traced H.

     This option is indicated by the percentage of contrast (from 1 to 100 percent). Try higher numbers for high-contrast images, and lower numbers for flatter, low-contrast images (just as with the Width option).
   - Frequency specifies how close the fastening points are to each other.

     For Frequency, enter a number from 1 to 100. In general, you'll need to use higher frequency values when the edge is very ragged or irregular I.
   - If you are using a stylus tablet, you can select the Stylus Pressure button to increase the stylus pressure and so decrease the edge width. That's right: With the button enabled, pressing harder on the stylus will yield a smaller, more precise edge.

TIP Press Alt/Option and click to use the Polygonal Lasso tool while the Magnetic Lasso tool is selected. Press Alt/Option and drag to use the Lasso tool.

Making Selections by Color

The Magic Wand and Quick Selection tools allow you to make selections based on a selected color or tonal value. These tools can seem truly magical—or wildly unpredictable—at first. When you select an area of an image with either tool, it selects all of the pixels within a color or tonal range close to the pixel you've initially selected.

The Magic Wand tool provides options for setting tolerance (the range of color or tonal values included in the selection around the pixel where you're clicking or dragging), anti-aliasing (smoothing), contiguousness (whether the pixels need to be connected to that first selected pixel), and whether to include all layers in the selection.

The Grow and Similar commands, found in the Select menu, can be used to expand the selection area. The Grow command expands the range of adjacent pixels, and the Similar command expands the selection based on the pixel colors.

Although the Quick Selection tool doesn't offer the options available with the Magic Wand, it will often make an accurate selection based solely on the areas you mark with the brush. In fact, it's the first selection tool I turn to.

To use the Quick Selection tool:

1. From the toolbar, choose the Quick Selection tool (or press A) **A**.
2. In the Tool Options bar, choose a brush size.
3. In the image window, click—or click and drag—in the area where you want to make your selection. As you drag, the selection is created **B**.

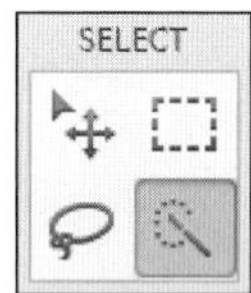

A The Quick Selection tool.

B Painting through an area with the Quick Selection tool creates a new selection.

C To add to a selection, paint in additional brushstrokes (Add to Selection is chosen by default).

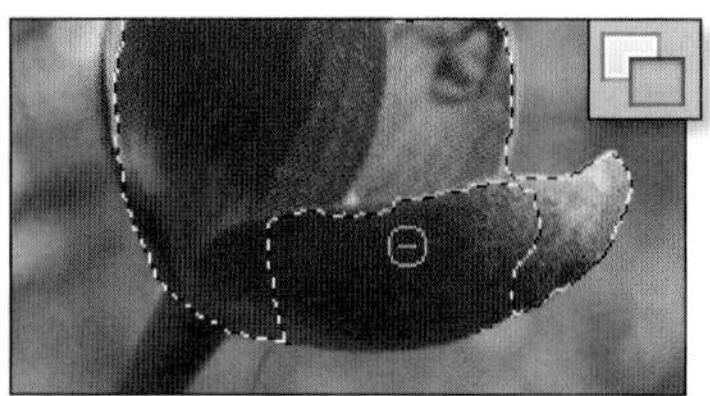

D Use Subtract from Selection to delete a portion of a selection.

E Access the Magic Wand in the Tool Options bar.

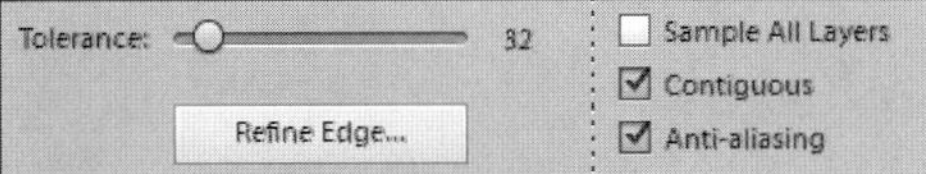

F The Magic Wand Tool Options bar controls.

G The Tolerance setting determines how wide a range of colors is included in the selection.

H Uncheck Contiguous if you want to select similar colors throughout the image.

4. To add to the selection, drag an area outside the current selection C.
5. To subtract from a selection, choose the Subtract from Selection button or hold down the Alt/Option key, and click (or drag) inside the selection area D.

To use the Magic Wand:

1. From the toolbar, choose the Quick Selection tool and then, in the Tool Options bar, select the Magic Wand (or press A until it's selected) E.
2. In the Tool Options bar, choose whether to create a new selection, add to or subtract from an existing selection, or intersect with an existing selection F.

   The default setting in the Tool Options bar creates a new selection.
3. Select the tolerance (a range of pixels from 0 to 255) to establish how wide a tonal range you want to include in your selection.

   The default tolerance level is 32 pixels. To pick colors or tonal values very close to the selected pixel, choose lower numbers. Entering higher numbers results in a wider selection of colors G.
4. If you want your selection to have a smooth edge, select Anti-aliasing.
5. If you want only pixels adjacent to the original pixel to be included in the selection, select Contiguous H.
6. If you want the selection to include pixels on all the layers, select Sample All Layers (see Chapter 7 for more on working with layers).
7. Click a color or tone in the image. Based on your settings, a group or range of pixels will be selected.

To expand the selection area:

1. Choose the Magic Wand tool.
2. Click a color or tonal value in the image.
3. From the Select menu, choose Grow to expand the selection of adjacent pixels.

   Each time you select Grow, the selection is expanded by the tolerance amount displayed in the Magic Wand's controls in the Tool Options bar **I**.

I Making a selection at left covers just part of the desired image. Choose Select > Grow to expand the selection to adjacent, similarly colored areas.

To include similar colors:

1. Choose the Magic Wand tool.
2. Click a color or tonal value in the image.
3. From the Select menu, choose Similar to expand the selection of nonadjacent pixels.

   The selection is extended through the image to similar tonal values using the tolerance amount set in the Tool Options bar **J**.

J Choose Select > Similar to add pixels to your selection throughout the image.

TIP When you make your original selection with the Magic Wand, it takes a color "sample" from your image. You can adjust the sample size with the Eyedropper tool. Select the tool and then change the option in the Sample Size drop-down menu: sample 1 pixel, or the average of a 3-by-3-pixel area (9 pixels total), or a 5-by-5-pixel area (25 pixels total). Whichever option is active determines how the Magic Wand establishes the sample color.

TIP You can also access the Grow command by right-clicking after you have made a selection with the Magic Wand. A contextual menu appears in the image window, which includes the Grow and Similar commands plus a number of other useful selection options.

Ⓐ Access the Selection Brush in the Tool Options bar.

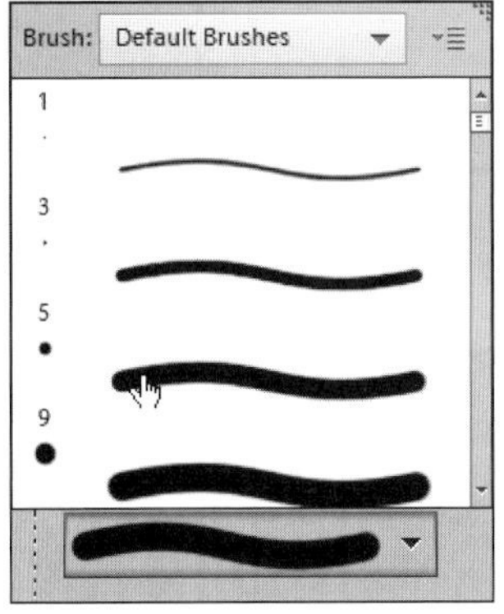

Ⓑ Choose from a wide variety of prebuilt brushes.

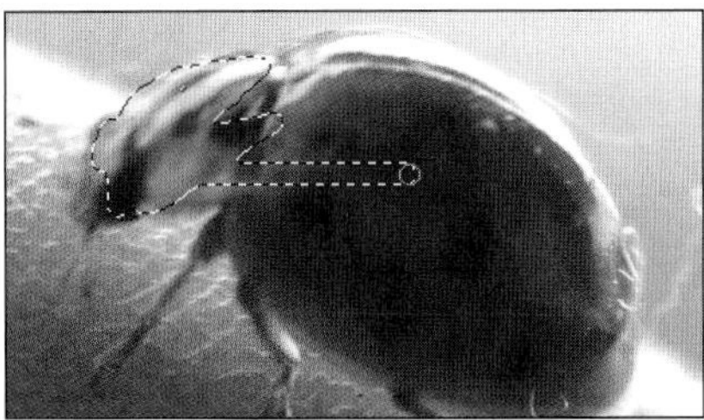

Ⓒ To make a selection, just "paint" over your image with the Selection Brush.

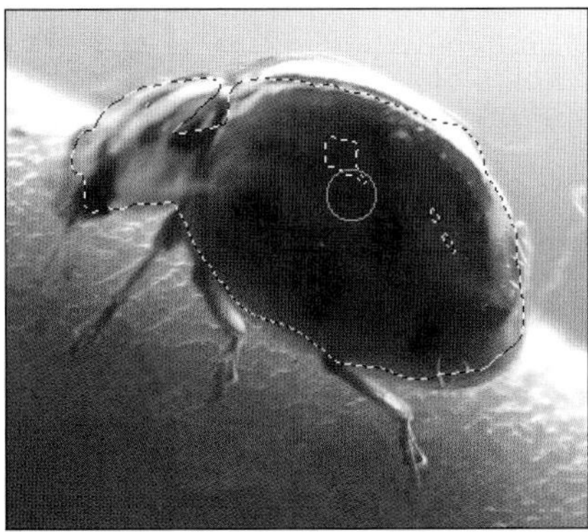

Ⓓ You can expand the selection by brushing around and through the original selection.

Using the Selection Brush Tool

The Selection Brush tool lets you make a selection by painting over an error; it differs from the Quick Selection tool by selecting only the areas covered by the brush's "paint," instead of contiguous areas of similar tonal values.

Unlike the other selection tools, the Selection Brush offers a Mask mode, which allows you to create a "protected" or unselected area. To work more easily with masked areas, you can control the opacity and color of the mask overlay. The two modes can be used together with great results. It's easier to make your initial selection in the default mode, and then switch to Mask mode to tune your selection.

To make a selection with the Selection Brush:

1. From the toolbar, choose the Selection Brush (or press A) Ⓐ.
2. Make sure the Mode menu in the Tool Options bar is set to Selection.
3. Choose a brush style and optionally choose values for the brush size and hardness Ⓑ.

   You can either enter values for the size and hardness, or drag the sliders until you get the setting you want.
4. Drag the brush tool over your image to make a selection Ⓒ.
5. To expand your selection, brush on the edge of the selected area Ⓓ. To make a selection in another portion of your image, click and drag away from the original selection.

continues on next page

6. To subtract from your selection, choose the Subtract from Selection button in the Tool Options bar, and then click and drag through any portion of the selection E.

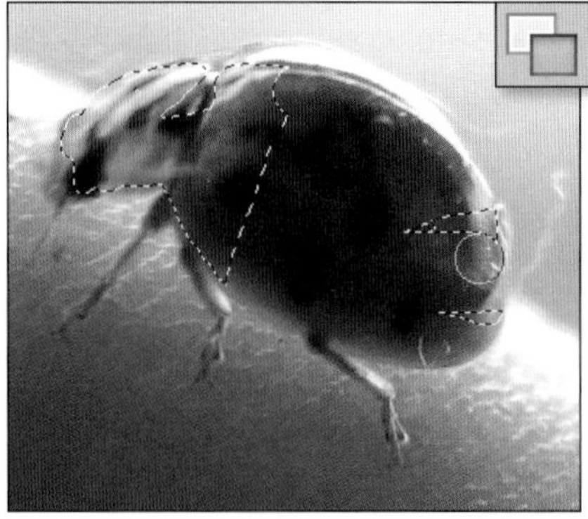

E Use the Subtract from Selection button in the Tool Options bar to remove areas of your selection.

To make a mask with the Selection Brush:

1. Choose the Selection Brush tool.
2. From the Mode menu in the Tool Options bar, choose Mask.
3. Choose a brush style, brush size, and hardness.
4. Set the opacity with the Overlay slider, or enter a percentage in the text field.
5. If your selection area is close to the overlay color (the default is red), click the Overlay Color box in the Tool Options bar, and then choose a different color from the Color Picker.
6. Drag the brush tool over your image to make a mask F.

   As soon as you select another tool, the mask overlay area changes to a selection border. The area is protected from any changes you apply to the image G. If you want to modify the mask, select the Brush Selection tool again. The mask automatically appears over the image, and you can continue to paint in additional masked areas.

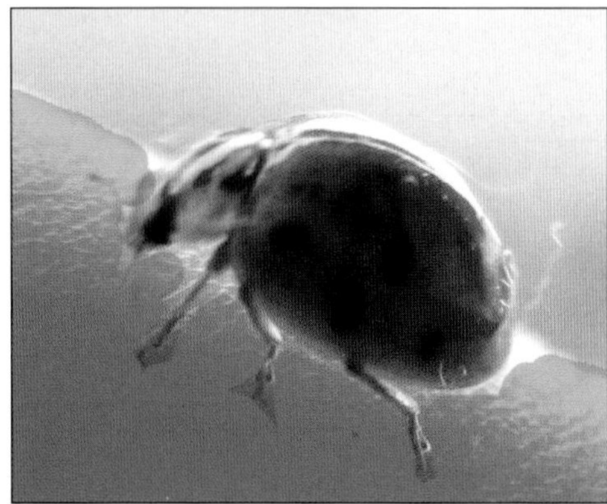

F When you paint with the Mask option on, the area becomes filled with the mask overlay (in pink).

TIP A quick way to change the size of the Selection Brush is to press the bracket keys on your keyboard: Press [to reduce size and] to increase size.

TIP The mask overlay is handy for inspecting selections and can be used with any selection tool. Whenever you have an active selection, click the Selection Brush tool and select the Mask option to see the masked area. When you're done viewing it in Mask mode, choose Selection from the Mode drop-down menu.

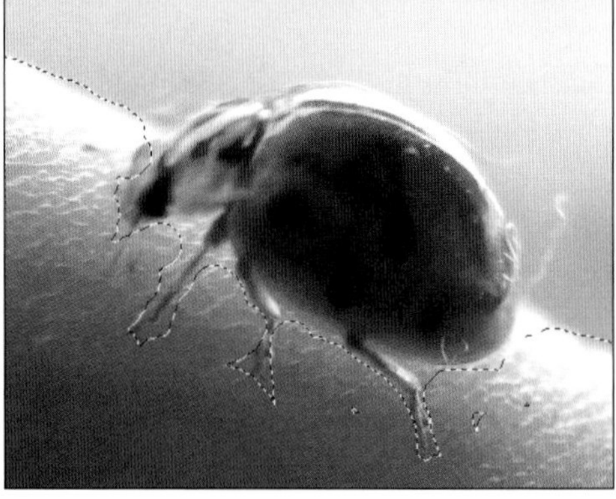

G In Mask mode, you paint a mask through any areas that you *do not* want to be selected.

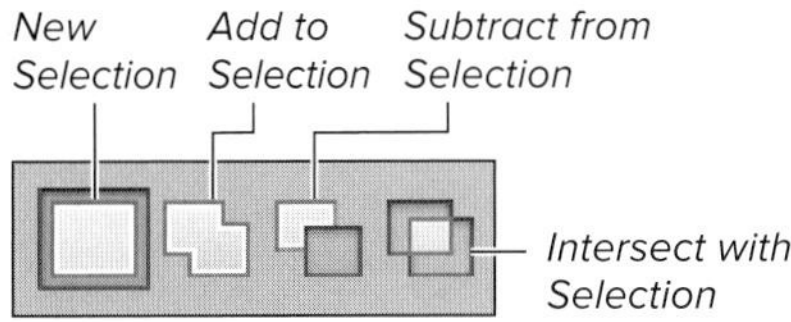

A To add to the current selection, either click the Add to Selection icon in the Tool Options bar or hold down the Shift key while making another selection.

B In this example, two selections combine to form a single selection.

Adjusting Selections

You can probably tell by now that a little fine-tuning is needed to make selections just the way you want them. For example, imagine you're using the Magnetic Lasso tool to trace the outline of a face, but then realize you didn't include the ear in your selection. Rather than start again from scratch, you can add to or subtract from your selection until you've included every part of the image you want. Photoshop Elements even lets you select the intersection (or overlapping area) of two independent selections. This feature offers an effective solution for constructing interesting selection areas that would be difficult to create with a single selection tool.

To add to a selection:

1. Make a selection in your image with any of the selection tools.
2. With the selection still active, do one of the following:
   - Using the same selection tool or after selecting another one, click the Add to Selection button in the Tool Options bar **A**.

     If the Add to Selection button is already highlighted, skip to step 3.
   - Hold down the Shift key, and, if you want, select a different selection tool.

     A plus sign appears, indicating that you are adding to the current selection.
3. Make a new selection in your image. If you want to add to your existing selection, make sure your new selection overlaps the original. If you want to create an additional selection, make sure you click outside of your original selection. The new selection area is added to your first selection **B**.

To subtract from a selection:

1. Make a selection with any of the selection tools.
2. With the selection still active, do one of the following:
   - Select the Subtract from Selection button in the Tool Options bar, optionally choosing a different selection tool.
   - Hold down the Alt/Option key.

   A minus sign appears, indicating that you are subtracting from the current selection.
3. Drag the pointer through the area you want to subtract.

   The area you defined is removed from the selection **C**.

C A pie-shaped cutout is left where the rectangle selection has been subtracted.

To select the intersection of two selections:

1. Make a selection with any of the Marquee or Lasso selection tools.
2. With the selection still active, do one of the following:
   - Select the Intersect with Selection button in the Tool Options bar and create a new selection that overlaps the current selection.
   - Hold Alt+Shift/Option-Shift and create a new selection that overlaps the current selection. An X appears, indicating that you are selecting an area of intersection.
3. A new selection area is formed based on the intersection of the two selections **D**.

D In this example, only the area of intersection remains.

E When you delete a selection, the selected area disappears, and your current background color shows through.

To deselect the current selection:

From the Select menu, choose Deselect, or press Ctrl+D/Command-D.

To reselect the last selection:

Choose Select > Reselect, or press Ctrl+Shift+D/Command-Shift-D.

To delete a selection:

Choose one of the following methods:

- From the menu bar, choose Edit > Cut, or press Ctrl+X/Command-X.
- Press Delete.

  When you delete a selection, the portion of the image within your selection disappears entirely, leaving a hole in your image E. If you accidentally delete a selection, choose Undo from the Edit menu or press Ctrl+Z/Command-Z.

To hide a selection border:

From the View menu, uncheck Selection, or press Ctrl+H/Command-H.

Sometimes, after you've made a selection, you want to hide the selection marquee while you edit the image; this prevents the selection border from obscuring your view. Be sure to press the same keyboard shortcut to display the selection once you're done—otherwise, you might lose track of it.

TIP You can deselect an entire selection at any time by pressing the Esc key.

Refining the Edges of a Selection

Selections often work best when their edges are smooth, instead of hard. Anti-aliasing adds blended pixels to create a smooth edge instead of a stairstepped or jagged edge **A**. Most selection tools offer an Anti-Alias checkbox in the Tool Options bar. That option is usually checked by default, and you almost always want to leave anti-aliasing enabled. When you're compositing images (combining several pieces into one), anti-aliasing smooths the border between elements.

Feathering blurs the edges of a selection. Set the amount of blurring in the Tool Options bar in the Feather box. Unlike anti-aliasing, which affects just the very edge of a selection, feathering creates a more dramatic, soft transition or halo effect around an image. Depending on the image selection, you may want to experiment with different feathering settings, because some detail is usually lost around the edges of a feathered selection.

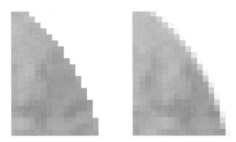

A Anti-aliasing automatically smooths a selection edge by adding pixels that blend the color transition.

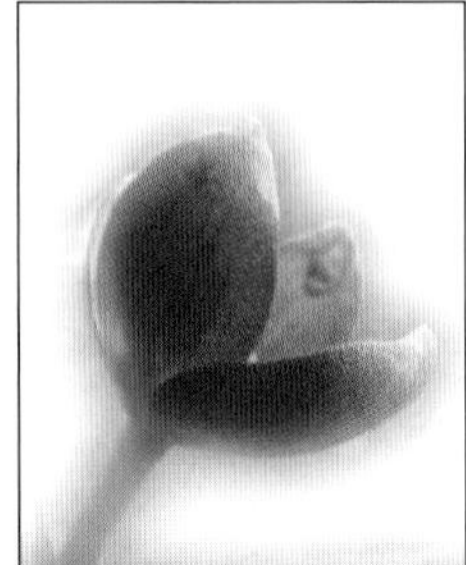

B The dogwood blossom at left was highlighted through the Quick Selection tool, and then Inverse was chosen from the Select menu. A 25-pixel Feather was applied and the background deleted to create the image at right.

To feather the edge of a selection:

1. From the toolbar, choose from any of the Marquee or Lasso tools.
2. In the Tool Options bar or in the Refine Edge dialog, select a value for the feather radius (from 0.1 to 250.0 pixels).
3. Make a selection. The resulting edge appears blurred, based on the number you entered for the Feather option **B**.

TIP You can apply feathering after you make a selection, unlike anti-aliasing. With your selection active, from the Select menu choose Feather or Refine Edge, and then enter a feather radius.

C The Border command lets you control the width of a selection border. In this example, a 15-pixel border is selected at left, then filled with color at right.

D You can expand or contract the size of a selection border from the Modify menu.

Modifying Selection Borders

You can make subtle—or not so subtle—changes to a selection border. The Border feature lets you change the width of the selection border. The Smooth command smooths out a jagged or irregular selection edge. To increase or reduce the size of a selection, use Expand or Contract. (In the Refine Edge dialog box, Expand/Contract is a slider from –100% to 100%.)

To change the width of the border:

1. Make a selection in your image with any of the selection tools.
2. From the Select menu, choose Modify > Border.
3. Enter a value for the border width.

   The selection border changes based on the number you enter **C**.

To smooth the edge of a selection:

1. From the Select menu, choose Modify > Smooth.
2. Enter a value for the radius of the smoothing effect.

   The radius values range from 1 to 100 and define how far away from the current edge the selection will move to create a new, smoother edge.

To expand or contract the selection area:

1. From the Select menu, choose Modify > Expand or Modify > Contract.
2. Enter a value for the number of pixels you would like the selection to either grow (expand) or shrink (contract) **D**.

Use the Refine Edge controls

The Refine Edge dialog combines several softening and selection modification tools in one place **E**.

To refine the edge of a selection:

1. Make a selection in your image.
2. Click the Refine Edge button in the Tool Options bar. Or, choose Select > Refine Edge.
3. Adjust the Radius slider to change the width of the selection edge **F**. With the Smart Radius checkbox selected, Elements analyzes the hard and soft areas of the border region. (Click Show Radius to view just the selection border.)
4. Drag the Adjust Edge sliders to smooth, feather, and increase contrast for the selection. You can also adjust the position of the selection using Shift Edge.
5. To reduce color fringing, select the Decontaminate Colors checkbox and set an amount using its associated slider.
6. From the Output To drop-down menu, choose how to save the refined edge: as a new selection, layer, or document, each with the option of defining the selection using a layer mask.

   Some of the adjustments, like Decontaminate Colors, can dramatically affect the pixels in the selection border, so I prefer to use New Layer with Layer Mask; it blends with the original layer if needed, and exists as a separate layer item in case you want to discard or adjust it later.
7. Click OK to apply the changes, which you can then use, for example, to add the selected item to another composition **G**.

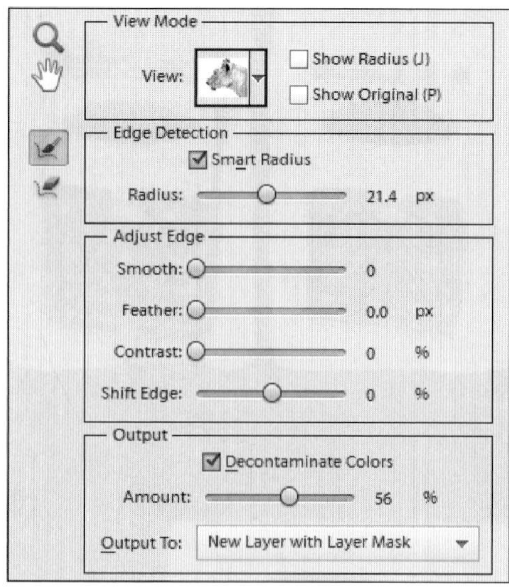

E The Refine Edge dialog combines softening and selection options.

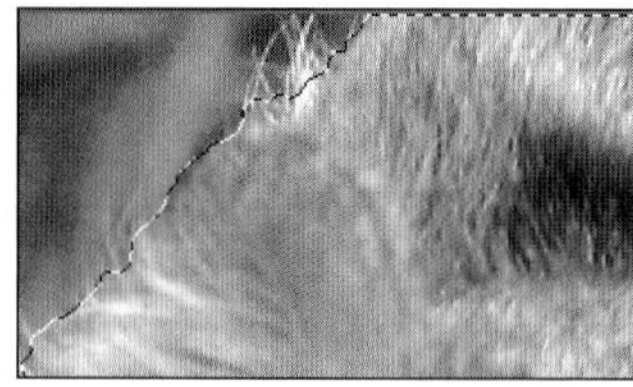

Original selection

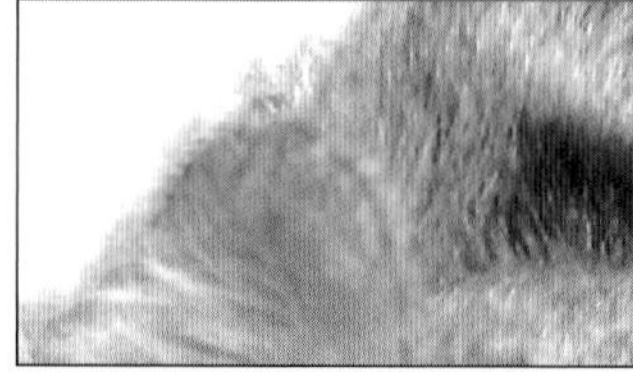

Edge refined

F Using the Refine Edge dialog, the selection's edge has been softened and made less green.

G The final composition.

Working with Layers

Photoshop Elements allows you to work on individual image layers, a feature that lets you make edits that don't permanently alter your original image. You can create and name new layers, and then reorder, group, and even merge selected layers.

Layers are also immensely important when making many edits to photos. Instead of altering the pixels on the image itself, you can add adjustment layers that change brightness, color, saturation, and other attributes. Separating the edit from the image on layers means you can try several settings without having to roll back your changes every time.

In this chapter, you'll learn how layers are created, and then explore several methods and techniques to help you take advantage of one of Elements' most powerful and creative features.

In This Chapter

Understanding Layers

When you first import or scan an image into Photoshop Elements, it consists of one default layer. When you begin working with some of the more involved and complex image manipulation and retouching tools, you'll find that layers make things a whole lot easier.

Layers act like clear, transparent sheets stacked one on top of another, and yet, when you view a final image, they appear as one unified picture **A**. As you copy and paste selections, you may notice these operations automatically create new layers in your image. You can edit only one layer at a time, which allows you to select and modify specific parts of your photo without affecting the information on other layers. This is the real beauty of layers: the ability to work on and experiment with one part of your image while leaving the rest of it completely untouched. Adjustment layers are even more flexible, letting you make color and tonal corrections to individual or multiple layers below them without changing the actual pixels.

Layers appear in your image in the same order as they appear in the Layers panel. The top layer of your image is the first layer listed on the Layers panel, and the background layer is positioned at the bottom of the list.

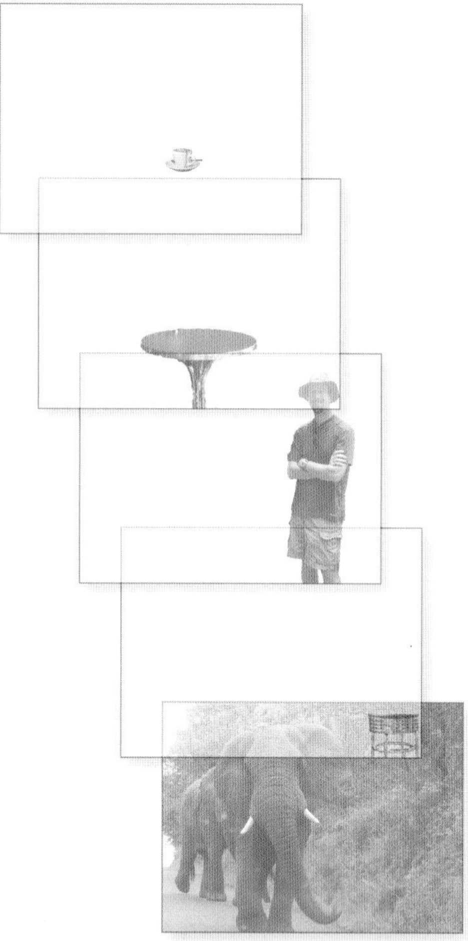

A Layers act like clear acetate sheets, where transparent areas let you see through to the layers below. (It's a good thing I showed the layers, or you might think the photo was undoctored!)

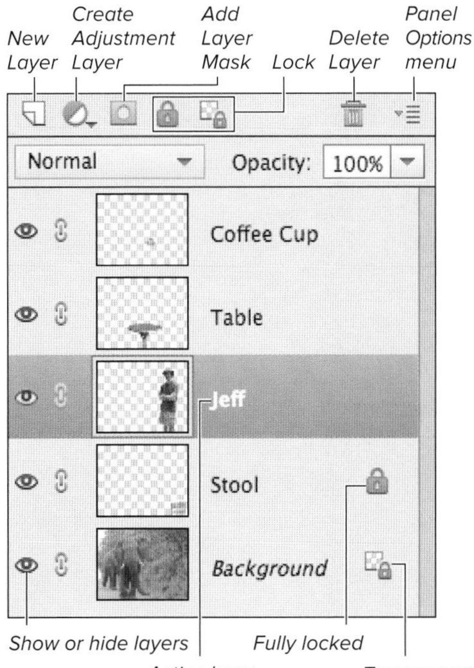

A The Layers panel shows stacked layers exactly as they're arranged in your image. This panel gives you complete control over the stacking order of your layers, whether they're visible or hidden.

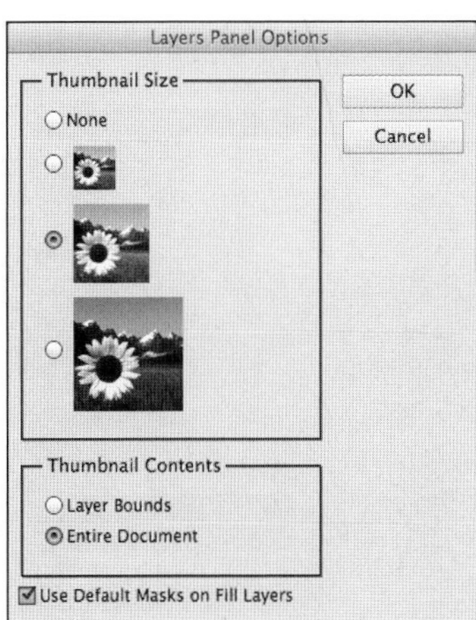

B Change thumbnail views from the Layers panel Options menu.

Using the Layers Panel

When you launch Photoshop Elements for the first time, the Layers panel automatically appears in the lower-right corner of your screen in the Panel Bin. You can use the Layers panel from within the Panel Bin, or drag it out into the work area.

You can select which layer to make the active layer, display and hide layers, and lock layers to protect them from unintentional changes **A**. You can also change layer names, set the opacity (transparency) of individual layers, and apply blending modes.

The panel menu offers quick access to many of the same commands found on the Layer menu, plus options for changing the appearance of the panel thumbnails.

To view the Layers panel:

Do one of the following:

- Choose Window > Layers.
- Click the Layers button in the Task bar.
- Choose Window > Reset Panels to return all the panels to their default locations, including Layers.

To view the Panel Options menu:

Click the Panel Options button in the top-right corner of the Layers panel.

Once the Layers panel menu is open, you can select a command from the menu.

TIP To change the appearance of the layer thumbnail views, choose Panel Options from the Layers panel menu and click the size you want B. The smaller the icon, the more layers you're able to view at one time on the panel.

Layer Basics

To begin working with layers, you need to master just a few fundamental tasks. Start by creating and naming a new layer, and then add an image (or portion of an image) to it.

Once you've constructed an image file of multiple layers, you need to select the individual layer before you can work on that layer's image. Keep in mind that any changes you make will affect only the selected (active) layer, and that only one layer can be active at a time.

To create a new layer:

1. From the Layer menu or from the Layers panel menu, select New > Layer, or press Ctrl+Shift+N/Command-Shift-N.
2. In the New Layer dialog, choose from the following options:
   - Rename the layer with a more meaningful and intuitive name. The default names are Layer 1, Layer 2, Layer 3, and so on **A**.
   - Choose a blending mode for the layer.

     The default blending mode is Normal, meaning that no change will be applied to the layer. You can experiment with other blending modes directly from the Layers panel.
   - Choose the layer's level of opacity.

     Opacity can also be adjusted at any time from the Layers panel.
   - Apply a clipping mask over a previous (or lower) layer.

     The lower layer acts as a window for the upper layer's image to show through. For a detailed description of layer grouping, see "Creating Clipping Masks," later in this chapter.

A Default layer names are Layer 1 for the first layer you create, Layer 2, Layer 3, and so on. You can enter a new name when creating a layer, or you can rename it later.

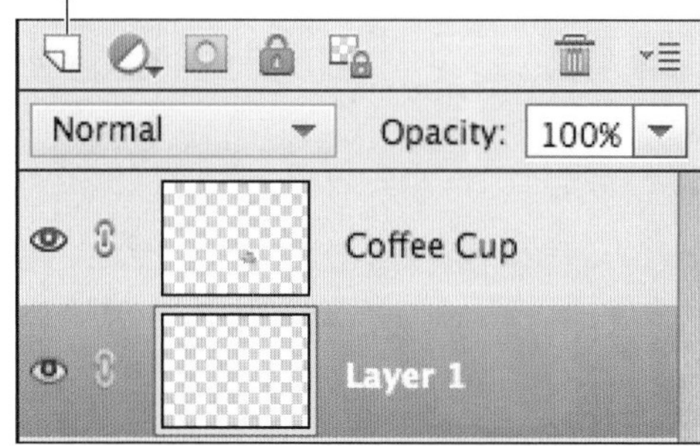

B Click the New Layer button to quickly create a new, blank layer.

TIP I prefer to quickly create a new layer by clicking the New Layer button B. The new layer appears as the top layer in the panel with the default blending and opacity modes applied. To rename the new layer, double-click its name in the Layers panel and enter a new name.

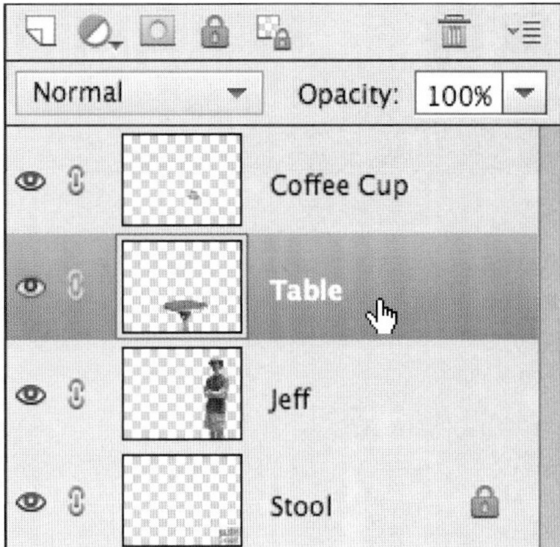

Ⓒ Click the layer name or thumbnail to make it the active (editable) layer.

Ⓓ When you click a layer image in the image window, a bounding box appears to show you that it is the selected, active layer.

Visible

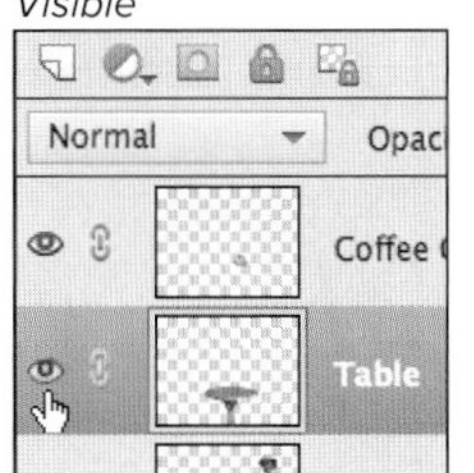

Hidden

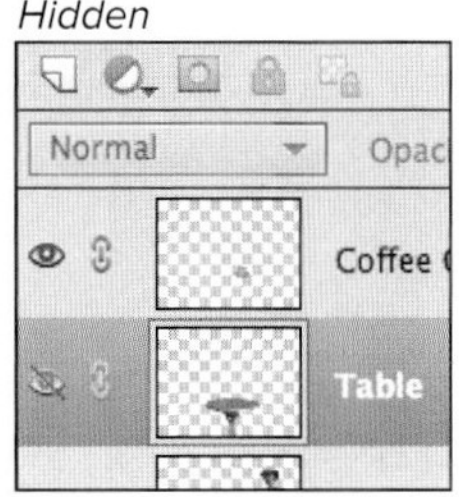

Ⓔ Click the eye icon to hide a layer; click again to make the layer visible.

To select a layer:

Do one of the following:

- On the Layers panel, click the Layer thumbnail or name to make that layer active Ⓒ.

  If you've imported an image from a digital camera, by default it will have only one layer—the background layer, which is selected automatically.

- Select the Move tool and click directly on a layer image in the image window. A border with selection handles appears around the layer image to indicate that it's selected Ⓓ.

To show or hide a layer:

On the Layers panel, click the eye icon to hide the layer (the eye disappears). Click again and the eye reappears, making the layer visible again in the image window Ⓔ.

TIP When you try to select or make changes to an area in your image, you might encounter weird and unexpected results. For example, your selection can't be copied, or you apply a filter but nothing happens. More often than not, this is because you don't have the correct layer selected. Just refer to the Layers panel to see if this is the case. Remember that the active layer is always highlighted in the Layers panel.

TIP Quickly show or hide multiple layers by clicking and dragging through the eye column.

TIP To quickly display just one layer, Alt-click/Option-click its eye icon. The other layers become hidden. Alt-click/Option-click again to show all layers.

To delete a layer:

1. Select a layer on the Layers panel.
2. Do one of the following:
   - With the layer selected, click the Trash icon on the Layers panel (F) and then click Yes in the dialog that appears.
   - From the Layer menu or from the Layers panel menu, choose Delete Layer.
   - Drag the layer to the Trash icon on the Layers panel.

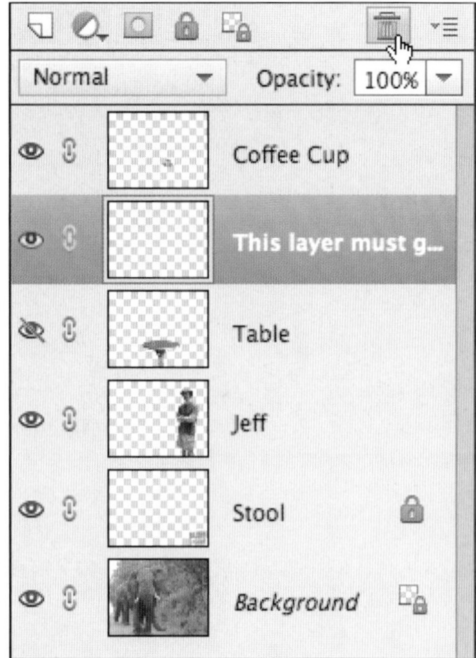

(F) Clicking the Trash icon also removes the selected layer.

Background Layers

When you open a photo imported from a digital camera or scanner, the photo appears on the background (or base) layer in Photoshop Elements. In fact, when you open an image file from just about any source, chances are it has been flattened and contains only a background layer. This layer cannot be reordered (that is, its relative position or level cannot be moved), and it cannot be given a blending mode, or assigned a different opacity.

When you create a new image and choose Transparent for its background, the bottom layer is called Layer 1. This layer can be reordered, and you can change its blending mode or opacity just as with any other layer.

A simple background layer can never be transparent, but that's okay if you're not concerned with changing opacity or applying blending modes. However, if you want to take advantage of the benefits transparency offers, start by creating an image with transparent background contents, or convert an existing background layer to a regular layer.

See "Converting and Duplicating Layers," later in this chapter, for details on turning background layers into regular layers (and vice versa).

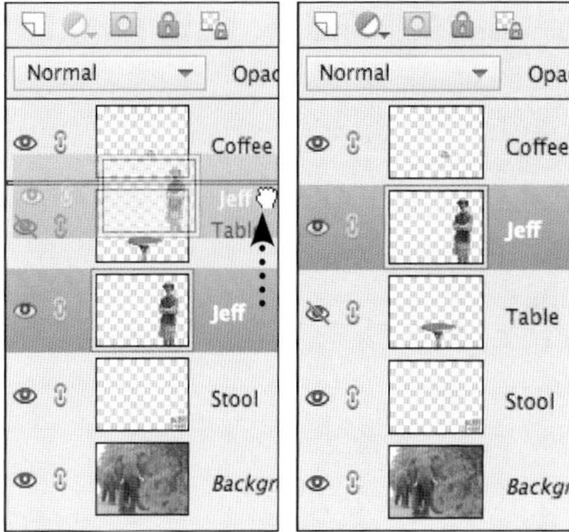

Ⓐ Drag a layer up or down on the Layers panel to change its stacking order.

Changing the Layer Order

The layer stacking order determines which layers are on top of others, and plays a big role in determining how your image looks. As you build a composition, you may decide you want to change the layer order, either to help you work more easily on a particular layer, or to get a particular result or effect. The actual, visible overlapping of elements is determined by the layer order, so you may need to reorder layers frequently when you work on complex images.

Elements provides two main ways to change the stacking order of your layers. The most common and versatile approach is to drag the layer within the Layers panel. The second way is to select the Layer > Arrange menu and then choose commands such as Bring to Front and Send to Back—a method similar to what you use to arrange objects in a drawing program.

To change the layer order by dragging:

1. On the Layers panel, select the layer you want to move.
2. Drag the layer up or down in the Layers panel Ⓐ.

   You will see a thick double line between the layers, indicating the new layer position.
3. Release the mouse button when the layer is in the desired location.

To change the layer order by arranging:

1. Select the layer you want to move on the Layers panel.
2. From the Layer menu, choose Arrange, and then select one of the following options from the submenu; or use the keyboard shortcuts noted for each **B**.
   - Bring to Front (Ctrl+Shift+]/Command-Shift-]) moves the layer to the top of the Layers panel and the image **C**.
   - Bring Forward (Ctrl+]/Command-]) moves the layer up by one step in the stacking order **D**.
   - Send Backward (Ctrl+[/Command-[) moves the layer down by one step in the stacking order.
   - Send to Back (Ctrl+Shift+[/Command-Shift-[) makes the layer the bottom layer on the Layers panel.

   You can also Shift-click to select two layers in the Layers panel, and select Reverse to swap their order in the layer stack.

TIP If your image contains a background layer and you choose the Send to Back command, you'll find that the background layer stubbornly remains at the bottom of your Layers panel. By default, background layers are locked in place and can't be moved. To get around this, just double-click and rename the background layer to convert it to a functional layer. Then you can move it wherever you like.

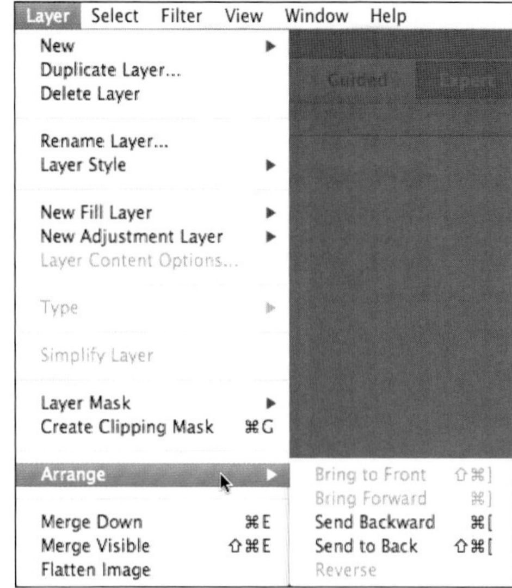

B You can also change a layer's position using the options on the Layer > Arrange menu.

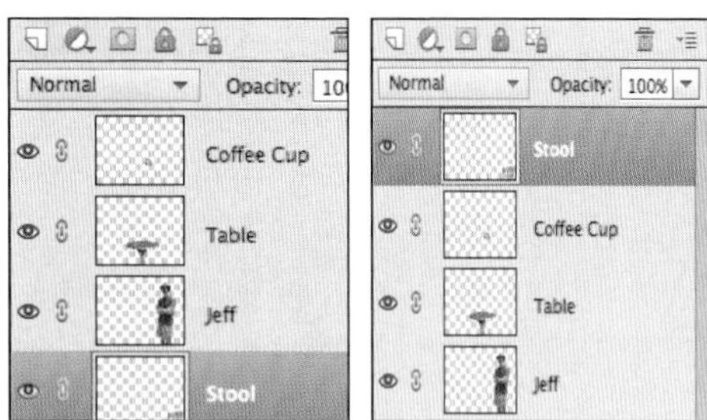

C The Bring to Front command moves the selected layer to the top level in your image.

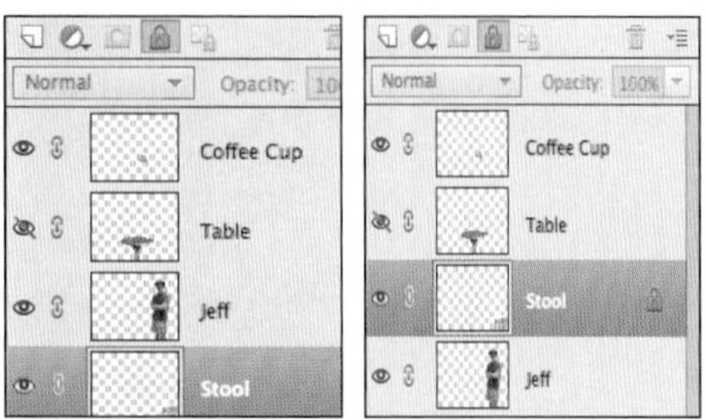

D The Bring Forward command moves the selected layer up just one level.

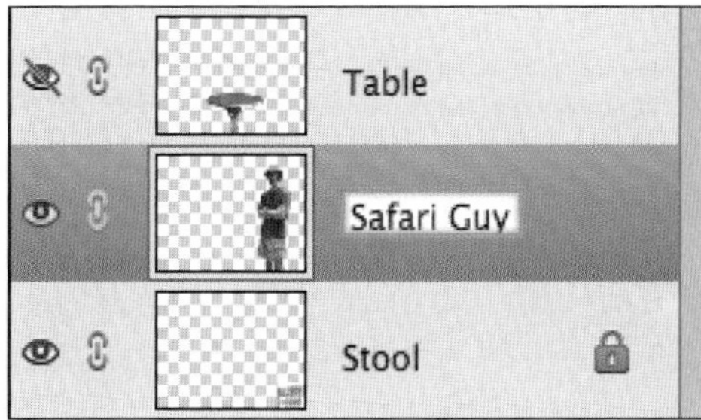

A To rename a layer, just double-click its name on the Layers panel.

B Link icons indicate which layers are linked together.

Managing Layers

As your image becomes more complex, consider renaming your layers—it's much easier to find a cloud image on a layer called "Clouds" than it is to remember that it's on "Layer 14."

You can also link layers together, so that any changes, such as moving and resizing, happen to two or more layers together.

And you can protect layers from unwanted changes by locking them. All layers can be fully locked, so that no pixels can be changed, or you can lock just the transparent pixels, so that any painting or other editing happens only where opaque (non-transparent) pixels already are present. This partial locking is useful if you know that you want to preserve certain areas as transparent (like for a graphic you want to incorporate into a Web page). Locking an image protects it in other ways, too: You can move a locked layer's stacking position on the Layers panel, but the layer can't be deleted.

To rename a layer:

1. Double-click the layer's name on the Layers panel to display the text cursor and make the name editable **A**.
2. Enter a new name for the layer and press the Enter key. The new name appears on the Layers panel.

To link layers:

1. Ctrl-click/Command-click to select the layers in the Layers panel that you want to link.
2. Click the Link button in any of the selected layers. The link icon appears in each linked layer, to the right of the layer name **B**.

To lock all pixels on a layer:

1. Select the layer on the Layers panel.
2. Click the Lock All button.

   The Lock All icon appears to the right of the layer name on the Layers panel **C**.

To lock transparent pixels on a layer:

1. Select the layer on the Layers panel.
2. Click the Lock Transparent Pixels button.

   The Lock Transparent Pixels icon appears to the right of the layer name on the Layers panel **D**.

C The Lock All icon indicates that the layer's pixels are completely locked.

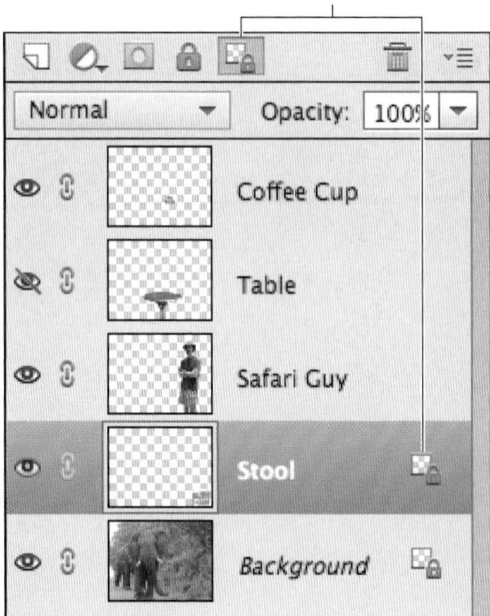

D The Lock Transparent Pixels icon indicates that the transparent pixels are locked.

A The top image is a composite of a number of layers from a 3D rendering program: a background layer, the pole, the sign's shadow on the pole, and three layers for the sign itself. To simplify the file, the three sign layers were merged into a single layer, and the pole and the shadow were combined (lower right). The finished image will look the same, but because it's composed of fewer layers, its file size will be significantly smaller.

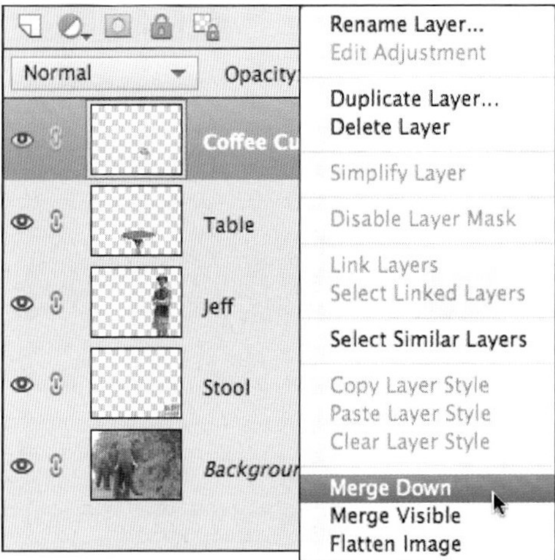

B Combine a single layer with the layer below it by using the Merge Down command.

Merging Layers

Once you begin to create projects of even moderate complexity, the number of layers in your project can add up fairly quickly. Although Elements lets you create an almost unlimited number of layers, there are a couple of reasons why you may want to consolidate some or all of them into a single layer **A**. For one thing, it's just good housekeeping. It doesn't take long before the Layers panel begins to fill, and you find yourself constantly scrolling up and down in search of a particular object or text layer. And every layer you add drains a little more from your system's memory. Continue to add layers, and, depending on available memory, you may notice a decrease in your computer's performance.

Photoshop Elements offers three approaches to merging image layers. You can merge just two at a time, merge multiple layers, or flatten your image into a single background layer.

To merge one layer with another:

1. On the Layers panel, identify the two layers you want to merge, and then select the topmost of the two.

   Photoshop Elements will merge two layers only when one is stacked directly above the other. If you want to merge two layers that are separated by one layer or more, you'll need to rearrange their order in the Layers panel before they can be merged.

2. From the Panel Options menu on the Layers panel, choose Merge Down **B**, or press Ctrl+E/Command-E. The two layers are merged into one.

To merge multiple layers:

1. On the Layers panel, identify the layers you want to merge, checking that the Visibility (eye) icon is on for just the layers you want to merge.
2. From the Panel Options menu on the Layers panel, choose Merge Visible **C**, or press Ctrl+Shift+E/Command-Shift-E.

   All of the visible layers are merged into one layer.

TIP You can create a new layer and then place a merged copy of all of the visible layers on that layer by holding the Alt/Option key while choosing Merge Visible from the Layers panel's Panel Options menu. The visible layers themselves aren't merged and so remain separate and intact D. This technique offers you a way to capture a merged snapshot of your current file without actually merging the physical layers. It can be a handy tool for brainstorming and comparing different versions of the same layered file. For instance, take a snapshot of a layered file, change the opacity and blending modes of several layers, and then take another snapshot. You can then compare the two snapshots to see what effect the different settings have on the entire file.

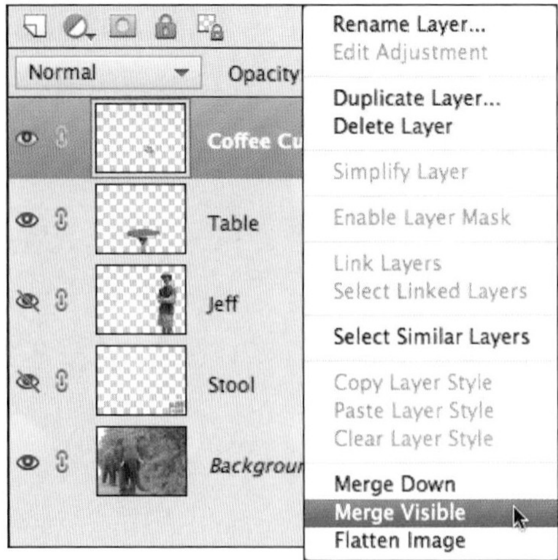

C Only the three visible layers will be merged into one using the Merge Visible command.

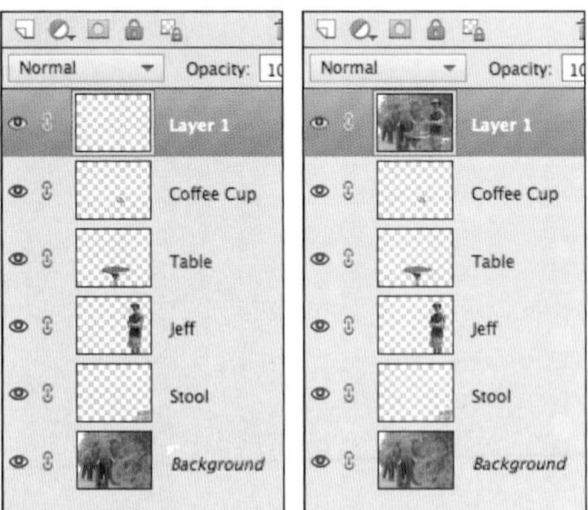

D On the left, a new layer has been created at the top of the Layers panel. If you hold the Alt/Option key while selecting Merge Visible from the panel menu, all visible layers are merged and copied to the new layer, as shown on the right.

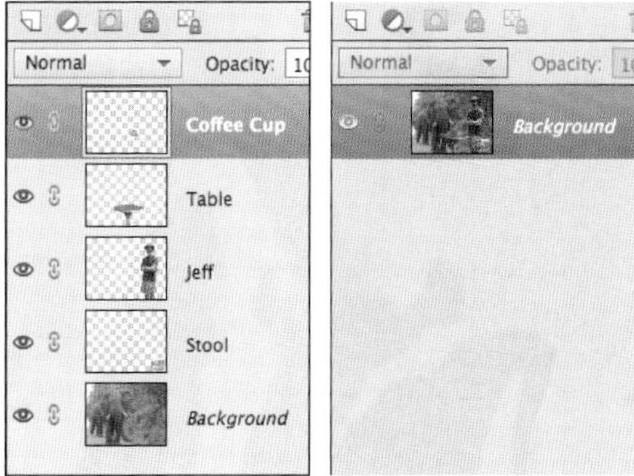

Ⓔ Use the Flatten Image command to combine all the layers in a project into a single layer.

To flatten an image:

1. In the Layers panel, click the More button to open the panel menu.
2. From the panel menu, select Flatten Image.
3. If any layers are invisible, a warning box appears asking if you want to discard the hidden layers. If so, click OK.

   The entire layered file is flattened into one layer Ⓔ.

TIP If there's any chance you may eventually want to make revisions to your layered image, always create a duplicate file before flattening so the layers are safely preserved in your original. Once you've flattened, saved, and closed a file, there's no way to recover those flattened layers.

Removing a Halo from an Image Layer

Often when you create a new image layer from a selection, you'll find you've inadvertently selected pixels you didn't want to include. This is a particularly common problem when you're trying to remove an image from its background using the Magic Wand or Quick Selection tools. On close inspection, what you thought was a clean selection actually includes a halo of colored background pixels.

Once you've pasted your selection into its new layer, choose Enhance > Adjust Color > Defringe Layer. In the Defringe dialog, enter a pixel width to control how much of the border of your image you want to affect—for high-resolution images, I usually start around 5. Then, click OK to see the results in the image window Ⓕ. If you're not happy with the results, undo the operation by pressing Ctrl+Z/Command-Z, then repeat the steps, entering a new pixel width in the Defringe dialog.

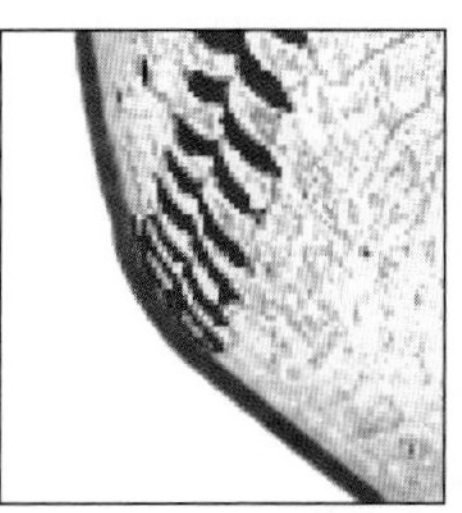
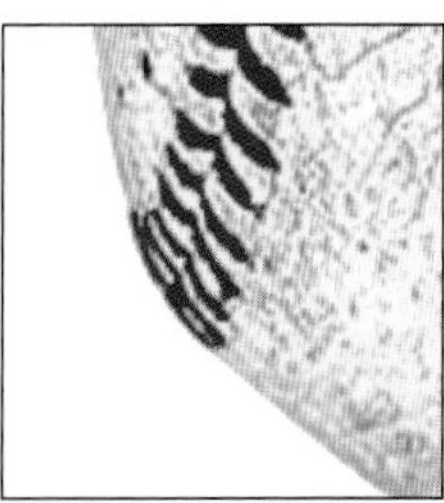

Ⓕ When zoomed in, it's apparent that the old, weathered baseball I've cut and pasted carried with it a halo of the background it was resting on (left). After applying Defringe, the colored halo has disappeared (right).

Converting and Duplicating Layers

You now know you can create a new layer using the Layer > New command; in addition, Elements creates layers in all sorts of sneaky ways. For example, whenever you copy and paste a selection into an image, it's automatically added to your image on a brand-new layer.

When you start editing an image, you'll often find it convenient to create a selection and convert it to a layer to keep it isolated and editable within your photo. It's also quite easy to duplicate a layer, which is useful when you want to copy an existing layer as is, or use it as a starting point and then make additional changes.

The background layer is unique and by default can't be moved, but sometimes you will need to move it, change its opacity, or apply a blending mode. To do any of those things, you'll need to convert it to a regular layer. And sometimes you'll want to convert an existing layer to the background.

Ⓐ Select an area to convert to its own layer.

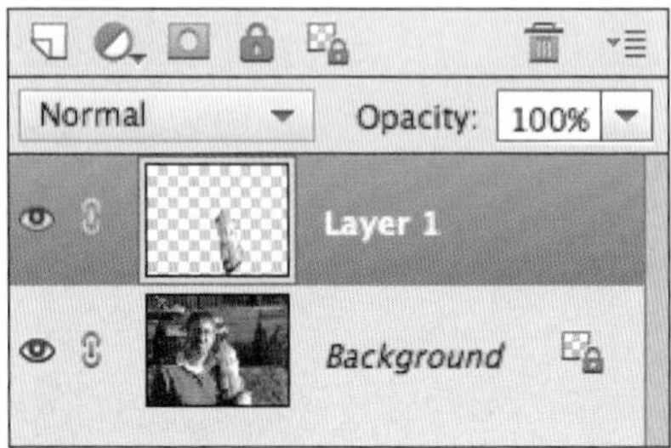

Ⓑ Copying a selection to a new layer leaves the original selection unchanged.

Ⓒ The Layer via Cut command cuts the selected pixels to a new layer. (The new layer has been hidden here to demonstrate that it's actually cut, not copied.)

To convert a selection to a layer:

1. Make a selection using any of the selection tools Ⓐ.
2. From the Layer menu, choose New; then perform one of the following commands:
   - Layer via Copy (Ctrl+J/Command-J). The selection is copied to a new layer, leaving the original selection unchanged Ⓑ.
   - Layer via Cut (Ctrl+Shift+J/Command-Shift-J). The selection is cut to a new layer, leaving a gaping hole in the original layer, with the current background color showing through Ⓒ.

D Use the Duplicate Layer dialog to rename your new duplicate layer.

E You can also duplicate a layer by dragging any existing layer to the New Layer button.

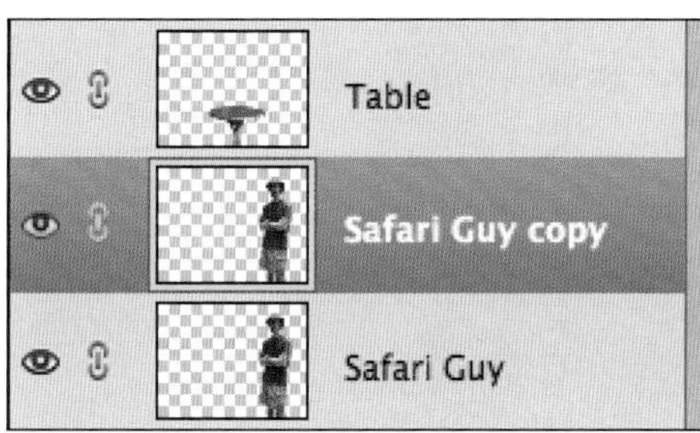

F The new layer appears right above the original layer on the Layers panel.

To duplicate a layer:

1. Select the layer on the Layers panel.
2. Duplicate the layer using one of the following methods:
   - If you want to create a new name for the layer, choose Layer > Duplicate Layer.

     The Duplicate Layer dialog appears, where you can rename the layer D. Note that you can also get to this dialog from the Layers panel menu.
   - If you're not concerned with renaming the layer right now, just drag the selected layer to the New Layer icon on the Layers panel E.

     The new layer appears above the original layer with a "copy" designation added to the name F.

TIP Perhaps this is because of the way I originally learned it, but I always duplicate layers by dragging them to the New Layer button. I then double-click the layer's name to type a new name.

To convert a background to a layer:

1. From the Layer menu, choose New > Layer from Background.
2. If desired, type a new name for the layer and click OK **G**.

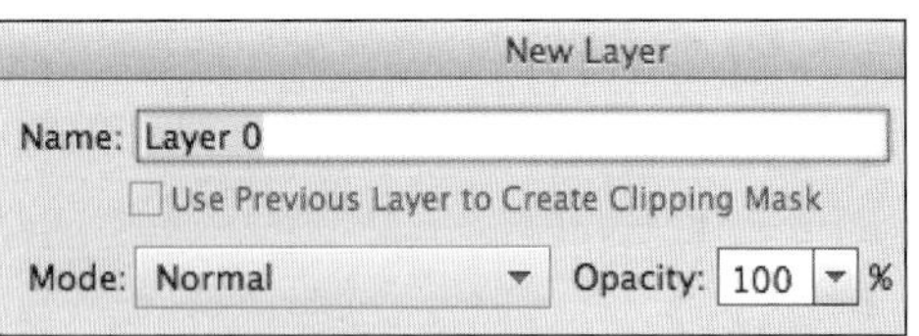

G You can convert the background to a layer and rename it during the conversion.

To convert a layer to a background:

1. Select a layer on the Layers panel.
2. From the Layer menu, choose New > Background From Layer **H**.
3. The new background appears at the bottom of the Layers panel **I**.

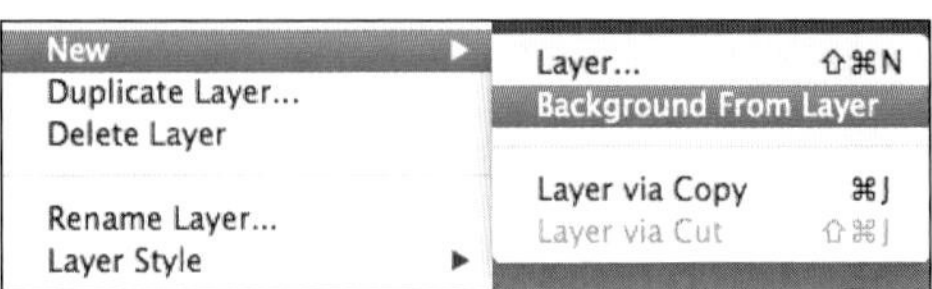

H You can convert a layer to a background by choosing Layer > New > Background From Layer.

TIP **You can also convert the background by double-clicking it on the Layers panel, which brings up the same New Layer dialog.**

TIP **The Type and Shape tools also each automatically generate a new layer when you use them, keeping those elements isolated on their own unique layers.**

TIP **The Background From Layer command won't work if you already have an existing background layer in your Layers panel. Why? Because no image can have two background layers at the same time. To get around this, convert the current background to a regular layer. Then, follow the steps to convert a regular layer into a background.**

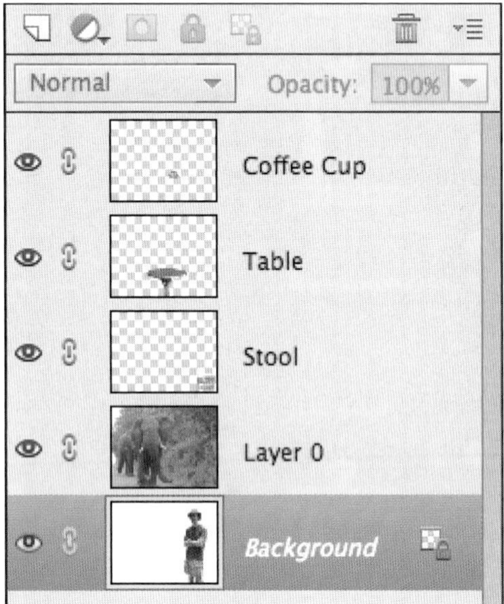

I New background layers always appear at the bottom of the Layers panel.

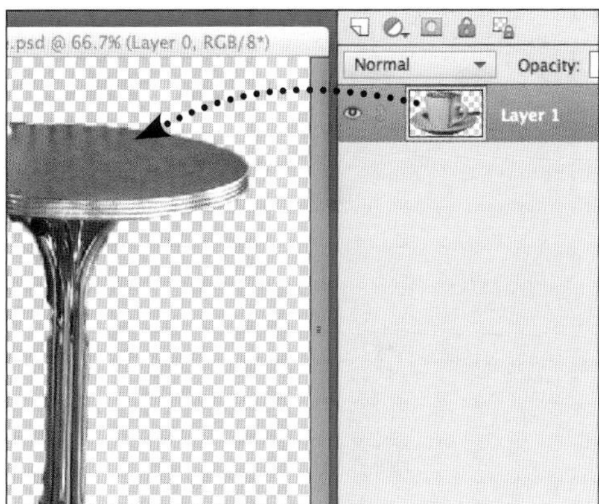

Ⓐ To copy a layer, just drag it from the Layers panel and drop it directly onto another image.

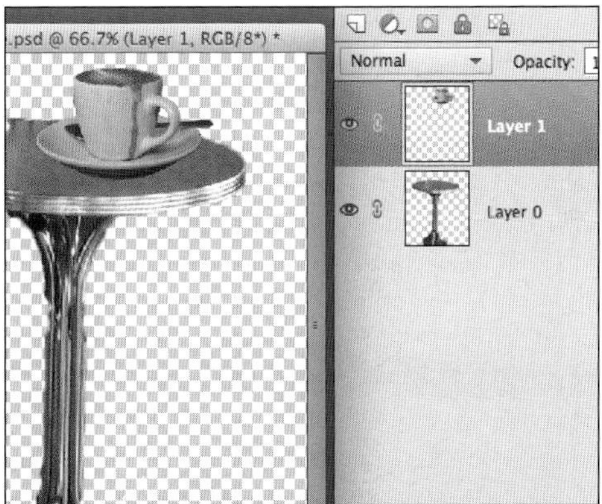

Ⓑ The new layer appears directly above the previously selected (active) layer in the destination image and in the Layers panel.

Copying Layers Between Images

It's extremely easy to copy layers from one Elements document to another. If you're used to the drag-and-drop technique, you'll be glad to know this method works well for copying layers as well as selections. Remember, as you copy and paste selections they end up on their own layers. So, layers often contain unique objects you can easily share between photos.

To drag and drop a layer from the Layers panel:

1. Open the two images you plan to use.
2. In the source image, select the layer you want to copy by clicking it in the Layers panel.
3. Drag the layer's name from the Layers panel into the destination image Ⓐ.

   The new layer appears both in the image window and on the Layers panel of the destination image Ⓑ. When you drag a layer from one image into another, the original, source image is not changed. The layer remains intact.

TIP In some cases, the layer in your source image may be larger than the destination, in which case not all of the layer will be visible. Use the Move tool to bring the desired area into view, and choose Image > Transform > Free Transform to resize as needed.

To drag and drop a layer using the Move tool:

1. Open the two images you plan to use.
2. Select the Move tool, and then in the source image window, select the layer you want to copy by clicking it.

   You can also select the layer by clicking its thumbnail in the Layers panel.
3. With the Move tool still selected, drag the actual image layer from the source image window to the destination image **C**.

   The copied layer appears on the Layers panel immediately above the previously active layer.

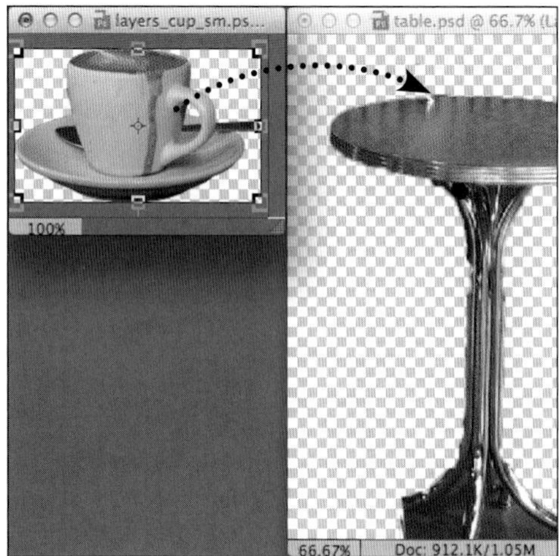

C The Move tool lets you copy a layer from one image window to another.

To copy and paste a layer between images:

1. In the source image, select the layer you want to copy from by clicking it either in the Layers panel or the image window.
2. Choose Select > All to select all of the pixels on the layer, or press Ctrl+A/Command-A.
3. Choose Edit > Copy to copy the layer to the clipboard, or press Ctrl+C/Command-C.
4. In the destination image, choose Edit > Paste, or press Ctrl+V/Command-V.

   The contents of the copied layer appears in the center of the destination image.

TIP If you're viewing open documents in tabbed view, drag an item to the tab of the file to which you want it added.

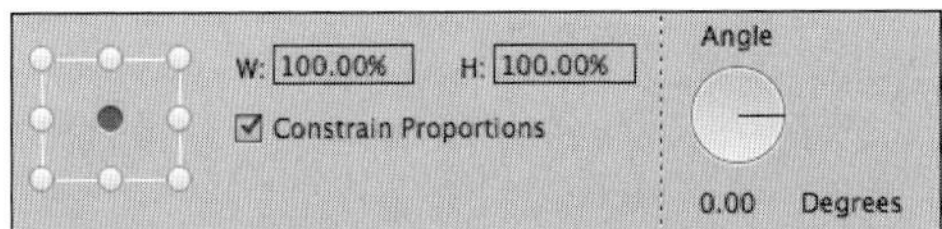

A Precise scale and rotation values can be entered for any shape.

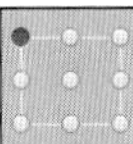

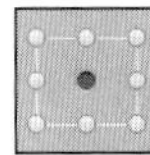

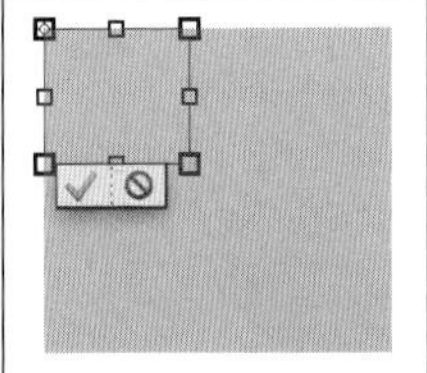

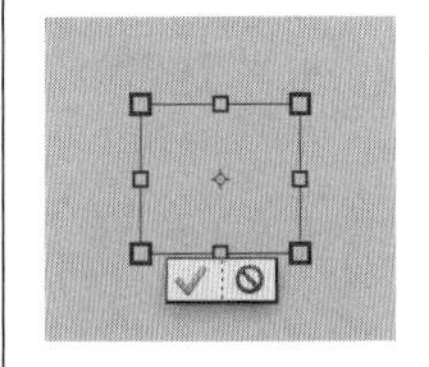

B Both of these squares are being reduced in size by about half. The one on the left is scaled toward its upper-left corner, and the one on the right is scaled toward its center.

C The Commit Transform button scales the image to the size you define.

Transforming Layers

You can also scale (resize), rotate, and distort layer images. They can be altered either numerically, by entering specific values on the options bar, or manually, by dragging their control handles in the image window. Constrain options, such as proportional scaling, are available for most transformations, and a set of keyboard shortcuts helps to simplify the process of adding distortion and perspective.

To scale a layer image:

1. Click a layer in the Layers panel to activate it; then from the Image menu, choose Transform > Free Transform, or press Ctrl+T/Command-T. The options bar displays the scale and rotation text fields and the reference point locator **A**.
2. On the options bar, click to set a reference point location **B**.

   The reference point determines what point your layer image will be scaled to: toward the center, toward a corner, and so on.
3. If you want to scale your layer image proportionately, click the Constrain Proportions checkbox.
4. Enter a value in either the height or width text field. The layer image is scaled accordingly.
5. At the lower-right corner of your layer image, click the Commit Transform button **C**, or press Enter.

TIP You can scale a layer image manually by selecting it with the Move tool and then dragging any one of the eight handles on the selection border. Constrain the scaling by holding down the Shift key while dragging one of the four corner handles.

To rotate a layer image:

1. Click a layer in the Layers panel; then from the Image menu, choose Rotate > Free Rotate Layer **D**.

   The options bar changes to show the scale and rotation text fields and the reference point locator.

2. On the options bar, click to set a reference point location **E**.
3. Enter a value in the rotate text field.

   The image will rotate accordingly.

4. Click the Commit Transform button, or press Enter.

TIP To rotate the image in 90- or 180-degree increments or to flip it horizontally or vertically, choose Image > Rotate; then choose from the list of five menu commands below the Free Rotate Layer command.

TIP You can rotate a layer image manually by selecting it with the Move tool and then moving the pointer outside of the selection border until it becomes a rotation cursor F. Drag around the outside of the selection border to rotate the image. In addition, you can constrain the rotation to 15-degree increments by holding down the Shift key while dragging the rotation cursor.

TIP If you simply want to reposition a layer image in the image window, click anywhere inside the image with the Move tool and then drag the image to its new position.

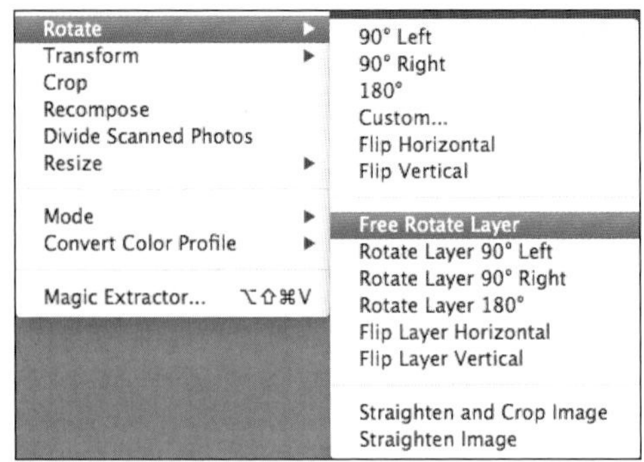

D You can apply any of the layer rotation menu commands to a layer image.

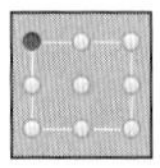
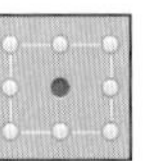
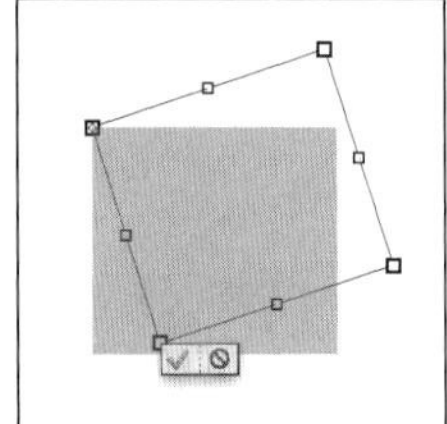
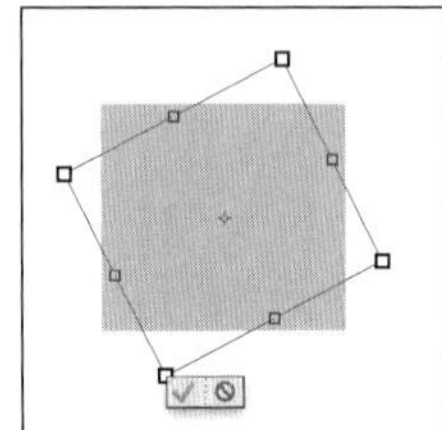

E Both of these squares are being rotated about 20 degrees. The one on the left is rotated around its upper-left corner, and the one on the right is rotated around its center.

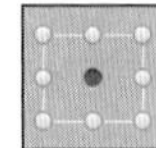
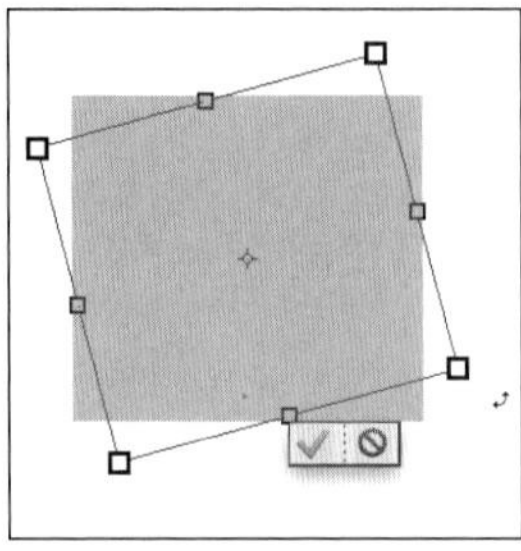

F Rotate any layer image manually by dragging it around its reference point with the rotation pointer.

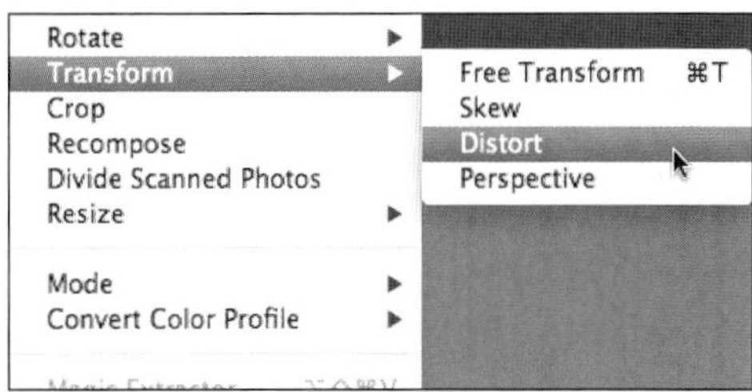

G Choose one of the three specific transformation commands.

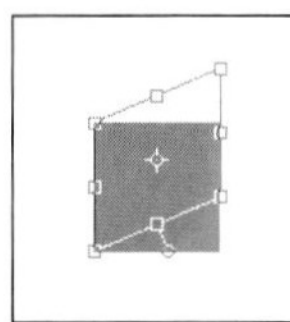
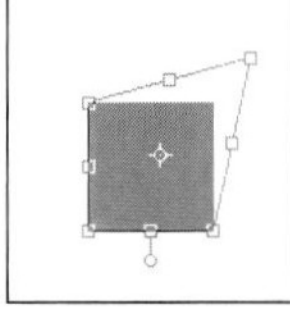
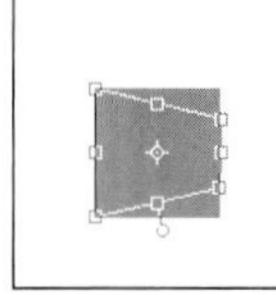

H The same square layer image transformed using Skew (left), Distort (center), and Perspective (right).

Before

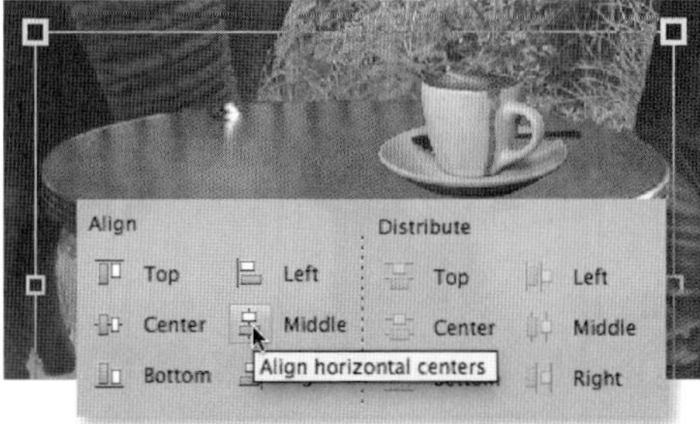

After

I You can align or distribute objects on different layers.

To distort a layer image:

1. Click a layer in the Layers panel to make it active. From the Image menu, choose Transform; then choose Skew, Distort, or Perspective G.
2. On the options bar, check that the reference point location is set to the center.

   The reference point can, of course, be set to any location, but the center seems to work best when applying any of the three distortions.
3. Drag any of the layer image's control handles to distort the image.

   Dragging the control handles will yield different results depending on the distort option you choose H.
4. On the options bar, click the Commit Transform button, or press Enter.
5. Click the Commit Transform button a second time (or press Enter) to deselect the image layer and hide the selection border.

To align or distribute layer objects:

1. Select two or more layers in the Layers panel; the Distribute command requires three or more selected layers.
2. Select the Move tool from the toolbox.
3. From the options bar, click the Align or Distribute drop-down menu and choose how you'd like the layer objects repositioned I.

About Opacity and Blending Modes

One of the most effective and simple ways to enhance your layered image is to create the illusion of combining one layer's image with another by blending their pixels. This differs from merging layers because the layers aren't actually combined, but rather appear to mix together. Photoshop Elements provides two easily accessible tools at the top of the Layers panel that can be used alone or in tandem for blending multiple layers: the Opacity slider and the Blending Modes drop-down menu.

The Opacity slider controls the degree of transparency of one layer over another. If a layer's opacity is set at 100 percent, the layer is totally opaque, and any layers beneath it are hidden. If a layer's opacity is set to 30 percent, 70 percent of any underlying layers are allowed to show through **A**.

Blending modes are a little trickier. Whereas Opacity settings strictly control the opaqueness of one layer over another, blending modes act by mixing or blending one layer's color and tonal value with the one below it. The Difference mode, for example, combines one layer's image with a second, and treats the top layer like a sort of negative filter, inverting colors and tonal values where dark areas blend with lighter ones **B**.

A Two separate layers (top) compose this image of me and a giant coffee cup. The lower-left image displays the top layer with an opacity setting of 100 percent. The lower-right image displays the top layer with an opacity setting of 50 percent.

B The image on the left contains no blending modes; the image on the right displays the top layer with the Difference blending mode applied.

C The top layer is selected on the Layers panel. Its opacity is set at 100 percent.

D You can change a layer's opacity from 0 to 100 percent by dragging the Opacity slider.

To set a layer's opacity:

1. On the Layers panel, select the layer whose opacity you want to change **C**.
2. To change the opacity, do one of the following:
   - Enter a percentage in the Opacity text field, which is located at the top of the Layers panel.
   - Click the arrow to activate the Opacity slider and then drag the slider to the desired opacity **D**.

TIP You can change the opacity settings in 10-percent increments directly from the keyboard. With a layer selected on the Layers panel, press any number key to change the opacity: 1 for 10 percent, 2 for 20 percent, and so on. Also, pressing two number keys in rapid succession will work—for example, 66 percent. If this technique doesn't seem to be working, make sure you don't have a painting or editing tool selected in the toolbox. Many of the brushes and effects tools can be sized and adjusted with the number keys, and if any of those tools are selected, they take priority over the Layers panel commands.

TIP A background layer contains no transparency, so you can't change its opacity until you first convert it to a regular layer (see "To convert a background to a layer," earlier in this chapter).

To apply a blending mode to a layer:

1. On the Layers panel, select the uppermost layer to which you want to apply the blending mode.

   Remember, blending modes work by mixing (blending) the image pixels of one layer with the layers below it, so your project will need to contain at least two layers in order for a blending mode to have any effect.

2. Select the desired blending mode from the Blending Mode drop-down menu **E**.

   The image on the layer to which you've applied the blending mode will appear to mix with the image layers below.

TIP You can apply only one blending mode to a layer, but it's still possible to apply more than one blending mode to the same image. After assigning a blending mode to a layer, duplicate the layer and then choose a different blending mode for the duplicate. There are no hard-and-fast rules to follow, and the various blending modes work so differently with one another that getting what you want is largely an exercise of trial and error. But a little experimentation with different blending mode combinations (and opacities) can yield some very interesting effects that you can't achieve any other way.

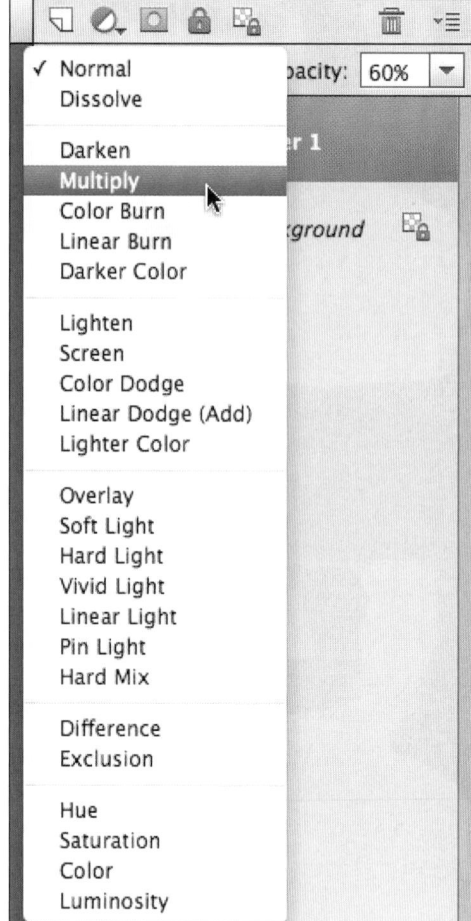

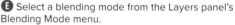

E Select a blending mode from the Layers panel's Blending Mode menu.

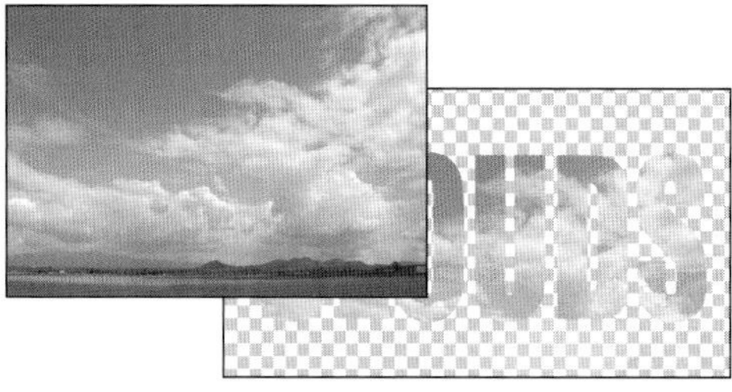

Ⓐ This project is composed of two layers: a photo of clouds and the CLOUDS text layer. The photo completely covers the text layer in the image at top, but when made a clipping mask, the clouds peek through only where the text is visible.

Ⓑ In this figure, the CLOUDS text layer serves as the base layer. It will soon be grouped with the Sky layer, which is directly above it.

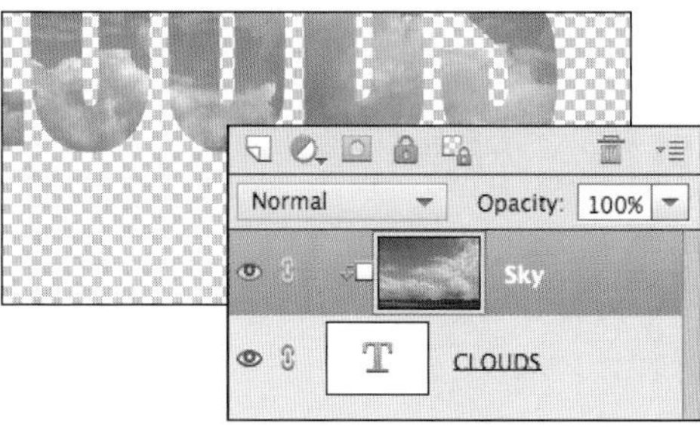

Ⓒ A clipping mask appears indented.

Creating Clipping Masks

Any object placed on a layer, including photographic images and lines of editable text, can be used as the basis for masking any number of layer objects above it. Think of the lower, or base layer, as a window through which the upper layers are allowed to show through Ⓐ. Once applied, any layer mask can be repositioned independently of the others, or all masks can be linked and moved as a group.

To create a clipping mask:

1. On the Layers panel, identify the layer you want to use as your base layer Ⓑ. Your layers must be arranged so that the layer you want to mask is directly above the base layer.
2. Still on the Layers panel, select the layer above the base layer; then from the Layer menu choose Create Clipping Mask, or press Ctrl+G/Command-G. The two layers are now grouped, and the upper layer is visible only in those areas where the base layer object is present.

   On the Layers panel, the base layer's name is underlined, and the masked layer is indented Ⓒ.

To remove a clipping mask:

1. On the Layers panel, select the base layer.
2. From the Layer menu, choose Release Clipping Mask, or press Ctrl+G/Command-G.

TIP For a faster way to create a clipping mask, Alt-click/Option-click the space between the two layers.

Using Layer Masks

In several examples in this chapter, objects (such as the coffee cup or table) have been removed from their backgrounds. In those cases, I made a selection, then deleted the surrounding pixels. The problem, of course, is that I can't get those pixels back without returning to the unedited source files.

Photoshop Elements offers a better way. Instead of deleting pixels, you can hide them using a layer mask. That enables you to edit what appears at any point, keeping your precious pixels intact.

Layer masks are always grayscale: black pixels hide content, white pixels reveal it. Gray pixels, however, become transparent depending on how dark they are, opening up all sorts of possibilities for compositions.

To create a layer mask:

1. Make a selection of the area in your image you want to keep visible.
2. Click the Add Layer Mask button in the Layers panel. A mask is created to the right of the image thumbnail **A**.

   To reverse the mask (make the selection transparent), Alt-click the Add Layer Mask button.

To edit a layer mask:

1. Click the layer mask thumbnail for the layer you want to edit.
2. Use the editing tools to change the contents of the mask. For example, paint with the brush tool set to black to make more areas transparent **B**.

TIP Since a mask is just a grayscale image, you can apply filters and other interesting effects to it C.

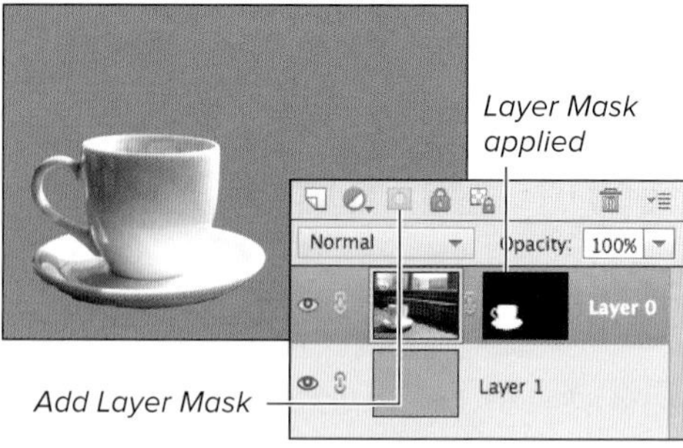

A The black areas of the mask hide the layer's pixels without deleting them.

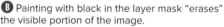

B Painting with black in the layer mask "erases" the visible portion of the image.

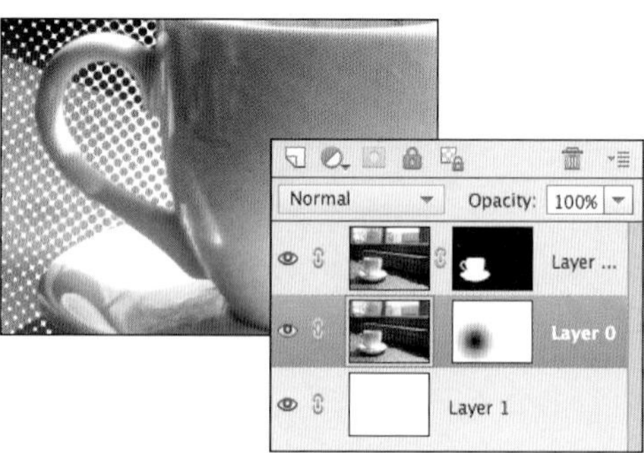

C To achieve this halftone highlight effect, I duplicated the image, created a circular gradient within the mask, and then applied the Color Halftone effect to the mask. To punch up the contrast, I changed the color of the underlying layer (which shows through the dark portions of the mask) to white.

D With the mask unlinked, moving its contents shifts the visible portion of the image, not the image itself.

E It's often helpful to turn off a mask without deleting it when you need to view the full image.

To unlink a layer mask:

Click the link icon between the image thumbnail and the mask thumbnail.

The mask can be repositioned independently of the image **D**.

To disable a layer mask:

With the layer selected, choose Layer > Layer Mask > Disable. A red X appears over the mask to indicate that it's not currently active **E**.

To turn it back on, choose Layer > Layer Mask > Enable.

To delete a layer mask:

Select the layer and choose Layer > Layer Mask > Delete. The mask is removed, leaving the image untouched.

To apply a layer mask:

If you want to make the mask permanent, choose Layer > Layer Mask > Apply. Transparent pixels are erased from the image on that layer.

TIP The layer mask commands are also available by right-clicking and choosing them from the contextual menu that appears. I much prefer this approach, since my cursor is usually already there within the Layers panel.

TIP Ctrl-click/Command-click a layer mask to select its contents without needing to make a new selection.

TIP Photoshop Elements has had layer masks for several revisions, but the feature wasn't as accessible as it is now. For example, when you make a selection in an image and apply an adjustment layer (described later in this chapter), Elements creates a layer mask so the effect is applied only to the selection.

Applying Effects with Layer Styles

With layer styles, you can add editable effects to individual layers within an image, and you can be as conservative or as wild as your heart desires. For example, you can add a subtle drop shadow to an object, or you can go in the opposite direction and set your friend's hair ablaze with the Fire layer style. Beveled edges, glowing borders, and even custom textures can all be applied to any object or text layer. The Layer Styles options in the Effects panel contain a series of style sets, grouped as galleries and accessed from the panel's drop-down menu. Once you've applied a layer style, you can choose to keep it as an active element of a layer and return to and adjust it at any time; or you can choose to merge the layer object and style together to simplify the layer.

Ⓐ Select a layer to apply a layer style.

Ⓑ The Effects pane allows you to select Filters, Layer Styles, and Photo Effects (or All).

To apply a layer style:

1. On the Layers panel, choose the layer to which you want to apply the style Ⓐ.
2. To open the Effects panel (if it's not already visible), do one of the following:
   - Click the Effects panel tab in the Task bar Ⓑ.
   - From the Window menu, choose Effects.
3. Click the Layer Styles icon at the top of the panel.
4. From the Library drop-down menu, choose a style set Ⓒ. The set you choose presents a gallery from which you can select a specific style.
5. In the style gallery, click the style you want to apply to your layer.

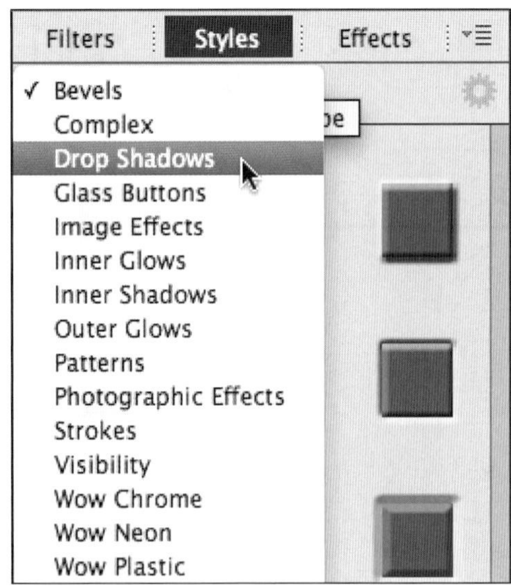

Ⓒ Layer styles are divided into different style sets.

D Choose a style from the panel gallery and click Apply to make the style active.

E When a layer style is applied, a Layer Style icon appears to the right of the layer name.

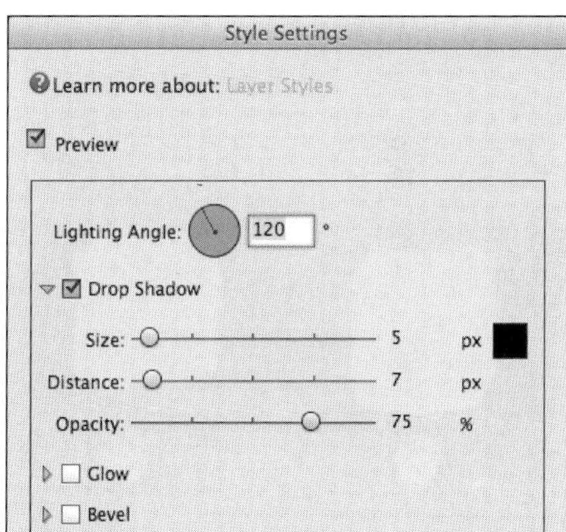

F Use sliders in the Style Settings dialog to modify the shadow, glow, bevel, and stroke styles.

6. Click the Apply button (or double-click the chosen style). The style is applied to the layer object **D**, and a Layer Style icon appears next to the layer name on the Layers panel.

To remove a layer style:

From the Layer menu, choose Layer Style > Clear Layer Style. The command removes all styles from the layer, no matter how many have been applied.

To edit a layer style:

1. On the Layers panel, double-click the Layer Style icon **E**. The Style Settings dialog opens.
2. Make sure the Preview box is selected; then refer to the image window while dragging the Size, Distance, and Opacity sliders **F**.

TIP Multiple layer styles can be assigned to a single layer; however, only one layer style from each set can be assigned at a time. In other words, you can assign a drop shadow, bevel, and outer glow style to the same layer all at once, but you can't assign two different bevel styles at the same time.

TIP Layer styles can be applied only to images or text on a regular, transparent layer. If you try to apply a style to a background layer, a warning box asks if you want to first make the background a layer. Click OK and the background is converted to a layer; the layer style will be applied automatically.

TIP Elements allows you to apply a layer style to a blank layer, but the layer style won't have any effect until text or an image is placed on the layer. When you place something on a layer with a previously assigned layer style, it will display with the layer style's attributes: drop shadow, beveled edge, and so on.

The Style Settings Dialog

Not all of the layer styles can be adjusted, but, using a series of sliders, a wheel, checkboxes, and radio buttons, you can make adjustments to drop shadows, inner and outer glows, bevels, and stroke styles. Here's a quick tour of the Style Settings dialog controls **A**.

Except for Lighting Angle and Bevel, each section contains a slider to determine how opaque the effect appears, as well as a color well for changing the effect's color. The distance and size slider values are all based on units of pixels. Click a style's checkbox to enable it.

- The Lighting Angle wheel controls the direction of the light source when a bevel or shadow style is applied. Changing the light angle will change which beveled surfaces are in highlight and which are in shadow, and will also control where a drop shadow falls behind an object **B**.
- The Drop Shadow's Distance slider controls the distance that a drop shadow is placed from an object. The larger the number, the more shadow is exposed from behind an object. If the distance is set to 0, the shadow is centered directly under the object and isn't visible. The Size slider determines how large the shadow appears.
- The Inner Glow Size slider lets you increase or decrease the amount of glow radiating in from the edges of an object.
- The Outer Glow Size slider lets you increase or decrease the amount of glow radiating out from the edges of an object.

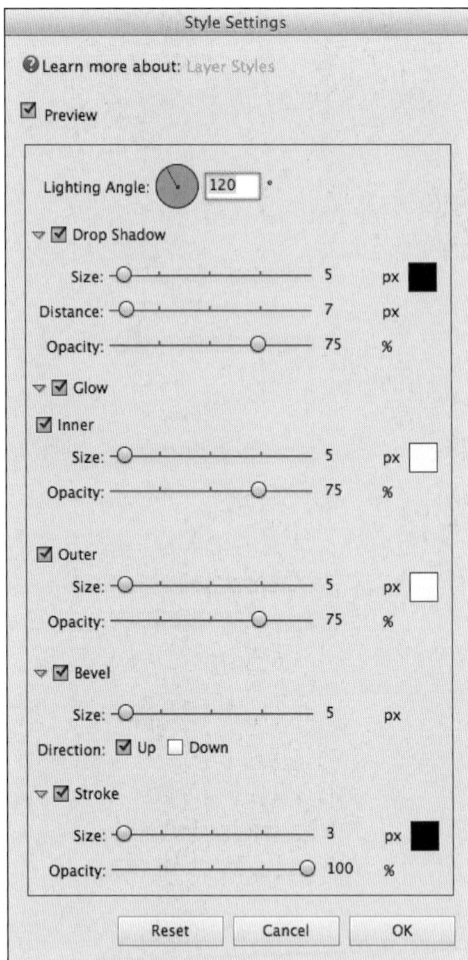

A Please, please, please, never use all of these effects at once! I'm just showing all options.

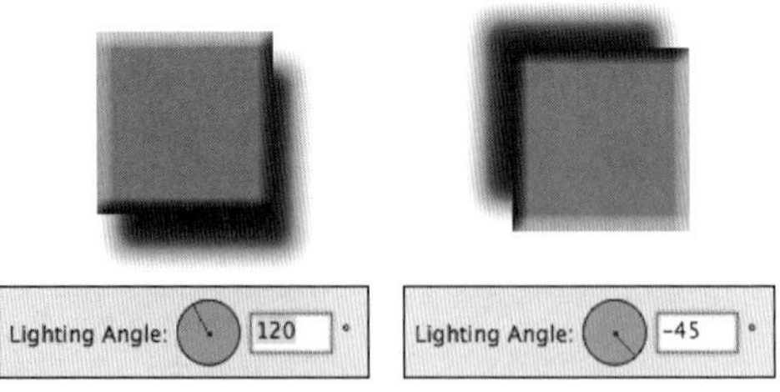

B The Lighting Angle wheel sets a light source for any bevel or drop shadow styles you apply, and can be set to light any object from any angle.

C When the bevel direction is set to Up, the object bevel appears to come forward (left). When the bevel direction is set to Down, the object bevel appears depressed (right).

- The Bevel Size slider controls the amount of beveled edge on your object. An inside bevel of 3 will be almost imperceptible, whereas larger values create an increasingly more pronounced bevel effect.
- The Bevel Direction radio buttons control the appearance of a bevel style. If the Up button is selected, the bevel will appear to extrude or come forward; if the Down button is selected, the bevel will appear to recede **C**.
- The Stroke effect draws a solid line around elements on the layer. The size slider sets the line's width.

Once you've applied a layer style, you can return to it at any time to modify it, but you also have the option of merging the layer style with its layer by simplifying. In effect, simplifying is like flattening an individual layer. Simplifying a layer permanently applies a layer style to its layer and can help to reduce the complexity and file size of your project.

To simplify a layer:

1. On the Layers panel, click to select the layer you want to simplify.
2. From the panel menu on the Layers panel, choose Simplify Layer.

   The layer style is merged with the layer, and the Layer Style icon disappears from the layer on the Layers panel.

Making Color and Tonal Changes with Adjustment Layers

Adjustment layers let you make color and tonal adjustments to your image (much like the commands discussed in Chapter 8) without changing the actual pixels in your image. Adjustment layers work like filters, resting above the actual image layers and affecting any image layers below them. They can be especially useful when you want to experiment with different settings or compare the effects of one setting over another.

Because you can apply opacity and blending mode changes to adjustment layers (just as you would to any other layer), they offer a level of creative freedom not available from their menu-command counterparts. For instance, you can create a Levels adjustment layer above an image, and then change the opacity of that adjustment layer to fine-tune the amount of tonal correction applied.

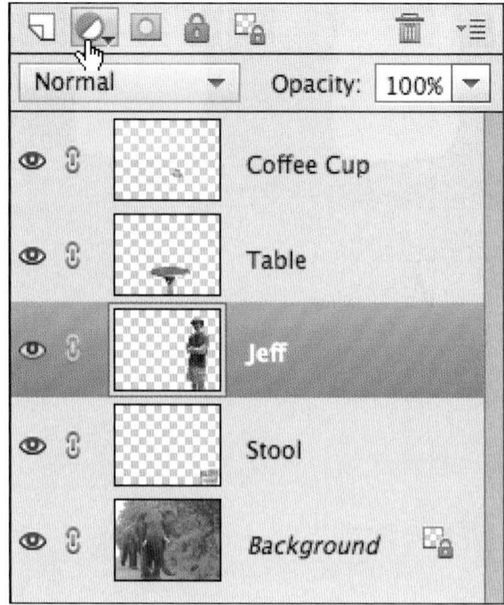

A Once you've selected a layer, click the Create Adjustment Layer button.

To create an adjustment layer:

1. On the Layers panel, identify the topmost layer to which you want the adjustment layer applied, and then select that layer.

   Remember that the adjustment layer affects all layers below it on the Layers panel, not just the one directly below it.

2. At the top of the Layers panel, click the Create Adjustment Layer button **A**.

B Choose an adjustment command from the drop-down menu.

C The edits you make in the adjustment dialog apply to all layers below the adjustment layer, but do not change those layers' pixels.

D The adjustment layer has been grouped with the object layer directly below it.

3. From the drop-down menu, choose from the list of adjustment layer options **B**.

   When you choose an adjustment layer option, its dialog opens and a new adjustment layer is created above the selected layer **C**.

4. Use the sliders to adjust the settings, and then click OK to close the dialog.

   If you want to return to the adjustment layer dialog later, just double-click its layer thumbnail on the Layers panel.

By default, an adjustment layer affects all the layers below it in the Layers panel. But if you create a clipping mask, the effects of the adjustment layer will be limited to one specific layer.

To apply an adjustment layer to a single layer:

1. In the Layers panel, move the adjustment layer directly above the layer to which you want it applied.

2. With the adjustment layer still selected in the Layers panel, choose Create Clipping Mask from the Layer menu, or press Ctrl+G/Command-G.

   The adjustment layer and the one directly below it are grouped, and the effects of the adjustment layer are applied only to that single layer **D**.

TIP A much faster way to create a clipping mask is to Alt-click/Option-click the space between the two layers.

Applying Texture or Color with Fill Layers

The Create Adjustment Layer drop-down menu includes not only tonal correction options such as Levels, but also three layer fill options: Solid Color, Gradient, and Pattern. When you combine them with the ability to make clipping masks, you can add a texture or color cast to an image.

For example, suppose you want to make a photo appear as if it were printed on rough paper stock. A Pattern fill layer works well.

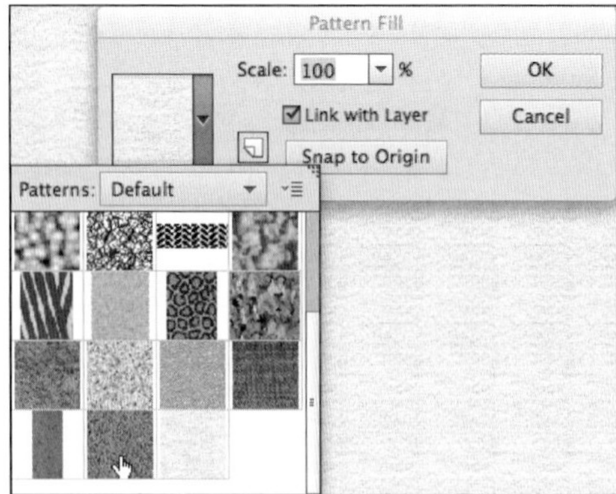

Ⓐ Choose a pattern to fill the layer.

To add a texture using a fill layer:

1. From the Create Adjustment Layer drop-down menu in the Layers panel, choose Pattern.
2. In the Pattern Fill dialog, click the pattern thumbnail at left to choose from a grid of available patterns Ⓐ.
3. Drag the Scale slider to make the pattern appear larger or smaller (usually making it coarser or finer).
4. Click OK. The pattern covers your photo at this point.
5. In the Layers panel, choose a blend mode and opacity for the fill layer to bring the photo back into view Ⓑ.
6. If you want to change the attributes of the pattern, double-click the fill layer to bring up the Pattern Fill dialog.
7. Experiment with the settings until you arrive at the look you want Ⓒ.

Ⓑ Reducing the opacity and setting the blend mode to Overlay reveals the photo.

Ⓒ Texture applied, before (left) and after (right).

TIP If you hit upon a combination of pattern and size that you want to reuse, click the Create a New Preset button (the document icon to the right of the pattern thumbnail) to save the settings.

Adjusting Lighting and Color

Almost any photograph can benefit from some simple color and lighting corrections. For example, you might find that a vivid sunset you photographed ends up looking rather dull and ordinary, or that a portrait taken outdoors is too dark to discern any details. Luckily, you're never stuck with a set of inferior images. Photoshop Elements provides a powerful set of lighting and color correction tools, with both automatic and manual adjustments, so you can fine-tune your images as much as you want.

In this chapter, I'll review Photoshop Elements' lighting and color correction tools and discuss which ones you may want to use, and when you'll most likely want to use them. I'll also show you how to help colors display and print accurately (also known as *color management*) and how to correct colors and tonal values in your images.

In This Chapter

Understanding Tonal Correction

Before we jump into buttons and sliders, let's step back and take a quick look at what we're doing. Tonal correction tends to be one of the least understood (and most intimidating) features of Elements. That's a shame, because there's really no magic involved.

In plain terms, correcting tonal range simply comes down to adjusting brightness and contrast. Elements offers several ways to make automatic brightness and contrast adjustments.

Understanding histograms

The histogram is a graphic representation of the tonal range of an image. The lengths of the bars represent the number of pixels at each brightness level: from the darkest on the left to the lightest on the right. If the bars on both sides extend all the way to the left and right edges of the histogram box, the darkest pixels in the image are black, the lightest pixels are white, and the image is said to have a full tonal range **A**.

If, as in many images, the bars stop short of the edges, the darkest and lightest pixels are some shade of gray, and the image may lack contrast. In extreme circumstances, the bars may be weighted heavily to the left or right, with the tonal range favoring either the shadows or highlights **B**. Whatever the tonal range, the brightness and contrast of an image can be adjusted using sliders located beneath the histogram in the Levels dialog or the Levels adjustment layer (see "Adjusting Levels Manually," a few pages ahead).

A A photo displaying full tonal range and its accompanying histogram. Note how the histogram extends all the way to the left and right, indicating that pure blacks are present in the darkest shadow areas and pure whites are present in the lightest highlight areas. The fairly uniform peaks and valleys throughout the middle portion of the histogram also indicate sufficient pixel data present in the midtones.

B Here's the same image, this time too bright and with insufficient contrast. Note the lack of data on the left end, indicating a lack of black pixels, and the abundance of data on the right, indicating very light tones.

Adjusting Lighting

No matter what the photo is, I always start editing by adjusting the lighting. Often a few pulls of a slider can bring out detail that otherwise appears muddy or faint.

A The photo on the top lacks sufficient tonal range, particularly in the highlight and lighter midtone areas. The photo on the bottom, corrected with the Auto Levels command, reveals more detail in both the shadow and highlight areas because the pixels have been distributed across the full tonal range.

Adjusting levels automatically

Although I recommend adjusting levels manually, the auto commands can be a good jumping-off point before launching into more controlled, manual image correction.

The auto commands tend to be most successful when applied to a photograph that contains an average tonal range; one where most of the image detail is concentrated about halfway between the darkest and lightest values. Severely overexposed or underexposed images may be beyond help. If the camera or scanner didn't capture the detail in the first place, it's not there to be corrected.

To apply Auto Levels to an image:

Do one of the following:

1. In the Layers panel, click the Create Adjustment Layer button and choose Levels.
2. In the Adjustments panel that appears, click the Auto button.

Or

- From the Enhance menu, choose Auto Levels, or press Ctrl+Shift+L/ Command-Shift-L.

  Photoshop Elements instantly adjusts the image's tonal range **A**.

If you're not happy with the result, select Edit > Undo Auto Levels, or press Ctrl+Z/ Command-Z.

Get Smart

Finessing an image's levels and other settings gives you an enormous amount of power to correct tonal ranges—but maybe you don't have the time or desire to be a slave to the sliders. The Auto Smart Fix command under the Enhance menu does it all for you. If you don't like the result, build from there or start over and tackle each setting yourself.

To apply Auto Contrast to an image:

1. From the Enhance menu, choose Auto Contrast, or press Alt+Ctrl+Shift+L/ Command-Option-Shift-L.

   Photoshop Elements instantly adjusts the image's contrast **B**.

2. To undo, choose Edit > Undo Auto Contrast, or press Ctrl+Z/Command-Z.

TIP As mentioned earlier, the auto commands work best in specific circumstances (as when the image's tonal range favors the midtones) and should be used sparingly. The Auto Levels command, in particular, can yield surprising and unexpected color shifts. In some instances it seems to overcompensate by swapping out one undesirable color cast for another, whereas in others it may ignore the color altogether and throw the contrast way out of whack. Give these auto commands a try, but be prepared to commit that Undo keyboard shortcut to memory.

TIP If you're looking for adjustments without all the detail, the Quick edit environment groups a cross-section of some of the more commonly used commands and functions into one convenient, interactive workspace. See Chapter 5 for more information.

B The photo on the top lacks sufficient contrast, so detail is lost in both the shadow and highlight areas. The photo on the bottom, corrected with Auto Contrast, reveals detail not present in the original.

Editing with Adjustment Layers versus Editing Image Layers

For what seems like ages, I applied levels adjustments directly to each image I edited. It works, certainly, but I've since seen the light: adjustment layers. The problem with correcting levels on the image layer is that the pixel values change—if you want to go back to a previous state, you must wipe out all changes you made in the interim.

Adding an adjustment layer gives you the same benefits without the inflexibility. A Levels adjustment layer makes the same changes but on a separate layer that can be hidden or deleted without affecting the image layer's original pixels. You can also add several adjustment layers to experiment with different looks. For example, one layer can be set for a high exposure while another emphasizes a darker look; toggle the visibility of each to see which you like better, without having to redo the sliders.

Adjustment layers aren't appropriate in all situations; for example, the Shadows/Highlights dialog can often create slightly better results than just adjusting midtones with a levels correction. But my advice is: If you can made an edit using an adjustment layer, try that first.

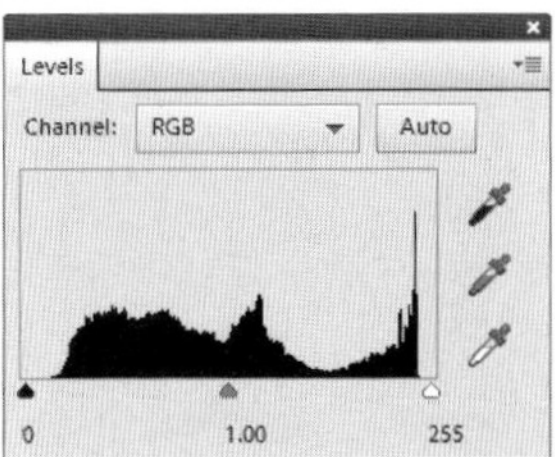

Ⓒ The Levels controls in the Adjustments panel.

Ⓓ Moving the left slider underneath the left edge of the histogram spreads the darker pixels more evenly into the dark areas of the midtones and shifts the darkest pixels to black.

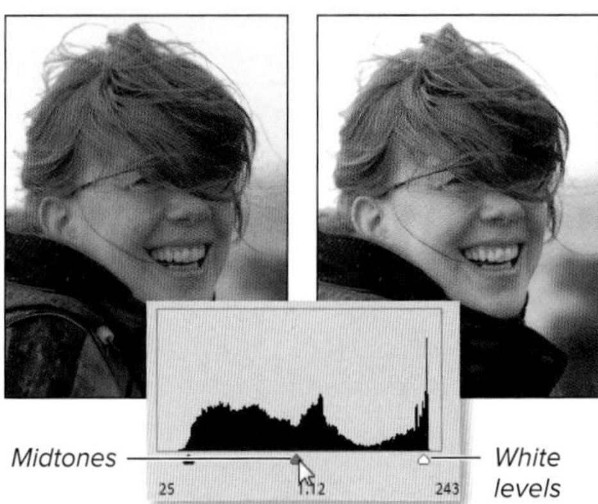

Ⓔ The right slider affects the lightest pixels in the image. Moving the right slider underneath the right edge of the histogram spreads the lighter pixels more evenly into the light areas of the midtones and shifts the lightest pixels to white, resulting in more detail in the highlight areas.

Adjusting levels manually

Is your image washed out or too dark? Adjusting the levels by hand gives you more control, and can result in dramatic improvements.

To adjust the tonal range:

1. Do one of the following:
   - In the Layers panel, click the Create Adjustment Layer button and choose Levels. The Adjustments panel opens with Levels settings Ⓒ.
   - From the Enhance menu, choose Adjust Lighting > Levels, or press Ctrl+L/Command-L to open the Levels dialog.
2. Drag the slider on the left until it rests directly below the left edge of the histogram Ⓓ. The image darkens as the darkest pixels in the image move closer to black.
3. Drag the slider on the right until it rests directly below the right edge of the graph. The image lightens as the lightest pixels move closer to white.
4. Drag the middle slider to the left or right to adjust the brightness level of the pixels that fall in the midtones Ⓔ.
5. If you're using the Levels dialog, click OK to close it.

TIP These adjustments apply to the entire color range of the image. To modify just the reds, greens, or blues, choose one from the drop-down menu above the histogram.

TIP What about the Brightness/Contrast adjustments? I never use them. Brightness/Contrast indiscriminately lightens or darkens pixels across the entire tonal range, typically creating more problems than it solves.

Adjusting shadows

Another way to fix images with overexposed background images and underexposed foreground subjects is the Shadows/Highlights dialog. Although you could adjust the midtones using a Levels adjustment layer, Elements uses its smarts in this feature to avoid making the image appear flat.

To lighten detail in shadow:

1. From the Enhance menu, choose Adjust Lighting > Shadows/Highlights.

   The Shadows/Highlights dialog appears **F**.

2. Do one or all of the following:
   - Drag the Lighten Shadows slider to the right to lessen the effect of the shadows, or to the left to introduce shadow back into the image.
   - Drag the Darken Highlights slider to the right until you're satisfied with the detail in the foreground or other brightly lit areas.
   - Drag the Midtone Contrast slider to the right to increase the contrast, or to the left to decrease the contrast.

3. Click OK to close the dialog and apply the changes **G**.

TIP I've found in many (if not most) images imported from a digital camera, the Shadows/Highlights dialog defaults work surprisingly well on their own, requiring just minor slider adjustments.

TIP In any case, use the Midtone Contrast slider sparingly. A little goes a long way, and adjustments of more than plus or minus 10 percent can quickly wash out or flatten an image's details.

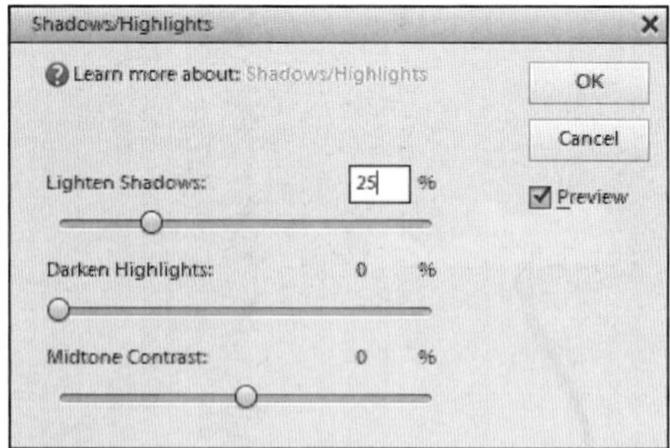

F The Shadows/Highlights dialog.

G The top photo is underexposed in the foreground, so detail in the girl's face is hidden in shadow. In the bottom photo, making adjustments with the Lighten Shadows and the Midtone Contrast sliders selectively brightens and enhances detail in both her face and shirt.

H I shot three different exposures to capture detail in the foreground and the background.

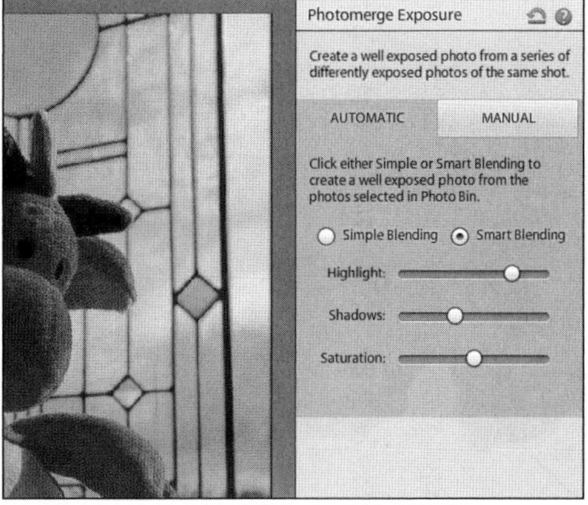

I The automatic merge did a pretty good job, but the colors are a bit too saturated.

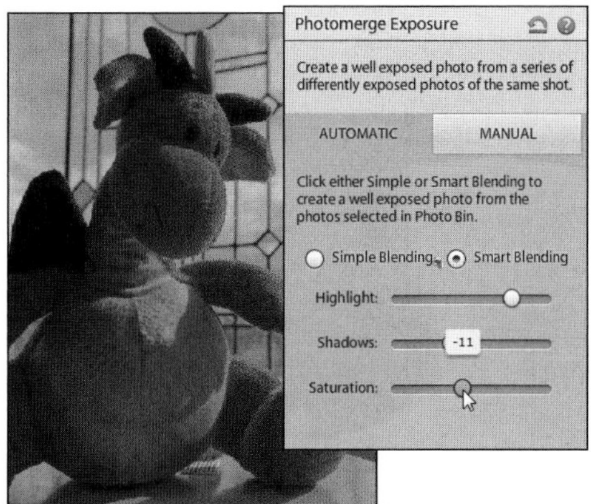

J Adjust the blend settings to balance highlights, shadows, and saturation.

Fixing lighting using Photomerge Exposure

Another way to deal with photos that contain over- or under-exposed areas is to run them through the Photomerge Exposure feature. When you're shooting, especially in difficult lighting situations, put your camera into its *bracketing* mode, which captures successive shots and applies a different level of exposure compensation for each; typically, you'll get three shots with EV (Exposure bias Value) settings of –1, 0, and +1. Capture them in burst mode to minimize movement between shots.

To fix lighting using Photomerge Exposure (Automatic mode):

1. Open two or more related images with different exposures **H** and select them in the Photo Bin.
2. Choose Enhance > Photomerge > Photomerge Exposure. Or, switch to the Guided Edit mode and click Exposure under the Photomerge heading.

   Elements examines the files and opens the Photomerge Exposure interface in Automatic mode **I**.
3. Use the following controls to adjust the appearance **J**:
   - Highlight adds more details to highlight areas, which can make the image darker.
   - Shadows lightens or darkens shadow areas.
   - Saturation boosts or tones down the colors.

   You can also switch from Smart Blending to Simple Blending, but doing so disables the additional controls.
4. Click Done.

To fix lighting using Photomerge Exposure (Manual mode):

1. If you're not happy with the automatic results, or you want more control over how the feature is applied, click the Manual tab.
2. In the Photo Bin, click a photo that has a good foreground exposure. That becomes the Source image.
3. Drag a photo with good background exposure to the Final pane **K**.
4. With the Selection Tool active, paint the foreground area you want to appear against the background image **L**. Use the Eraser Tool to clean up edges of your selection.
5. Use the Opacity slider to control how much the areas are blended—this is helpful if the foreground image is too bright, for example.
6. Click the Edge Blending checkbox to smooth the areas that overlap in the final image.
7. Click Done to create a new merged image **M**.

TIP For best results, mount your camera on a tripod to take shots destined for the Photomerge Exposure tool.

TIP In the Manual mode, click Advanced Options to reveal controls for aligning the images by hand.

TIP When taking pictures of people, a fast burst rate is essential; differences in body position between images creates a blurred, ghosting effect.

K The image with the yellow border here has a better sky, so I'm using it as the background.

L Paint an area from the foreground image to selectively choose what appears in the final image.

M The final image retains the dramatic background and sheds more light on the poor soul who woke up early to capture this photo.

Before *After*

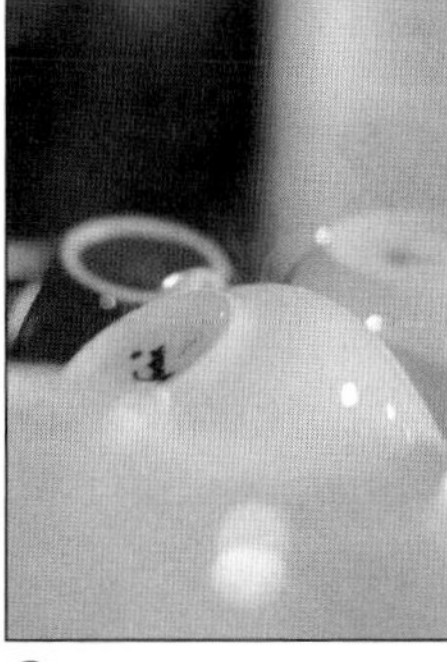

A Choose Auto Color Correction from the Enhance menu to automatically remove color cast from your image.

Your Friend, Roy G. Biv (RGB)

RGB stands for red, green, and blue, which are the three color channels your eyes perceive, the three color phosphors used in your computer monitor to display color, and the three channels digital cameras record **B**. The combination of these channels creates the full-color image you see. Many correction tools allow you to adjust these colors independently.

Red *Green* *Blue*

B Grayscale versions of each channel's hues.

Adjusting Color

Color cast refers to a general shift of color to one extreme or another: An image can be said to have a yellow or red cast, for instance. Although sometimes introduced into images intentionally (to create a certain mood or effect), color casts are usually unhappy accidents. They can result from any number of circumstances, from a scanner in need of calibrating to light from a fluorescent bulb.

Elements gives you several ways to deal with color cast or adjust colors that are a little out of whack.

To adjust color with the Auto Color Correction command:

From the Enhance menu, choose Auto Color Correction, or press Ctrl+Shift+B/ Command-Shift-B.

That's it. Photoshop Elements performs some elegant, behind-the-scenes magic, examining the image's color channels and histogram and performing a little math, and voilà—no more color cast **A**.

To remove a color cast:

1. If you're specifically adjusting for an image's color cast, another option to try is to choose Enhance > Adjust Color > Remove Color Cast.
2. Using the eyedropper provided, click an area of the image that should be white, gray, or black.
3. Click OK to accept the adjustment.

TIP I'm constantly amazed at how well Auto Color Correction works, and usually give it a try even if I don't perceive a color cast. It almost always offers some degree of improvement to the color.

To adjust hue and saturation:

1. Do one of the following:
   - In the Layers panel, click the Create Adjustment Layer button and choose Hue/Saturation.
   - Choose Enhance > Adjust Color > Adjust Hue/Saturation, or press Ctrl+U/Command-U to open the Hue/Saturation dialog.
2. Adjust the Saturation slider to increase or decrease the saturation **C**.
3. If the hue is slightly off, or if you want to pull the colors in one direction (suppose you want more blues, for example), adjust the Hue slider.
4. Use the Lightness slider to increase or decrease the brightness of the effect.
5. To adjust the hue, saturation, or lightness of a particular range of colors, choose from the drop-down menu at the top of the panel **D**. ("Master" refers to the entire image.)

To adjust color using color curves:

1. Choose Enhance > Adjust Color > Adjust Color Curves to open the Adjust Color Curves dialog.
2. To go with one of Elements' suggestions, click one of the styles at left **E**. You can also drag the sliders under Adjust Sliders to manually tweak highlights, midtone brightness and contrast, or shadows. The points on the color curve to the right represent each setting.
3. Click OK to apply the color changes.

Before

After

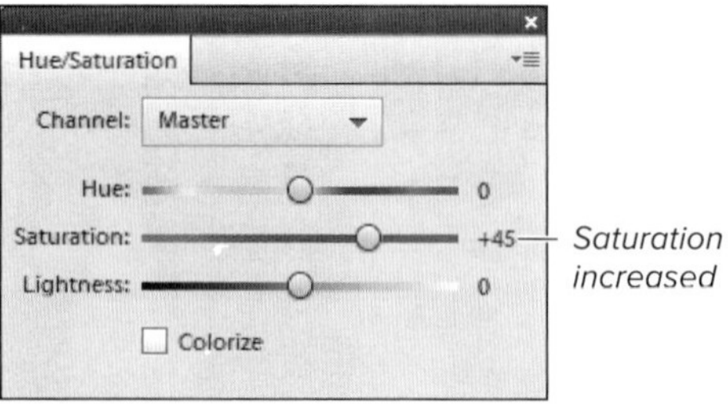

C Increasing the saturation can punch up the colors in a photo.

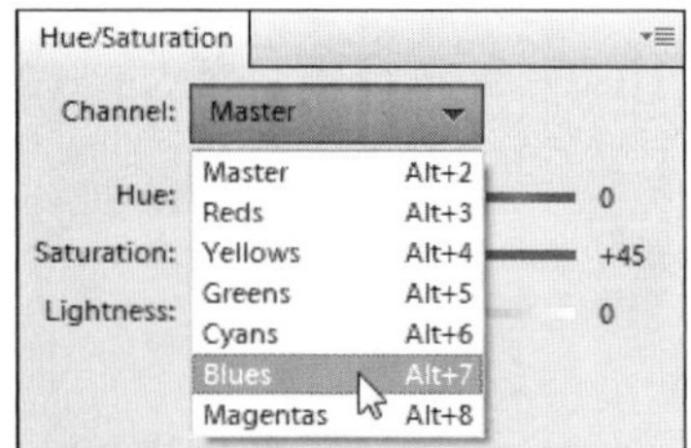

D Adjust particular color ranges instead of the entire spectrum.

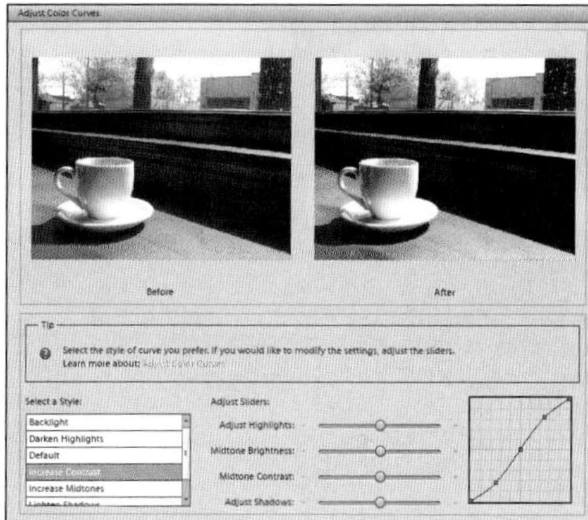

E The Adjust Color Curves feature provides one more way of fine-tuning an image's color.

F The eyedropper samples skin tones in a photo and then makes a best-guess color correction.

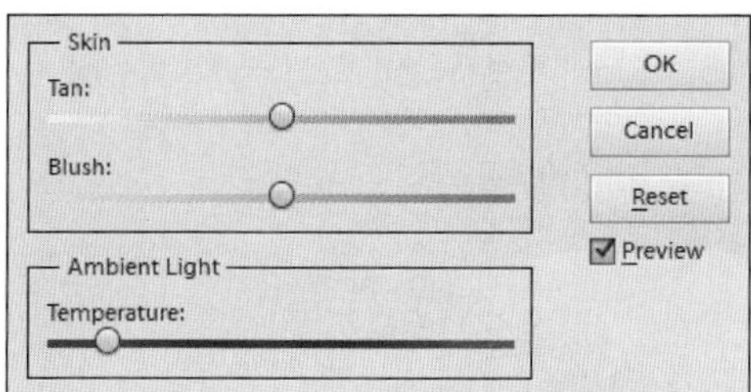

G Use dialog sliders to make manual skin tone corrections.

To adjust color in an image based on skin tones:

1. Choose Enhance > Adjust Color > Adjust Color for Skin Tone.
2. Check that the Preview checkbox is selected, and then move the cursor onto the photo until it becomes an eyedropper. Click with the eyedropper on any part of a person's skin **F**.

   Photoshop Elements adjusts the color in the entire image, but pays special attention to the skin tones.
3. If you're not satisfied with the results, click a different area of skin, or use the sliders to fine-tune the color change **G**.
4. Click OK to close the dialog and set the color changes.

Converting to Black and White

Taking a color photograph and making it black and white (well, technically *grayscale*) can involve more than just draining the color. The RGB values can be adjusted to highlight different tones in the final image and the contrast can be changed—edits you could perform separately later. But the Convert to Black and White dialog rolls them into one place and throws in some handy presets, too.

To convert an image to black and white:

1. Open the image you want to convert.
2. Choose Enhance > Convert to Black and White (or press Ctrl+Alt+B/ Command-Option-B) to open the similarly named dialog **A**.
3. Optionally, choose a preset from the Select a style list that matches the type of image you're editing **B**.
4. If you want to change the black and white photo's appearance, use the Adjust Intensity sliders **C**.
5. When you're satisfied with the result in the preview, click OK. The photo is converted to black and white **D**.

TIP Duplicate the layer the image is on in the Layers panel before you open the Convert to Black and White dialog, and then apply the command to that layer. The feature applies only to the active layer, not the entire image as if you had switched to Grayscale mode.

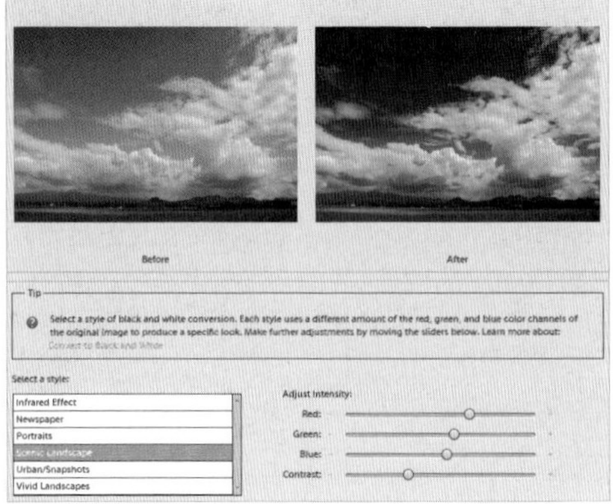

A The Convert to Black and White dialog includes many adjustments you likely would have made anyway.

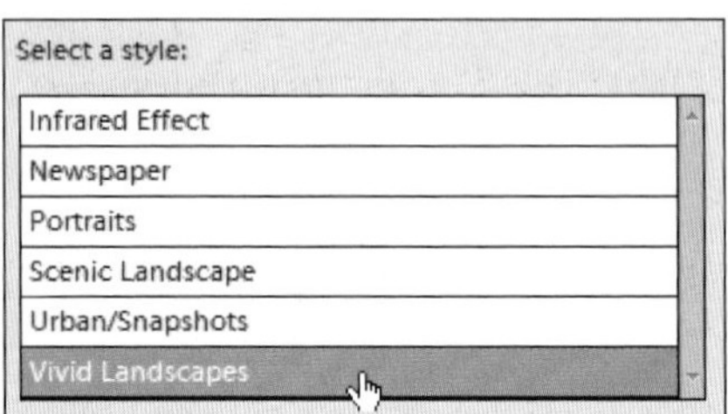

B Elements includes several preset styles that can get you started.

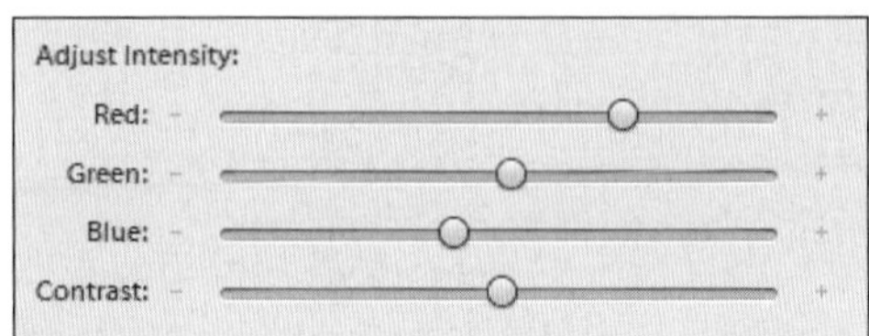

C Experiment with the Adjust Intensity sliders to get the look you want.

D You may not be Ansel, but you're getting there.

Ⓐ Select the area you want to convert to grayscale.

Ⓑ The color in the selection is removed.

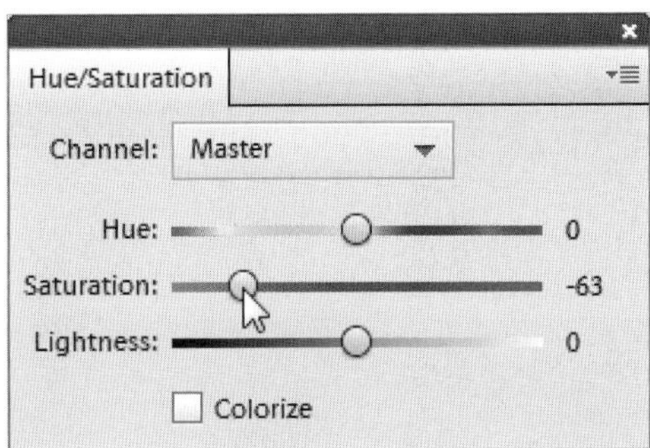

Ⓒ Use the Saturation slider in the Adjustments panel to control the amount of color you remove from an image.

Removing Color

Unlike converting to black and white (which removes all color information from an image), you can use the Remove Color command to remove color from just a portion of an image. This feature can be used to great effect for highlighting or dimming specific areas, creating neutral fields in which to place type, or as a first step before applying a colorization or color tint effect.

To apply the Remove Color command:

1. Using any of the selection or marquee tools, select the area of your image from which you want to remove the color Ⓐ.
2. Choose Enhance > Adjust Color > Remove Color, or press Ctrl+Shift+U/Command-Shift-U.

   All color is removed from the selected areas of the image and replaced by levels of gray Ⓑ.

TIP You can also control how much color to remove from an image or selection by decreasing saturation. In the Layers panel, create a new Hue/Saturation adjustment layer. Then, move the Saturation slider to the left until you achieve the desired effect Ⓒ. The value 0 on the saturation scale represents normal color saturation, whereas –100 (all the way to the left) represents completely desaturated color, or grayscale.

Replacing Color

The Replace Color command does just what you would expect it to do, and does it very well indeed. In a nutshell, it allows you to select a specific color, either across an entire image or in an isolated area of an image, and then change not only the color but its saturation and lightness values as well. Eyedropper tools let you add and subtract colors to be replaced, whereas a slider control softens the transition between the colors you choose and those around them. I've seen this used to great effect on projects as varied as experimenting with different color schemes before painting a house's trim to changing the color of a favorite uncle's tie so that it no longer clashes with his suit.

To replace color across an entire image:

1. Choose Enhance > Adjust Color > Replace Color.
2. In the Replace Color dialog, click the Selection radio button under the image preview box **A**.

   When the Replace Color dialog is open, your pointer will automatically change to an eyedropper tool when you move it over your image.
3. With the eyedropper tool, click in the image to select the color you want to change **B**.

   The color selection appears as a white area in the image preview of the Replace Color dialog **C**.
4. To expand the selection and include similar colors, drag the Fuzziness slider to the right. To contract the selection and exclude similar colors, drag the Fuzziness slider to the left.

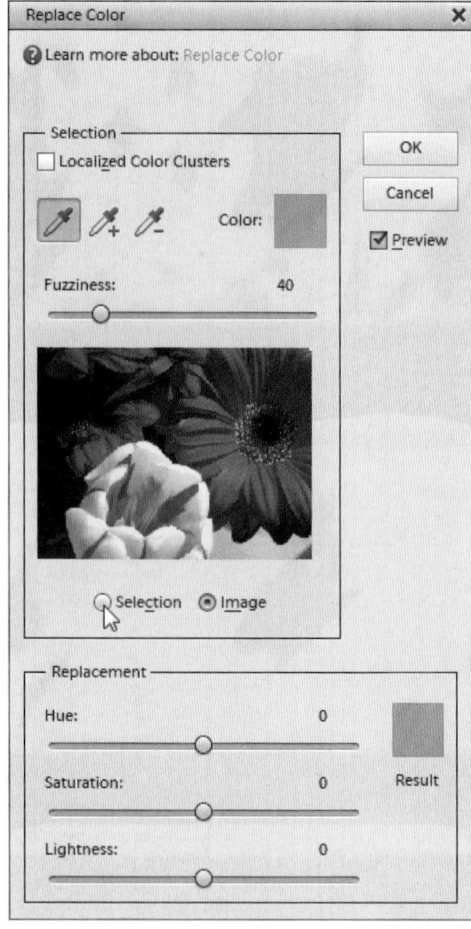

A Options under the image preview box let you choose whether to view your color selections or just the image.

B Click the actual image in the image window to make a color selection.

C The image preview area of the Replace Color dialog shows selected colors as white or shades of gray.

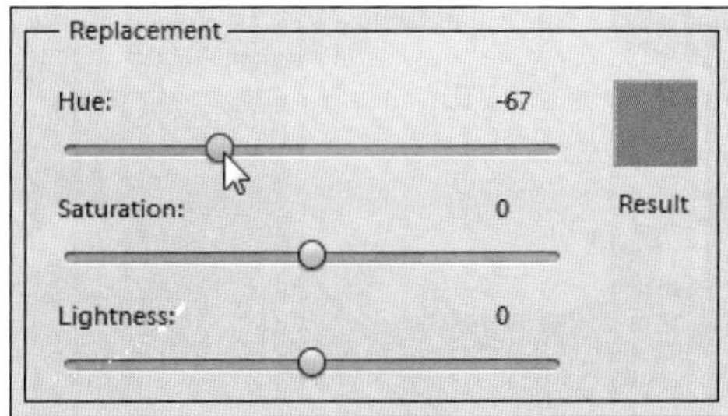

D Drag the Hue, Saturation, and Lightness sliders until you capture the right color effect. You may have to experiment a little until you get it just right.

You may want to expand or contract your selection beyond the limits of the Fuzziness slider. If parts of a selection fall too heavily in shadow or highlight, or have very reflective surfaces, you may need to make additional color selections or deletions.

5. To add a color to the selection, Shift-click the eyedropper tool in another area of the image. To subtract a color from the selection, press Alt and click.

   The dialog contains separate add and subtract eyedropper tools, but the keyboard shortcuts provide a much more efficient way to modify your color selections.

6. With the Preview checkbox selected, drag the Hue, Saturation, and Lightness sliders **D** until you achieve the desired color effect.

   These sliders operate just like those in the Hue/Saturation dialog. The Hue slider controls the actual color change; the Saturation slider controls the intensity of the color, from muted to pure; and the Lightness slider controls the color's brightness value, adding either black or white.

7. Click OK to close the Replace Color dialog and view your corrected image.

Adding a Color Tint to an Image

Using a technique called colorization, you can add a single color tint to your images, simulating the look of a hand-applied color wash or the warm, antique glow of an old sepia-toned photograph.

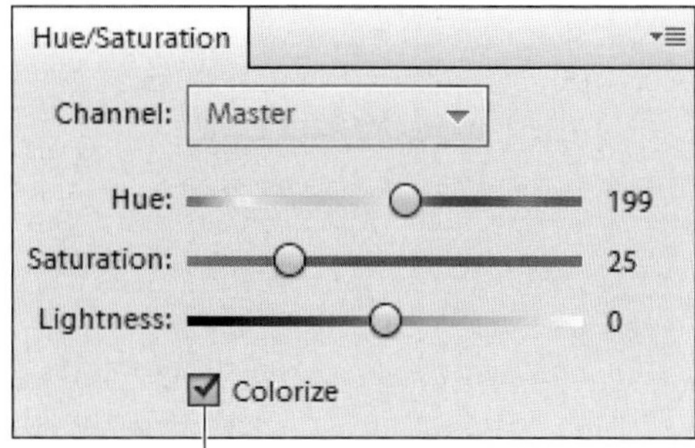

A The position of the Hue slider determines the color your tinted image will be.

B When selectively colorizing your image, you'll get more flexibility by using an adjustment layer.

To colorize an area of an image:

1. Using any of the selection or marquee tools, select the area of your image you want to colorize. If you want to colorize an entire image, it's not necessary to make a selection.
2. Do one of the following:
   - In the Layers panel, click the Create Adjustment Layer button and choose Hue/Saturation.
   - From the Enhance menu, choose Adjust Color > Adjust Hue/Saturation, or press Ctrl+U/Command-U to open the Hue/Saturation dialog.
3. Click the Colorize checkbox **A** to convert all the color in the image to a single hue.
4. Drag the Hue slider right or left until you arrive at the color you like.
5. Drag the Saturation slider to adjust its values.
6. Drag the Lightness slider to adjust the color's brightness values.
7. If you opened the Hue/Saturation dialog, click OK to close it.

TIP When you're applying a color tint to just a portion of your image, creating a new Hue/Saturation adjustment layer in the Layers panel is definitely the way to go B.

Color Management Is an Imperfect Science

As you start selecting and adjusting colors in Photoshop Elements, it's important to understand that the term *color management* can be a little misleading.

Color management operates under the assumption that we're creating artwork at our calibrated monitors under specific, controlled lighting conditions, and that our desktop printers work at peak performance at all times. In other words, it assumes controlled, uncompromised perfection.

At the time of this writing, the late afternoon sun is casting some lovely warm reflections off the blinds of the window and onto the wall directly behind my computer monitor, and is competing for attention with the glow from the 40-watt, soft-white bulb in my desk lamp. Therein lies the problem: The vast majority of Photoshop Elements users are working in similarly imperfect conditions.

In addition to trying to make a perfect science out of a host of imperfect variables, color management all but ignores one of the most imperfect sciences of all: our very human, very subjective perception. I may print out an image I find perfectly acceptable, whereas you may look at the same image and decide to push the color one way or another to try to create a different mood or atmosphere. That's what makes everything I create so different. That's what makes it art. And that's (at least in part) what makes color management an imperfect science. So, keep in mind that your images will never look precisely the same when viewed by different users on different monitors. And that's perfectly all right.

Managing Color Settings in Elements

No matter how your images got into the computer, whether from a digital camera, a scanner, or downloaded from the Internet, the version of the image stored on your hard disk can only approximate the colors of the original scene. A computer is only capable of dealing with numbers, so it somehow has to come up with numerical equivalents of the colors perceived by our eyes.

Computers use number systems, called color models, to display and reproduce color. Almost everything you do in Elements is in RGB (red, green, and blue; see the sidebar "Your Friend, Roy G. Biv (RGB)" earlier in the chapter), but it's also possible to convert images to grayscale, bitmap (black and white only), and indexed color (used for some Web images). One color mode not supported is CMYK (cyan, magenta, yellow, and black), which is used in professional publishing. If you need to output images in CMYK, you must get the full version of Photoshop CS.

This information is important because cameras, displays, and printers often don't process color information in the same way. However, you can take a couple of steps to help ensure that the color you view on your computer monitor will be close to what Elements outputs for screens or for print.

Calibrating your display

Fortunately, color management in Elements is simple and doesn't require any labor-intensive chores on your part.

You should first make sure the colors you see on the monitor are reasonably accurate and represent what others will see on their monitors. Calibrating your monitor is a particularly good idea if you have an older monitor or have inherited it from a friend or relative (you don't know what they might have done to the monitor settings). If you have a newer monitor, it probably came with an accurate calibration from the factory.

Windows 7 and Mac OS X both include color calibration tools in the Displays preferences. Or, turn to tools such as Datacolor's Spyder (spyder.datacolor.com).

Choose color settings in Elements

If you prefer, you can also choose color settings optimized for either Web graphics or color printing.

To choose color settings:

From the Edit menu, choose Color Settings.

The Color Settings dialog appears with three color management options plus the option to choose No Color Management **A**.

- Always Optimize Colors for Computer Screens displays images based on the sRGB (standard RGB) color profile and is the default setting. It's a good all-around solution, particularly if you are creating images to be viewed primarily onscreen.
- Always Optimize for Printing displays color based on the AdobeRGB profile. Although the image you see onscreen may display with only subtle color differences (as compared to sRGB), you will generally get truer, more accurate color when you send the image to print.
- Allow Me to Choose will default to sRGB, but if the image contains no color profile, you'll have the option of choosing AdobeRGB.

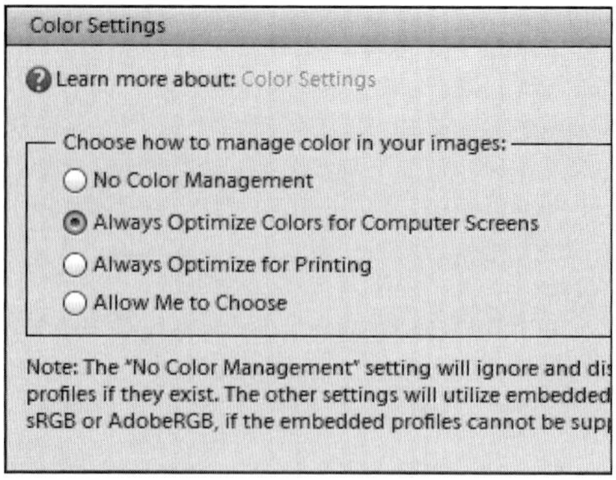

A Choose a color management option best suited to the final output of your image.

About Color Profiles

The choices you make in the Color Settings dialog affect only the display of an image onscreen and won't affect how an image is printed. The Always Optimize for Printing option, for instance, will simulate the AdobeRGB color spectrum on your monitor but will not assign the AdobeRGB color profile to an image. A color profile is information embedded in an image and stored in the background until it's required (usually by a printer). The color profile helps to interpret the RGB color information in an image and convert it to a color language that a printer can understand, and so reproduce the most accurate color possible. You can assign a color profile to an image at any time regardless of the option you've set in the Color Settings dialog. With an image open, simply choose Convert Color Mode from the Image menu. From the Convert Color Profile submenu, you can remove an unwanted profile (sRGB, for example) and apply the profile more suitable for printing: AdobeRGB.

Fixing and Retouching Photos

How often have you thumbed through photo albums and found images you wished were better composed or lit more evenly? Or maybe you've sorted through shoeboxes from the attic, disappointed that time and age have taken their toll on those wonderful old photographs of your dad in his high school band uniform and your grandparents honeymooning at the lake. Until recently, there was no simple way to correct or repair photographs regardless of whether they were out of focus, water damaged, or poorly composed.

Happily, things have changed. In this chapter, you'll learn how to perform a wide variety of photo fixes. I also discuss several clever and time-saving features such as the Photomerge Scene Cleaner (which removes unwanted objects from photos), the Smart Brush tool for painting effects on an image, and much more.

In This Chapter

Repairing Flaws and Imperfections

Little maladies, such as torn edges, water stains, scratches, even specks of dust on a scanner's glass or the camera's sensor, are the bane of the photo-retouch artist, and are problems all too common when you set to the task of digitizing and restoring old photographs. Even when you're shooting, dust on the lens or the camera sensor can cause unwanted pixels and flaws. To the rescue come three similar but distinctly different repair and retouch tools.

The Spot Healing Brush tool is the perfect tool for removing small imperfections like dust or tiny scratches. With a single click, the Spot Healing brush samples (copies) pixels from around the area of a trouble spot and creates a small patch that covers up the flaw and blends in smoothly with its surrounding area.

The Clone Stamp tool is versatile not just for cleaning up and restoring photos, but for any number of special effects and enhancements. It works on the simple principle of copying and duplicating (cloning) image pixels from one part of an image to another. Although ideal for repairing tears or holes in photographs, it can also be used to add or duplicate objects in a photograph. For example, you can create a hedgerow from one small bush or add more clouds to a nearly cloudless sky.

The Healing Brush tool operates like a combination of the Clone Stamp and Spot Healing Brush tools. As with the Clone Stamp tool, it first samples pixels from one area of your image to another. Then, like the Spot Healing Brush tool, it blends those pixels seamlessly with the area you want to repair **A**.

A With just a little patience and the Healing Brush and Clone Stamp tools, imperfections caused by a poor scan or dust on the camera lens can be easily removed or repaired.

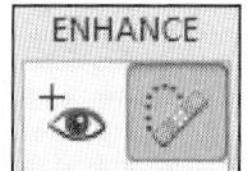

B The Spot Healing Brush tool.

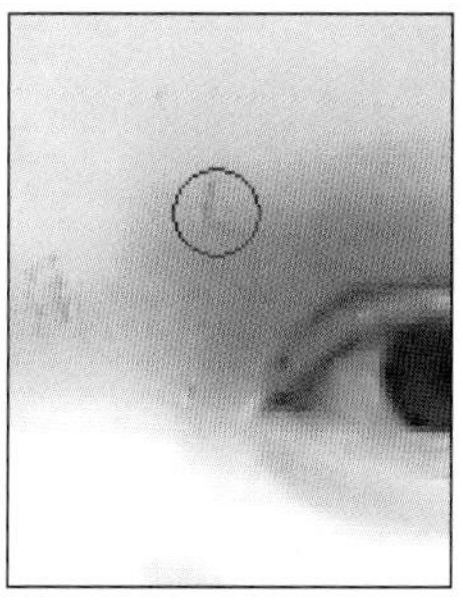

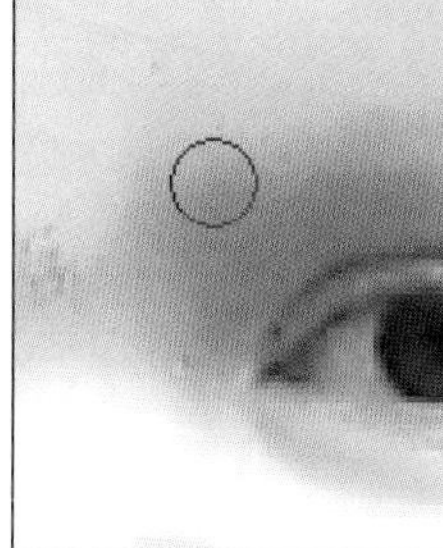

C With a single mouse click, each dust speck is removed.

TIP **Alternately, click and drag through a slightly larger area with the Spot Healing Brush tool.**

To clean up small areas with the Spot Healing Brush tool:

1. Select the Spot Healing Brush tool from the Tools pane, or press J **B**.
2. In the Tool Options bar, select a healing method from the radio buttons.
   - Proximity Match samples pixels from around the edge of your brush shape to create the patch over the area you want to repair.
   - Create Texture uses the pixels directly beneath the brush shape to create a soft, mottled texture.
   - Content-Aware uses advanced algorithms to intelligently fill the affected area (see the sidebar on the next page for more information).
3. Also in the Tool Options bar, select a brush size using the brush Size slider.

   Try to size your brush to fit snugly around the flaw you're covering.
4. Click and release the mouse button to apply the patch **C**.

Clone and Healing Overlays

Photoshop Elements has an interesting retouching tool in its arsenal: the overlay. When using the Healing Brush or the Clone Stamp tools, set the origin point and notice that a preview of what you will paint appears under the brush head. It's also possible to view a translucent overlay of the full image; the mouse pointer remains fixed on the origin point, so you can see what will be drawn when you click the mouse button **D**. With this approach, you don't have to click blindly and hope the edit you're about to make is the one you envisioned.

To make the full overlay appear, click the Clone Overlay button in the Tool Options bar and disable the Clipped checkbox. You can also set the opacity here, hide it as you paint, or disable the feature entirely.

D The overlay lets you preview what will be drawn (left) when you start drawing (right).

Making Content-Aware Repairs

The Spot Healing Brush tool utilizes one of the best features in Photoshop Elements: content-aware fill. Using technology borrowed from Photoshop CS, the Spot Healing Brush can not only sample surrounding pixels to make repairs, but can also reconstruct areas based on the image's content.

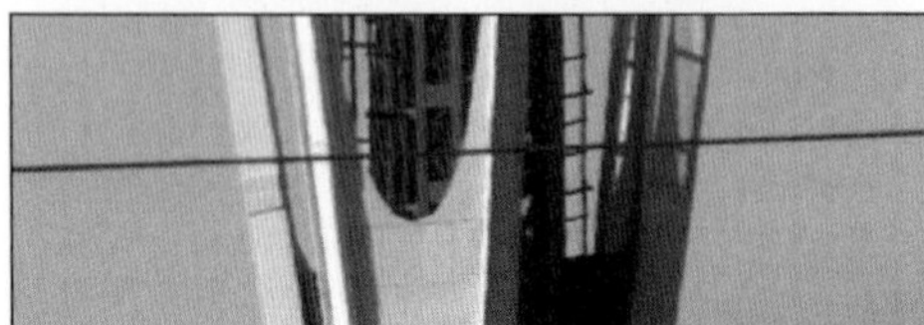

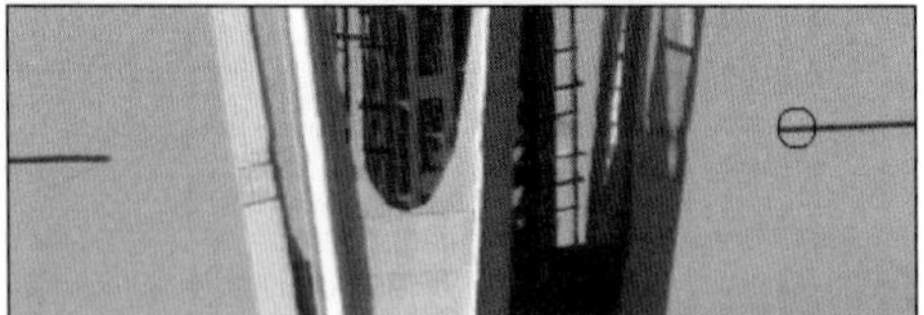

E I painted over the power line (just once) using the Spot Healing Brush set to Content-Aware.

In most cases, the practical benefit is less time spent making repairs, because Photoshop Elements is applying more "thought" to how to fix an area. You don't need to go over it several times with the Clone Brush as you would have in the past.

For example, when removing power lines from a photo, the Spot Healing Brush also intelligently fills in more complicated areas of the landmark as well as the blue sky **E**.

You can also attempt more dramatic content-aware repairs successfully (**F** and **G**). Of course, results will vary depending on the content of the image.

TIP If a repaired area doesn't look right, hit it again with the Spot Healing Brush. In G, for example, I'd want to clean up the grass clumps that appeared where the girl's shadow had been.

F Painting over the girl and her shadow...

G ...fills the space with content that wasn't there before.

H The Clone Stamp tool.

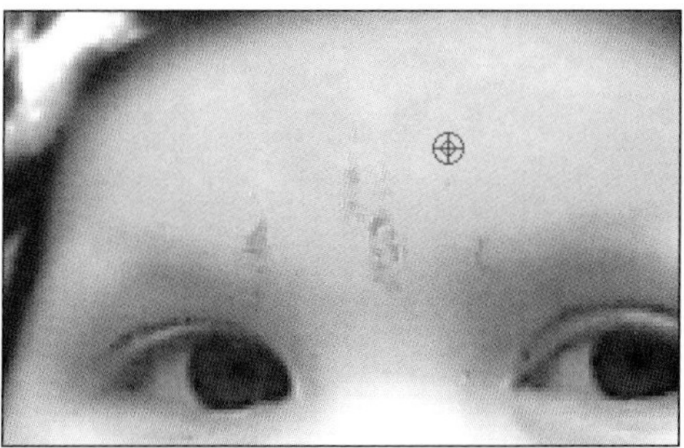

I Clearly, someone needs to clean his scanner! Once you've found an area of your image you want to clone, hold down the Alt key; your pointer turns into a bull's-eye target. Click to set that area as the origin.

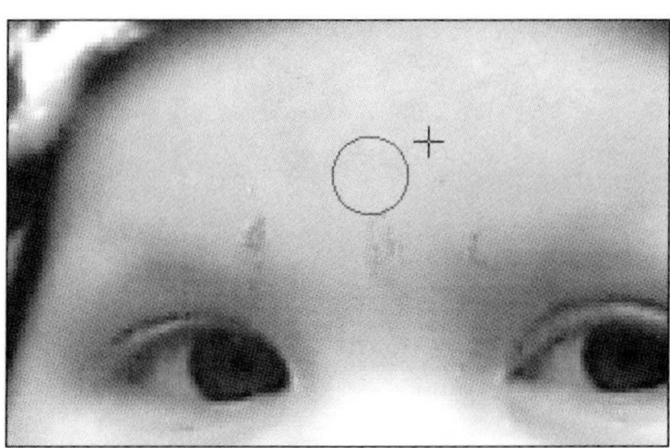

J Drag the Clone Stamp tool over the portion of the image you want to replace. As you drag, crosshairs appear, providing a constant reference point of the cloned pixels as you paint over the image.

To retouch an image with the Clone Stamp tool:

1. Select the Clone Stamp tool from the Tools pane, or press S H.
2. In the Tool Options bar, select a brush size using the brush Size slider.

   The brush size you choose will vary depending on the area you have available to clone from and the area you're trying to repair. Larger brush sizes work well for larger open areas like skies or simple, even-toned backdrops, whereas smaller brushes work well for textured surfaces or areas with a lot of detail.
3. Move the pointer over the area of your image you want to clone (the pointer becomes a circle, representing the brush size you've specified), and then hold down the Alt/Option key.

   The pointer becomes a target I.
4. Click once to select the area you want to sample; then, release the Alt/Option key and move the pointer to the area to which you want the clone applied J.
5. Hold down the mouse button, and drag to "paint" the cloned portion over the new area.

   The original image is replaced with a clone of the sampled image.

TIP Here's one of my favorite Elements tips, which oddly works only on the Mac: To quickly change your brush size (in any tool that uses a brush), hold Option-Control and drag left or right to decrease or increase the diameter, respectively.

To copy images from one picture to another with the Clone Stamp tool:

1. Select the Clone Stamp tool from the Tools pane and then select a brush size from the Tool Options bar.
2. Still In the Tool Options bar, check that the Aligned option is selected.

   With the Aligned option selected, the Clone Stamp tool will always copy pixels relative to the initial sampling point, even if you release the mouse button and press it again to continue. With the Aligned option deselected, each time you release the mouse button and press to resume cloning, you will copy pixels starting from the initial sampling point **K**.
3. Holding down the Alt/Option key, click in the first picture to select the area you want to sample.
4. Click the second picture's image window to make it active, and then drag to paint a clone of the sampled image.
5. The original image in the second picture is replaced with a clone of the sampled image from the first **L**.

TIP Before experimenting with the Clone tool, it's good practice to first create a new, blank image layer. Creating a separate layer not only protects your original image by leaving it unchanged, but it gives you more creative flexibility. You can apply different cloned areas to different layers and then compare the effect of each by turning the layer visibility settings off and on. And if you apply different cloned areas on separate layers, you can experiment further by applying different blending mode and opacity settings to each clone. See Chapter 7.

K Using the image on the left as a source, the image in the middle was cloned with the Aligned option selected. Although the mouse button was released and depressed several times, the image was still copied *relative* to the initial sampling point. The image on the right was cloned with the Aligned option deselected. Notice that each time the mouse button was released and depressed, the clone again *started* from the initial reference point.

L The Clone tool provides a controlled method for combining parts of one image with another.

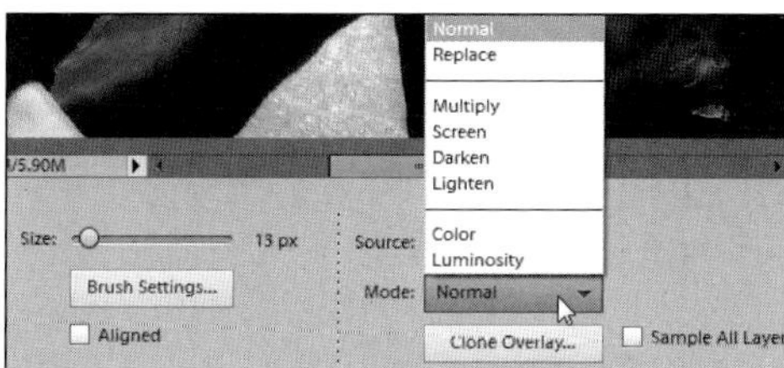

Ⓜ Although several healing modes are available, most often the Healing Brush tool works best in Normal mode.

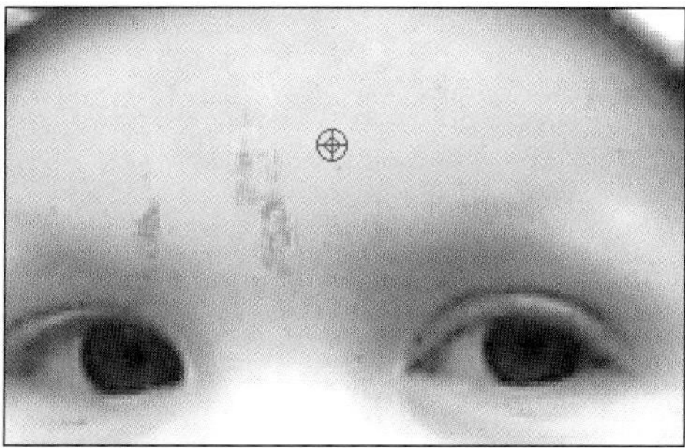

Ⓝ Once you've found an area of your image to use as a patch, hold down the Alt key and click to select it. Your pointer turns into a bull's-eye target.

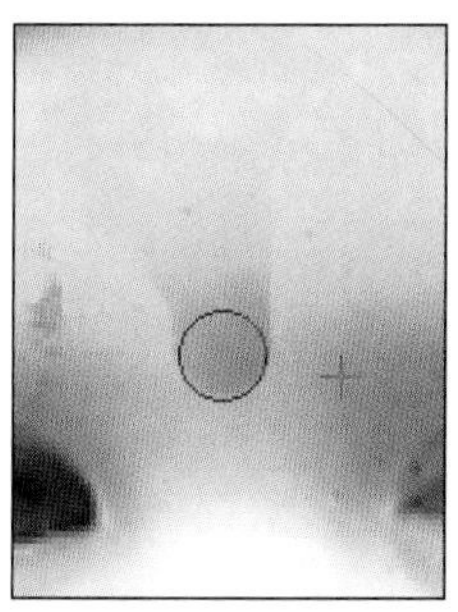

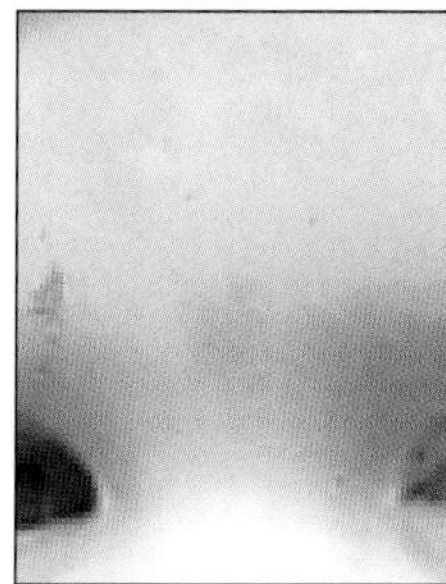

Ⓞ As you draw, the Healing Brush picks up the pixels relative to the origin point, just like the Clone Stamp tool (left). After you release the mouse button, Elements blends the values in the area (right).

To remove flaws with the Healing Brush tool:

1. In the Tools pane, select the Spot Healing Brush tool. Then, click the Healing Brush tool in the Tool Options bar.
2. From the Mode drop-down menu in the Tool Options bar, check that Normal is selected Ⓜ.

   Normal mode blends sampled pixels with the area you're repairing to create a smooth transition with the area surrounding the repair. Replace mode does little more than duplicate the behavior of the Clone Stamp tool. For information on the other effect modes available from the drop-down menu, see "About Opacity and Blending Modes" in Chapter 7.
3. In the Tool Options bar, select a brush size using the brush Size slider.

   The brush size you choose will vary depending on the area you have available to sample from and the area that you're trying to repair.
4. Move the pointer over the area of your image you want to sample and hold down the Alt/Option key. The pointer becomes a target Ⓝ.
5. Click once to select the area you want to sample; then release the Alt/Option key and move the pointer to the area you want to repair.
6. Hold down the mouse button and drag to "paint" the sampled image over the new area Ⓞ.

   The sampled image blends with the repair area to cover any flaws and imperfections.

Sharpening Image Detail

Generally speaking, you want most of your photos to be in focus—which can be surprisingly difficult to achieve, depending on surrounding movement, zoom level, or even just plain shaky fingers (maybe cut back on the caffeine). Even then, photos may not quite "pop" the way you'd like them to. In addition, any time you resize an image by resampling, pixels may be lost in the process, and so you also lose some degree of image detail.

Elements offers an Auto Sharpen command, but you may want more control. Look to the Adjust Sharpness command, which finds pixels with different tonal values and slightly increases the contrast between those adjoining pixels, creating a sharper edge. The resulting correction can help to enhance detail and bring blurred or fuzzy areas throughout an image into clearer focus.

To sharpen an image:

1. From the Enhance menu, choose Adjust Sharpness to open the Adjust Sharpness dialog **A**.
2. Make sure the Preview box is checked; then drag the following sliders to adjust the image's sharpness:
   - The Amount slider sets the percentage of contrast applied to the pixels and so determines the degree of sharpness you apply. For high-resolution images (those above around 150 pixels per inch), set the Amount slider to between 150 and 200 percent. For low-resolution images, use settings somewhere around 30 to 80 percent **B**.

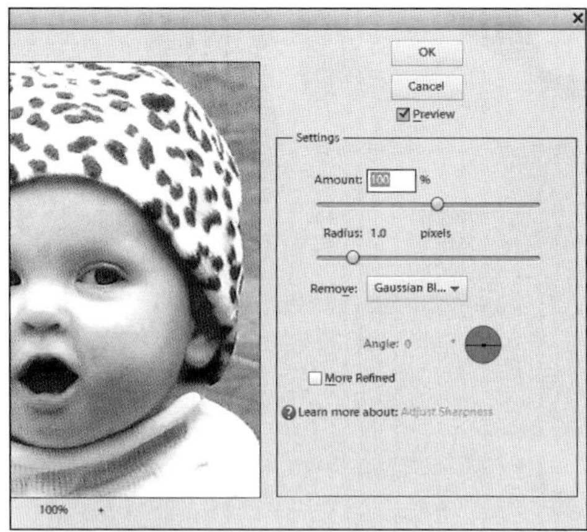

A The Adjust Sharpness dialog's sliders adjust the degree of sharpening you apply.

Original *Amount: 80%*

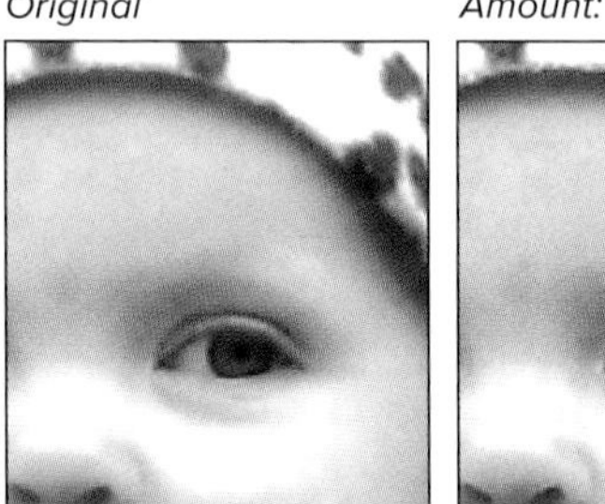

Original *Amount: 150%*

B The Amount slider controls the percentage of sharpness applied to your image. The difference here is most pronounced around the eyelid and in the pattern on the hat. Also, the sharpening appears too aggressive in the 150 percent version when zoomed-in so close, but at normal size may look just fine. Feel free to experiment quite a bit to achieve your desired image.

C The Radius slider controls the number of pixels included in any sharpened edge. Smaller numbers include fewer pixels, and larger numbers include more pixels (exaggerated here for effect).

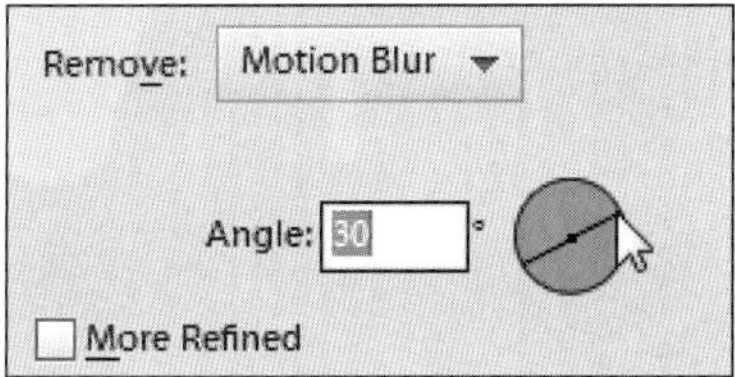

D If the blur is caused by movement of the camera or subject, Motion Blur can compensate.

Adjust Sharpness vs. Unsharp Mask

If you've used Photoshop or another image editor in the past, you may be familiar with the Unsharp Mask command (under the Enhance menu). It provides the same controls as the Remove: Gaussian Blur option of the Adjust Sharpness dialog, and I suspect Adobe kept it in Elements for people who've been using that feature for years. The Adjust Sharpness feature, however, adds compensation for motion blur, which I find to be more common. Depending on the severity of the blur, Adjust Sharpness can salvage a shot that otherwise would have to be rejected.

- The Radius slider determines the number of pixels surrounding the contrasting edge pixels that will also be sharpened. Although the radius can be set all the way to 64, you should never have to enter a value much higher than 2, unless you're trying to achieve a strong, high-contrast special effect **C**.
- The More Refined checkbox offers higher quality, but requires more processing time and power. If you're experimenting with the settings, keep this option disabled until you reach the level of sharpening you want.
- The Remove drop-down menu offers three types of correction: Gaussian Blur applies the effect to the entire image; Lens Blur detects edges in its sharpening; and Motion Blur works to reverse the blur caused by camera movement. If Motion Blur is enabled, adjust the Angle setting to match the angle of the movement **D**.
- Use the preview area to see a detailed view of your image as you apply the changes. You can move to a different area of an image by holding down the mouse button and dragging with the hand pointer in the preview screen. You can also zoom in or out of an area using the minus and plus buttons below the preview.

3. When you're satisfied with the results, click OK to close the dialog and apply the changes.

Enhancing Image Detail

The Adjust Sharpness command works best on entire images or large portions of images. A couple of other tools are better suited for making sharpening and focus adjustments in smaller, more specific areas of an image. Not surprisingly, the Blur tool softens the focus in an image by reducing the detail, and the Sharpen tool helps bring areas into focus. For instance, you can create a sense of depth by blurring selected background areas while keeping foreground subjects in focus, or enhance the focus of a specific foreground subject so that it better stands out from others.

To blur a specific area or object:

1. Select the Blur tool from the Tools pane, or press R **A**.
2. In the Tool Options bar, select a brush size using the brush Size slider.

   If you want, you can also select a blend mode and enter a Strength percentage. The higher the percentage, the more the affected area is blurred.
3. Move the brush pointer to the area of your image you want to blur; then hold down the mouse button and drag through the area **B**.

   As you drag, the area is blurred.

TIP Working on a portrait? Another tool to consider is the Surface Blur filter (Filter > Blur > Surface Blur), which smooths surface areas like skin without blurring edges. It's an easy way to minimize wrinkles and other sharp details in faces.

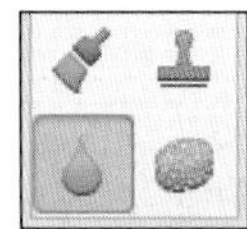

A The Blur tool.

Original *After Blur tool applied*

B Drag the brush through the area you want to blur. You can resize the brush as you work on larger and smaller areas.

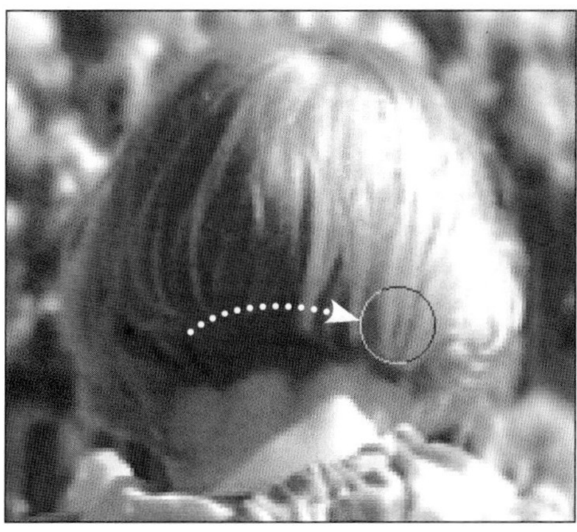

Original *After Sharpen applied*

C I can pull more detail out of the girl's hair and coat by dragging the Sharpen tool over that area.

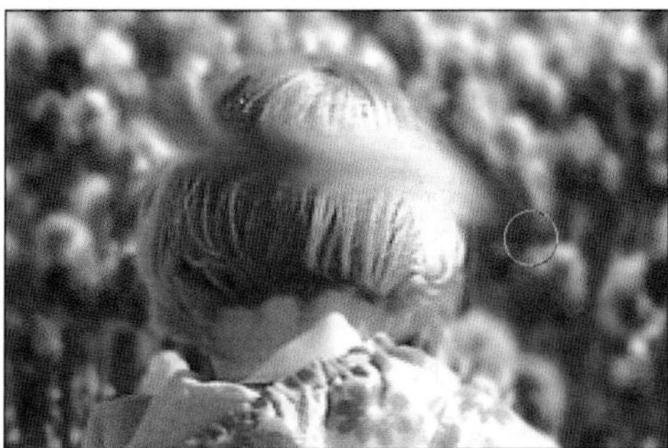

D The Smudge tool can easily do more harm than good, so use it sparingly.

To sharpen a specific area or object:

1. Select the Blur tool from the Tools pane and then click the Sharpen tool in the Tool Options bar. Or, press R to toggle through the enhance tools to the Sharpen tool.
2. In the Tool Options bar, select a brush size. If you prefer, choose a blend mode and enter a Strength percentage. The higher the percentage, the more the affected area is sharpened.
3. Move the brush pointer to the area of your image you want to sharpen; then hold down the mouse button and drag through the area **C**.

   As you drag, the area is sharpened.

To use the Smudge tool:

1. Select the Smudge tool in the Tool Options bar, or press R to toggle through the enhance tools to the Smudge tool.
2. In the Tool Options bar, select a brush size using the brush Size slider.

   Just as with the Blur and Sharpen tools, you can select a blend mode and enter a Strength percentage. The higher the percentage, the more the affected area is smudged.
3. Move the brush pointer to the area of your image you want to smudge; then hold down the mouse button and drag through the area **D**. As you drag, the area is softened and blended.

TIP Use the Blur and Sharpen tools together when you want to draw attention to a particular person or object. First, use the Blur tool to soften the focus and detail of the subjects you want to appear to recede into the background. Then use the Sharpen tool to bring the subject of primary interest into sharp focus.

Using the Tonal Adjustment Tools

In traditional photography, technicians control darkness and lightness values on specific parts of an image by masking one area of film while exposing another. In the process, selected areas are either burned in (darkened) or dodged (lightened). The Burn and Dodge tools replicate this effect without the bother of creating masks. Drag an adjustable tool's brush pointer through the area you want to affect. If one portion of an image is dramatically overexposed or washed out, and another portion is underexposed, the Dodge and Burn tools can be used to target and correct just those specific problem areas.

The Sponge tool increases or decreases the intensity of the color. Use the Sponge tool to bring colors back to life in badly faded, older photographs; or, work in the opposite direction, pulling the color out of a newer photo to create an antique effect.

To lighten a portion of an image with the Dodge tool:

1. Select the Sponge tool from the Tools pane and then select the Dodge tool in the Tool Options bar **A**. Or, press O to toggle to the Dodge tool.
2. In the Tool Options bar, select a brush size using the brush Size slider. Choose a size appropriate to your image (between 20 and 40 pixels is a good start).

   Using the Range and Exposure settings, you can also select a specific tonal range to lighten (shadows, midtones, or highlights) and control the amount of lightness applied **B**.

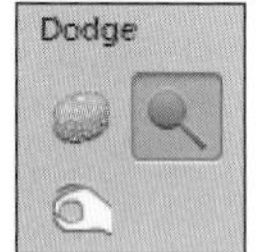

A The Dodge tool in the Tool Options bar.

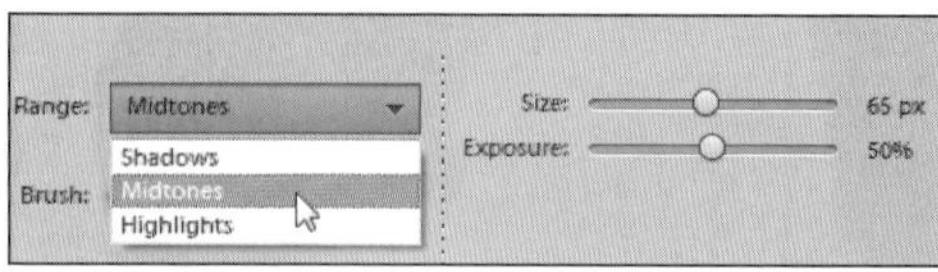

B Select the part of the tonal range you most want to affect with Photoshop Elements' tonal adjustment tools. With both the Dodge and Burn tools, you can choose to limit your changes to just the shadow, midtone, or highlight areas.

C Drag the Dodge or Burn brush through any area to lighten or darken the pixels while preserving image detail. Here, I've used the Dodge tool to lighten the child and chair, keeping the tones in the window (which would get blown out if I were to lighten the entire image).

D The Burn tool in the Tool Options bar.

E In this image, the leopard is washed out and blends into the background (top). The Burn tool added some much needed form and dimension by darkening the pixels in the shadow and midtone areas (bottom).

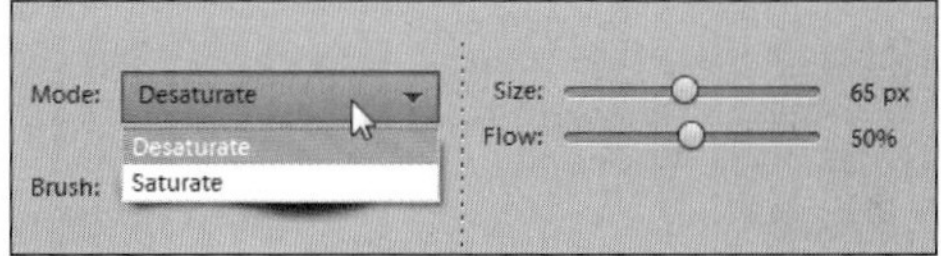

F In the Tool Options bar, choose whether you want the Sponge tool to add color or subtract it.

3. Move the brush pointer to the area of your image you want to lighten; then hold down the mouse button and drag through the area C.

To darken a portion of an image with the Burn tool:

1. Select the Burn tool in the Tools pane, or press O to toggle through the tonal adjustment tools to the Burn tool D.
2. In the Tool Options bar, select a brush size using the brush Size slider.

   If you like, select a specific tonal range to darken (shadows, midtones, or highlights) and control the amount of darkness applied with the Exposure setting.
3. Move the brush pointer to the area of your image you want to darken; then hold down the mouse button and drag through the area E.

To adjust the color saturation with the Sponge tool:

1. Select the Sponge tool in the Tools pane, or press O to toggle through the tonal adjustment tools to the Sponge tool.
2. In the Tool Options bar, select a brush size using the brush Size slider.
3. From the Mode drop-down menu, select whether you want to saturate (add) or desaturate (subtract) color F.

   You can also adjust the amount of color to be added or subtracted using the Flow percentage slider.
4. Move the brush pointer to the area of your image where you want to change the color's intensity; then hold down the mouse button and drag through the area.

Erasing Backgrounds and Other Large Areas

The Background Eraser tool is an intelligent (and really quite amazing) feature. Not only does it remove the background from around very complex shapes, but it does so in a way that leaves a natural, softened, anti-aliased edge around the foreground object left behind. Additionally, because the Background Eraser tool always erases to transparency, if you use it to remove the background from even a flattened layer, it automatically converts that layer to a floating, transparent one. This allows you to easily place a new background behind a foreground image, or to move it into a different photo composition altogether.

A The Background Eraser tool in the Tool Options bar.

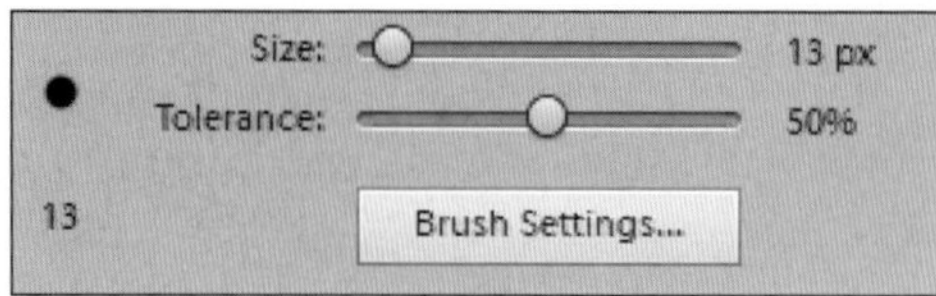

B Use the Tolerance slider to increase or decrease the number of pixels sampled based on their similarity to one another.

To use the Background Eraser tool:

1. Select the Eraser tool in the Tools pane and then select the Background Eraser tool in the Tool Options bar **A**.

   Alternatively, you can press E to select the Eraser tool and then press E again to toggle to the Background Eraser tool.

2. In the Tool Options bar, select a size using the brush Size slider.
3. Select one of the limit modes:
   - Contiguous mode erases any pixels within the brush area that are the same as those currently beneath the crosshairs, as long as they're touching one another.
   - Discontiguous mode erases all pixels within the brush area that are the same as those beneath the crosshairs, even if they're not touching one another.
4. Select a Tolerance value using the Tolerance slider **B**. The value controls

C Begin by placing the crosshairs of the brush in the background portion of the image (top), then drag the brush along the outside edge of the foreground object to erase the background (bottom). Continue around the edge of the foreground object until it's completely separated from the background.

which pixels are erased according to how similar they are to the pixels beneath the eraser crosshairs. Higher Tolerance values increase the range of colors that are erased, and lower values limit the range of colors erased.

5. In the image window, position the eraser pointer on the edge where the background and foreground images meet, and then drag along the edge.

   The background portion of the image is erased, leaving behind the foreground image on a transparent background **C**. The brush erases only pixels similar to those directly below the crosshairs, so the entire background can be completely erased while leaving the foreground image intact.

TIP It's okay if the circle (indicating the brush size) overlaps onto the foreground image, but be sure to keep the crosshairs over just the background area. The Background Eraser tool, of course, doesn't really know the difference between background and foreground images, and is simply erasing based on the colors selected, or sampled, beneath the crosshairs. If the crosshairs stray into the foreground image, that part of the image will be erased, too.

TIP There's a third eraser tool—the Magic Eraser tool—that I've chosen not to cover here because, frankly, it doesn't work very well. It operates on the same principle as the Magic Wand tool by deleting like pixels based on color or tonal value. That's all well and good, but you're not given any feedback or opportunity to modify your selection. You just click, and poof—a large area of color is gone. Since the erasure typically is either not quite enough or a little too much, you undo, reset the tolerance, try again, undo—well, you get the idea.

Removing a Foreground Image from Its Background

The Magic Extractor works much the same way as the Background Eraser tool, but distinguishes itself with speed and added control. Using brushes, mark and identify first the foreground image you want to save, and then the background image you want to delete. A set of additional tools helps you to fine-tune your foreground and background selections.

Ⓐ Open the Magic Extractor dialog.

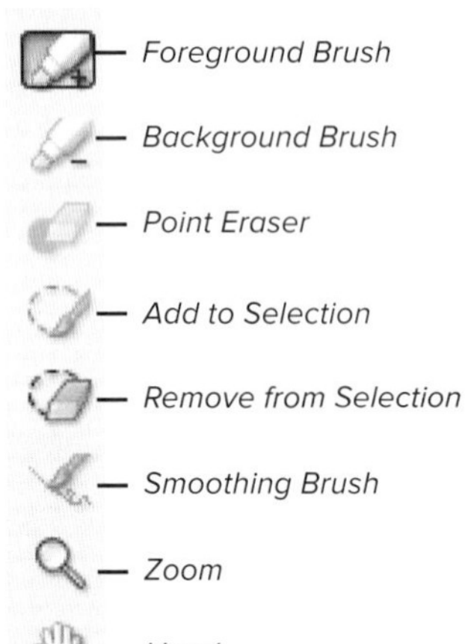

Ⓑ The Magic Extractor tool set.

To use the Magic Extractor tool:

1. From the Image menu, choose Magic Extractor to open the Magic Extractor dialog Ⓐ.
2. From the tool area on the left side of the dialog, select the Foreground Brush tool Ⓑ.
3. Use the brush Size slider, if necessary, to adjust the size of your brush, and then use the brush to mark the foreground area of the image—the area of the image you want to preserve.

   You can mark the foreground with a series of either dots or scribbles, or a combination of the two. The idea is to use the brush to get a good cross-sampling of all the different pixel colors and tones in the foreground Ⓒ.
4. Select the Background Brush tool, and in the same manner, mark the area of the image you want to remove.
5. Click the Preview button to see the results of your work Ⓓ.

   Use the Zoom and Hand tools to get a closer look at the transitions

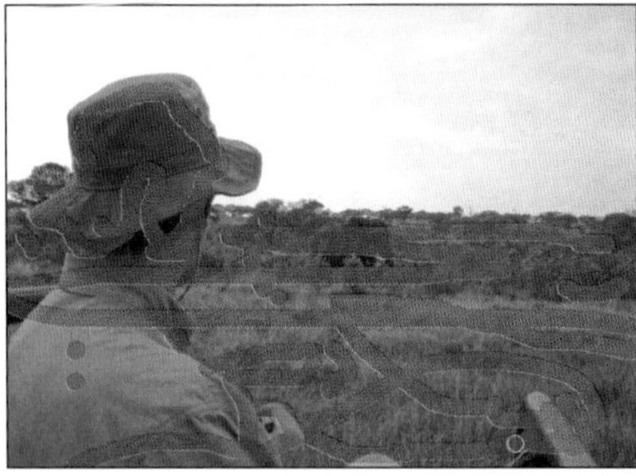

Ⓒ Identify the foreground area with a series of dots and scribbles.

D Click Preview to see the changes you've made to your image in the preview window.

E The Magic Extractor identified the foreground and background areas of the image, and then deleted the background.

between the foreground image and the background.

6. If necessary, use one of the touch-up tools to modify or clean up the transitions between the foreground image and background:
   - The Point Eraser tool removes portions of marks you've made. When you remove a portion of a mark from the background area, for instance, you're telling the Magic Extractor that you don't want to erase pixels of a particular tonal or color range.
   - The Add to Selection tool allows you to paint back in areas of the foreground image that may have been mistakenly removed along with the background.
   - The Remove from Selection tool works like an eraser to remove areas of the foreground image.
   - The Smoothing Brush softens the transition between the foreground image and transparent background by adding a halo of deleted background color to the edge of the foreground image.
7. If necessary, use the options in the Touch Up area of the dialog to further refine the foreground image.
8. Click OK to finish **E**.

TIP In the Magic Extractor dialog, you can only Undo (Ctrl+Z/Command-Z) the action of two tools: the Remove from Selection tool and the Smoothing Brush tool. But if you're not happy with the results you're getting, you can start over by clicking either the Reset or Cancel buttons. Clicking the Reset button will undo every action in the Preview window but will leave the dialog open, whereas clicking Cancel will exit the dialog altogether without applying any changes.

Removing Objects from a Scene

You've probably seen the photo on the Web or forwarded via e-mail from a friend: A couple in full wedding attire are exchanging vows on the beach, the ocean meeting the sky in the background, and...what's that? Yes, a topless sunbather is walking into the frame, ruining an otherwise romantic wedding photo. In Elements, however, that photo would be easily salvageable.

The Photomerge Scene Cleaner lets you take a collection of similar images and selectively "paint out" objects you'd prefer weren't in the photo. Select two or more images that contain an element you want to remove; scenes where people are moving are ideal, because Elements takes areas from the background and superimposes them over the person you wish to hide. (In fact, the early name for Scene Cleaner was "Tourist Remover.")

To remove objects from a scene:

1. Open two or more photos of the scene you want to clean in the Editor, and select them in the Photo Bin.
2. Choose Enhance > Photomerge > Photomerge Scene Cleaner.

   The first image appears in the Source pane on the left, with an empty Final pane on the right.
3. Choose the image that will be the basis for the finished photo and drag it to the Final pane **A**.
4. Click a photo in the Photo Bin that contains background in the area where you want to remove an object from the Final image **B**.

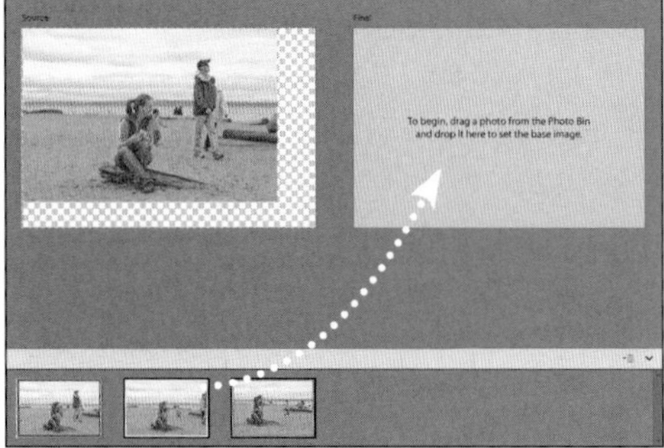

A Drag the photo you want to use as a base into the Final pane.

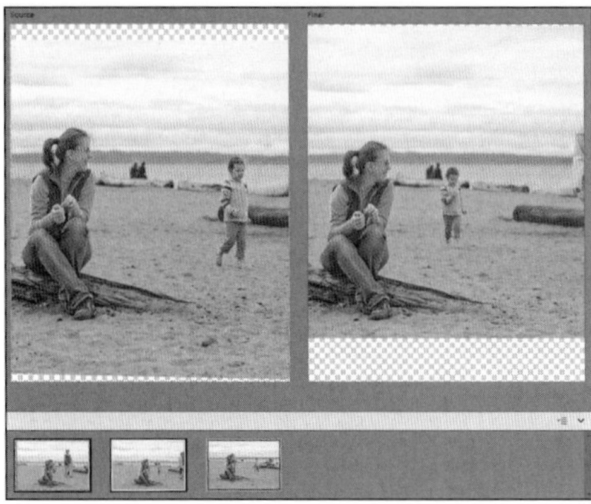

B I want to remove the little girl from the Final image, so I click a photo that has a corresponding empty area—in this case, a shot after she's taken a few steps—to load into the Source pane.

(C) Drawing over the girl in the Final image at right grabs the corresponding pixels from the Source, removing her.

(D) Two people appeared at the edge of the Final photo, so here I click a third photo (with the blue outline) and paint them out in the Source image. With regions visible, you can see which portions are being copied.

(E) I've cropped the final photo to remove artifacts left over from blending the images.

5. With the Pencil tool selected, draw over the object to be removed in the Final image (C). Elements copies that area from the selected Source image to make the object vanish.

   Repeat steps 4 and 5 to remove other objects from the scene. (Move the mouse pointer off the Final image to preview it without pencil strokes.) The ink color corresponds to the outline surrounding each source image, so you can easily tell which areas are being used. You can also click the Show Regions checkbox to view the patchwork Elements created (D).

6. To fine-tune the effect, you may need to use the Eraser tool to erase some of your pencil marks in the Final image.

7. Click Done. Elements saves the image in a new layered file.

TIP Depending on how well the source images lined up, you may need to crop the final image to remove blending irregularities (E).

TIP Elements attempts to align the source images based on their contents, but sometimes things end up a little off. If that's the case, click the Advanced Options expansion triangle to reveal the Alignment tool, which you can use to mark three points the images share. Click the Align Photos button to realign them.

TIP Click the Pixel Blending checkbox to get a higher-quality, but slower and more processor-intensive, result.

TIP A tool like Photomerge Scene Cleaner is a great reason to take multiple shots of a scene while you're shooting. With digital photography, you can fire off lots of exposures and end up with plenty of choices.

Recomposing a Scene

When you're taking photos, especially photos of groups, it's not always possible to line people up the way you'd like them to appear. The Recompose tool can help by shifting objects that you choose while retaining a workable background. Like the Photomerge Scene Cleaner, the tool lets you paint areas of an image to choose which objects to retain and which to merge or remove.

Unlike the Photomerge tools, however, the Recompose tool doesn't sport its own interface. It's a cousin to the Crop tool, and performs its magic when you adjust an image's borders.

To recompose a scene:

1. Choose the Recompose tool from the Tools pane, or press W **A**. The image gains control handles as if you were using the Crop tool.
2. Drag a handle to resize the image **B**. The tool calculates which areas can be removed or compressed.

   If you like the end result, click the Commit button to finish. If the effect needs more attention, click the Cancel button (or press Esc) and continue to the next step.
3. To gain greater control over which areas are preserved, use the marking tools in the Tool Options bar. With the Mark for Protection brush, paint areas that should remain intact **C**. Use the Mark for Removal brush to specify areas that should definitely be removed.

A The Recompose tool.

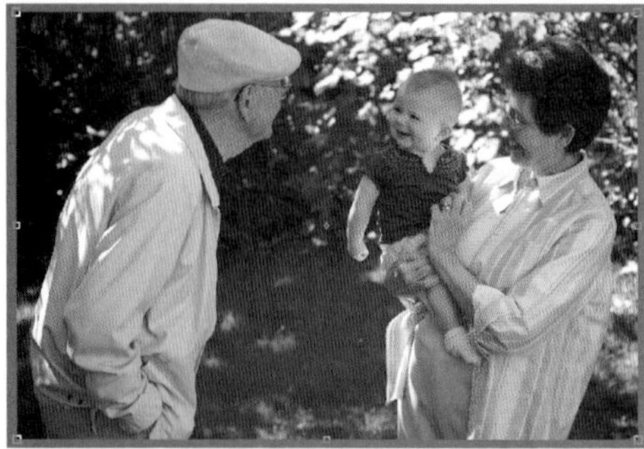

B We want to bring the man and baby closer together. Drag a handle to recompose the scene. In this case, however, the man's face is compressed.

C The Mark for Protection Brush preserves its painted pixels.

D Areas marked for protection are left unharmed, while the background gets compressed.

E Highlight Skin Tones marks people (or people-colored things) for protection.

4. Drag a handle again to resize the image **D**. You may need to fine-tune the marked areas to get a smoother result.
5. Click the Commit button to apply the edit.

TIP You'll probably want to switch to the Crop tool after committing the edit to remove the area that's no longer used in the image.

TIP Is something unwanted in the middle of your scene? Use the Mark for Removal tool to completely paint it out; Elements removes those pixels first.

TIP Choose a size from the Preset menu in the Tool Options bar to restrain how the image is resized (for example, to keep the original aspect ratio).

TIP Figuring that this feature would get the most use in bringing people together (or moving them apart), Adobe added a button in the Tool Options bar: Highlight Skin Tones. (It's located to the right of the aspect ratio drop-down menu.) Click it to apply the Mark for Protection brush to areas matching skin tones E.

Compositing Images

Compositing is the art of combining multiple images to create a single merged image. Combine different digital photos or scanned images to create effects that range from subtle to spectacular to silly. For example, you can replace a landscape's clear blue sky with a dramatic sunset; create complex, multilayered photo collages; or replace the face of the Mona Lisa with that of your Uncle Harold.

To replace part of an image with another image:

1. Open an image that contains an area you want to replace. I'll call this the "target" image.

   In this example, the sky isn't as dynamic as it could be **A**. Since the edges are well defined, the image is a good candidate for the Background Eraser tool.

2. From the Tools pane, select the Background Eraser tool; then adjust its brush size and tolerance values.
3. Position the Background Eraser tool along the outside edge of the foreground shape (the tower). Making sure the brush crosshairs are over the background (sky), drag along the edge to erase the background. Continue to erase the background until the area is completely transparent **B**.
4. Open the image you want to use to replace the transparent pixels in your original image. I'll call this the "source" image.

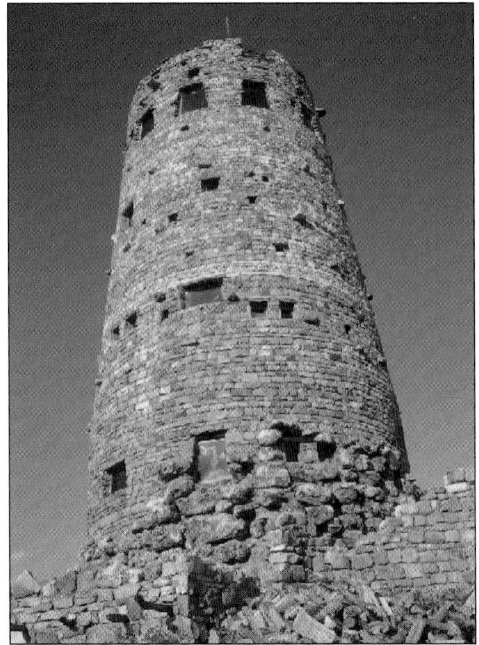

A I'll enhance this image by replacing its background with something more dynamic.

B Use the Background Eraser tool to remove the sky and create a transparent background.

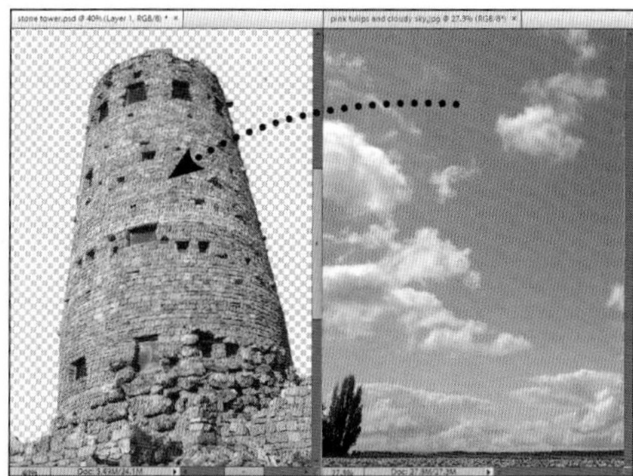

C Drag the source image (the sky) into the target image (the tower).

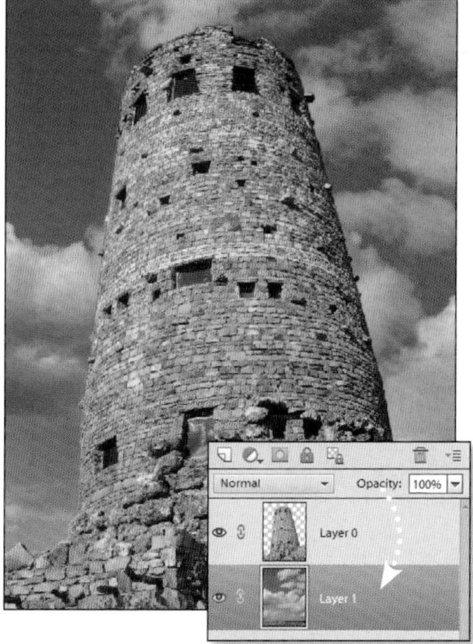

D Move the sky layer below the tower layer on the Layers panel and adjust the position in the image window.

5. Make both images visible by clicking the Layout button on the Task bar and choosing a layout scheme (such as All Column).
6. Select the Move tool and drag the source image into the target image **C**.

   In the example, the sky image is larger than the empty background area, which allows flexibility in positioning the new sky in the composition.

   You can also use the selection tools to select just a portion of the source image, then drag just that selection into the target image.
7. On the Layers panel, drag the source layer below the target layer **D**.
8. In the image window, use the Move tool to adjust the position of the source image until you're satisfied with the composition.

TIP It's always good to save a copy of your composition retaining the layers in case you want to make further adjustments. Layered files should be saved as Photoshop Elements (PSD) files.

TIP Instead of using the Background Eraser tool, you could have just as easily used the Magic Extractor in Step 3 to clear the background.

Merging Portions of Multiple Photos

My instructions were simple: Get a good photo of my niece and nephew together. It sounds easy, but you can't assume that a five-year-old and his little sister will sit still. If it weren't for my camera's ability to shoot multiple frames per second, I think I'd still be trying to get the shot.

Elements makes that quandary much easier with Photomerge, an impressive feature that lets you combine areas of multiple photos into one nearly seamless composition.

To merge portions of multiple photos:

1. Open two or more similar photos in the Editor.
2. Select the photos you want to use in the Photo Bin. (If you don't initially, Elements will ask you to do so.)
3. Choose Enhance > Photomerge > Photomerge Group Shot.

   The first image appears in the Source pane on the left, with an empty Final pane on the right.
4. Drag one of the images to the Final pane **A**. This image is the end result, so it should have the fewest imperfections (such as people's heads turned away from the camera, motion blur, or other issues).
5. Click to select a photo in the Photo Bin that contains an element (a better facial expression, for example) you want merged into the Final pane. The photo appears in the Source pane **B**.

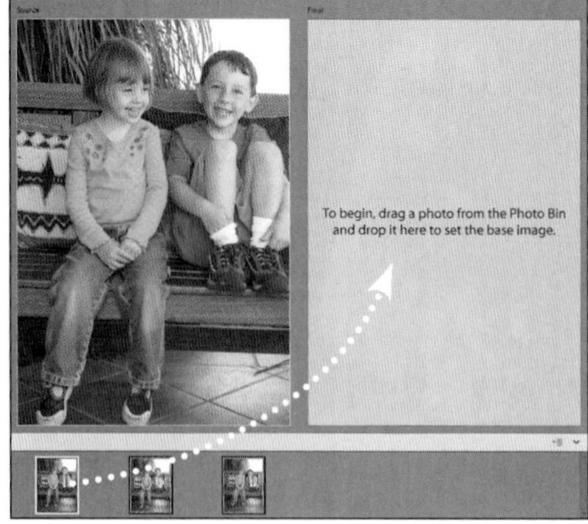

A Drag the photo you want to use as a base into the Final pane. In this case, the boy's facial expression is my favorite of the three, so I'm building on the first image.

B I like the girl's expression in the third image, so I've clicked it in the Photo Bin to load it into the Source pane. Elements uses colored borders to help you track which photo is which.

C Elements calculates the pixels surrounding the areas I've drawn and merges them into the Final image.

D I drew over the boy's legs from the second image to merge them into the Final image. I've also enabled the Show Regions option to see how Elements has patched the photo together.

E In the previous figure, the girl's left arm ended up deformed as a result of the merge. To remedy, I used the Eraser tool to shave some of the blue line on the boy's right arm.

6. Select the Pencil tool (if it's not already selected) and, in the Source pane, draw over the area you want to transfer to the Final image **C**. When you release the mouse button, Elements incorporates that area into the Final image.

   Repeat Steps 5 and 6 for other areas you want to merge **D**.

7. Elements does an amazing job of automatically merging images, but it's not perfect. If you need to adjust some areas, use the Eraser tool to edit the drawing lines in the Source pane **E**.

8. Click Done to exit the Photomerge interface. Elements creates the image in a new layered file.

TIP After you exit Photomerge, you may still need to perform some clean-up editing on the image in the Full Edit mode. The merged image appears on a new layer above the Source image. Use the Clone Stamp tool (or the other tools covered in this chapter) to fine-tune the image.

TIP Elements attempts to align the source images based on their contents, but sometimes things end up a little off—due to different image sizes, slightly different camera angles, and so forth. If that's the case, click the Advanced Options expansion triangle to reveal the Alignment tool, which you can use to mark three points the images share. Click the Align Photos button to realign them.

TIP Click the Pixel Blending checkbox to get a higher-quality, but slower and more processor-intensive, result.

TIP The Photomerge Faces feature works similarly to Group Shot, but requires you to set alignment points first. It's great rainy-day fun!

Using the Smart Brush

The Smart Brush applies many effects—called Smart Paints—to make common edits as easy as selecting areas of your image. You can also edit the appearance of a Smart Paint effect after you've applied it.

What's behind the magic? Each Smart Paint application is a new adjustment layer; a layer mask defines the area where the effect is applied.

To apply a Smart Paint effect:

1. With an image open in Expert edit mode, select the Smart Brush tool from the Tools pane **A** or press F.
2. In the Smart Paint menu in the Tool Options bar, choose an effect **B**; click the drop-down menu at top to list categories of effects, and then click a Smart Paint style to use it.
3. Paint over an area of your photo. Elements creates a selection and applies the Smart Paint effect **C**.

   You can adjust the brush size using the Brush pop-up menu in the Tool Options bar.

TIP When you apply a new Smart Paint to an image, a new selection is created. To switch easily between multiple Smart Paint areas, click the layer pin that appears. Right-clicking the pin brings up options for refining the area, deleting the effect, or hiding the selection border.

A The Smart Brush tool.

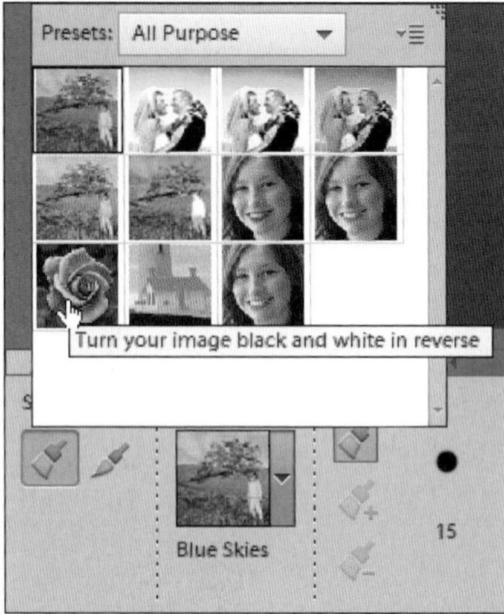

B The Smart Paint menu and category drop-down menu list the various Smart Brush effects.

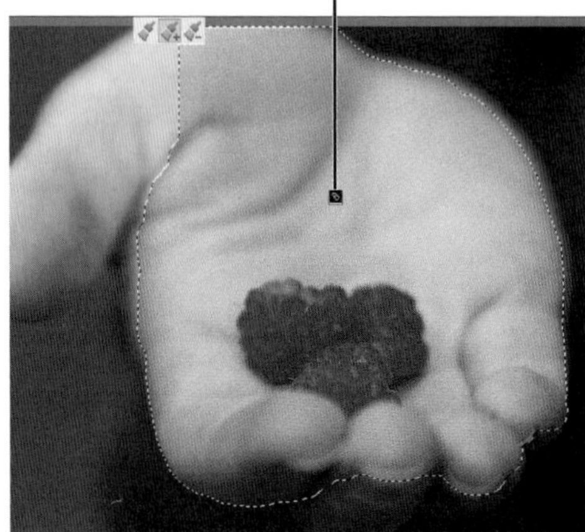

C Paint the area to be affected by the Smart Paint effect (Reverse–Black And White shown here).

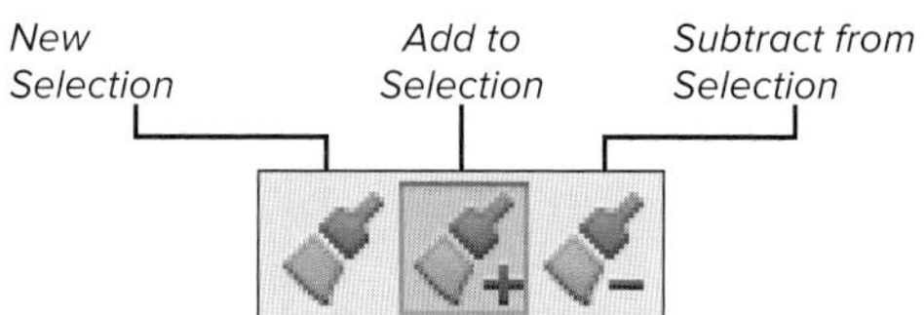

D The selection tools appear above the Smart Paint area.

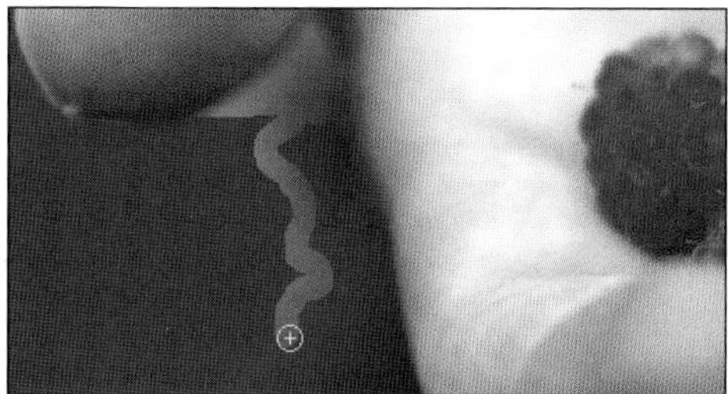

E Use the Detail Smart Brush tool to draw directly on the layer mask for a more precise selection.

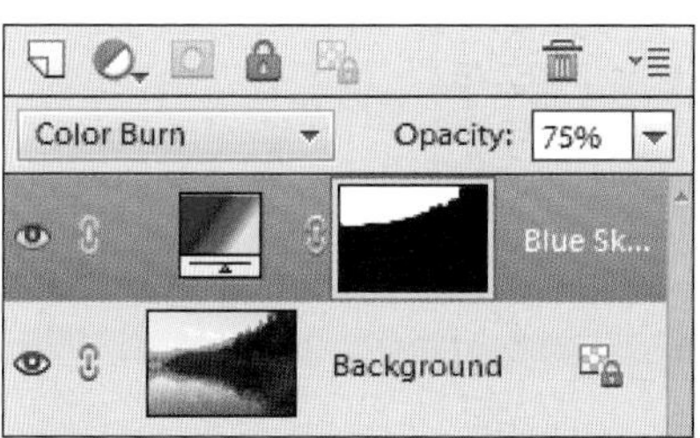

F Smart Paints are actually just adjustment layers.

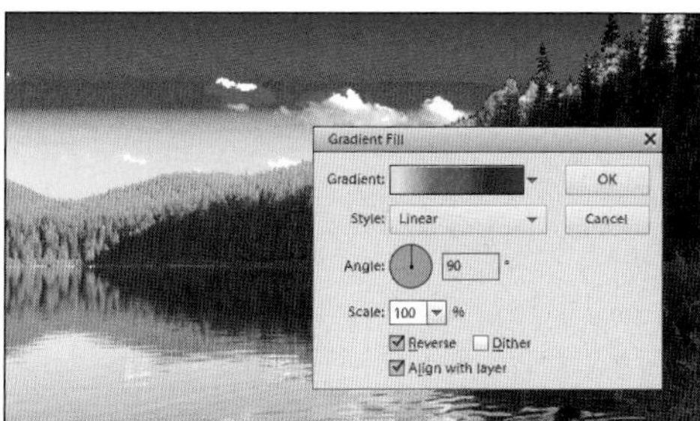

G The Blue Skies Smart Paint effect applies a gradient fill to the selected area, which you can edit (but please, not like this, I beg you).

To edit a Smart Paint selection area:

- Once you start painting, the brush is in Add to Selection mode so additional areas you paint are added to the selection.
- To apply the Smart Paint to a different area of the image, click the New Selection button and begin painting.
- To deselect part of the Smart Paint area, click the Subtract from Selection button in the Tool Options bar or in the toolbar that accompanies the selection **D**.
- Click the Refine Edge button in the Tool Options bar to feather, contract or expand, or smooth the edge. The Inverse checkbox inverts the selection.
- To fine-tune the selection, switch to the Detail Smart Brush tool (press F again). The selection border disappears, letting you add to, or subtract from, the mask that defines the area **E**.

To change Smart Paint settings:

In the Layers panel, double-click the adjustment layer that corresponds with the Smart Paint effect **F**.

The dialog that appears depends on the effect you chose; for example, Blue Skies applies a gradient to the area, so the Gradient Fill dialog appears. You can then edit the gradient **G**.

TIP Some Smart Paints, such as the Black and White Yellow Lens Filter, are not editable. Double-clicking the layer reveals that the effect was created in the full version of Photoshop. That actually means Elements has no interface or capability to edit the effect, even though the program is clearly capable of applying it.

Matching the Style of Another Image

One of the best ways to improve one's photography is to emulate what other people have done. I may not have a burning desire to become a landscape photographer (which requires getting up *really* early in the morning for the best light), but when I'm in the right environment you can bet I'm thinking, "I want this shot to look like something Ansel Adams would have made."

Alas, I'm not Ansel Adams, but with the help of Photoshop Elements, I can get my images a little closer to his style. The Photomerge Style Match feature examines a source image and attempts to replicate its style to one of your images.

Adobe provides a handful of source images, but you can also use one of your own (or one you downloaded from the Internet).

To match the style of another image:

1. Open the image you want to edit in the Editor.
2. Choose Enhance > Photomerge > Photomerge Style Match.
3. Drag a style image from the Style Bin below the previews **A**. Elements analyzes the source and does its best to apply the same style to your image.
4. To match the coloring of the style image, such as a black-and-white or sepia image, click the Transfer Tones checkbox **B**.

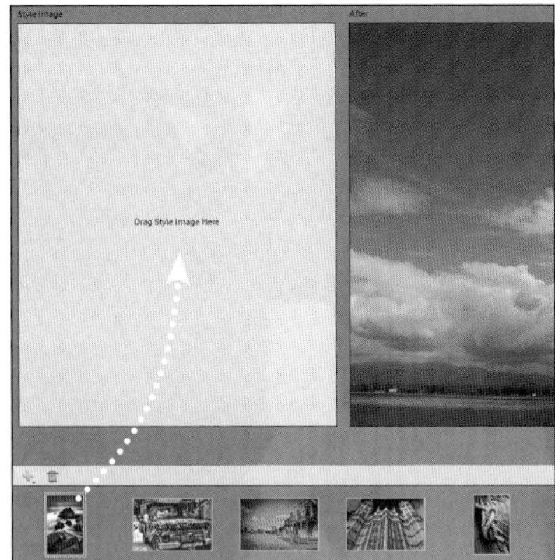

A Adobe provides a few source photos in the Style Bin. Drag one to the Style Image area.

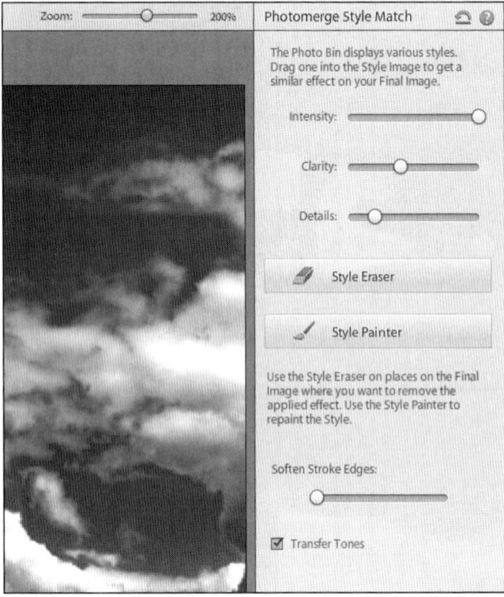

B Enabling the Transfer Tones option carries over custom coloring, such as a black and white image.

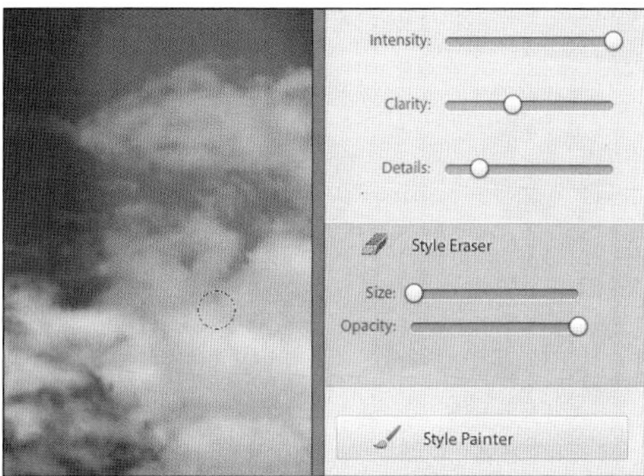

C The style is applied to the entire image, but you can erase areas to further control how the effect appears.

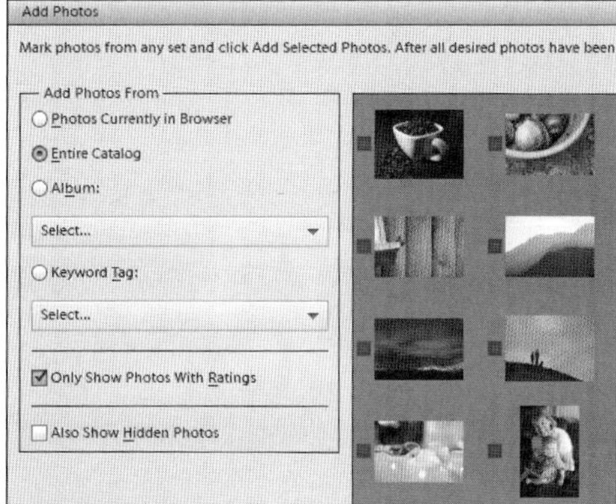

D Use your own images as style sources.

TIP **There is no Undo command when erasing selected areas, so you need to repaint them to get the style back (or just click Reset and then reapply the style image).**

TIP **I find the Style Match feature to be heavy-handed at times; it often posterizes images and blows out highlights. For this reason, I typically reduce the Details slider. You can also pull back on the Intensity amount, but that also minimizes the Transfer Tones feature.**

5. Adjust how the effect is applied by manipulating the following sliders:
   - Intensity affects the overall amount of the matched style.
   - Clarity adjusts the contrast level of the style.
   - Details adjusts the sharpness of the effect.
6. If you don't like the effect, click the Reset button or select a different photo as the style image.
7. Click Done to apply the effect.

To apply a style to selected areas:

1. After applying the style to the entire image, click the Style Eraser button.
2. Paint the areas where you want the original image to show through **C**. The brush size and intensity is controlled In the Tool Options bar.

   Use the Style Painter brush to reapply the style to areas where needed.
3. To feather the edges of your area, drag the Soften Stroke Edges slider.

To add style source images:

1. In the Style Bin, click the Add (+) button
2. From the drop-down menu, choose Add Style Images from Organizer to bring up the Add Photos dialog. (Choosing the hard disk option presents a regular Open dialog to let you find a file.)
3. Click the checkbox next to images you want to add to the Style Bin **D**. To narrow the number of options, use the filters in the Add Photos From area.
4. Click the Add Selected Photos button to add the pictures, then click Done.

Creating Panoramas

With Photoshop Elements, you can create wide, panoramic images that would be difficult to capture with a single shot from a standard camera. The Photomerge Panorama command analyzes your individual photos and assembles them into a single panoramic image **A**.

A Photomerge combines several separate photos into a single panoramic picture.

Taking pictures for panoramas

If you're getting ready to snap some scenic photos and know you want to assemble them into a panorama later, making a few camera adjustments will make it easier to assemble a seamless panorama.

- Use a consistent zoom level when taking the pictures.
- Use a consistent focus. If your subject matter is far away, set your camera's focus to infinity, if the option is available.
- Use consistent exposure. A panorama with widely varied lighting will be difficult to merge seamlessly. Set your camera's exposure manually or lock the exposure setting if possible. Photomerge Panorama can make slight adjustments for images with different exposures, but it is not as effective when the image exposure varies greatly.
- If possible, use a tripod. You can take pictures for a panorama with a handheld camera, but you might find it difficult to keep all of the images perfectly level.
- Overlap sequential images by about 15 to 40 percent **B**. Photomerge looks for similar detail in the edges of your images to match consecutive pictures. Try to capture as much detail throughout the frame to give Photomerge more reference points to match up.

B The more your images overlap, the better your chances of successfully merging them. Try for an overlap of between 15 and 40 percent.

TIP Try taking *two* versions of panorama images: one with the camera held horizontally and one with the camera held vertically. See which option makes a better panorama.

TIP You're not limited to creating horizontal panoramas. You can also create vertical panoramas of tall subjects, such as skyscrapers or redwood trees.

TIP Some digital cameras include a feature that helps you compose multiple overlapping photos when you shoot.

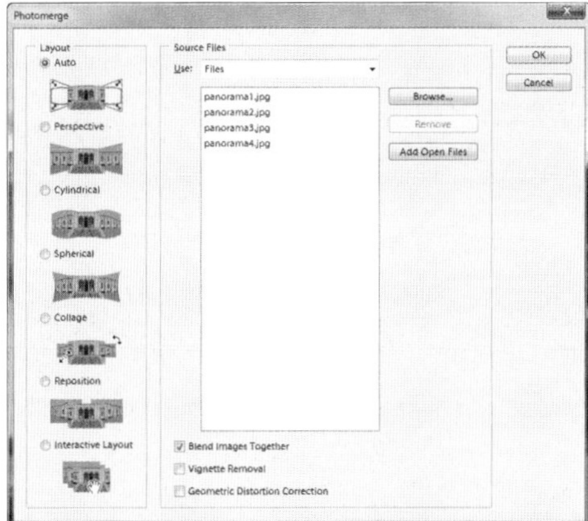

C Browse for photos to merge in the Photomerge dialog.

D When you click OK, your merged images open in a new Elements file.

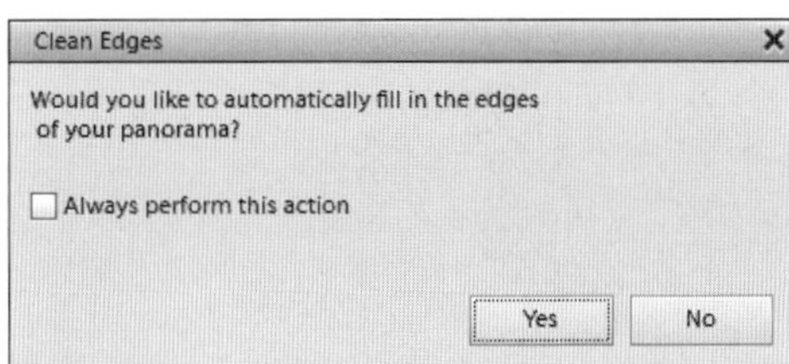

E Choose to fill in the edges using content-aware technology.

F The edges are filled in (with varying levels of success due to the image contents, especially at the bottom).

Assembling images into a panorama

To create a panoramic image, select the images you want to merge and then let Photomerge work its magic.

To create a panorama:

1. Open the images you want to merge.

   If you want to make any adjustments, such as tonal corrections or cropping, make your corrections first, before you begin assembling the images.

2. Choose Enhance > Photomerge > Photomerge Panorama **C**.

3. Click the Add Open Files button to use the images from Step 1. If you need to delete a file from the list, select it and then click the Remove button.

   If you want to add more images, click the Browse button to open the Open dialog; then navigate to the folder containing the images you want to merge.

4. Choose a panorama style from the Layout column based on your source images. For example, you'd choose Cylindrical if you shot a 360-degree revolution around one point.

   The Interactive Layout option works differently than the rest, as you'll see on the following pages; for now, don't choose it.

5. When you have all of the images you want in the Source Files list, click OK.

   Photoshop Elements automatically merges them into a single image **D**.

6. Elements can attempt to fill in the empty area using its content-aware technology. In the dialog that appears, choose whether to apply the fix (**E** and **F**).

continues on next page

TIP You may see an alert message telling you that some images can't be assembled. If Photomerge can't find enough common details in your images, it will ignore those files. See the next page for a solution.

TIP Once you click OK to create your panorama, there's no returning to the Photomerge dialog to make further adjustments. If you're not happy with the way the panorama rendered, you'll need to start over. Refer to the following topics for further instruction on how to make additional adjustments to your panorama before you click the OK button.

TIP If seams are still visible in the panorama, try touching up the areas with the Spot Healing Brush or the Clone tool.

TIP Use the Crop tool to remove those rough edges and give your panorama a nice, crisp rectangular border **G**.

TIP Before you print your final panorama, take the time to examine its size in the Image Size dialog (from the File menu, choose Resize > Image Size). Depending on the size and resolution of the images you've used, your panoramas can quickly grow to exceed the standard paper stock sizes for your printer (which are usually no larger than 8.5 x 14 or 11 x 17 inches). Once you've determined the final image dimensions, use either the Image Size dialog or the controls in the Print Preview dialog to resize your image so it will fit on whatever paper stock you have available.

G After creating the panorama, you can use the Crop tool to trim the image.

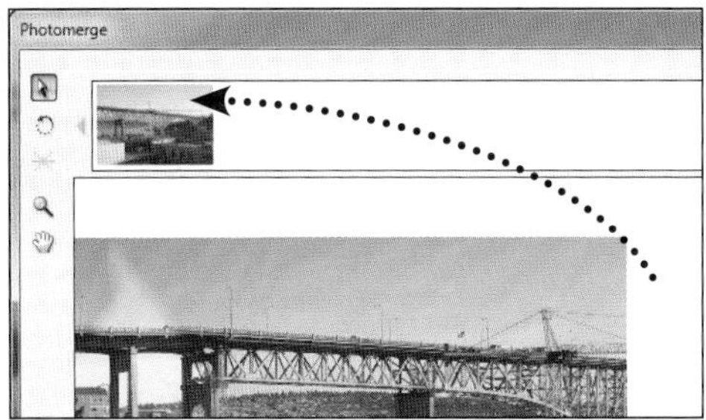

H Drag an image in the work area to the Lightbox.

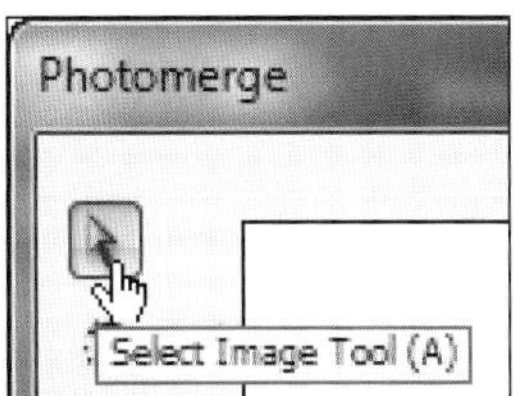

I The Select Image tool.

J When you drag one image over another, the top image becomes semitransparent, allowing you to align the images.

Adjusting images using the Interactive Layout

When you choose the Interactive Layout option in the initial Photomerge dialog, Elements merges the selected images, but then opens a new window where you can fine-tune the composition.

To reposition images in the panorama:

1. If you want to remove an image from the panorama before repositioning it, drag it from the work area into the Lightbox (just above the main preview area) H.
2. Check that the Select Image tool is highlighted in the Photomerge dialog I.
3. Drag the image over the image with which it should merge. As you drag, the image becomes partially transparent so you can more easily line it up with the one below it J.
4. When the two images match up, release the mouse button.

   If Snap to Image is selected in the dialog, any two overlapping images will automatically try to match up with one another. If Snap to Image is not selected, Photomerge allows you to align the overlapping image manually.

   Turning off Snap to Image allows you to move the images in small increments if they are not matching up exactly. You may also need to rotate an image slightly to make it match up with its neighbor correctly.

continues on next page

5. Select the Rotate Image tool, and then drag to rotate the selected image if needed **K**.

   The Photomerge dialog offers several options for moving through its work area while composing your panoramas, including its own built-in navigator.

6. To navigate through the work area, do one of the following:

   - Select the Move View tool (the hand icon) in the dialog and drag in the work area.
   - In the Navigator, drag the view box. This changes the view in the work area **L**.
   - Use the scroll bars at the bottom and right edges of the work area.

7. To change the zoom level in the work area, do one of the following:

   - Select the Zoom tool in the dialog and click in the work area to zoom in.
   - Hold down the Alt/Option key while clicking to zoom out.
   - Move the slider under the thumbnail in the Navigator.
   - Click the Zoom icons under the thumbnail in the Navigator section of the dialog.

TIP You may see some tonal variation as a result of merging the images in the Interactive Layout (as in the images on the next page). However, Elements smooths those when the final panorama is constructed.

K You can rotate images to help align them in the work area.

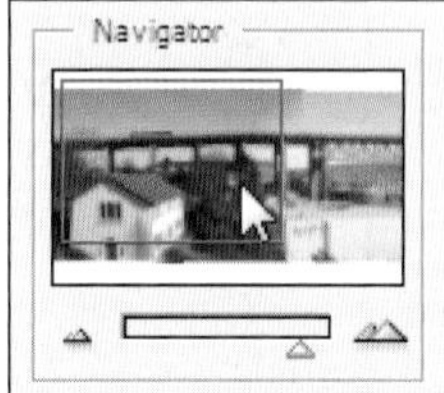

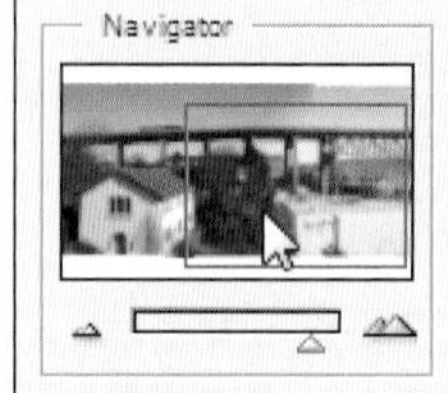

L Drag the view box in the Navigator to change the view in the work area.

Enhancing perspective

Even the most sophisticated camera lenses tend to flatten what little depth or perspective is present in the landscapes or objects they capture. Photomerge Panorama lets you restore that lost perspective to create a more natural-looking panoramic image. In addition, you can adjust the vanishing point (the point where natural perspective recedes into the distance) to help draw attention to a specific area or object in the panorama.

To add perspective to a panorama:

1. In the Settings section of the dialog, select the Perspective option Ⓜ.

   The outside edges of the panorama are distorted, creating a more dramatic, and sometimes more realistic, perspective view Ⓝ. The middle of the center image is designated as the vanishing point, and the outside images appear to recede into its center. The vanishing point image is identified by a blue outline when it's selected.

2. To make a different image the vanishing point image, first select the Set Vanishing Point tool.
3. Click a different image in the work area. The panorama changes the perspective to make it look as if the other images now recede into the new Vanishing Point image Ⓞ.
4. If the Perspective option doesn't give you the effect you'd hoped for, select the Reposition Only option in the Settings section of the dialog to return your panorama to its original state.

   You can also remove the perspective from your panorama by dragging the Vanishing Point image to the Lightbox.

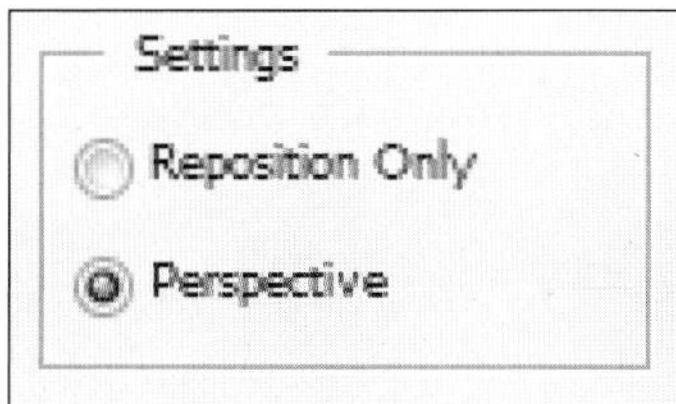

Ⓜ Click the Perspective radio button to add exaggerated perspective to your merged composition.

Ⓝ When you select the Perspective setting, Elements adjusts and distorts the images to create the illusion of a vanishing point. Here, the vanishing point image is identified by the light blue outline.

Ⓞ When you change the Vanishing Point image, the other images adjust and distort in response to change the perspective.

Correcting Red Eye

When you're in an indoor or darkened space, your pupils grow larger to let in more light. The pupils can't shrink fast enough to compensate for a camera's flash, so when that light reflects off the back of the eye, it causes red eye. Many cameras pre-flash before the picture is actually snapped, giving the subject's pupils a chance to contract and greatly reduce the effects of red eye. But chances are you still have some older photos lying around you'd like to repair. The Red Eye Removal tool offers an effective way to remove red eye, simply by changing pixels from one color to another.

To remove red eye from a photo:

1. Select the Red Eye Removal tool from the Tools pane, or press Y **A**.
2. In the Tool Options bar, set the Pupil Size slider to match the proportional size of the pupil (the red part of the eye that you want to turn black) to the colored portion of the eye. Then, use the Darken Amount slider to control the darkness of the retouched pupil **B**.

   Although these settings are not inconsequential, the defaults of 50 percent work fine in most cases I've tried.
3. If necessary, zoom in on the area you want to correct; then click and drag to draw a selection over the colored portion of one eye **C**.
4. Release the mouse button to remove the red eye effect. If you're not quite satisfied with the results the first time, press Ctrl+Z/Command-Z to undo the operation, and then repeat steps 2 through 4, revising the option bar settings or changing the size of the selection before you click and drag.

A The Red Eye Removal tool.

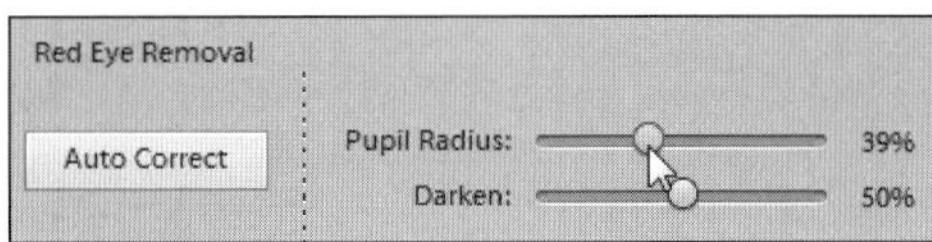

B Two sliders In the Tool Options bar help you to adjust red eye removal.

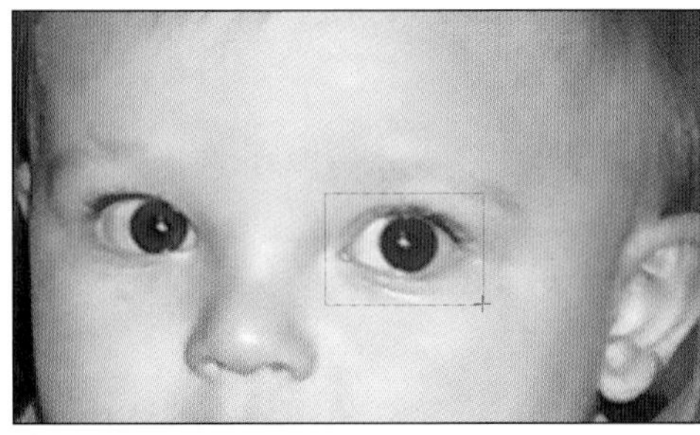

C To remove red eye, draw a selection around the eye and release the mouse button.

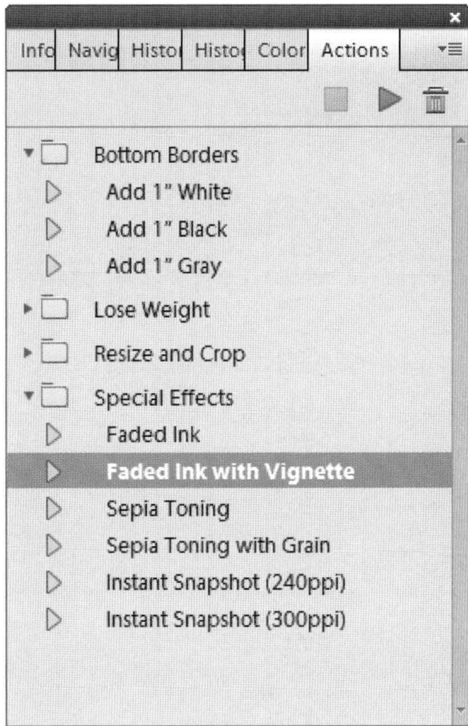

Ⓐ The Actions panel can run automated combinations of adjustments.

Run Automated Actions

One benefit of sharing the same code base as Photoshop CS is that Elements has more power under the surface than is apparent. For example, Elements can run Photoshop actions, which are scripts that execute commands in succession so you don't have to do them all manually. This way, you can apply a series of levels adjustments and a vignette by clicking a single button. The new Actions panel includes a bunch of operations to add borders, resize and crop, and apply special effects to images.

The downside is that you can't create actions in Elements—that's a feature Adobe reserves for Photoshop CS. However, you can import actions created by Photoshop and run them in the Editor. So, for example, if a friend of yours uses Photoshop extensively and has created an action that resizes an image and adds a border and photo credit, you could run that action in Elements instead of performing each step. (Elements can currently only run actions, not create them.)

To run actions:

1. Choose Window > Actions to bring up the Actions panel Ⓐ.
2. Select an action to run.
3. Press the Play button.

To load actions:

1. Click the flyout menu in the Actions panel and choose Load Actions.
2. Locate a Photoshop action file—it ends in the extension .atn. The actions it contains appear in the Actions panel.

TIP When creating actions in Photoshop CS, you can save only sets of actions, not single actions themselves. Select a set and choose Save Actions from the flyout menu.

TIP Actions aren't actually new in Photoshop Elements 11. They've been around for several versions, but were accessible only as a Guided Edit feature. Loading new actions also involved copying files to areas of the operating system that were difficult to access.

Working with Camera Raw Photos

Most digital cameras save photos in the JPEG format, which is highly compressed. The processor in the camera analyzes the image, applies automatic corrections, and tosses out pixels to reduce the size of the file. Usually, you won't notice a difference—JPEG is optimized to produce images that are pleasing to the eye.

As good as this process is, it still throws away data. And when you're editing photos, you want to start with as much data as possible.

Many cameras—not just DSLRs—have the capability to save the unedited data captured by the camera's image sensor, which is commonly known as *camera raw*. Each manufacturer uses its own proprietary specifications, so you may see files ending in .NEF, .CRW, or others.

Camera raw gives you more data to work with, which means more flexibility when adjusting white balance or tonal range—the camera hasn't already made choices for sharpening or tonal balance for you. Then, when you're done making raw adjustments, you can continue to edit the image using the other tools in Elements.

In This Chapter

Working in Adobe Camera Raw

When you open one or more raw files in the Editor, a separate utility called Adobe Camera Raw (often referred to as just ACR) appears **A**. ACR includes many of the same correction tools found in the Editor—in some cases you may want to do most of your adjustments in ACR alone.

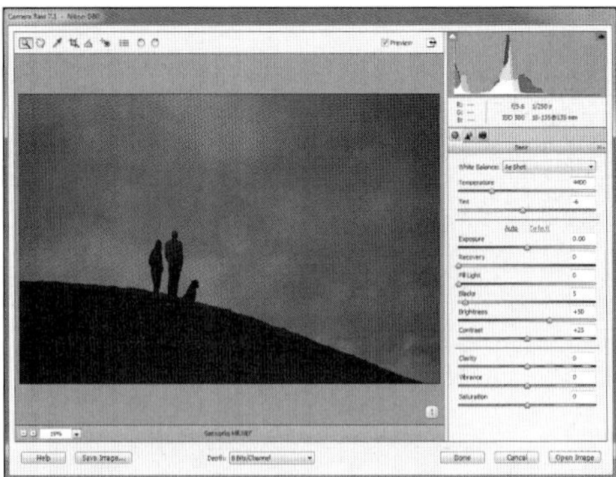

A Camera Raw gives you an opportunity to adjust the raw, unedited image data.

Using camera profiles

Before we jump into manipulating sliders (because you know how much Adobe loves sliders), I want to talk briefly about camera raw profiles.

The camera manufacturers tweak their raw algorithms to fit each camera, which is why it's often necessary to install updates that provide raw support for the newest cameras on the market. ACR uses that information to determine how to display the image in a few common areas such as Landscape, Portrait, and Vivid. Although I typically stick with the ACR default (Adobe Standard), it's worth checking out the others as a starting point for your adjustments.

Camera Calibration button

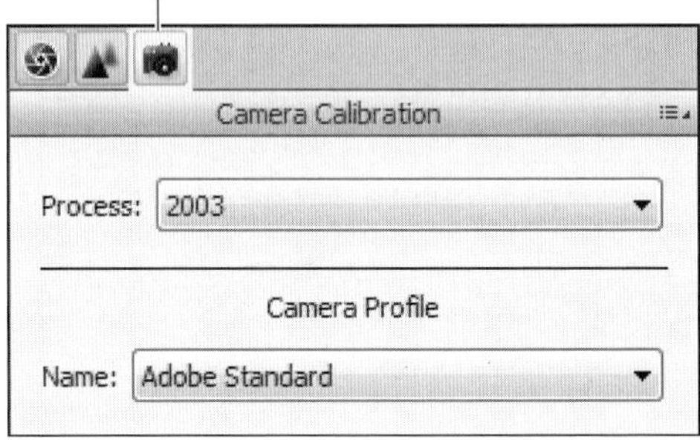

B Camera profiles apply presets for common photo situations.

To choose a camera profile:

1. In the Adobe Camera Raw window, click the Camera Calibration button **B**.
2. Choose a camera profile from the Name drop-down menu. Adobe Standard is a good all-around option, but feel free to explore the camera-specific profiles depending on the type of photo **C**. (You won't see specific camera models listed; your camera's raw profiles are activated in the "Camera [setting]" profiles.)

Adobe Standard

Camera Vivid

C Two profiles appear different even without making slider adjustments.

Process version warning

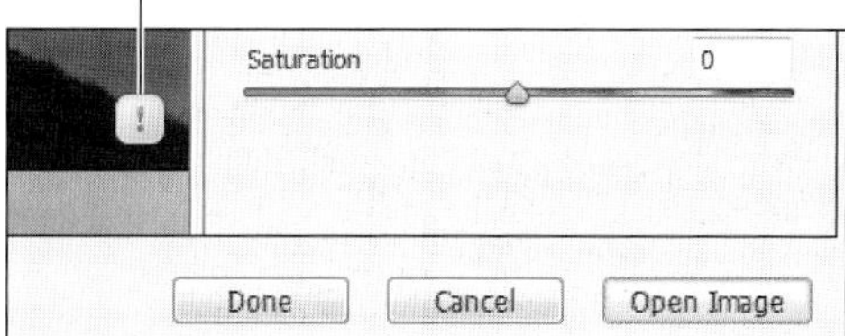

D A warning icon appears if an earlier process version is applied.

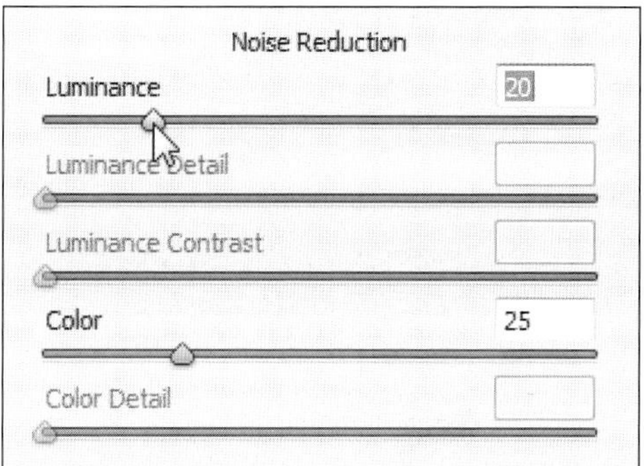

E Images with older process versions can't take advantage of the latest controls until they're converted to the current process.

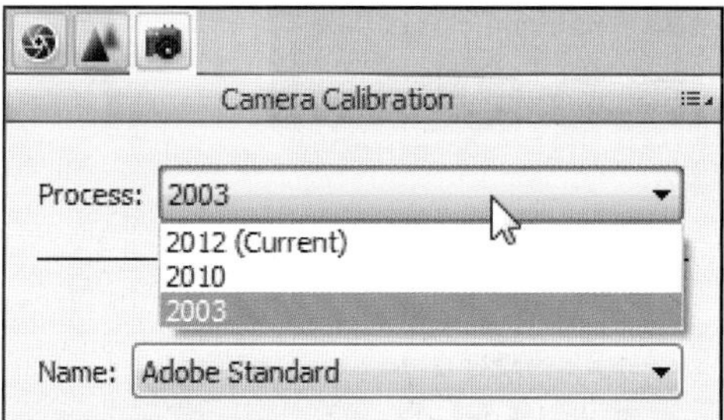

F Choose a process version in the Camera Calibration tab.

Understanding process versions

Not only do camera manufacturers adjust their raw algorithms for each camera model, Adobe is also evolving the way its software handles raw files. Every few years, it incorporates a new *process version* into ACR to better decode the raw data with new or improved features.

Any new raw file you open uses the 2012 process. If you open a file that was previously processed using an earlier version of ACR, it will open with the 2010 or 2003 process applied. You can tell right away if a warning icon appears **D**.

What's the difference? An image with the 2003 process, for example, lacks the ability to adjust Luminance Detail, Luminance Contrast, and Color Detail controls in the Noise Reduction section of ACR **E**. You will probably also notice slight visual differences when selecting the different processes.

You don't need to update to the latest process version—you may have spent considerable time on the image originally, and don't want to throw away that work. But if you decide to apply the current process, here's how to do it.

To update the process version:

- Click the process warning icon to update to the current version.

Or,

1. Click the Camera Calibration tab.
2. Choose a version from the Process drop-down menu **F**.

Adjusting White Balance

If I do nothing else in ACR, I adjust the white balance setting in images that need it. Although you can compensate for color casts in the Editor, the White Balance slider makes the process much easier. It also offers presets that match cameras' white balance modes.

To adjust white balance:

- Choose a preset from the White Balance drop-down menu Ⓐ.

Or,

1. Drag the Temperature slider to warm up or cool down the image Ⓑ.
2. To adjust the color tint—for example, to remove a green color cast—drag the Tint slider.

Or,

1. Select the White Balance Tool from the toolbar (or press I).
2. Click a white, black, or gray area of your image Ⓒ. The white balance changes based on where you click.

TIP Adjusting the white balance is a great way to add warmth to an overcast day, or even to add some personalization to a photo without going extreme with filters. In my example photo of a cider press Ⓑ, I deliberately wanted a much warmer image to emphasize the deep color of the cider being produced.

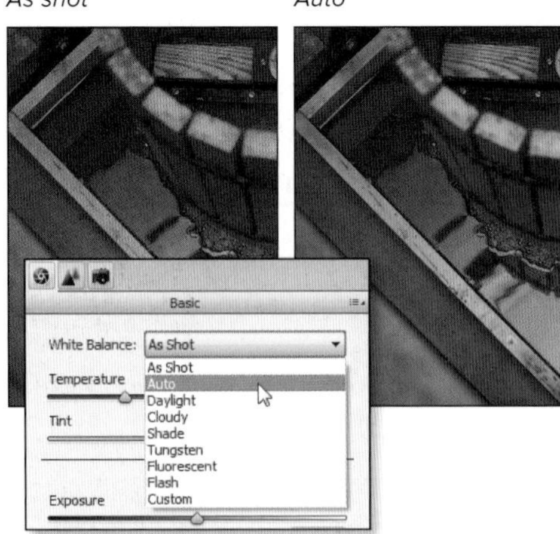

Ⓐ White Balance options mirror the settings used by your camera.

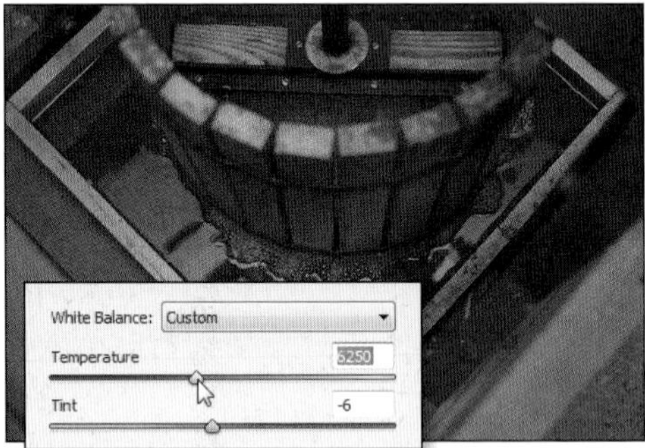

Ⓑ Warm or cool an image using the Temperature slider, or shift color casts using the Tint slider.

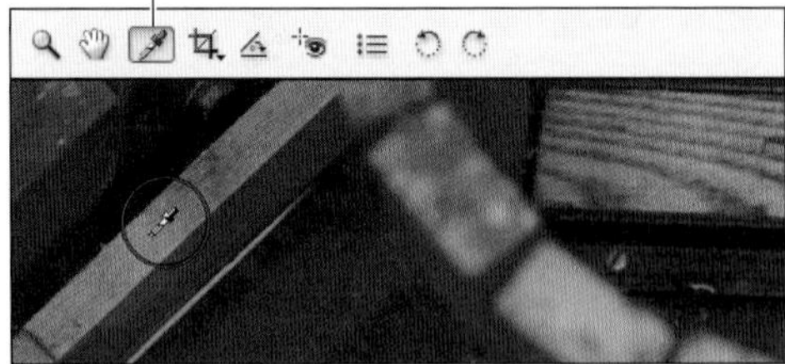

Ⓒ Another option is to use the White Balance Tool to sample white, black, or gray areas.

Original Auto

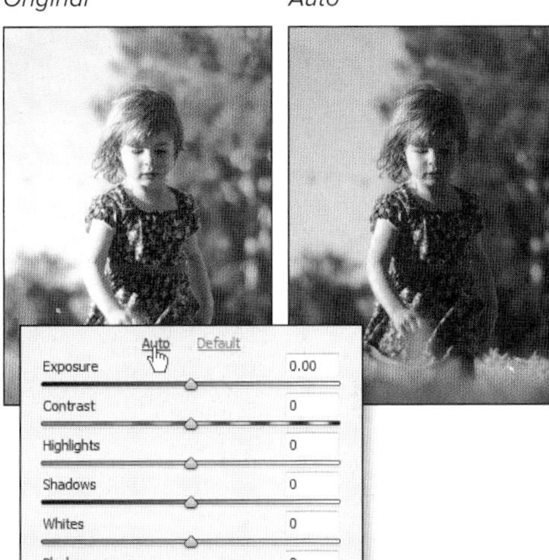

Ⓐ Clicking Auto is a great first lighting adjustment.

Shadow Clipping Warning

Highlight Clipping Warning

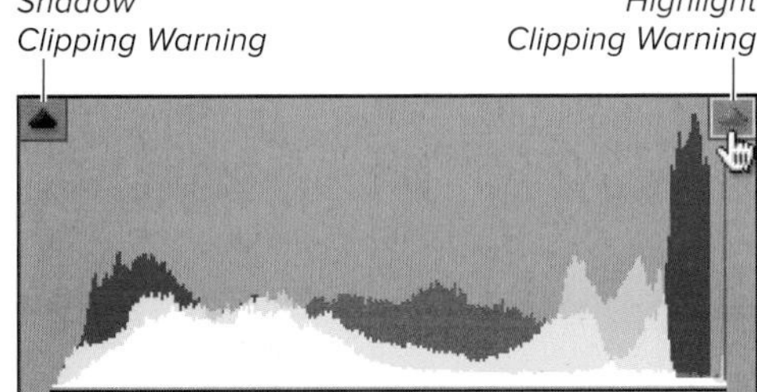

Ⓑ Display the clipping warnings to identify dark or bright problem areas.

Overexposed areas

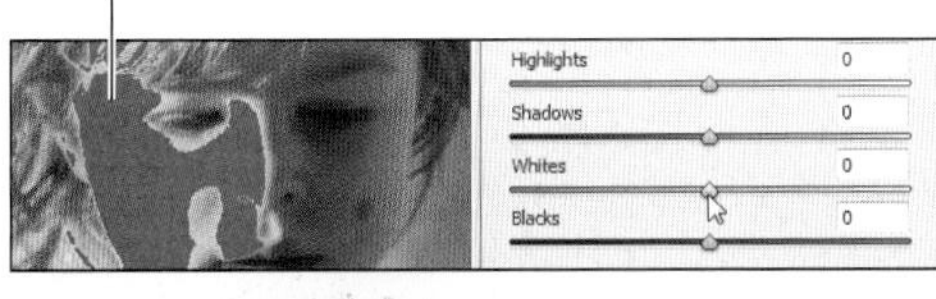

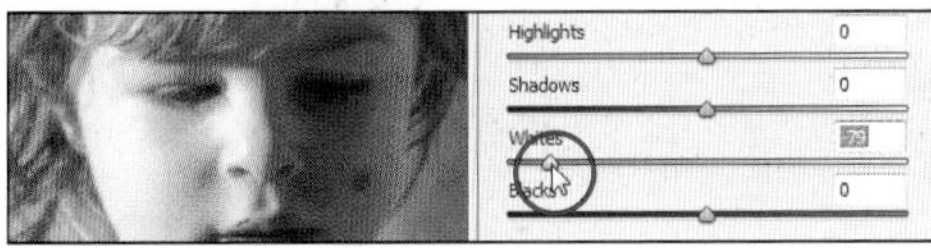

Ⓒ Increasing the Whites value brings tones back into overexposed areas.

Adjusting Lighting

The lighting adjustments in Adobe Camera Raw really demonstrate the advantages of shooting in raw. For example, overexposed areas that in a JPEG would be hopelessly blown out can sometimes be rescued.

The lighting controls are similar to many of the features covered in Chapter 8, but are conveniently grouped into one section.

To adjust lighting:

1. As with most adjustments, I recommend clicking the Auto button to see what ACR suggests Ⓐ. To return to the image's original state, click the Default button.
2. If you want to identify areas that are too dark or too light, click the Shadow and Highlight Clipping Warning buttons in the histogram Ⓑ.
3. Manipulate the individual sliders according to the photo's needs:
   - Exposure brightens or darkens the image.
   - Contrast applies contrast to the image's midtones.
   - Highlights tempers very bright, blown-out areas.
   - Shadows brightens or darkens midtones.
   - Whites brightens or darkens white values, which helps for overexposed areas Ⓒ.
   - Blacks pushes darker areas to black or brightens them up a little.

TIP Are you seeing different sliders than what's shown here? These options appear in the 2012 process version. See "Understanding process versions," two pages back.

Adjusting Clarity and Color Saturation

The version of Adobe Camera Raw that ships with Photoshop Elements isn't as robust as what you'll find in the full version of Photoshop CS. You can't adjust colors independently, but you can boost or reduce overall color saturation, including the "vibrance" of an image.

ACR also lets you modify "clarity," which is a smart method of sharpening the photo.

To adjust clarity:

- Drag the Clarity slider, which sharpens the image by detecting and working on edges, as opposed to sharpening everything.

To adjust color saturation:

- Drag the Vibrance or Saturation sliders:
  - Vibrance applies saturation but doesn't allow colors to become clipped. More importantly, Vibrance keeps skin tones intact **A**.
  - Saturation increases or decreases the color intensity as a whole.

TIP If you're not dealing with skin tones, you can often get more mileage out of the Saturation slider. But be careful, it's easy to overdo it and end up with a photo that looks more like pop art (which could be the effect you're looking for).

Vibrance +50, Saturation 0

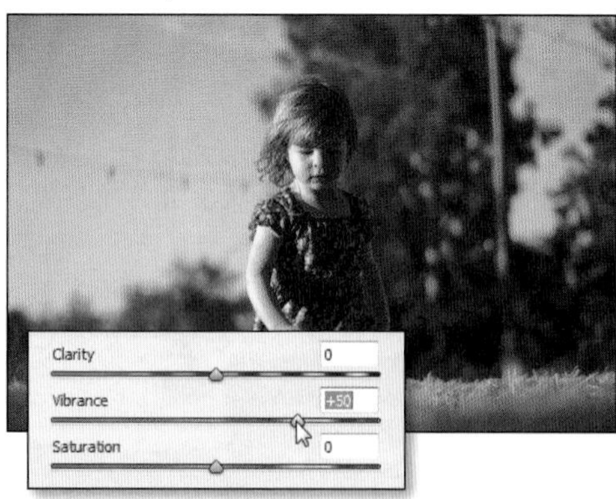

Vibrance 0, Saturation +50

A Applying Vibrance (top) boosts saturation but doesn't make skin tones appear discolored—here quite yellow—as the Saturation control can do (bottom).

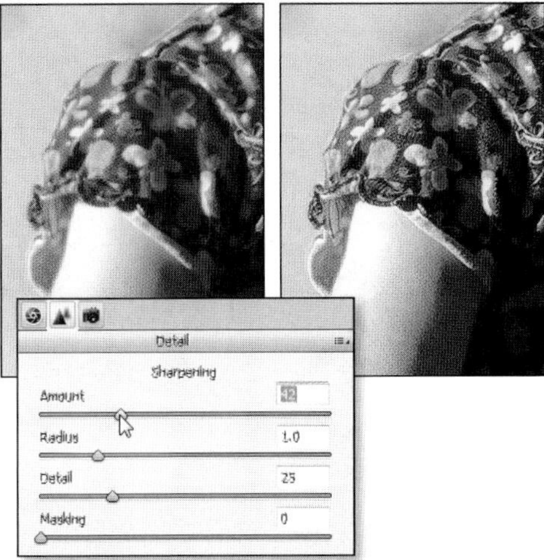

A I've set a high sharpening Amount value on the right (139) to exaggerate the effect.

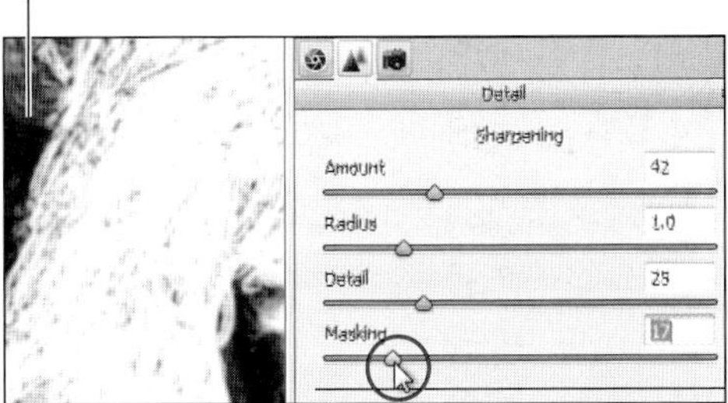

B Hold Alt/Option while dragging to view which areas are not sharpened due to the mask.

TIP Hold the Alt/Option key as you drag a slider to view a colorless version of the adjustment to better see the effect. The Amount slider switches to grayscale; Radius and Detail display a flat gray version that shows only the sharpened areas; and the Mask slider identifies sharpened areas in white and masked areas in black B.

TIP Camera raw algorithms automatically apply some amount of sharpening, which is why you'll see an Amount value higher than zero even when you've made no adjustments.

Sharpening the Image

The sharpening capabilities of ACR are impressive, but I must interject an important caveat. Sharpening is almost always best done after most of your other edits are completed, because making adjustments in the Editor can exaggerate the sharpening and cause unwanted halos or artifacts. If you're doing most of your correction in ACR, though, you'll appreciate being able to sharpen at this stage.

To sharpen an image:

1. Click the Detail button in the sidebar.
2. Using the Zoom tool, or the Select Zoom Level field in the lower-left corner of the window, increase magnification to 100% to best view how the sharpening appears.

   You can also press Control-Alt-0 (zero)/Command-Option-0 (zero) to quickly zoom to 100%.
3. Use the Sharpening sliders to modify the image:
   - The Amount slider controls how much sharpening to apply A.
   - Radius sets how many pixels to sample when applying the sharpening.
   - Detail determines how fine the sharpening is to be applied. A lower value sticks to obvious edges, while a higher value emphasizes details such as textures.
   - Mask locates edges and excludes areas that are likely to add noise in broad areas where you don't want it. For example, sharpening a sky can accentuate subtle color variations, but using a high Mask value excludes the sky.

Reducing Noise

When you're shooting in low-light conditions or want to capture objects moving fast, increasing the ISO (light sensitivity) setting on your camera enables you to get shots you might lose. But high ISO comes with a price: more digital noise. The noise reduction sliders can work to remove that digital spottiness.

To reduce noise:

1. Click the Detail button in the sidebar.
2. Using the Zoom tool, or the Select Zoom Level field in the lower-left corner of the window, increase magnification to 100% or more to see the noise.
3. Drag one or both of the Noise Reduction sliders, depending on the nature of the noise **A**.

   The Luminance slider applies to grayscale noise; the Color slider affects chroma noise, or noise made up of multiple colors.

TIP Noise reduction works by smoothing pixel values, so although you can get rid of unwanted pixelation, you'll also create a softer image overall, especially with the Luminance and Color sliders set to high values. Experiment to determine a good balance between noise and softness.

Original

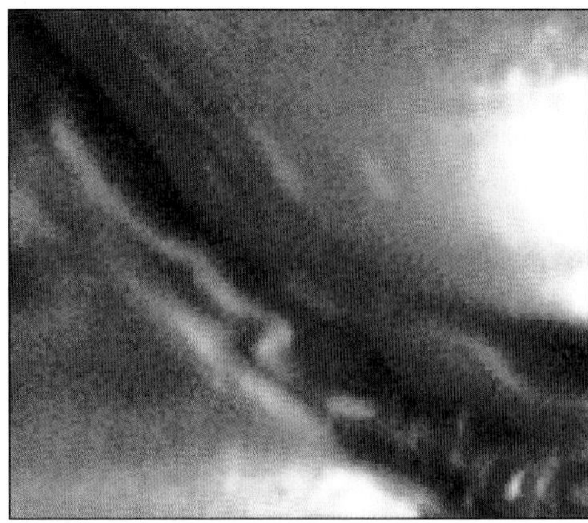

Luminance noise reduction applied

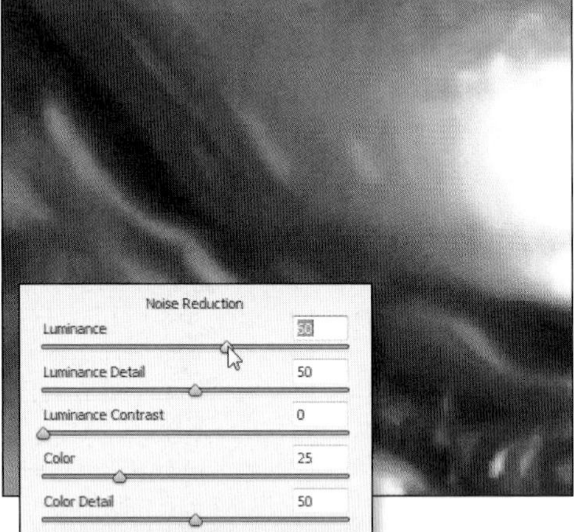

A Increasing the Luminance noise reduction smooths the pixels in this low-light photo.

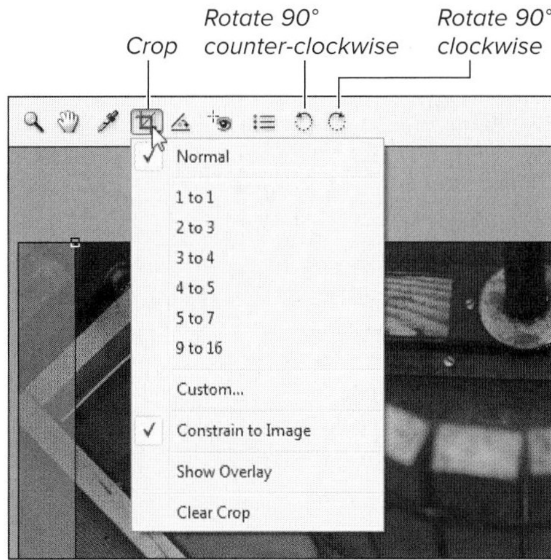

Ⓐ Choose an aspect ratio from the Crop tool's drop-down menu, or draw the crop area yourself.

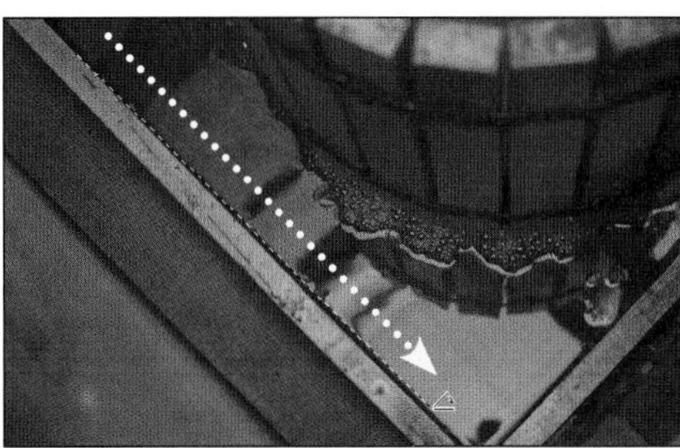

Ⓑ Drag where you want the "horizon line" to be.

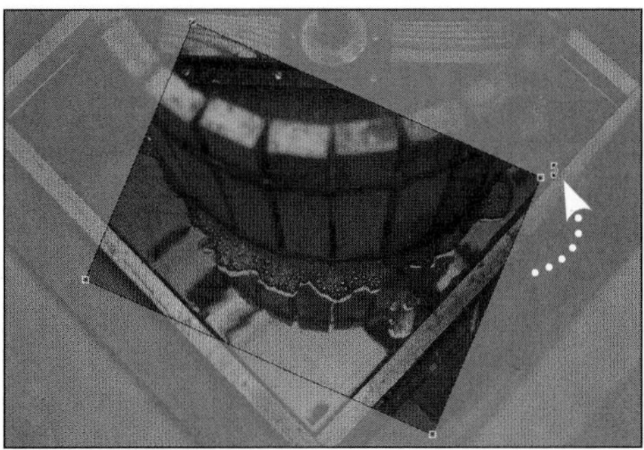

Ⓒ Refine the rotation and crop size.

Cropping and Rotating the Image

Cropping and rotating (and straightening) are actions you can take in the Editor, but if you're already working in Adobe Camera Raw, it's convenient to do it now.

To crop the image:

1. Click to select the Crop tool in the toolbar, or press C.
2. If you want to constrain the crop area to a specific aspect ratio, click and hold the Crop tool to bring up the Crop drop-down menu Ⓐ.
3. Double-click the crop area to apply the crop. Or, choose Clear Crop from the drop-down menu to cancel the crop and start over.

To rotate the image:

- Click the Rotate 90° Counter-clockwise button, or press L. Or, click the Rotate 90° Clockwise button, or press R.

To straighten the image:

1. Click to select the Straighten tool in the toolbar, or press A.
2. Drag a horizontal line that compensates for the amount of rotation you want to apply Ⓑ. Instead of rotating the image, ACR creates a crop rectangle representing the rotation once applied.
3. Drag outside a corner to refine the rotation. You can also resize and reposition the crop box Ⓒ.
4. Double-click the crop area to apply the crop. Or, choose Clear Crop from the drop-down menu to cancel the crop and start over.

Saving Raw Files

"Saving" seems a little disingenuous here, since in most cases your adjustments in ACR are just the first step before working with an image in the Editor. But making that step does involve saving, and in the case of raw files it's not straightforward.

ACR correctly treats your raw file as a "digital negative," an untouchable original that you can always go back to if needed. So, any adjustments you make are saved in "sidecar" files—separate XML-formatted text files that describe the edits you performed **A**. Opening the raw file in other editors that support sidecar files (such as Photoshop Lightroom) gives you the same changes you previously applied. However, if you delete the sidecar file and open the raw file, your image appears as it originally did out of the camera.

When you've finished making adjustments in ACR, a number of actions are available.

To save a raw file:

- Click the Open Image button to exit ACR and switch to the Editor. The adjustments you made are saved to a sidecar file. At this point you can't change any of the adjustments without re-opening the raw file again in ACR.
- If you want to switch to the Editor but not save the sidecar information, hold the Alt/Option key and click the Open Copy button (which is normally the Open Image button) **B**.
- Click Done to save the changes to the sidecar and close the file without opening it in the Editor.

continues on next page

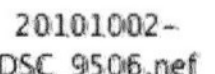

A Raw edits are stored in a separate .xmp sidecar file.

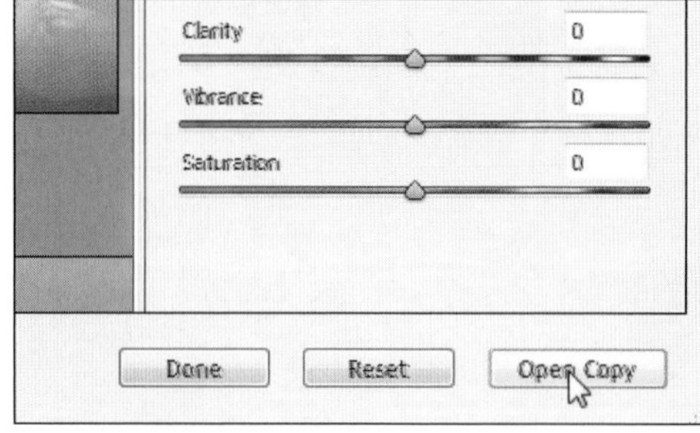

B Hold Alt/Option to open the image in the Editor without saving your adjustments first.

Applying Adjustments to Multiple Files

This chapter focuses on editing individual images, but you can also edit several raw files at once (helpful if you're editing photos from the same shoot):

1. Open the raw files you want to edit.
2. Click the Select All button at the top of the list of open images.
3. Make any adjustments; they're applied to each image as you work. Double-click an image thumbnail to view it in the editing area.
4. Click the Open Images button (or Open Copies with Alt/Option held).

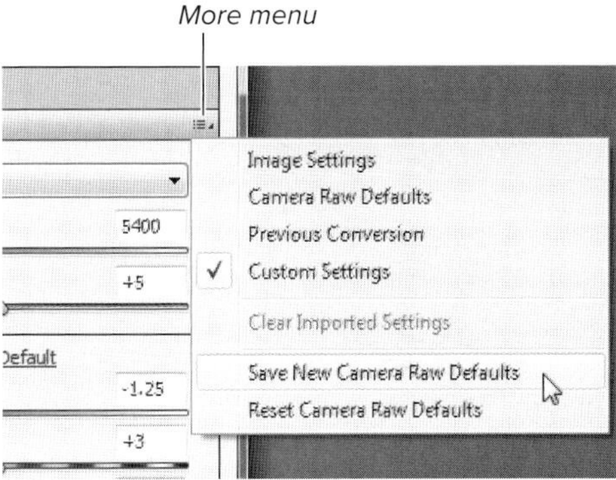

Ⓒ Save new defaults to avoid repetition.

Limitations of 16-bit Depth

At the bottom of the ACR window is a Depth drop-down menu that lets you choose between 16 Bits/Channel and 8 Bits/Channel. Raw images are often captured in 16-bit, which stores much more image data than 8-bit.

However, there's a problem: Although the Editor can open and work with 16-bit files, many features, such as adjustment layers, only work on 8-bit images and aren't accessible. (Also JPEG images are 8-bit, so if you want to save a copy of your photo as a JPEG, you must first switch to 8-bit.)

The solution is to either switch to 8 Bits/Channel in ACR, or choose Image > Mode > 8 Bits/Channel in the Editor.

- As you might expect, clicking the Cancel button exits ACR without applying any changes. However, hold Alt/Option and the Cancel button becomes the Reset button, which removes any edits you've made so far but keeps the file open.
- If you want to save a copy of the file as an Adobe .DNG (digital negative) file—a separate file format—click the Save Image button.

Changing Adobe Camera Raw defaults

If you find yourself making the same adjustments for every photo, you can save your settings as the ACR default. For example, let's say you always want to increase the Clarity by 10 and the Vibrance by 20.

To change ACR defaults:

1. Open a raw file and make the adjustments that you want to stick.
2. Click the More menu and choose Save New Camera Raw Defaults Ⓒ.

   The next time you open a raw file, those settings will be applied. You can go back to the original defaults by choosing Reset Camera Raw Defaults from the More menu.

Filters and Effects

For decades, photographers have used lens filters to improve and alter the look of their photographs when shooting—to change the intensity of color values, or lighten certain tones and darken others. For more creative effects, they would also rely on darkroom and printing techniques.

Thanks to the advancements of digital technology, though, you don't have to fiddle with chemicals or additional camera equipment to enhance your photographs. The filters and effects included in Photoshop Elements go far beyond what's been possible in traditional photography. Many of these filters (such as the Blur filters) allow you to make subtle corrections and improvements to your photos, whereas other filters (such as Artistic, Stylize, and Sketch) can transform an image into a completely new piece of artwork. Photoshop Elements also provides effects you can add to your photos, including striking image effects (lizard skin, anyone?) as well as type effects and unique textures.

In This Chapter

Using the Effects Panel

Photoshop Elements offers you almost unlimited possibilities for tweaking and enhancing your images. Most filters include a dialog where you can preview any changes and adjust the settings for either a subtle or dramatic effect. And some of the filters (such as the Liquify filter) are so comprehensive, they seem like separate applications within Photoshop Elements.

Effects work a bit differently than filters. When you apply an effect, Elements runs through a series of automatic actions in which a number of filters and layer styles are applied to your image. If you want to add a drop shadow, picture frame, or brushed-metal type to a photo, browse through the Effects panel to see what's available.

To view the Effects panel:

1. In the Editor, choose Window > Effects, or click the Effects button on the Task bar.
2. Click either the Filters or Photo Effects icon at the top of the Effects panel **A**.

A Access filters and photo effects from the Effects panel.

Filter and Effect Plug-ins

Plug-ins provide a nifty way to extend your Photoshop Elements experience. Want to add some sophisticated 3D shadows or translucent effects to your photos? If you can't find the effect or filter you want in Photoshop Elements, chances are good that a plug-in might do the trick. Most of the plug-ins designed for Photoshop will work just as well in Photoshop Elements, since both applications use the same file format (PSD). Some plug-in packages, clearly meant for professionals and creative types, don't come cheap—they can cost a few hundred dollars. But many plug-ins are available free of charge. One of the best places to start looking for filter and effect plug-ins is at the Adobe Exchange site (www.adobestudioexchange.com), where you can download and share filters, effects, and other plug-in goodies with other Photoshop and Photoshop Elements users.

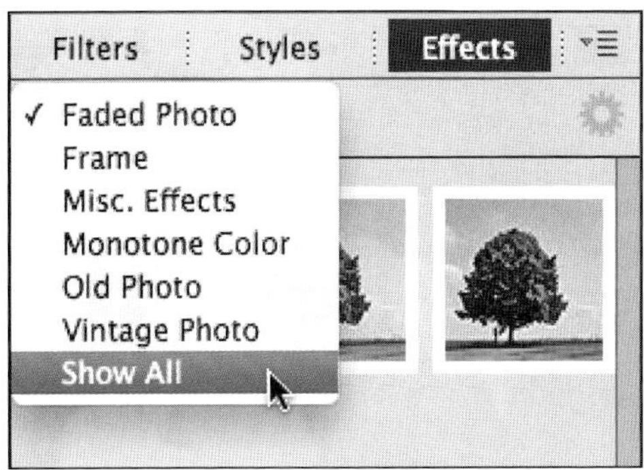

B When you select Show All from the Library drop-down menu, all filters or effects in their respective libraries are displayed at once.

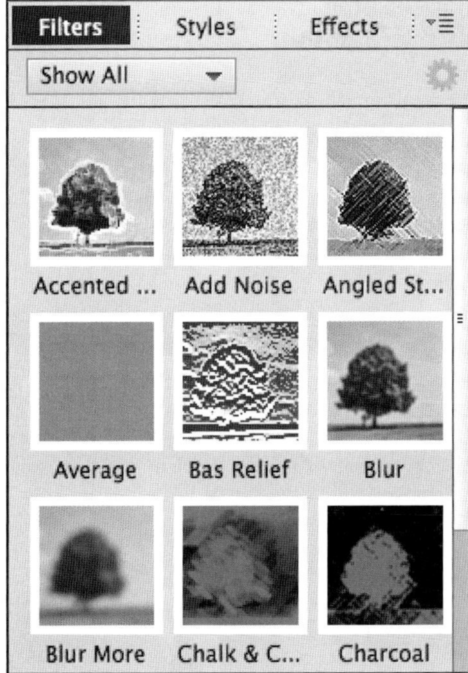

C Select Show Names from the Panel Options menu to display filters or effects with their names.

To change the number of filters or effects displayed in the panel:

Do one of the following:

- If it's not already selected, choose Show All from the Library drop-down menu to see all filters or effects **B**.
- Select a set of filters or effects from the Library drop-down menu to see just the ones in that set.

To change the panel view:

Do one of the following:

- From the Panel Options menu, choose Small, Medium, or Large Thumbnail View to change the size of the filters or effect previews. Medium is the default.
- From the Panel Options menu, choose Show Names to view the filters or effects with their identifying names **C**.

TIP Filter plug-ins created by third-party developers usually appear at the bottom of the Filters panel menu.

Applying Filters and Effects

Effects don't include a preview window, but you'll find useful examples of each effect on the Effects panel. For many filters and effects, a good approach is to select a small area of your image and apply the change to see the results—that way, you don't waste a lot of time waiting for your computer to process changes to the entire image. The exceptions are effects like Frames, where the effect is designed to be applied to your entire image. A few effects (such as the Cutout and Recessed frame effects) require you to make a selection before you can apply the effect.

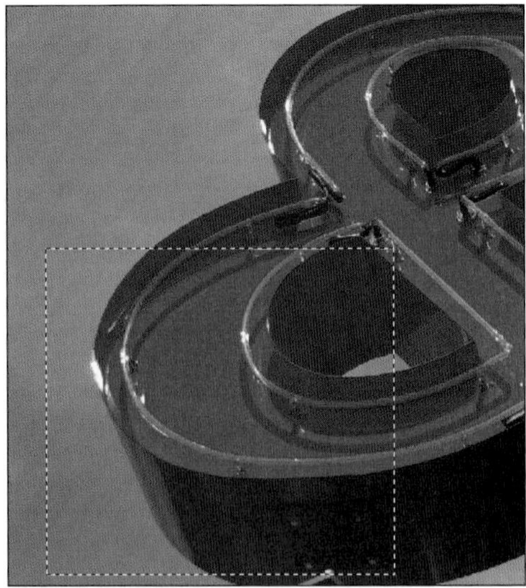

Ⓐ Filters and effects can be applied to an entire layer or to a selection.

To apply a filter:

1. To apply a filter to an entire layer, select the layer on the Layers panel to make the layer active. To apply a filter to just a portion of your image, select an area with one of the selection tools Ⓐ.
2. Do one of the following:
   - To immediately apply the filter or effect, double-click its button on the Effects panel; or, drag any filter from the Effects panel onto your image in the image window.
   - If you want to control how the effect appears, go to the Filter menu and choose a filter from one of the submenus. The Filter Options dialog appears Ⓑ. Continue following the next steps.
3. In the Filter Options dialog, experiment with the available values and options until you get the look you want.

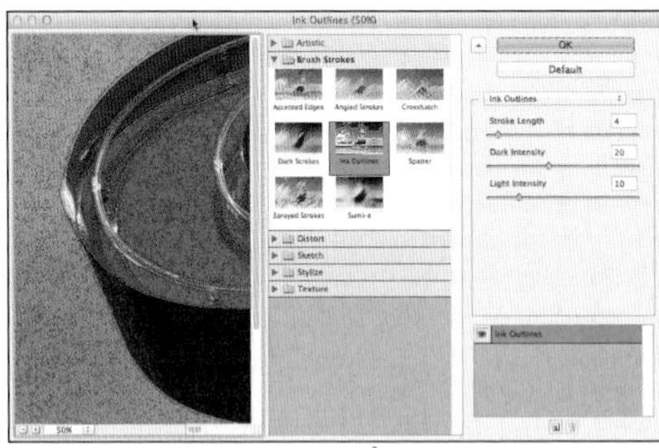

Ⓑ The Filter Options dialog includes a large preview window and sliders you can use to adjust a filter's settings.

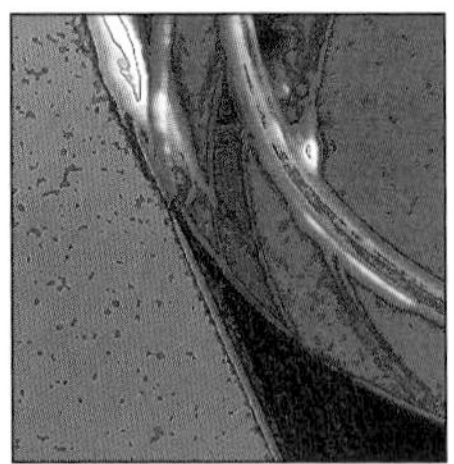

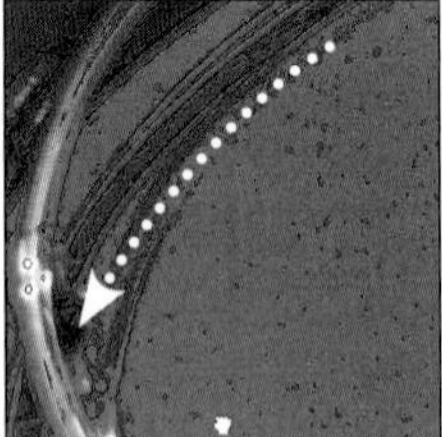

Ⓒ To move around (or pan) the preview image, just click and drag to move the image.

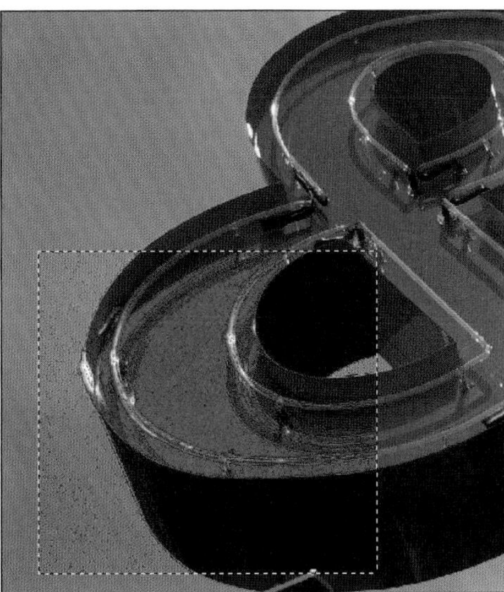

D After you click OK, the filter is applied to your image.

The Filter Dialogs

Given the sheer number of filters in Photoshop Elements, there's no way to cover the specific steps for each filter in the space of this book. Fortunately, the vast majority of these filters work the same way. So once you've used a couple of them, you can figure out the rest pretty easily. Most filters use the same Filter Options dialog with a preview window and slider bars that allow you to control the level and intensity of the filter. When using a filter for the first time, you should preview the default filter setting and apply it by clicking OK. Not what you wanted? Just press Ctrl+Z/Command-Z to undo your changes and start over. When you're back in the filter's dialog, you can experiment by adjusting the sliders to preview more (or less) dramatic results in your photo.

4. In the dialog preview window, you can change the view by doing one of the following:
   - To zoom in or out, click either the Zoom In (plus sign) or Zoom Out (minus sign) button.
   - To see a specific area of your image, click and drag within the preview window C.
5. Click OK. The filter is applied to your image D. If you're not happy with the result, choose Edit > Undo or select the previous state from the Undo History panel.

TIP Filters with additional options include ellipses (...) after their names.

TIP The list in the lower-right corner of the Filter Options dialog lets you add multiple filters before applying them to your image. Click the New Filter Layer button (the document icon) and choose another filter to see how it affects the image.

TIP As you add filters, you'll notice that you're presented with two different types of Option dialogs. The Add Noise filter, for instance, opens to a dialog specific to that filter. But filters contained in the Artistic, Brush Strokes, Distort, Sketch, Stylize, and Texture groups open to an Option dialog where you can not only adjust the settings for the filter you've selected, but also choose a completely different filter from a filter set menu in the center of the dialog. Just click any of the filter set names to open them, and then choose a new filter by clicking its thumbnail. A preview window changes to reflect the new filter you've selected.

To apply effects:

1. To apply an effect to an entire layer, select the layer to make it active. To apply an effect to just a portion of the image, select an area using one of the selection tools.
2. In the Effects panel, double-click the chosen effect **E**.

   If you prefer, you can also drag any effect from the Effects panel directly onto your image.

   When you apply an effect, it creates one or more new layers immediately above the selected layer **F**.

TIP To reduce the visible impact of an effect, change the opacity of the effect layer using the Opacity slider on the Layers panel.

TIP Sometimes the filter and effect names, and their thumbnails, don't represent the variety of results you might get by applying them to an image. Experiment by pushing the filter and effect options to extreme limits. You'll often be surprised by the results. Print a copy of your image for future reference and to use on other photos. It's also a good idea to rename the layer with a descriptive name related to the effect you used: for instance, Blizzard 30%.

TIP To change the look of an effect, experiment with the various blend modes on the Layers panel.

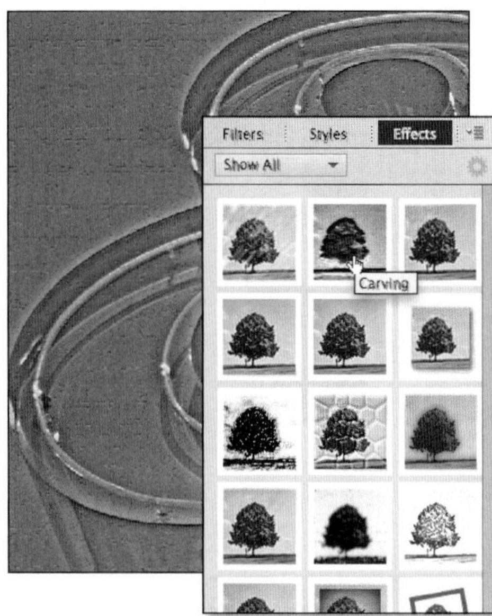

E Double-click any effect in the Effects panel to apply it to an image or selection. You can also drag an effect or filter from the panel into the image window.

F When you apply an effect, it generates one or more layers above the selected layer. The number of new layers depends on the series of actions required to create the specific effect.

A You can apply the Motion Blur filter to an entire layer or to a selection, as I'll do in this photo.

B Once you've chosen a layer or selection, double-click the Motion Blur thumbnail.

Simulating Action with the Blur Filters

Photoshop Elements includes a few blur filters that can create a sense of motion where none exists. In many cases, you'll want to select a specific area in your photo when using these filters, so that the motion or movement is applied to one object, such as a person, your dog, or a pair of shoes.

The Motion Blur filter blurs a layer or selection in a specific direction and intensity. The result simulates the look of taking a picture of a moving object with a fixed exposure or of panning a camera across a still scene.

The Radial Blur filter creates the impression of a camera zoom or of an object moving toward or away from you. You can also create the impression of an object spinning at variable rates of speed. In either case, the Radial Blur filter lets you control the center of the effect and the amount of blurring or motion.

To add a motion blur to an image:

1. Select the desired layer to make it active. To create a feeling of motion in just a portion of your image, select an area with one of the selection tools A.
2. Do one of the following:
   - To apply the default settings, choose Blur from the Library drop-down menu on the Effects panel, and double-click the Motion Blur filter B.
   - To customize the settings, go to the Filter menu and choose Blur > Motion Blur. The Motion Blur dialog appears with options for the motion angle and distance.

continues on next page

3. Set the Angle and Distance options to get the look you want **C**. You can refer to the preview window in the dialog, and if the Preview option is checked, you can also see the results in the main image window.

   By default, the Angle option is set to 0°, meaning that the pixels will be blurred along the horizontal axis as shown next to the Angle text field. So, the impression of motion will be right to left (or left to right) across your screen. You can change the angle by dragging the line on the Angle icon or by entering a number of degrees in the Angle text box.

   The Distance option determines the number of pixels included in the linear blur, with the default set to 10 pixels (a moderate amount of blurring). When you reach the upper limits of this option (999 pixels), the objects in your photo may become barely recognizable.

4. When you are satisfied with the effect, click OK to apply it to your image **D**.

TIP It may look more realistic if you feather your selection before applying the blur (choose Select > Feather). See Chapter 6 for more on feathering selections.

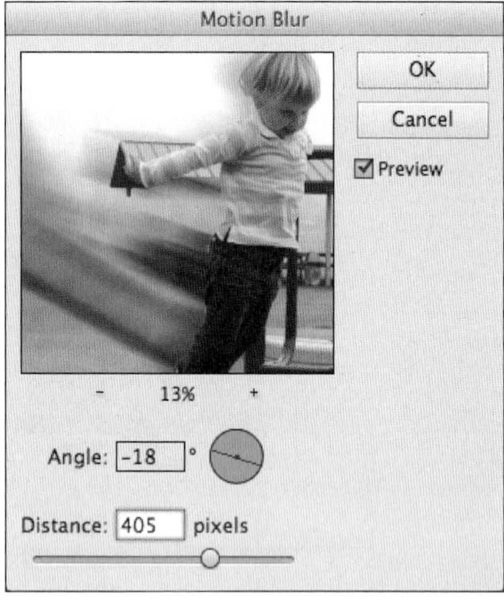

C The Motion Blur dialog includes options for the angle and distance of the effect.

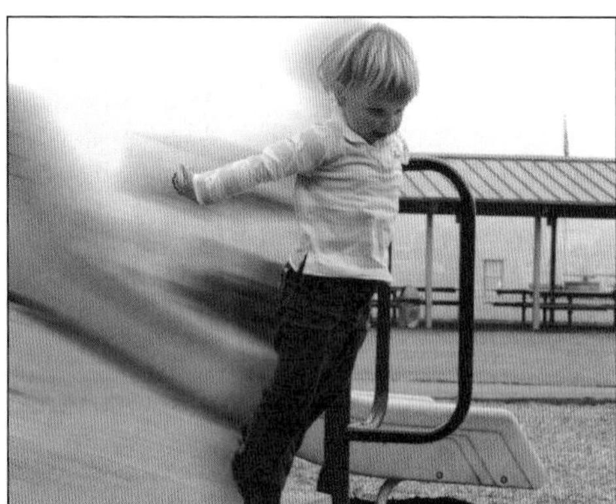

D Click OK to see the Motion Blur filter applied to your image. If you want to back up and try again, just choose Edit > Undo and experiment with different settings.

E The Radial Blur dialog does not include a preview, but the Quality options include Draft, which you can use to quickly apply and view the effects of the filter on your image.

Spin *Zoom*

F To change the center point, drag the preview in the Blur Center window.

To add a circular blur to an image:

1. Select the desired layer to make it active. To create a feeling of radial motion in just a portion of your image, select an area with one of the selection tools.

   A circular (elliptical) selection works especially well when you want to create a circular effect.

2. Select the Radial Blur by doing one of the following:
   - To apply the effect's default settings, double-click the Radial Blur filter on the Effects panel.
   - To specify the settings, go to the Filter menu and choose Blur > Radial Blur. The Radial Blur dialog appears, with options for amount of blur, blur center, blur method, and quality **E**.

3. Set the Amount and Blur Center values.

   The two Blur Method options are Spin and Zoom **F**. Choose Spin to blur along circular lines or Zoom to blur along lines radiating from the center, as if you were zooming in or out of an image.

4. Select a Quality option for the filter.

   Draft quality produces a quicker rendering of the filter, but with slightly coarse results. The Good and Best options both take a bit longer to render, but provide a smoother look; there's not a big difference between the latter two options.

5. When you are satisfied with the effect, click OK to apply it to your image.

TIP The Radial Blur filter doesn't include a preview window, so if you aren't happy with the results and want to try different settings, just click the Edit Undo button (or press Ctrl+Z/Command-Z) to try again.

To simulate depth of field with Lens Blur:

1. Duplicate the image layer so you're working on a copy.
2. Use the selection tools to select the area you want to keep in focus.
3. Click the Add a Mask button in the Layers panel to create a mask **G**.
4. Click the layer thumbnail so the mask isn't selected.
5. Choose Filter > Blur > Lens Blur to open the Lens Blur dialog.
6. In the Depth Map area, click the Source drop-down menu and choose Layer Mask.
7. In the Iris area, increase the Radius setting to blur portions of the image **H**.
8. Use the Blur Focal Distance to set which areas are to be in focus: a low setting is closer to the camera, while a high setting is farther away **I**. Click the Invert button to swap the depths if that's convenient.
9. Use the other Iris, Specular Highlights, and Noise settings to adjust how the image appears.
10. Click OK to finish.
11. In the Layers panel, right-click the layer mask and choose Disable Layer Mask to make the blur effect visible **J**.

TIP If you don't want to isolate specific elements in a photo, you can skip the selection in step 2. When you make a layer mask, fill it with a gradient (using the Gradient tool). The effect is a graduated falloff of focus from the darkest pixels of the mask to the lightest pixels.

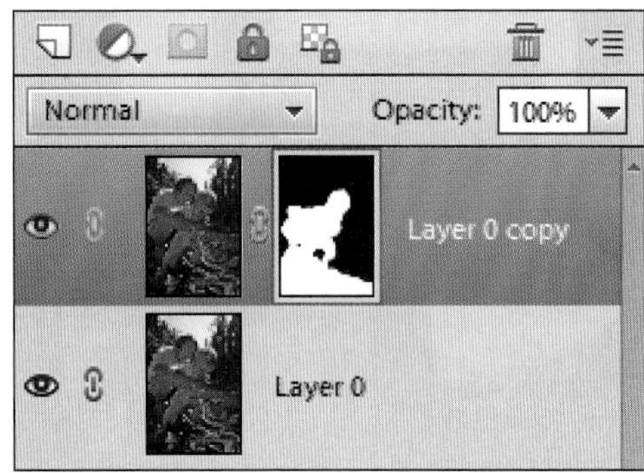

G Setting a layer mask defines which areas will be blurred using the Lens Blur filter.

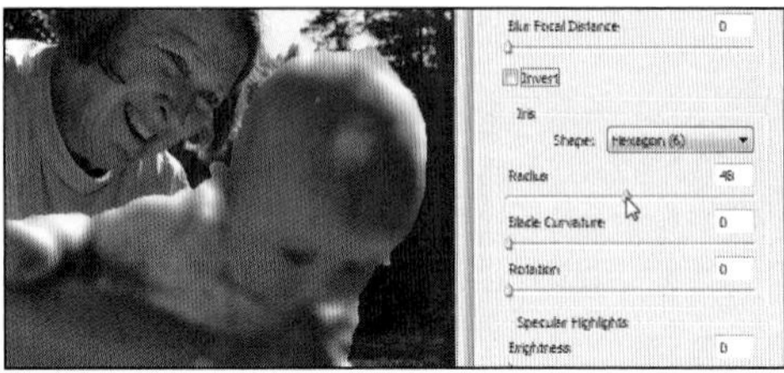

H Change the Radius value to set the amount of blur to simulate depth of field.

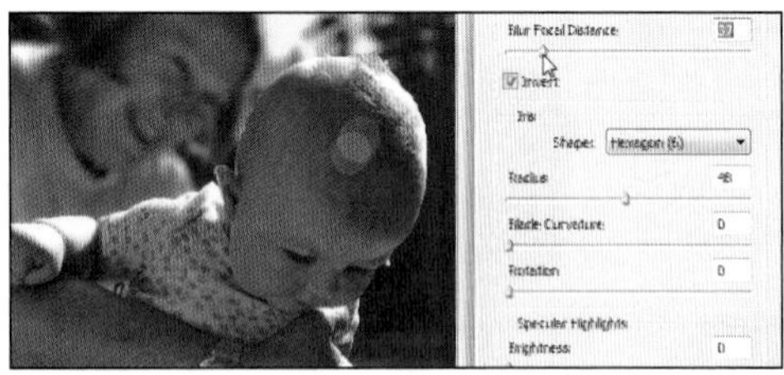

I The Blur Focal Distance slider determines how close or far the effect appears.

Original

Lens Zoom applied

J The finished effect.

The Liquify Tools

Warp lets you push pixels around as you drag with the mouse.

Turbulence is similar to the Warp tool, but it incorporates some actions of the other Liquify tools to create random variations, or turbulence. You can change the amount of turbulence with the Turbulence Jitter slider in the tool options.

Twirl Clockwise and **Twirl Counterclockwise** rotate pixels in either direction.

Pucker moves pixels toward the center of the brush area.

Bloat moves pixels away from the brush center and toward the edges of your brush.

Shift Pixels moves pixels perpendicular to the direction of your brush stroke.

Reflection copies pixels to the brush area, allowing you to create effects similar to a reflection in water.

Reconstruct restores distorted areas to their original state. As you brush over areas with this tool, your image gradually returns to its original state, undoing each change you've made with the Liquify tools. You can stop the reconstruction at any point and continue from there.

The **Zoom** and **Hand** tools work just like those on the Photoshop Elements toolbar.

Distorting Images

The Distort filters include an amazing array of options that let you ripple, pinch, shear, and twist your images. Experiment with all of the Distort filters to get a feel for the different effects you can apply to your images. One filter in particular stands above the others in its power and flexibility: Liquify.

The Liquify filter creates amazing effects by letting you warp, twirl, stretch, and twist pixels beyond the normal laws of physics. You've probably seen plenty of examples of this filter, where someone's face is wildly distorted with bulging eyes and a puckered mouth. However, you can also use the Liquify filter to create more subtle changes and achieve effects that would be impossible with any other tool.

The Liquify filter is unique in that it includes a dialog with its own complete set of image manipulation tools. And because the Liquify filter works within its own dialog box, you can't undo specific changes with the Edit > Undo command or Undo History panel. Fortunately, the Liquify filter offers its own Reconstruct tool to restore any area to its original (or less contorted) state. The Reconstruct tool allows you to "paint" over your image and gradually return to the original version, or stop at any state along the way. If you just want to go back and start over, clicking the Revert button is the quickest method.

To distort an image with the Liquify filter:

1. Select an entire layer, or make a selection of the area you want to change.
2. From the Filter menu, choose Distort > Liquify; or, on the Effects panel, choose Distort from the Library drop-down menu and double-click the Liquify filter.

   If your image includes a type layer, you will be prompted to simplify the type to continue. This means the type layer will be flattened into the rest of your image's layers. Be aware that if you click OK, the type will no longer be editable.

   The Liquify dialog appears, including a preview of the layer or selection area. The Warp tool is selected by default, with a brush size of 64 and a pressure of 50 **A**.

   You'll probably want to change the brush size and pressure during the course of your work.
3. To change the brush settings, do one of the following:
   - To change the brush size, drag the slider or enter a value in the option box. The brush size ranges from 1 to 600 pixels.
   - To change the brush pressure, drag the slider or enter a value in the option box. The brush pressure ranges from 1 to 100 percent.
4. Distort your image with any of the Liquify tools located on the left side of the dialog **B** until you achieve the look you want. To use any tool, simply select it (just as you do tools on the main toolbar) and then move your pointer into the image **C**.

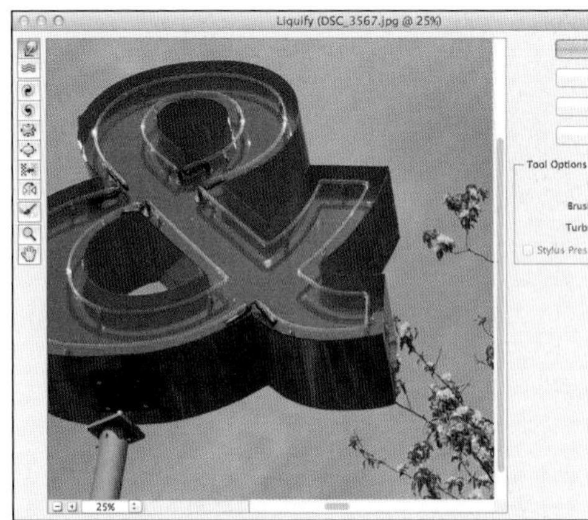

A The Liquify dialog includes its own set of distortion tools as well as options for changing the brush size and pressure.

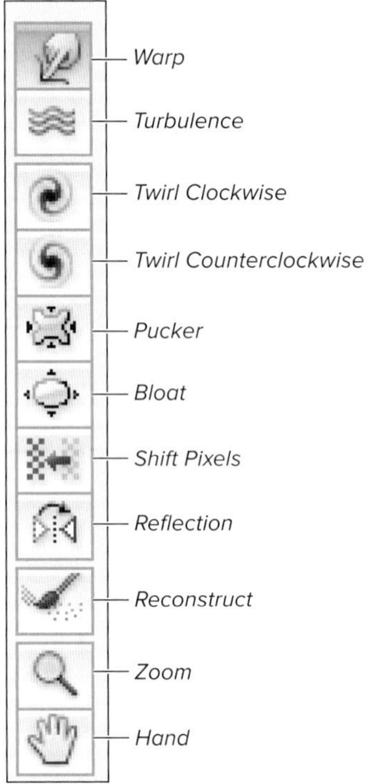

B The Liquify tool set.

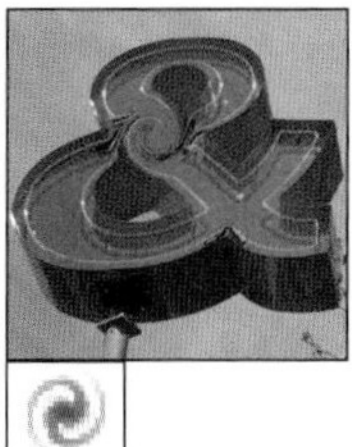
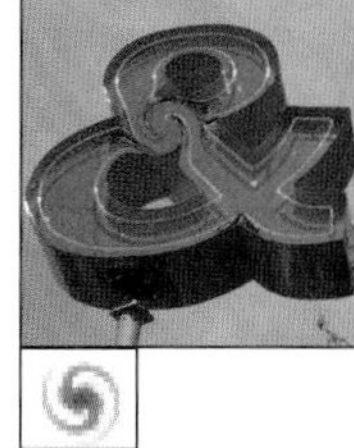

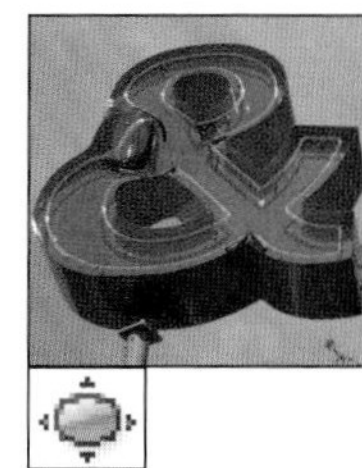
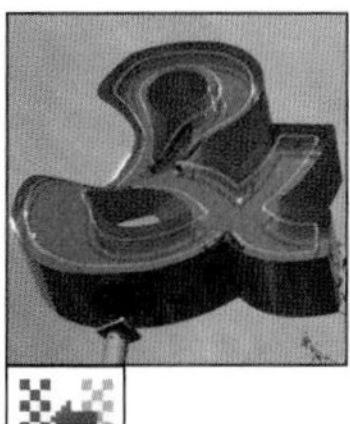

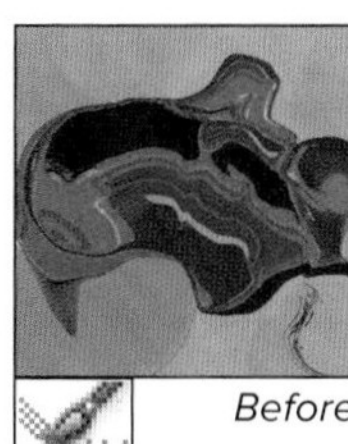
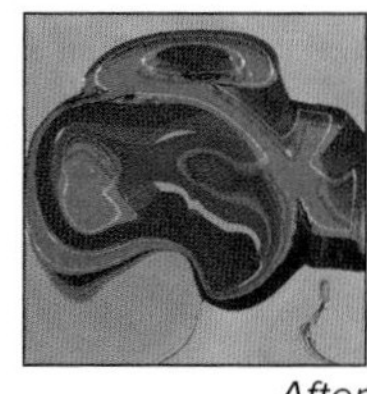

Before *After*

C The best way to become familiar with the Liquify distortion tools is to experiment with them on a variety of images, as in this series of photos.

To undo changes:

In the Liquify dialog, click the Reconstruct tool. Then, while holding down your mouse button, "brush" over your image to gradually undo each change you've made.

To undo all Liquify changes:

In the Liquify dialog, click the Revert button to return the image to its original state.

TIP **Here's another way to undo Liquify changes: In the Liquify dialog, hold down the Alt/Option key. The Cancel button changes to Reset. Click the Reset button to undo any changes you've made with the Liquify tools. The Revert and Reset buttons work the same way, but the Reset button, true to its name, also resets the Liquify tools to their original settings.**

TIP **The Reflection tool can be a little hard to master. You may find it works better if you use a large brush size and 100 percent pressure. Also, the direction of your stroke determines which way the image is reflected.**

Correcting Camera Distortion

Most cameras may be digital these days, but it's still an optical medium, and every camera has tradeoffs; for example, some lenses offer incredible zoom, but at the expense of introducing barrel distortion around the edges. The Correct Camera Distortion filter provides tools to compensate.

To correct camera distortion:

1. Select a layer or make a selection to edit.
2. From the Filter menu, choose Correct Camera Distortion. The dialog of the same name appears **A**.
3. Apply the following controls based on the distortion found in your image:
   - Remove Distortion. Drag the slider to the left to bloat the image or to the right to pinch it **B**.
   - Vignette. To add or remove a vignette (such as found in old photographs), drag the Amount slider to match the vignette area. Use the Midpoint slider to adjust the vignette's size.
   - Perspective Control. Drag the Vertical and Horizontal Perspective sliders to tilt the image. The Angle control rotates the image.
   - Edge Extension. After using the controls above, you may want to scale the image with Edge Extension to crop unwanted blank areas caused by the adjustments.
4. Click OK to apply the changes.

TIP As with most adjustment dialogs, hold Alt/Option and click the Cancel button if you want to reset the dialog's settings.

A Correct Camera Distortion fixes many common photographic gaffes.

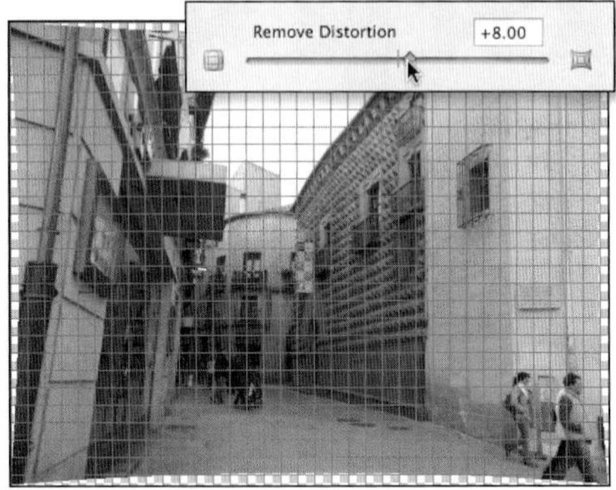

B The corner of the building on the left curves due to lens distortion (top), so I've applied a small amount of Remove Distortion to pinch the image slightly and straighten the curve (bottom).

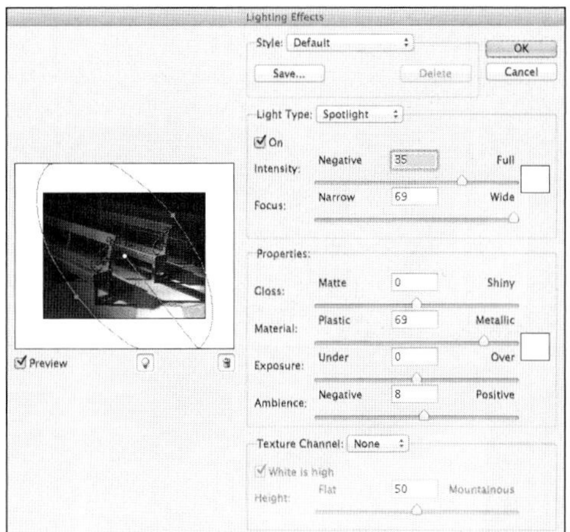

Ⓐ When you first open the Lighting Effects dialog, it may seem a bit intimidating. But it only takes a little experimentation with the settings to see the range of effects possible with this filter.

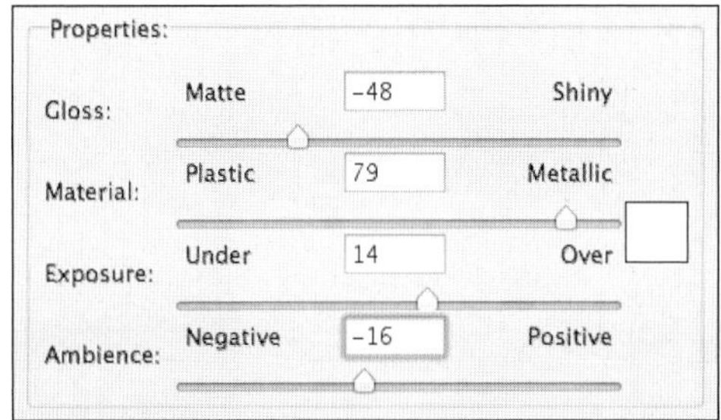

Ⓑ The Properties area offers an almost infinite combination of settings you can use to change the appearance and intensity of the lighting.

Ⓒ The Triple Spotlight filter has been applied to this image.

Creating Lights and Shadows

Lights and shadows add drama to almost any photograph. It's always best to plan your lighting before you take your picture, but there are times when you just can't control these factors. Elements includes some nifty filters to help you enhance the lighting after the fact. The Lighting Effects filter lets you create a seemingly infinite number of effects through a combination of light styles, properties, and even a texture channel. It's almost like having your own lighting studio.

To add lighting effects to an image:

1. Select the desired layer to make it active. To confine the lighting effect to just a portion of your image, select an area using one of the selection tools.
2. Select the Lighting Effects filter by doing one of the following:
   - To apply a default effect, go to the Effects panel, choose Render from the Library drop-down menu, and double-click the Lighting Effects filter.
   - To adjust the settings, go to the Filter menu and choose Render > Lighting Effects. The Lighting Effects dialog appears Ⓐ.
3. Choose a predefined Style, or create your own using the following controls:
   - Choose a Light Type from the drop-down menu, which includes Directional, Omni, and Spotlight options. Each lighting style is based on one of these three light types.
   - Set light properties Ⓑ.
4. When you are satisfied with the effect, click OK to apply it to your image Ⓒ.

Light styles and types

The Lighting Effects dialog offers a mind-boggling number of properties, light types, and styles, making it more than a little difficult to figure out where to start. Here's a list of some of the most useful lighting styles and types.

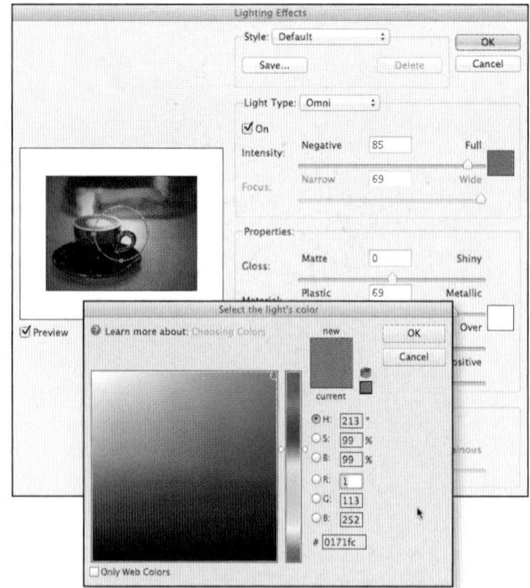

D Some lighting styles, such as Blue Omni, include colored lights. Change the color by clicking the lighting color box, which opens the Color Picker.

Lighting styles

- Flashlight focuses a direct spotlight on the center of the image, with the rest of the image darkened. It's set at a medium intensity with a slightly yellow cast.
- Floodlight has a wider focus and casts a white light on your image.
- Soft Omni and Soft Spotlight provide gentle lightbulb and spotlight effects respectively, and work well for many different kinds of images.
- Blue Omni adds a blue overhead light to your image and offers insight into how lighting styles and types work together. If you select this light type, you'll see a blue color box in the Light Type area of the dialog. If you click on this box, the Color Picker appears **D**, letting you change the color to anything you want. Once you've chosen a new color, click OK to apply your custom lighting style to your photo.
- Most of the remaining lighting styles create more dramatic and specialized effects (for example, RGB Lights consists of red, green, and blue spotlights), but are worth exploring.

E The Directional light produces a light source that shines in one direction across your photo, as indicated by the line in the image preview window.

Light types

- Directional creates an angled light that shines from one direction across your photo **E**.

F The Omni light creates the impression of a light shining directly onto your photo. To change the size of the lit area, drag one of the boundary handles.

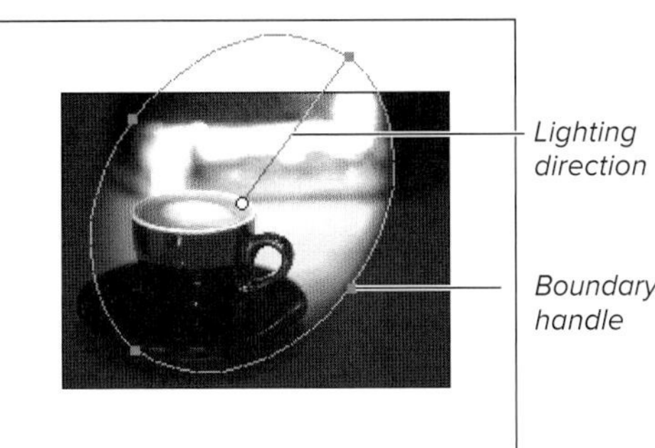

G The Spotlight is represented by an elliptical boundary in the preview. Drag a handle to change the area being lit, and drag the lighting direction line to change the direction of the light source.

- Omni produces a light that shines down on your image from above **F**.
- Spotlight creates a round spotlight in the center of your image. In preview mode, you'll see that the boundaries of the light look like an ellipse. You can change the size of the ellipse by dragging any of the handles. To change the direction of the light, just drag to move the line **G**.

When you select a light style, it automatically defaults to whichever light type best supports that look—so, for example, the Floodlight style uses the Spotlight type.

Light properties

Once you've chosen a light style and type, you have complete control over four different lighting properties.

- Gloss establishes how much light reflects off your image and can be set from Matte (less reflection) to Shiny (more reflection).
- Material determines the surface properties of your image. It can be set from Plastic to Metallic. As you move the setting toward Plastic, the highlights scatter across the surface more; with Metallic, the highlights are more contained.
- Exposure increases or decreases the light. If you click through the light types, you'll notice that most of them leave this setting at, or close to, 0. This is one setting you may just want to leave as is or only subtly change since it has such a pronounced impact on the light.
- Ambience refers to ambient lighting, or how much you combine the particular lighting effect with the existing light in your photo. Positive values allow in more ambient light, and negative values allow less.

To add a lens flare:

1. Select the desired layer to make it active. To confine the lighting effect to just a portion of your image, select an area using one of the selection tools.
2. Select the Lens Flare filter by doing one of the following:
   - To apply a default setting, go to the Effects panel, choose Render from the Library drop-down menu, and double-click the Lens Flare filter.
   - To specify settings, go to the Filter menu and choose Render > Lens Flare. The Lens Flare dialog appears, with options for the brightness, flare center, and lens type **H**.
3. Set the brightness option by dragging the slider to the right to increase or to the left to decrease the brightness.
4. To move the flare center, just click the image preview to move the crosshairs to another location.
5. Set the Lens Type options as desired, and when you're happy with what you see, click OK to apply the filter to your image **I**.

   The options include settings for three common camera lenses (50–300mm Zoom, 35mm, and 105mm), plus Movie Prime, and the filter creates a look similar to the refraction or lens flare you'd get with each one **J**.

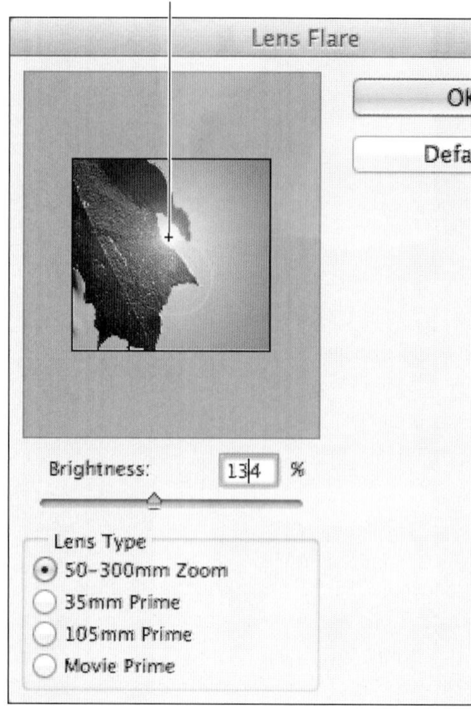

H The Lens Flare dialog adjusts the brightness, flare center, and lens type.

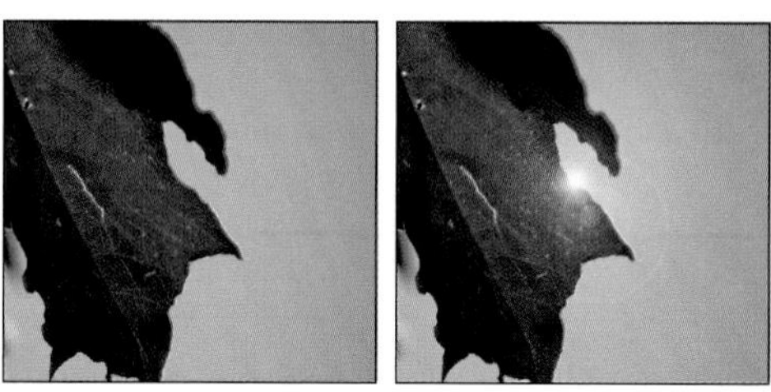

I I applied the Lens Flare filter with the default brightness and lens type options.

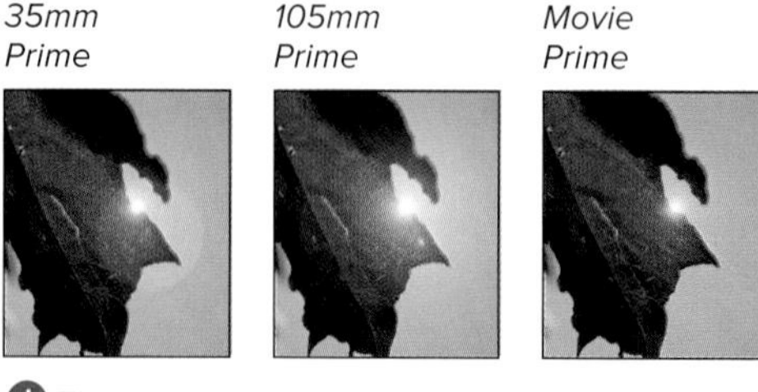

J The lens options can be subtle.

Painting and Drawing

A lifetime ago (in computer years, anyway) a little company just south of San Francisco introduced a small beige box with a tiny 9-inch keyhole of a monitor and a mouse resembling a bar of soap. It could display and print only in black and white, was incapable of reproducing even remotely convincing photographic images, and was strictly limited to a resolution of 72 pixels per inch. And yet graphic artists smiled a collective smile, because bundled in its modest software suite, alongside its stunted little word processor, Apple's Macintosh gave the world MacPaint.

Painting and drawing programs have jumped by leaps and bounds since taking those first, early baby steps, but one feature remains the same: They're still fun to use!

In this chapter, you'll learn how to use Photoshop Elements' built-in drawing and painting tools to create original artwork or to enhance your digital photos—whether you're filling parts of your image with color, adding a decorative stroked border to a logo or design element, or "painting" a photo with Impressionist-style brushstrokes.

In This Chapter

About Bitmap Images and Vector Graphics

Photoshop Elements' painting and drawing tools render artwork in two fundamentally different ways.

The painting tools, including all the varied fills, gradients, brushes, and erasers, work by making changes to pixels—adding them, removing them, or changing their colors. A bitmap image is composed entirely of tiny pixels; and digital photos, the mainstay of Photoshop Elements, are bitmap images. Although you can apply paintbrushes, color fills, special effects, and filters to bitmaps, they simply don't resize well. If you try to enlarge a digital photo, for example, you'll see that its image quality suffers as the pixels get bigger, resulting in a blurry mess.

The drawing tools (shape creation tools, really) form images not by manipulating pixels but by constructing geometric paths based on precise mathematical coordinates, or vectors. Images created with these drawing tools, known as vector graphics, hold one decided advantage over their bitmap cousins: They can be scaled up or down, virtually infinitely, with no loss of detail or resolution **A**. Elements' scalable fonts, for example, are based on vector shapes, so they can be stretched, warped, and resized to your heart's content. Vector graphics files also tend to be smaller than comparable bitmap image files, since a path shape requires less information for your computer to process and render than a similar shape constructed of pixels.

Although designed to work with different kinds of graphics, the painting and drawing tools are equally easy to use, and work well together if you want to combine vector and bitmap graphics—such as adding type or custom shapes to a favorite photo.

A A photographic bitmap image is constructed of pixels (top). Any attempt to zoom in on or enlarge a portion of the image can make the pixels more pronounced and the image more pixelated. A vector image (bottom) is drawn with a series of geometric paths rather than pixels. Vector graphics can be enlarged or reduced with no loss of detail or resolution.

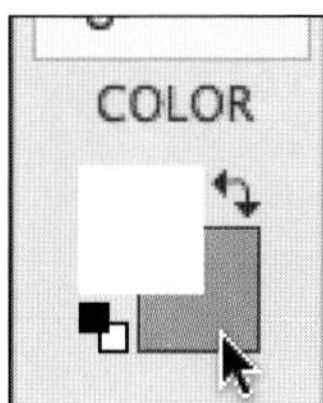

A Clicking the foreground or background color swatch in the Tools pane opens the Color Picker.

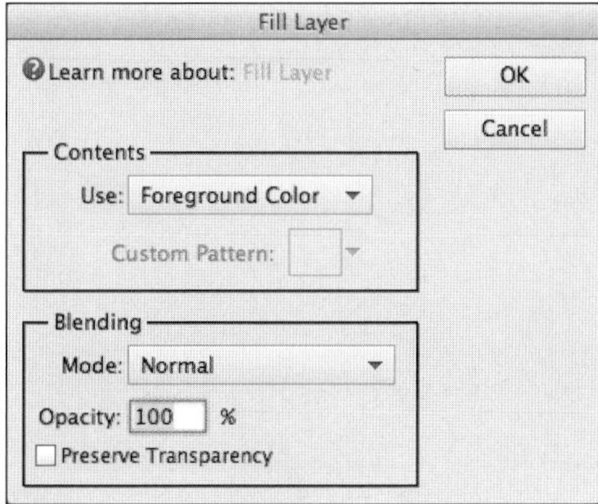

B The Fill Layer dialog offers several options for filling a layer or selection with color.

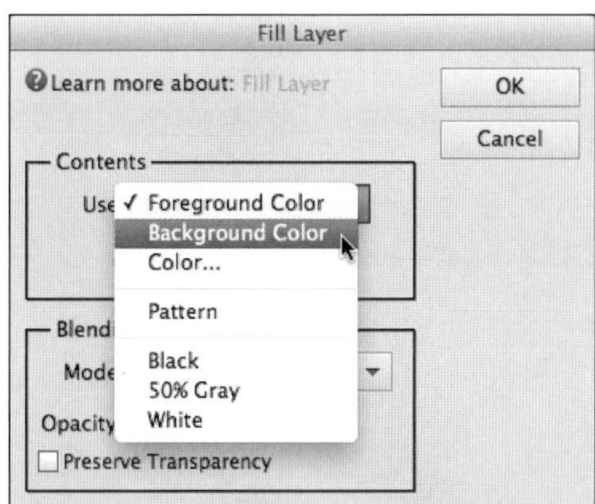

C The Use drop-down menu contains various sources from which to choose a fill color. Choose the Foreground Color option to apply a specific color chosen from the Color Picker or Swatches panel.

Filling Areas with Color

You have two primary ways of filling areas with a solid color. With the Fill dialog, you can quickly blanket an entire layer or a selected area of a layer with color. The Paint Bucket tool operates in a more controlled manner, filling only portions of areas based on properties that you set on the Tool Options bar. Either method works especially well for those times when you want to cover large, expansive areas with a single color.

To fill a selection or layer with color:

1. Using any of the selection or marquee tools, select the area of your image you want to fill with color.

   If you want to fill an entire layer, it's not necessary to make a selection.

2. To select a fill color, do one of the following:

   - Click either the current foreground or background color swatch at the bottom of the Tools pane **A** to open the Color Picker; then select a color.
   - Make the Color Swatches panel visible and click any color.

3. From the Edit menu, choose either Fill Selection or Fill Layer to open the Fill Layer dialog **B**.

4. From the Use drop-down menu, choose a source for your fill color **C**.

   In addition to the foreground and background colors, you can use the Fill command to fill a selection or area with a pattern or with black, white, or 50-percent gray. Or you can choose Color to open the Color Picker and select a different color altogether.

continues on next page

5. From the Blending area of the dialog, select a blending mode and opacity for your fill. (For more information on blending modes, see "About Opacity and Blending Modes" in Chapter 7.)
6. Click the Preserve Transparency checkbox if you want to maintain a layer's transparency when you apply the fill.
7. Click OK to close the dialog.

   The selection or layer is filled with the color and properties you specified D.

D In this example, an area of the Background layer is selected (left), then filled with a color using the Fill dialog (right).

TIP To save time, use simple keyboard shortcuts to fill a selection or layer with either the current foreground or background color. Alt+Delete/Option-Delete will fill a selection or layer with the current foreground color, and Ctrl+Delete/Command-Delete applies the current background color.

TIP To swap the foreground and background color swatches in the Tools pane, press X.

TIP To convert the foreground and background color to black and white (the defaults), press D.

About Preserving Transparency

The Preserve Transparency checkbox works just like the Lock Transparent Pixels button on the Layers panel. If the checkbox is highlighted and you fill a layer that has both opaque and transparent pixels, the transparent areas will be locked (or protected), and only the opaque areas of the layer will be filled E. If you check Preserve Transparency and then try to fill an empty layer (one containing only transparent pixels), the layer remains unfilled. That's because the whole layer, being transparent, is locked. If you fill a flattened layer, like Photoshop Elements' default background layer, the checkbox is dimmed and the option isn't available because a background layer contains no transparency.

E When a layer (left) is filled using the Preserve Transparency option, the transparent areas of the layer remain protected and untouched, and only the layer object accepts the fill color (right).

F The Paint Bucket tool.

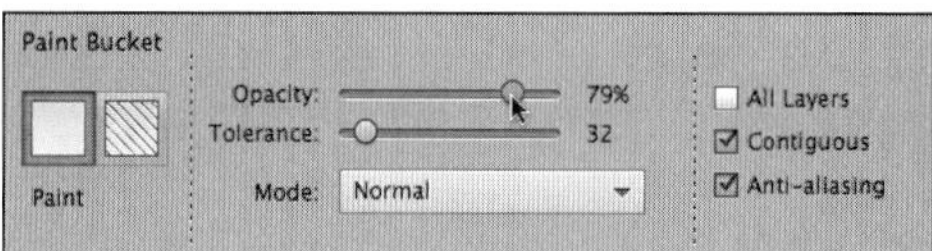

G The Paint Bucket tool takes advantage of all of Photoshop Elements' blending modes and opacity options.

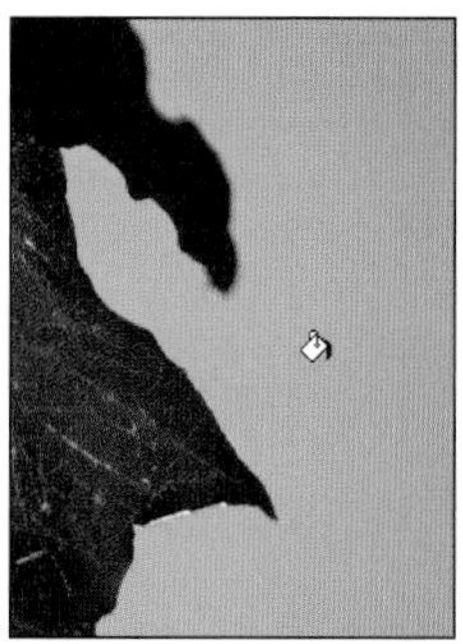

H The Paint Bucket tool fills areas based on their tonal values. Here it automatically selects and fills just the light-colored background area.

To apply fill color with the Paint Bucket tool:

1. Select the Paint Bucket tool from the Tools pane (or press K) **F**.
2. Select a foreground color from either the Color Picker or the Color Swatches panel.
3. On the Tool Options bar, select a blending mode and opacity setting if you want **G**.
4. Still on the Tool Options bar, set a Tolerance value; then specify whether you want the colored fill to be anti-aliased, to fill only contiguous pixels, or to affect all layers.

   For more information on these options, see the sidebar "How Does that Paint Bucket Tool Work, Anyway?" on the next page.
5. Click the area of your image where you want to apply the colored fill.

   The selected color is painted into your image **H**.

How Does That Paint Bucket Tool Work, Anyway?

If you're familiar with other painting and drawing programs, Photoshop Elements' Paint Bucket tool may leave you scratching your head. In many paint programs, the Paint Bucket tool does little more than indiscriminately dump color across large areas of an image. But Elements' Paint Bucket tool is much more intelligent and selective about where it applies color. Depending on the parameters you set in the Tool Options bar, it fills areas based on the tonal values of their pixels.

The Tolerance slider determines the range of pixels the Paint Bucket fills. The greater the value, the larger the range of pixels filled.

Click Anti-aliasing to add a smooth, soft transition to the edges of your color fill.

Click Contiguous to limit the fill to pixels similar in color or tonal value that touch, or are contiguous with, one another. If you're using the Paint Bucket tool to switch your car's color from green to blue, this ensures that only the car's green pixels are turned blue—not all the green pixels within the entire image.

If you select the All Layers checkbox, Photoshop Elements recognizes and considers pixel colors and values across all layers, but the fill is applied only to the active layer. This means if you click the Paint Bucket tool in an area of any inactive layer, the fill will be applied to the current active layer **I**.

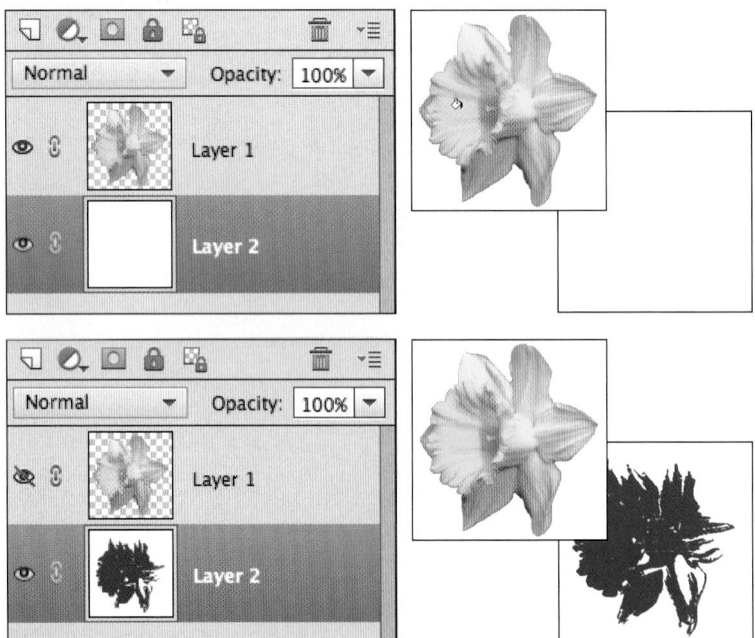

I If the All Layers checkbox is selected and you click the Paint Bucket tool in an inactive layer (top), the fill for that specific area is applied to the active layer (bottom).

Ⓐ The Gradient tool.

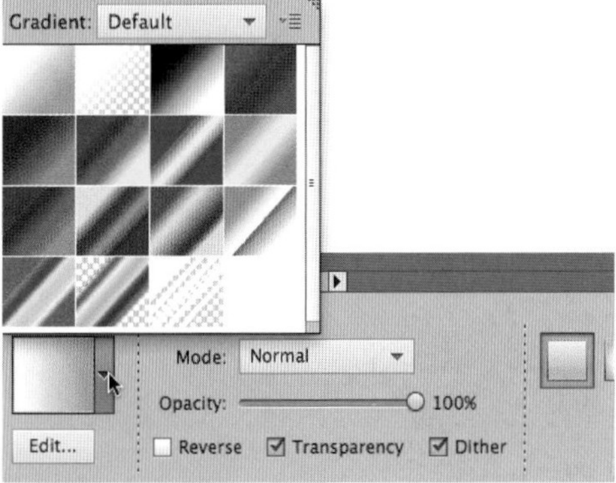

Ⓑ Open the Gradient Picker to select from sets of gradient thumbnails.

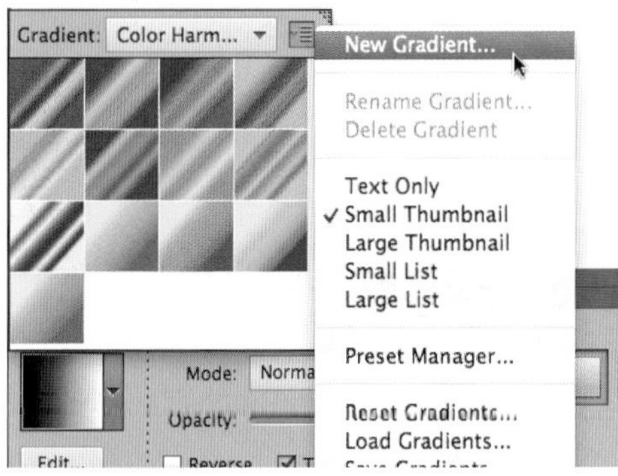

Ⓒ The Gradient Picker menu offers several picker display options plus access to a variety of gradient sets.

Filling Areas with a Gradient

The Gradient tool fills any selection or layer with smooth transitions of color, one blending gradually into the next. It can be rendered as an opaque fill or seamlessly incorporated into a layered project using any of Elements' blending modes and opacity settings. Use a gradient to create an effective background image for a photo, to screen back a portion of an image, or to create an area on which to place type. Or you can apply it to any shape or object to simulate the surface texture of metal or glass.

To apply a gradient fill:

1. Using any of the selection or marquee tools, select the area of your image where you want to apply the gradient.

   If you want to fill an entire layer, you don't need to make a selection.

2. Select the Gradient tool from the Tools pane (or press G) Ⓐ.

3. On the Tool Options bar, click to open the Gradient Picker Ⓑ.

4. Click to choose from the list of default gradients, or if you want to view additional gradient sets, click the More button (the triangles to the right of the thumbnail images) to open the Gradient Picker menu Ⓒ.

   Gradient sets are located at the bottom of the menu. When you select a new gradient set, it replaces the set displayed in the Gradient Picker.

continues on next page

5. In the Tool Options bar, click to choose a gradient style **D**.

   Choose from five gradient styles: Linear, Radial, Angle, Reflected, and Diamond.

6. In the image window, click and drag in the area where you want to apply the gradient **E**.

   The selection or layer is filled with the gradient.

TIP Hold down the Shift key to constrain a gradient horizontally, vertically, or at a 45-degree angle.

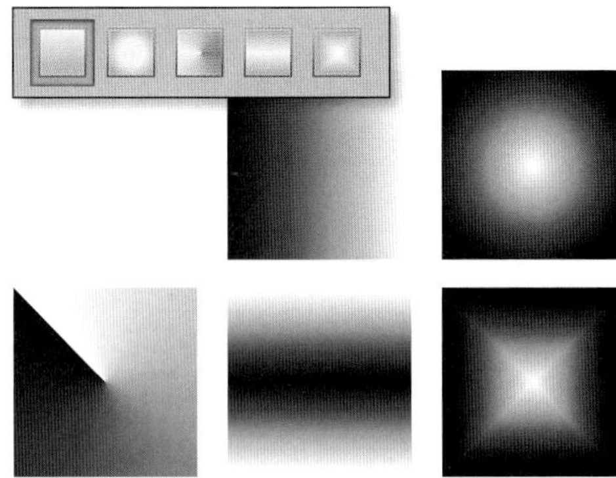

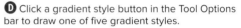

D Click a gradient style button in the Tool Options bar to draw one of five gradient styles.

E Drag from the center to the edge to create a halo effect with the Radial gradient.

Gradient Types

You can create two gradient types from the Gradient Editor: Solid and Noise.

Solid is the default gradient type. When creating or editing a gradient in Solid mode, you can add color and opacity stops and adjust the smoothness of the transition between colors with a percentage slider. You can also change the location of the Color and Opacity stops and their midpoints.

Noise is, well, largely useless. Noise creates random bands of color based on either the RGB or HSB color model, and although there must be some good application for it somewhere, I have yet to stumble on what it might be. Feel free to experiment with this gradient, but you probably won't end up using it much.

Adding a Stroke to a Selection or Layer

Photoshop Elements' Stroke command adds a colored rule or border around any selected object or layer. With the Stroke command, you can easily trace around almost anything, from simple rectangle or ellipse selections to complex typographic characters. Because you can control both the stroke's thickness and where the stroke is drawn in relation to a selection (inside, outside, or centered), you can create everything from delicate, single-ruled outlines to decorative, multiple-stroked borders and frames.

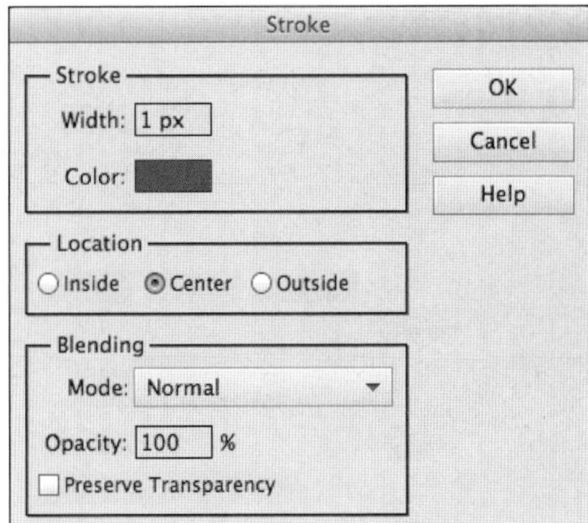

Ⓐ Draw lines around selections using the Stroke dialog.

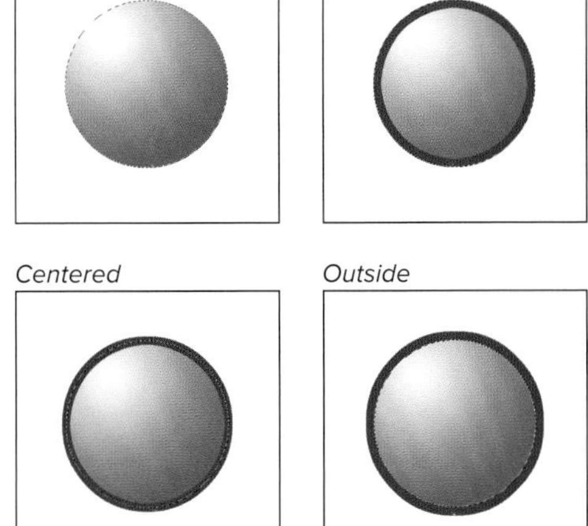

Ⓑ Once an object is selected, you can stroke it either inside, centered on, or outside of the selection.

To apply a stroke:

1. Using any of the selection or marquee tools, select the area of your image to which you want to add a stroke.

   If you're adding a stroke to an object on its own transparent layer, there's no need to make a selection. Instead, just check that the layer is active on the Layers panel.

2. From the Edit menu, choose Stroke (Outline) Selection to open the Stroke dialog Ⓐ.
3. In the Width text field, enter the stroke width, in pixels.

   There's no need to enter the pixel abbreviation (px) following the number value.

4. Change the stroke color by clicking the Color box and opening the Color Picker.
5. Select the location of the stroke. The location determines where the stroke is drawn: inside, outside, or centered directly on the selection Ⓑ.

continues on next page

6. Ignore the Blending portion of the dialog for now.
7. Click OK to apply the stroke to your selection or layer C.

TIP Photoshop Elements uses the foreground color for the stroke color unless you change the color in the Stroke dialog. So if you want to pick a stroke color from the Color Swatches panel, click the Color Swatches panel to assign the foreground color before anything else; then choose Stroke from the Edit menu. The color you choose from the Color Swatches panel will appear as the stroke color in the dialog.

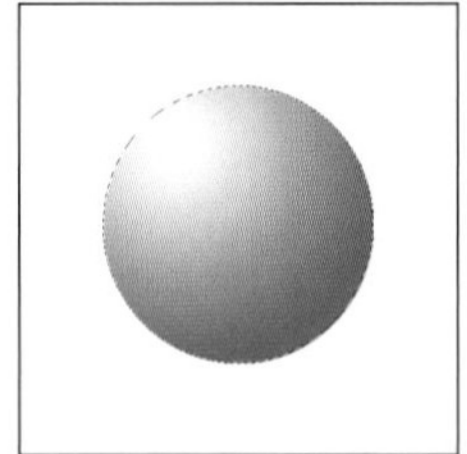

C Select an object (left), and then choose the Stroke command to apply a stroke (right).

Creating a Stroke Layer

It's a good habit to create a new layer before applying strokes to your image. That way, you can control attributes such as opacity and blending modes right on the Layers panel. You can even turn strokes off and on by clicking the stroke layer's visibility icon. If you're adding a stroke to a selection, simply create a new layer and then follow the steps in the task "To apply a stroke." If you're stroking an object on a transparent layer and want its stroke on a separate layer, you need to perform some additional steps:

1. Identify the object to which you want to add a stroke; then press Ctrl/Command and click once on the layer on the Layers panel. The object is automatically selected in the image window D.
2. Create a new layer by clicking the New Layer button at the top of the Layers panel.
3. With the new layer selected on the Layers panel, choose Stroke (Outline) Selection from the Edit menu; then follow steps 3 through 7 of "To apply a stroke," above.

A stroke is created for the object, but placed on its own layer.

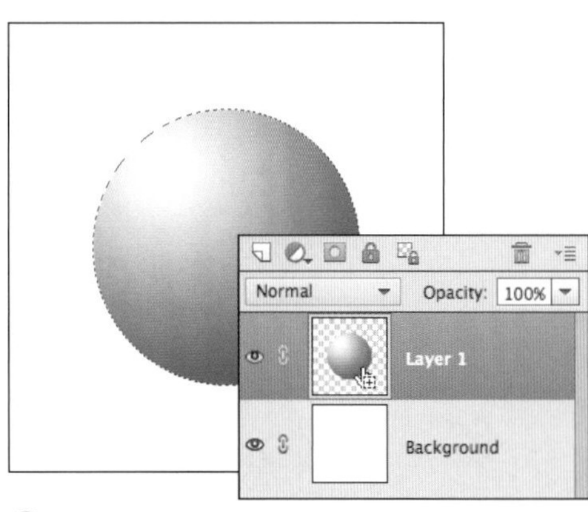

D Ctrl-click/Command-click the Layers panel to create a selection around a layer object.

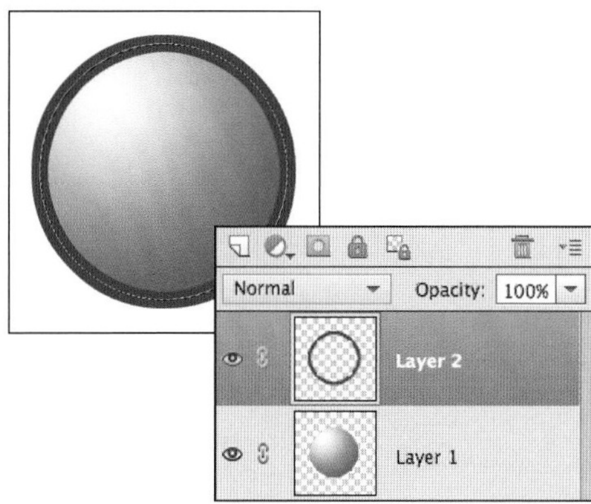

E The first step in creating a multiruled border is to create a thick stroke. Here, I used a stroke of 15 pixels.

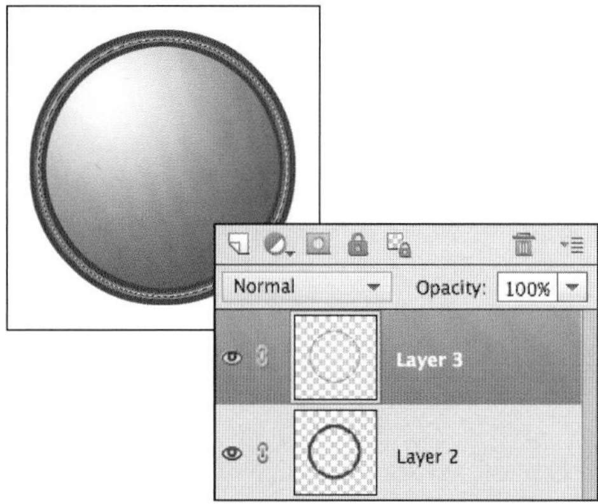

F Placing a narrow stroke of a different color over the broad first stroke creates an attractive three-ruled border.

To create a decorative border:

1. Make a selection, either by using one of the selection or marquee tools, or by selecting an object on a transparent layer as described in the "Creating a Stroke Layer" sidebar.
2. Create a new layer; then apply a wide stroke to the selection E.

   In this example, I used a stroke of 15 pixels.
3. With the selection still active, create a new layer above the first.
4. Apply a stroke narrower than the first and in a contrasting color or value F.
5. Continue to add stroke layers until you achieve the desired result.

TIP You can create different effects by adding inside and outside strokes.

Using the Brush Tool

The Brush tool is a near limitless reservoir of hundreds of different and unique brushes. You can apply painted brushstrokes directly to the surface of any photograph, or open a new file to serve as a blank canvas upon which you can create an original work of fine art. The dozen preset brush libraries offer selections as varied as Calligraphic, Wet Media, and Special Effect, and any brush can be resized from 1 pixel to a staggering 2500 pixels in diameter. You can paint using any of Photoshop Elements' blending modes and opacity settings, and you can turn any brush into an airbrush with a single click of a button. So whether you're a budding Van Gogh, would like to add a color-tint effect to an antique black-and-white photograph, or just enjoy doodling while talking on the phone, Photoshop Elements' brushes can help to bring out your inner artist.

To paint with the Brush tool:

1. To select a paint color, do one of the following:
   - Click the current foreground color swatch at the bottom of the Tools pane to open the Color Picker.
   - Choose a color from the Color Swatches panel.
2. Select the Brush tool in the Tools pane (or press B) **A**.
3. On the Tool Options bar, click to open the Brush Preset Picker **B**.
4. Click to choose from the list of default brushes, or select a different brush set from the Brushes drop-down menu **C**.

A The Brush tool.

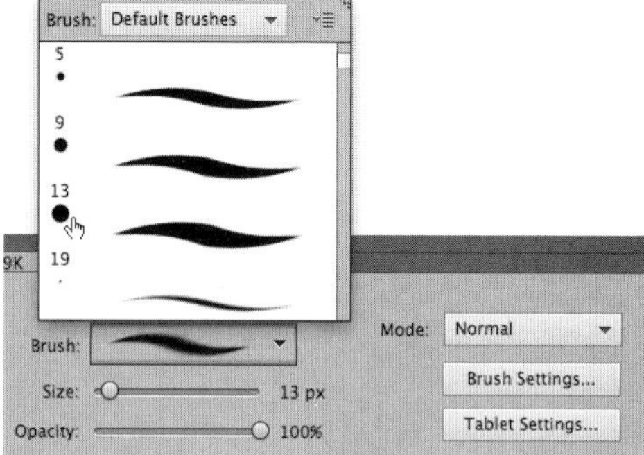

B Open the Brush Preset Picker to select from sets of different brushes.

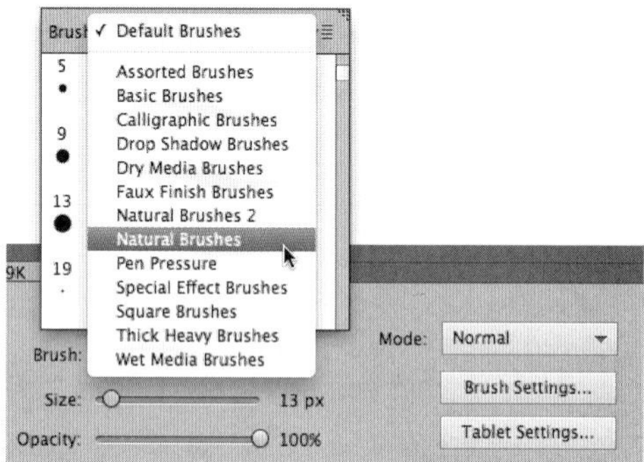

C The Brushes drop-down menu gives you access to a variety of brush sets.

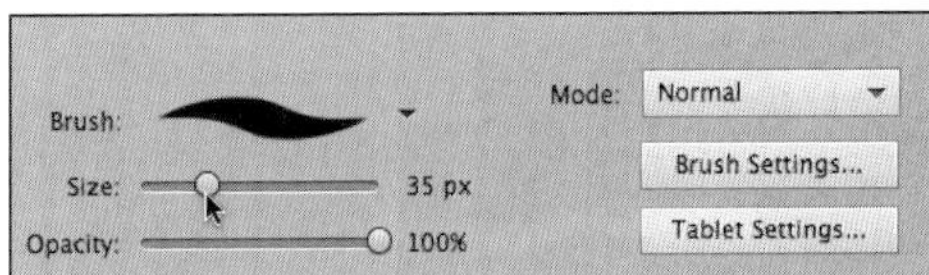

D Use the brush Size slider to resize your brush.

E Create realistic brush effects simply by dragging through the image window.

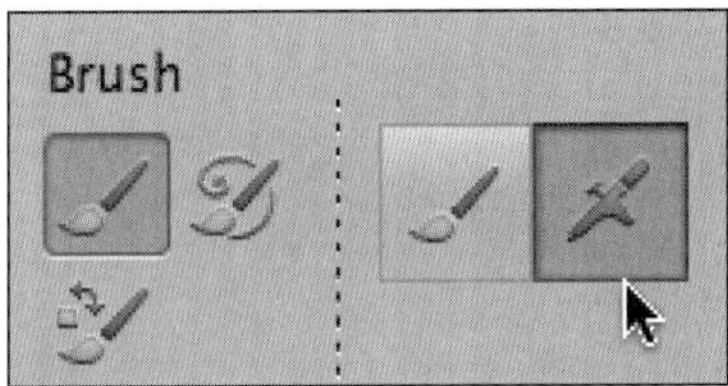

F Click the Airbrush button in the Tool Options bar to give a brush the characteristics of an airbrush.

Once you've selected a brush, you can use it at its predefined size, or you can resize it using the brush Size slider on the Tool Options bar D.

5. Again on the Tool Options bar, select a blend mode and opacity setting.
6. In the image window, drag to paint a brushstroke E.

TIP You can easily resize brushes on the fly using simple keyboard shortcuts. Once a brush of any size is selected, press the] or [key to increase or decrease the current brush size to the nearest unit of 10 pixels. Thus, if you're painting with a brush size of 23 pixels and press the] key, the brush size increases to 30 pixels and then grows in increments of 10 each subsequent time you press]. Conversely, a brush size of 56 pixels is reduced to 50 pixels when you press the [key, and the brush continues to shrink by 10 pixels each time thereafter that you press [.

TIP On the Mac, resize a brush by holding the Control and Option keys, and then dragging left (to reduce) or right (to enlarge).

TIP When any tool that uses a brush-type pointer is selected (the Eraser, Blur, Sharpen, and Clone tools, for instance), use the same keyboard shortcuts above.

TIP Almost any brush can be made to behave like an airbrush by clicking the Airbrush button on the Tool Options bar F. With the Airbrush activated, paint flows more slowly from the brush and gradually builds denser tones of color. The Airbrush option is most effective when applied to soft, round brushes or to brushes with scatter and spacing properties. (For more information on scatter and spacing properties, see the sidebar "Understanding the Brush Settings Panel" later in this chapter.)

Creating and Saving Custom Brushes

With so many different brushes and brush sets at your disposal, you may be surprised to discover you can change not only the size of brushes, but other characteristics such as flow, shape, and color. Photoshop Elements provides you with all the tools you need to modify existing brushes and create your own from photographs or scanned objects, such as leaves or flower petals. Once you've created a new brush, you can store it temporarily in an existing brush set or save and organize it into a new brush set of your own. Any new brush sets you create are then accessed and loaded from the Brushes drop-down menu on the Brush Preset Picker.

To create a custom brush:

1. Select the Brush tool from the Tools pane (or press B).
2. From the list of preset brushes on the Tool Options bar, click to select a brush you want to customize Ⓐ.
3. On the Tool Options bar, click the Brush Settings button to open its panel Ⓑ.
4. Use the sliders on the panel to modify the Fade, Hue Jitter, Scatter, Spacing, and Hardness, Roundness, and Angle properties of the brush Ⓒ.

   For more information on these slider controls, see the "Understanding the Brush Settings Panel" sidebar later in this chapter.

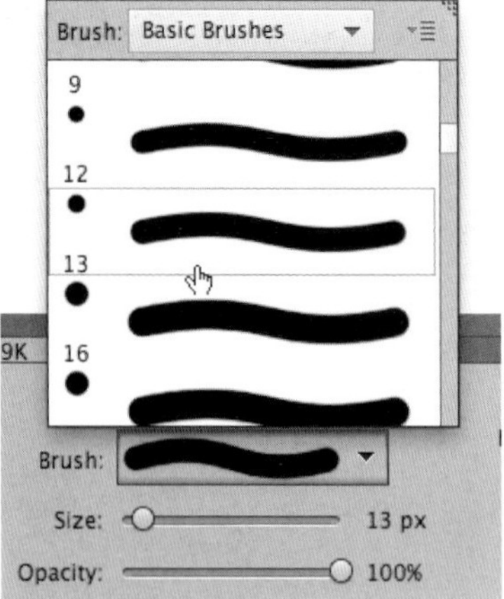

Ⓐ To create a new brush, select an existing brush and customize its properties.

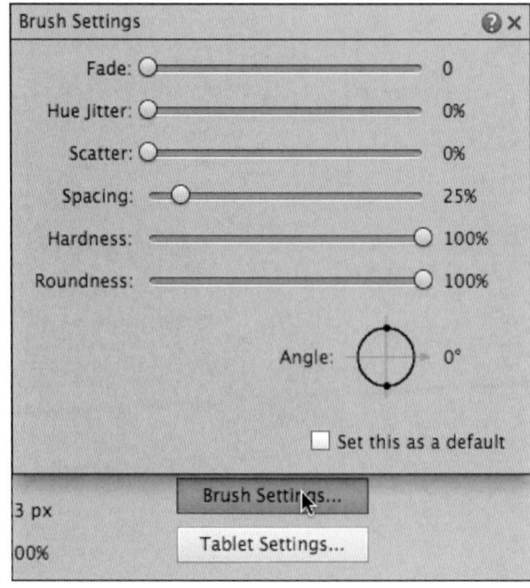

Ⓑ The Brush Settings panel contains sliders to modify a brush shape.

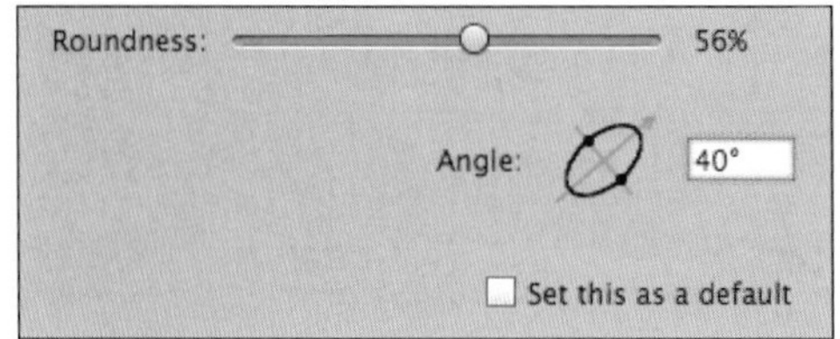

Ⓒ Control angle and roundness of a brush.

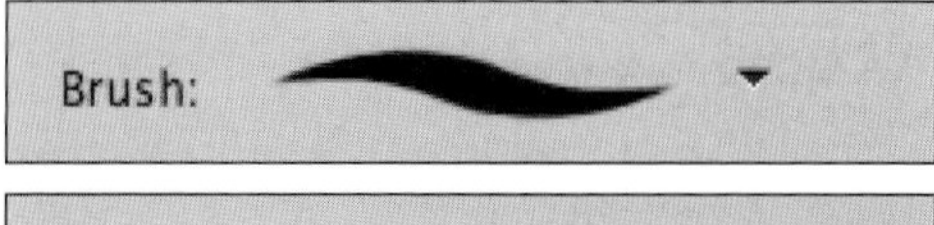

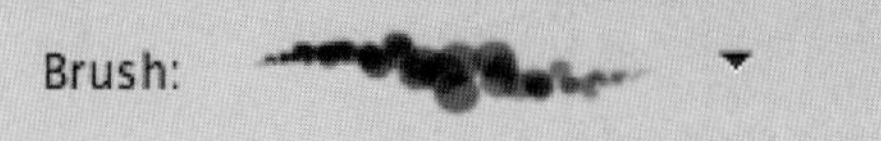

D The Brush Presets preview area here shows an original brush (top) and the same brush customized (bottom).

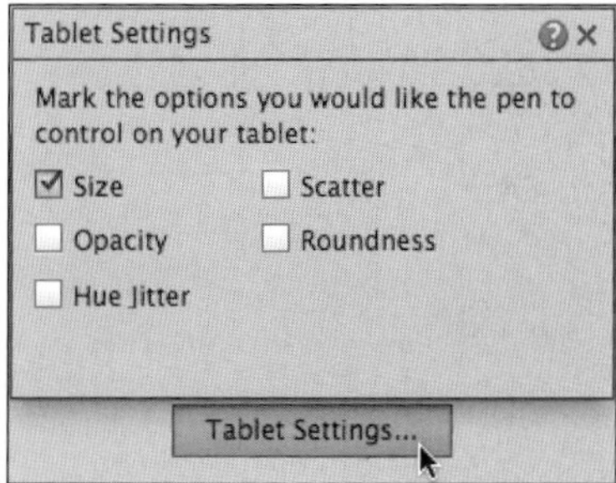

E Tablet Settings controls how pen pressure affects certain brush behaviors.

F Save your customized brushes.

G The new brush appears at the bottom of the panel list.

As you make adjustments, refer to the brush presets preview on the Tool Options bar to see the effects of your changes. All but the Hue Jitter property will be reflected in the preview on the Tool Options bar **D**.

5. If you have a pressure-sensitive digital tablet connected to your computer, you can control how the pen's pressure will affect your brush settings.

   In the Tool Options bar, click the Tablet Settings button, then check the boxes for the brush settings you want the pen pressure to control **E**.

6. When you're satisfied with your changes, click anywhere in the Tool Options bar to close the panel.

7. In the Tool Options bar, use the brush Size slider to size your brush.

8. Still in the Tool Options bar, open the Brush Preset Picker; then select Save Brush from the Panel Options menu **F**.

   The Brush Name dialog opens.

9. Type a name and click OK.

   Your new brush appears at the bottom of the current brush presets list on the Brush Preset Picker **G**.

To create a brush from a photographic object:

1. Open an image that contains an object or area from which you want to create a new brush.
2. To select an object from the image, do one of the following:
   - Using one of the selection tools, select the object or portion of a photograph you want to make into a brush. The Selection Brush and Magnetic Lasso tools both work well for this kind of selection H.
   - If you already have an object on its own transparent layer, hold down Ctrl/Command and click on the layer thumbnail in the Layers panel.
3. From the Edit menu, choose Define Brush from Selection. The Brush Name dialog opens with a representation of your new brush in its preview box I.
4. Enter a name for the brush and click OK to close the dialog.
5. Select the Brush tool from the Tools pane; then from the Tool Options bar, open the Brush Preset Picker. Your new brush appears at the bottom of the current brush presets list J.
6. Click to select the new brush; then in the Tool Options bar, click the More Options button to open the Brush Settings panel.
7. Use the sliders on the panel to modify the brush attributes; then click anywhere in the Tool Options bar to close the panel.

TIP Images with high contrast generally work best as brush shapes. Remember that you're not saving any color information—just the object's shape and its tonal values—so you'll want to use shapes with as much defined detail as possible.

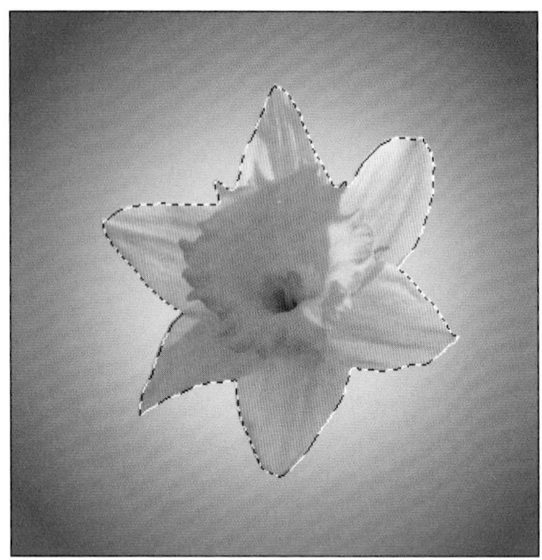

H A custom brush can be made out of virtually any selected object. In this example, I've selected a large flower.

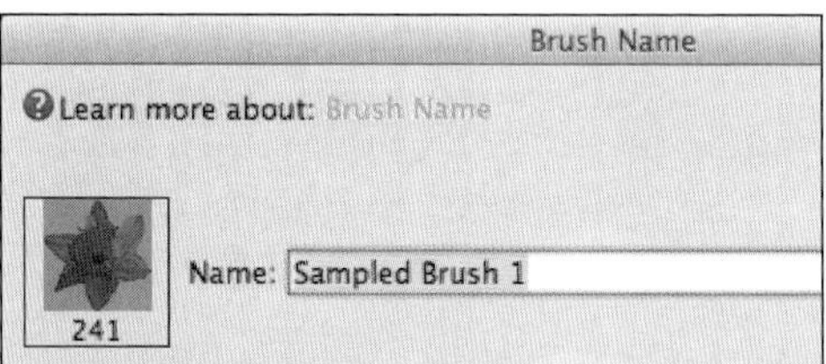

I The selection appears in the brush preview of the Brush Name dialog.

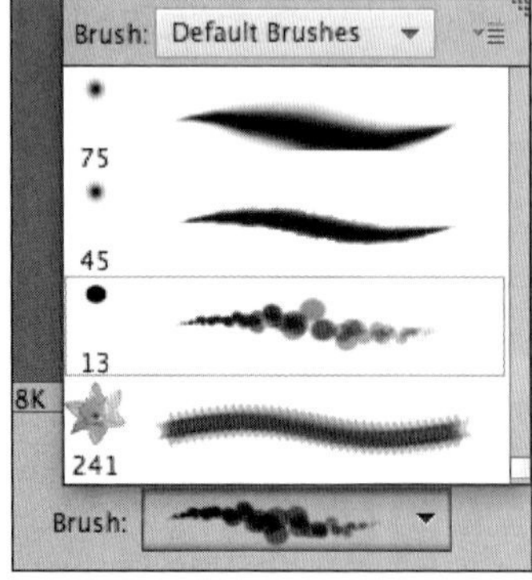

J Once saved, your new brush appears in the brush presets list.

Understanding the Brush Settings Panel

With a bit of exploration, you'll find the Brush Settings panel to be a useful tool for creating new brushes and modifying existing ones.

The Spacing slider controls the spacing of the brush shape and is based on a percentage of the brush's current size K. The default for most round brushes is 25 percent; 5 percent seems to be the optimum for most of the fine-art brushes such as Chalks, Pastels, and Loaded Watercolor.

The Fade slider sets the number of steps a brush takes to fade to transparent and can simulate the effect of a brush running out of paint as it draws across a surface. One step is equal to a brush width, so the fade effect is dependent on Spacing L.

The Hue Jitter slider determines how randomly the brush renders color, based on the foreground and background colors. The lower the jitter percentage, the more the foreground color is favored. If the percentage is set to the maximum of 100, the foreground and background colors (and mixtures of the two colors combined) are represented in equal measure throughout the brushstroke.

The Hardness slider controls the hardness or softness of a brushstroke's edges. A Hardness value of 100 percent creates a solid brushstroke with no soft edges M.

The Scatter slider determines how much a brush shape is spread around with each stroke. The higher the percentage, the more brush shapes are scattered and spread. Lower percentages create almost no scatter at all N.

The Angle value allows you to rotate a brush shape to any angle, and the Roundness value can be used to flatten or squish a brush shape.

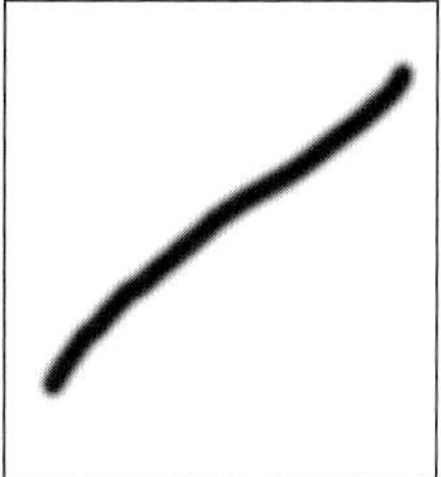
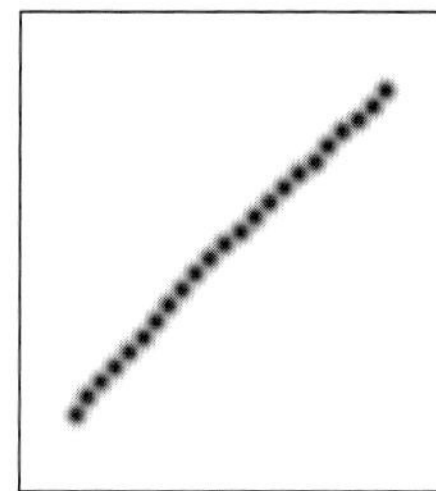

K A brush spacing value of 25 percent (left) and 75 percent (right).

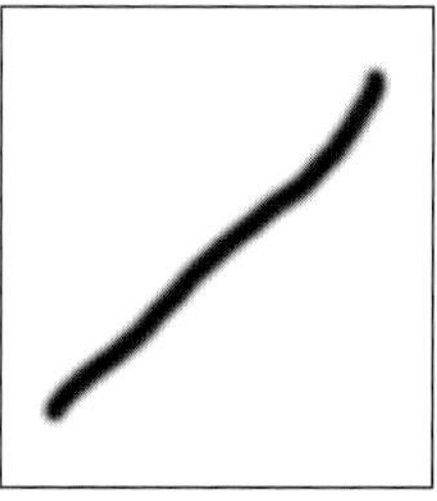

L A brush fade value of 0 (left) and 15 (right).

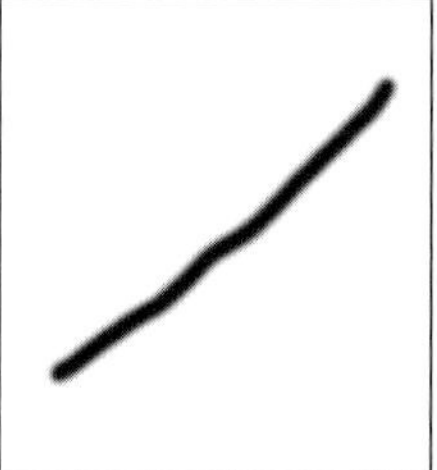
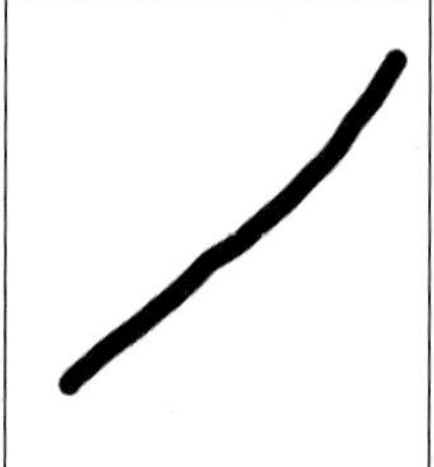

M A brush hardness value of 0 percent (left) and 100 percent (right).

N A brush scatter value of 0 percent (left) and 30 percent (right).

Managing brush sets

Managing brushes is no different than managing other presets (such as gradients and patterns). When you create a new brush, it's saved in the presets file. But once you reset the brushes on the Brush Preset Picker or select a different brush set, any new brushes you've created will be lost. Use the Preset Manager to create and save new brush sets.

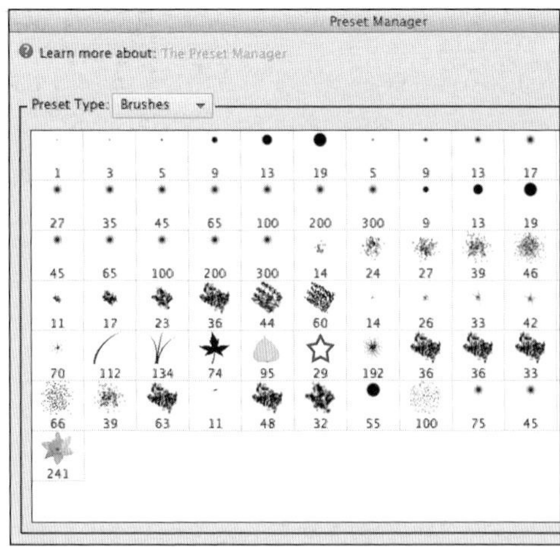

Ⓞ The Brushes Preset Manager.

To create a new brush set:

1. Create as many new brushes as you like, as described in the previous procedures.
2. From the Brush Preset Picker, choose Preset Manager.

   The Preset Manager dialog opens to the current brush set displayed on the Brush Preset Picker Ⓞ.
3. Scroll through the thumbnail views until you find the brushes you want to include in your new set.
4. In the thumbnail area, Ctrl-click/Command-click to select all of the brushes you want to include Ⓟ.

   If you select a brush by mistake, you can deselect it by holding down Ctrl/Command and clicking the thumbnail a second time.
5. Click the Save Set button to open the Save dialog.
6. In the File name text field, enter a new name to describe your brush set and click Save. Your brush set is saved with the brushes you selected in step 4, but it won't appear on either the More menu in the Preset Manager or the Brushes drop-down menu on the Brush Preset Picker until after you quit and then restart Photoshop Elements.

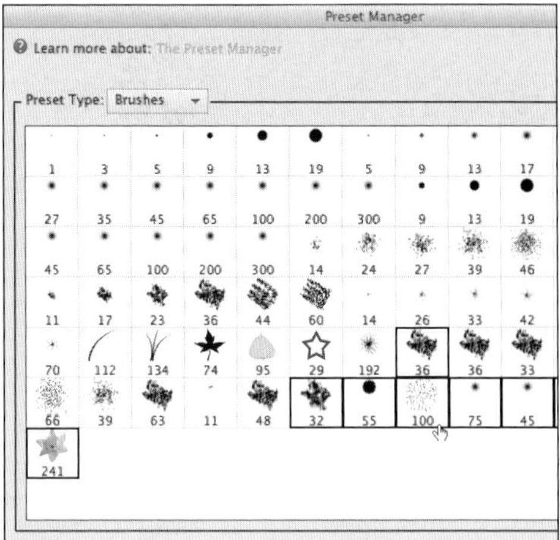

Ⓟ Select brushes you want included in your new brush set.

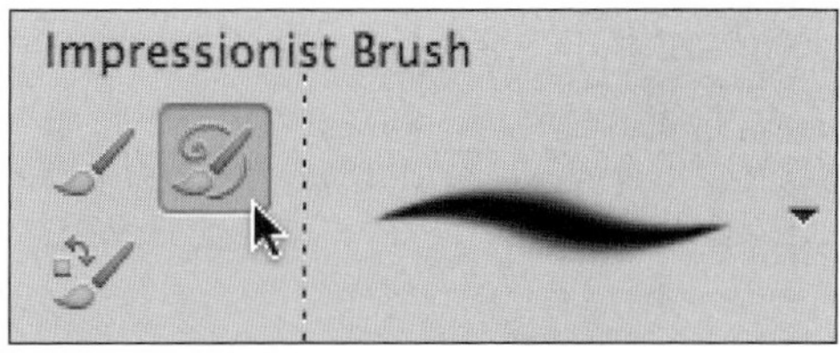

Ⓐ The Impressionist Brush tool.

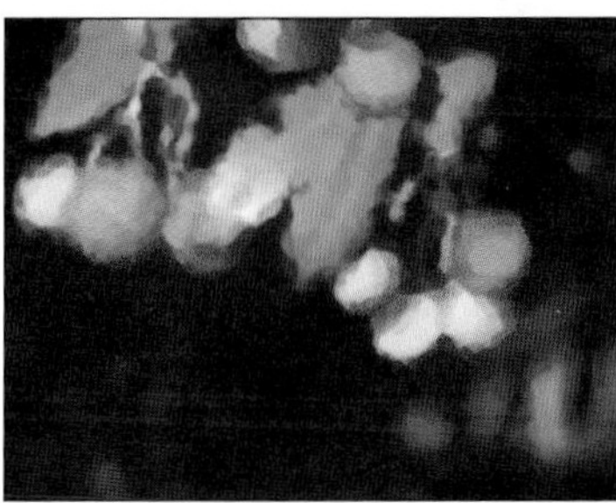

Ⓑ The brush size can have quite an impact on the way the Impressionist Brush tool affects your photograph. In the top photo, I painted with a brushstroke of 10 pixels. In the bottom photo, I changed the brushstroke to 20 pixels.

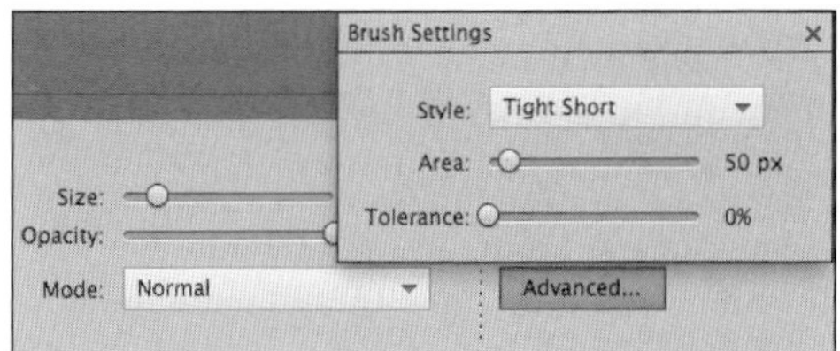

Ⓒ The Impressionist Brush Options panel has controls for different brush styles and the amount of image area they affect with each brushstroke.

Creating Special Painting Effects

The Impressionist Brush tool adds a painterly look to any photographic image. Although similar in effect to some of the Artistic and Brush Stroke filters, the Impressionist Brush tool allows you to be much more selective about which areas of an image it's applied to. That's because it uses the same scaleable, editable brushes as the Brush tool.

To paint with the Impressionist Brush tool:

1. Open the image to which you want to apply the Impressionist Brush effect.
2. Select the Brush tool, and then select the Impressionist Brush tool in the Tools pane Ⓐ.

   Alternatively, press B to select the Brush tool and press B again to toggle to the Impressionist Brush tool.
3. In the Tool Options bar, select a brush from the Brush Preset Picker.

   You can, of course, use any brush with the Impressionist Brush tool, but the round, soft-sided brush that Photoshop Elements picks as the default works especially well.
4. Again in the Tool Options bar, select a size with the brush Size slider Ⓑ.

   You can also select a mode and an opacity option, although in most cases the defaults of Normal and 100 percent are fine.
5. Still in the Tool Options bar, click the Advanced button to open the Impressionist Brush Settings panel Ⓒ.

continues on next page

6. From the Style drop-down menu, select a brush style **D**.

   I tend not to stray much beyond the top three styles (Tight Short, Medium, and Long), although the Dab style also creates some pretty effects.

7. In the Area text field, enter a value, in pixels, for the amount of area you want to affect with each stroke of the brush.

   For example, say you start with a brush that makes a single brush mark 10 pixels wide, and then select an Area value of 80 pixels. As you move the brush through the image—and depending on the brush style you chose—it will swoosh around an area of 80 x 80 pixels, distributing the paint in 10-pixel dollops.

8. If desired, select a Tolerance setting to determine the range of pixels affected.

   You may want to keep the Tolerance slider set at 0 percent and leave it alone. In use with the Impressionist brush, this setting seems wildly erratic and not worth the trouble.

9. In the image window, drag the brush through your image. The image takes on a painterly look wherever the brush is drawn through it **E**.

TIP Images with resolutions of 150 pixels per inch and higher make the best candidates for the Impressionist Brush tool, because the higher resolution helps to preserve detail when the effect is applied.

TIP Stick to using smaller brush sizes, particularly on low-resolution images. Although any rules of thumb vary from image to image, a good starting place is a brush size between 6 and 10 pixels and an Area setting between 30 and 50.

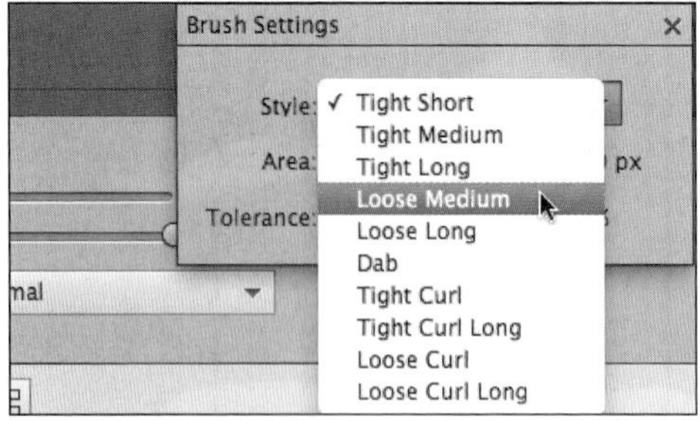

D Brush styles vary from subtle (Dab) to extravagant (Loose Curl Long).

E Simply drag the brush through your photo to create a work of art.

Painting with Texture

You can add texture to an image by painting a pattern onto it using the Pattern Stamp tool. The Editor includes some stock patterns, but you can also use your own images.

Ⓐ Define a pattern using an interesting texture.

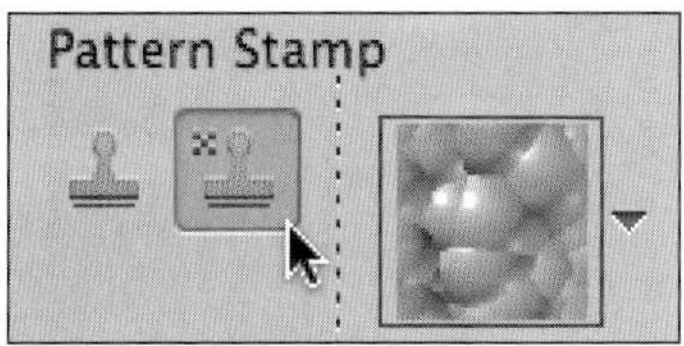

Ⓑ The Pattern Stamp tool.

Ⓒ Choose the pattern you created.

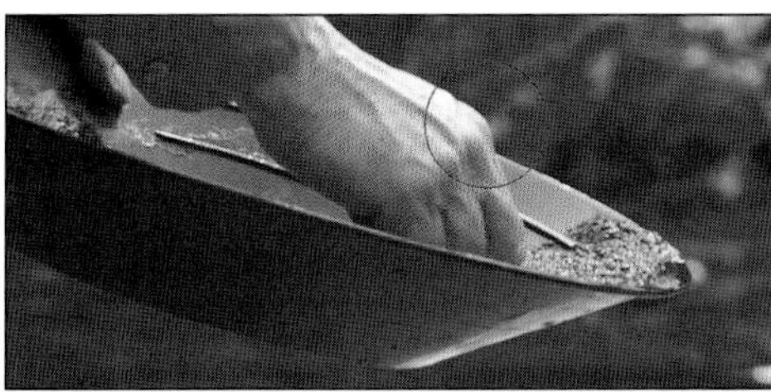

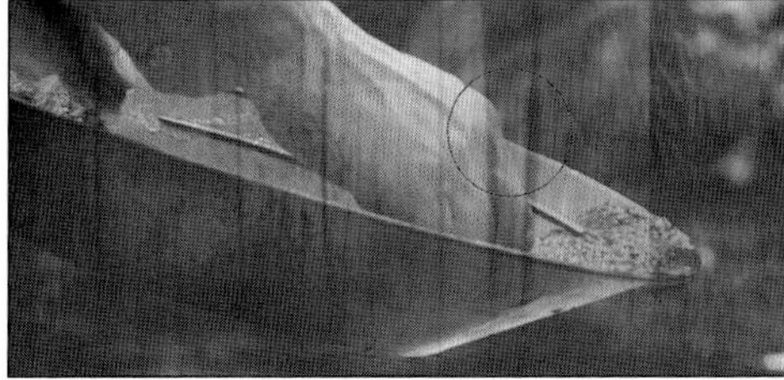

Ⓓ Paint the pattern onto the photo.

To define a pattern:

1. Open a photo you want to use as a texture. Also, consider switching the image to grayscale so the photo's colors don't interfere with the texture.
2. Select an area of the photo to define the texture, or select nothing to use the entire image Ⓐ.
3. Choose Edit > Define Pattern (or Define Pattern from Selection if you selected an area).
4. Give the pattern a name and click OK.

To paint with texture:

1. In the image on which you want to apply the texture, create a new layer in the Layers panel (so you're not drawing directly on your image).
2. Select the Pattern Stamp tool (S) Ⓑ.
3. In the Tool Options bar, click the Pattern Picker and choose a pattern Ⓒ.
4. Also in the Tool Options bar, choose a brush size, blend mode, and opacity for the Pattern Stamp tool. Those settings apply to the painting you're about to do, not everything you do on the layer, so you'll probably find yourself mixing and matching settings as you paint.
5. Click or drag to paint the pattern in the layer you created in step 1 to create the texture Ⓓ.

Erasing with Customizable Brush Shapes

The images or brushstrokes you choose to remove from a photograph are often as important as those you decide to add or leave behind. The basic Eraser feature is a powerful tool for cleaning up and fine-tuning your images, taking full advantage of every brush style and size that Elements has to offer. Not only can you perform routine erasing tasks such as rubbing away stray pixels, you can also customize an eraser's brush and opacity settings to create unique texture, color, and pattern effects.

To use the Eraser tool:

1. Select the Eraser tool from the Tools pane (or press E) **A**.
2. In the Tool Options bar, select a brush from the Brush Preset Picker **B**.
3. Again in the Tool Options bar, select a size using the brush Size slider.
4. Select an eraser type: Pencil, Brush, or Block.

   If you select a soft, anti-aliased brush and then choose the Pencil type, the eraser becomes coarse and aliased **C**.
5. Still in the Tool Options bar, select an opacity using the Opacity slider.
6. In the image window, drag the eraser through your image.

   The image is erased according to the attributes you've applied to the eraser.

A The Eraser tool.

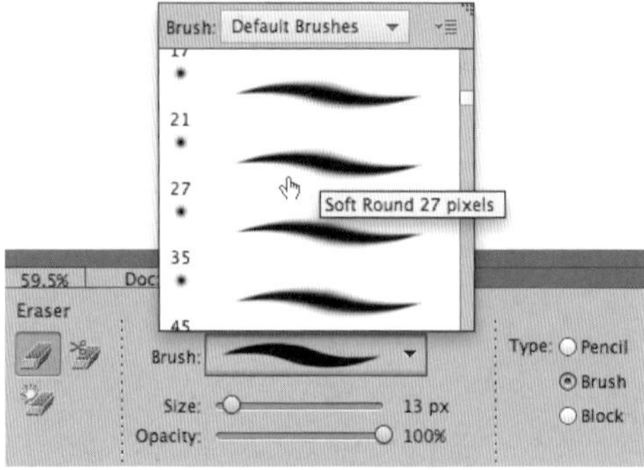

B The same brush presets are available for the Eraser tool as for the Brush tool.

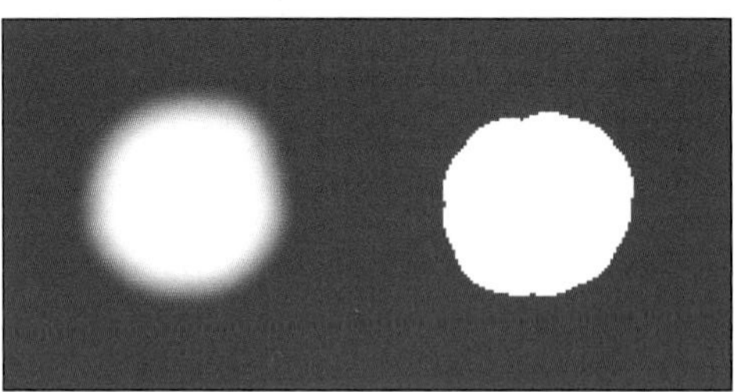

C An eraser in Brush mode (left) and in Pencil mode (right).

Erasing on Flattened vs. Layered Images

The Eraser tool functions in a fundamentally different way, depending on whether it's erasing on a flattened image, such as Photoshop Elements' default background, or on a layer of a multilayered file. When erasing on a flattened image, the Eraser tool doesn't really erase at all. Instead, it replaces the image with the current background color displayed in the Tools pane. In other words, it simply paints over the image with the background color D.

On the other hand, when erasing a portion of an image from a layer, the Eraser tool actually removes the pixels from the layer, creating a transparent hole and exposing the image on the layer directly below it E.

TIP You're not limited to round or square brush shapes for your erasers. Any brush, even pictorial ones (for instance, Maple Leaves and Dune Grass) or photographic ones (like Scattered Leaves) can be used as erasers. Try experimenting with different brush shapes and opacity settings to create unusual textures and patterns in your photographs.

D On a flattened image layer, the Eraser tool paints with the current background color wherever the eraser is dragged.

E When erasing on a layer with transparency, the Eraser tool actually removes image pixels (here, the center of the flower layer) and exposes the image on the layer below (the leaf).

Understanding Shapes

In Photoshop Elements, you create shapes not by rendering them with pixels, but by constructing them from vector paths, which are actually vector masks. I'll use some simple circle and square shapes to illustrate what that means.

Each time you draw a shape with one of the shape tools, Photoshop Elements is performing a little behind-the-scenes sleight of hand. Although it may appear that you're drawing a solid, filled circle, for instance, what you're really creating is a new layer containing both a colored fill and a mask with a circle-shaped cutout Ⓐ. When you move, reshape, or resize a shape, you're actually just moving or reshaping the cutout and revealing a different area of the colored fill below it Ⓑ. When you add to or subtract from a shape by drawing additional shapes, you're simply revealing or hiding more of the same colored layer Ⓒ.

Every time you create a new shape, a new shape layer is added to the Layers panel. A shape layer is represented in the panel thumbnails by a gray background (the mask) and a white shape (the mask cutout, or path). Since a shape's outline isn't always visible in the image window—if you deselect it, for instance—the Layers panel provides a handy, visual reference for every shape in your project Ⓓ. And as with any other layered image, you can use the Layers panel to hide a shape's visibility and even change its opacity and its blending mode.

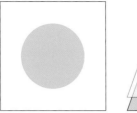
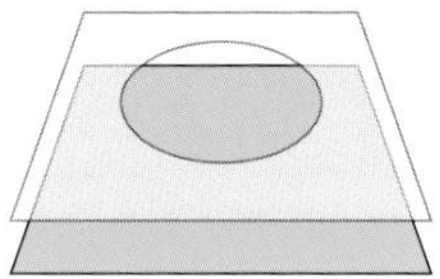

Ⓐ When you draw a shape, you're actually drawing a shape mask.

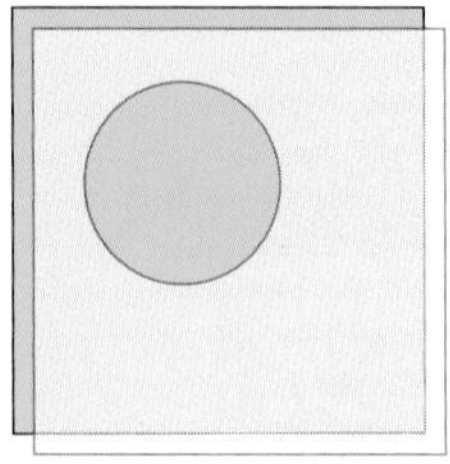
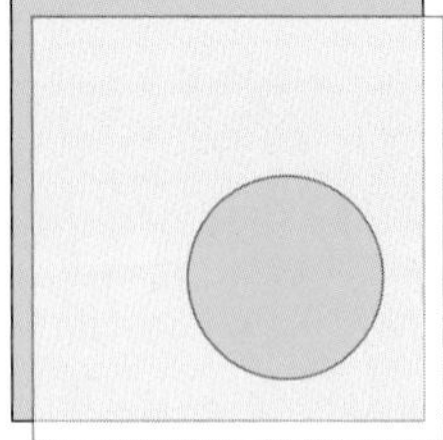

Ⓑ Moving a shape really means moving the cutout portion of the mask.

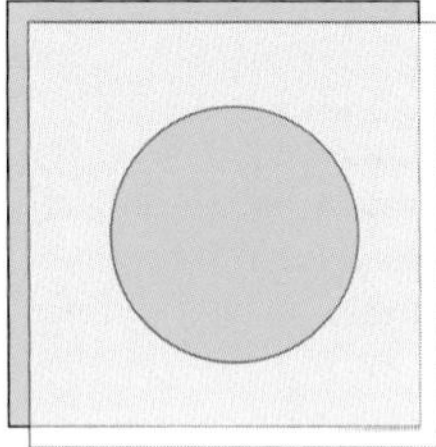
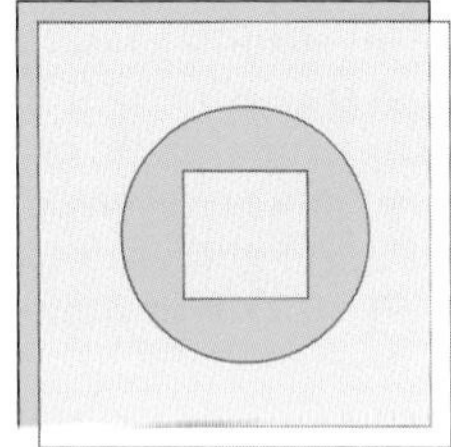

Ⓒ Adding a shape to a layer masks off another portion of the colored fill below it, in this case giving the illusion that the circle has a square hole in its center.

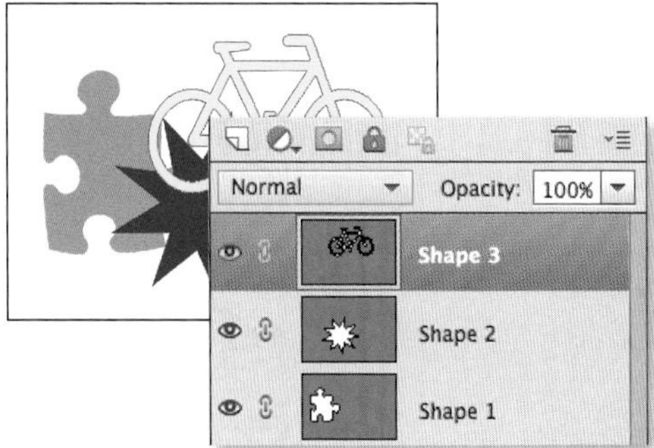

Ⓓ Shapes appear on their own layers.

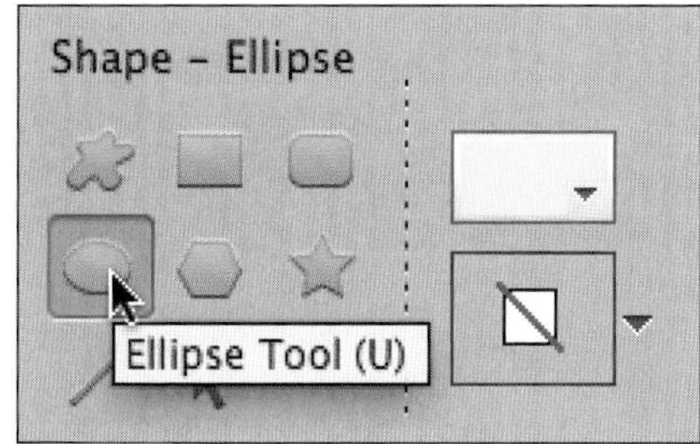

Ⓐ The Ellipse shape tool in the Tool Options bar.

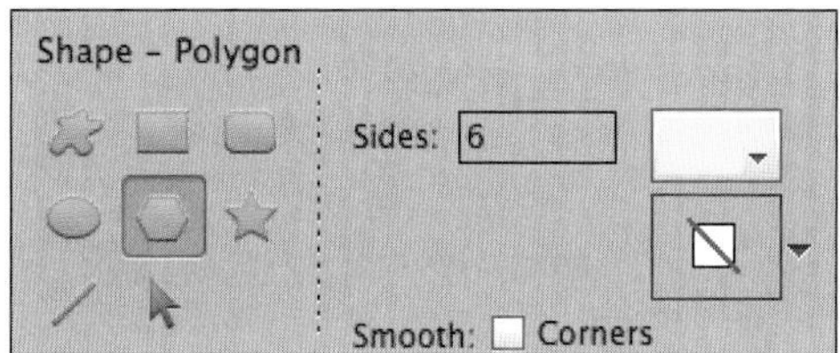

Ⓑ Some shape tools, such as the Polygon tool, have properties you can set in the Tool Options bar.

Drawing Basic Shapes

In Photoshop Elements, you can draw five basic geometric shapes (a shape selection tool and a tool for creating custom shapes are discussed in detail later in this chapter). Shapes can be drawn freely by clicking and dragging, or they can be constrained according to your specification of size, proportion, and special characteristics. You can use the shape tools to create logos or geometric designs; or, because a new layer is created with every shape you draw, you can draw shapes directly over any photo or scanned image without fear of damaging the image.

To draw a shape:

1. Select the shape tool from the Tools pane (or press U), and then select a shape in the Tool Options bar Ⓐ.

   To cycle through the shape tools, press U again until you arrive at the shape you want.

2. To select a shape color, do one of the following:

   - Click the current foreground color swatch at the bottom of the Tools pane, or click the color box in the Tool Options bar to open the Color Picker.
   - Choose a color from the Color Swatches panel.

3. If they're available for the tool you've selected, you can set special properties for your shape before you draw. In the Tool Options bar, enter values specific to the shape you've chosen Ⓑ.

   For example, for the Polygon tool, you can enter the number of sides. For the Line tool, you can enter a pixel weight.

continues on next page

4. In the Tool Options bar, select from the available options for that particular shape or leave the options set to the default of Unconstrained **C**.
5. In the image window, click and drag to draw the shape **D**.

   If you like, you can add a style to your shape from the Shape tool's built-in Style Picker.
6. In the Tool Options bar, click the icon or arrow to open the Style Picker **E**.
7. Choose from the list of available styles or click the Styles drop-down menu to view the available sets.
8. Click a style in the Style Picker to apply it to your shape **F**.
9. To deselect the shape and hide the path outline, press Enter.

TIP If you decide to remove a style from a shape, you have two options. With the shape layer selected in the Layers panel, open the Styles panel menu in the Tool Options bar, click the Panel Options menu, and then choose Remove Style. Or, right-click the Layer Style icon on the desired layer in the Layers panel and choose Clear Layer Style.

TIP To constrain the proportions of any shape (to make a rectangle a perfect square or an ellipse a perfect circle, for example), hold down the Shift key as you drag.

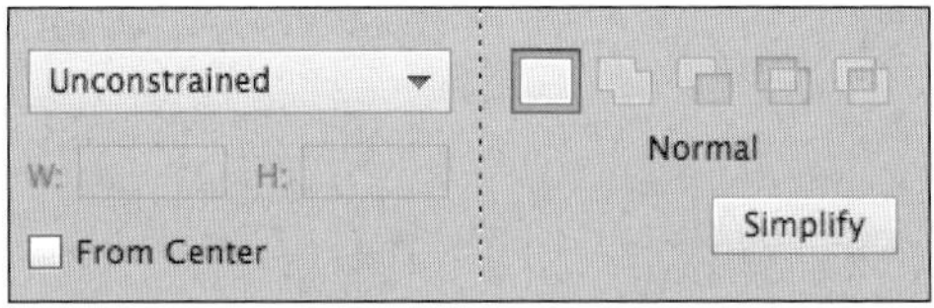

C Every shape tool has its own particular set of geometry options.

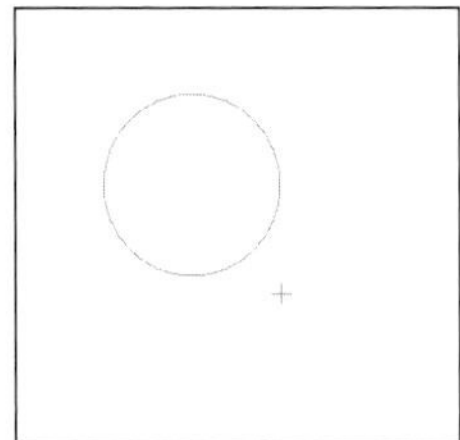

D Drawing a shape is as simple as clicking and dragging.

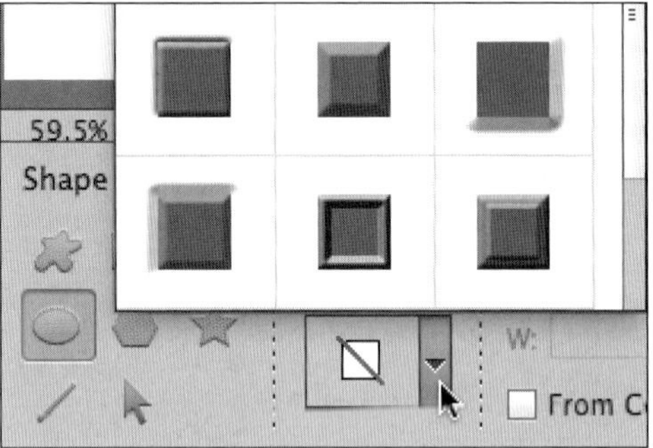

E When any shape tool is selected, the shape tool Style Picker appears in the Tool Options bar.

F A simple circle drawn with the ellipse shape tool (left) is transformed into a glossy button (right) using a style from the Style Picker.

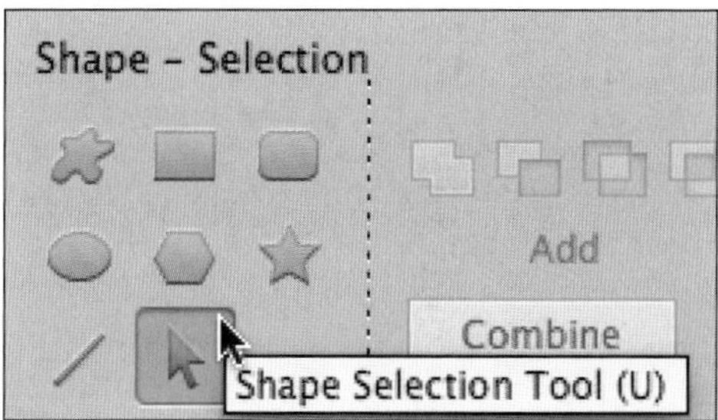

Ⓐ The Shape Selection tool, accessed from the Tool Options bar.

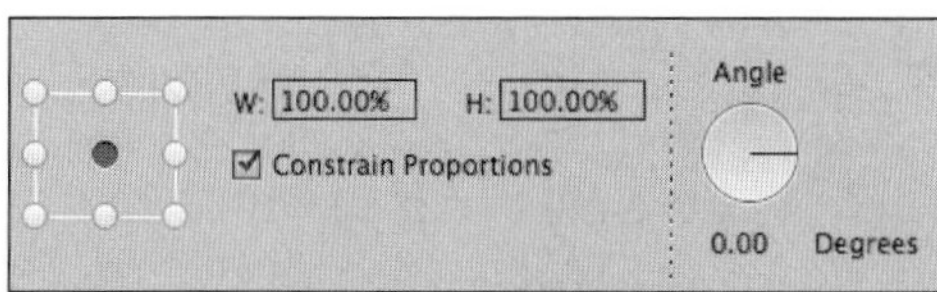

Ⓑ Precise scale and rotation values can be entered for any shape.

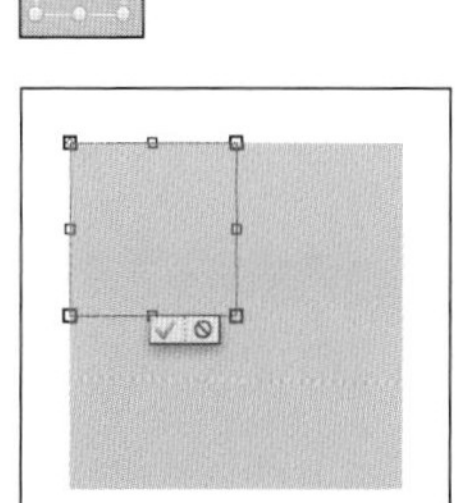

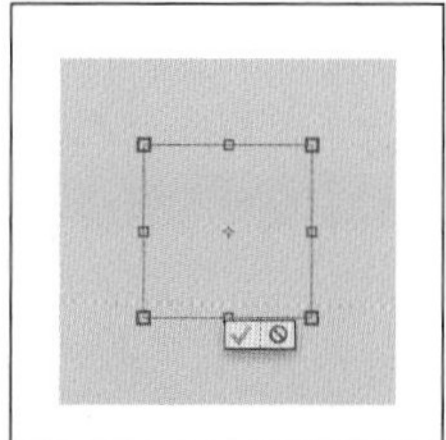

Ⓒ These squares are both being reduced in size by about half. The one on the left is scaled toward its upper-left corner, and the one on the right is scaled toward its center.

Transforming Shapes

You're not limited to just creating shapes in Photoshop Elements. You can also scale (resize), rotate, and distort them to your liking. Shapes can be altered either numerically, by entering specific values in the Tool Options bar, or manually, by dragging their control handles in the image window. Constrain options, such as proportional scaling, are also available for most transformations.

To scale a shape:

1. Select the Shape Selection tool by doing any of the following:
   - Choose the Shape Selection tool from beneath the current shape tool in the Tools pane Ⓐ.
   - Press U to select any shape tool and then press U again until you toggle to the Shape Selection tool.
   - Select any shape tool in the Tools pane, and then choose the Shape Selection tool from the Tool Options bar (it looks like an arrow).
2. In the image window, select the shape with the Shape Selection tool.
3. From the Image menu, choose Transform Shape > Free Transform Shape, or press Ctrl+T/Command-T.

   The Tool Options bar changes to show the scale and rotation text fields, and the reference point locator Ⓑ.
4. In the Tool Options bar, click to set a reference point location. The reference point determines what point your shape will be scaled to: toward the center, toward a corner, and so on Ⓒ.

continues on next page

5. If you want to scale your shape proportionately, click the Constrain Proportions checkbox.
6. Enter a value in either the height or width text field. The shape is scaled accordingly.
7. Click the Commit Transform button **D**, or press Enter.

To rotate a shape:

1. Select the Shape Selection tool from the Tools pane or Tool Options bar.
2. In the image window, select the shape with the Shape Selection tool.
3. From the Image menu, choose Rotate > Free Rotate Layer **E**.

   The Tool Options bar changes to show the scale and rotation text fields, and the reference point locator.
4. In the Tool Options bar, click to set a reference point location.

   The reference point determines the point around which your shape will be rotated **F**.
5. Enter a value in the rotate text field.

   The shape rotates accordingly.
6. Click the Commit Transform button, or press Enter.

TIP You can scale a shape manually by selecting it with the Shape Selection tool and then dragging any one of the eight handles on the selection border. Constrain the scaling by holding down the Shift key while dragging one of the four corner handles.

TIP If you want to simply reposition a shape in the image window, click anywhere inside the shape with the Shape Selection tool and then drag the shape to its new position.

D The Commit Transform button scales the shape to the size you define.

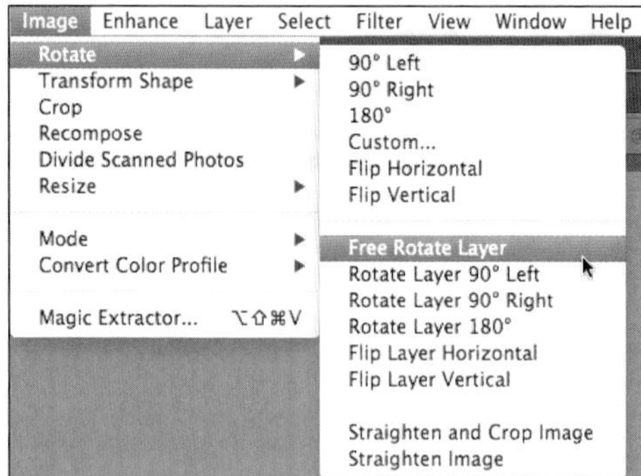

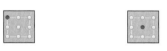

E You can apply any of the layer rotation menu commands to your shapes.

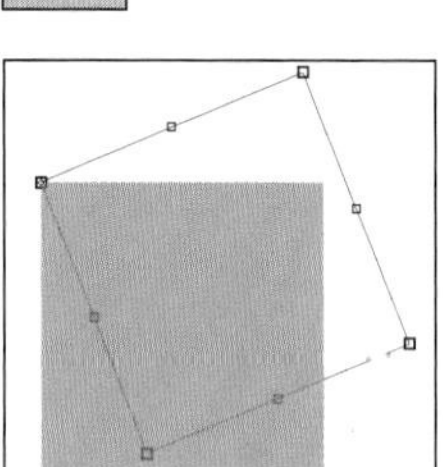
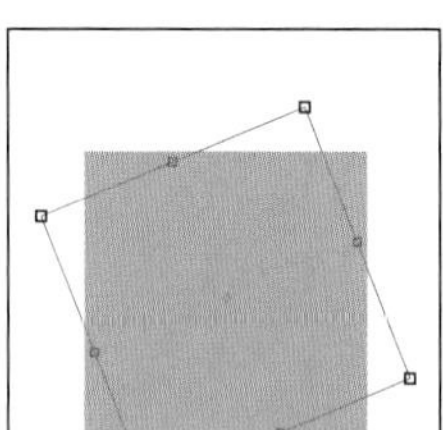

F These squares are both being rotated about 20 degrees. The one on the left is rotated around its upper-left corner, and the one on the right is rotated around its center.

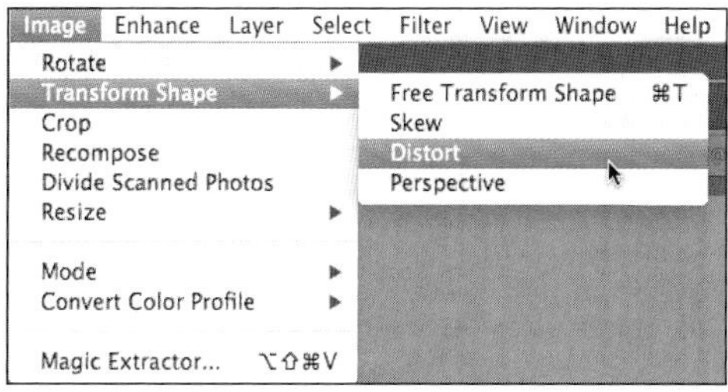

G Choose one of the three specific transformation commands.

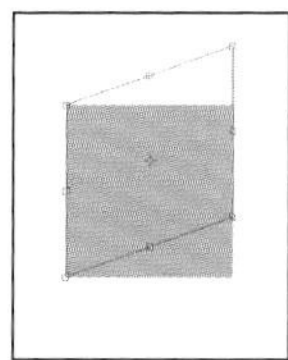 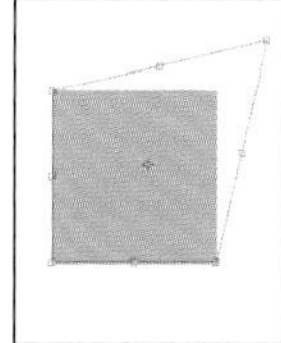 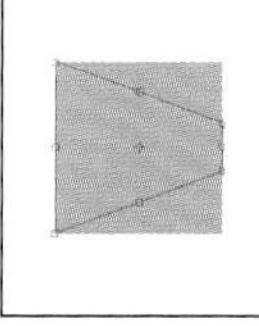

H The same square shape transformed using Skew (left), Distort (center), and Perspective (right).

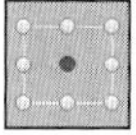

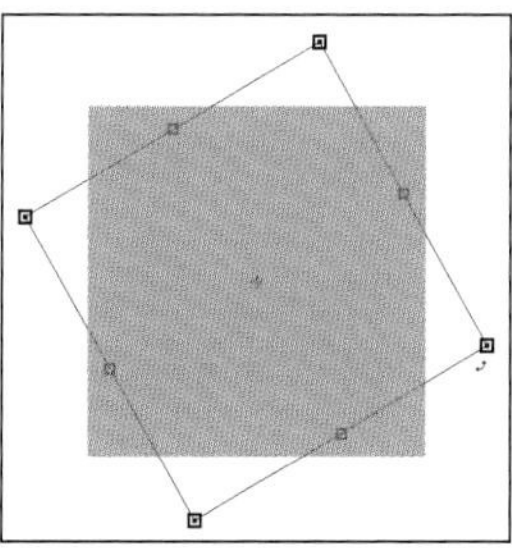

I Rotate any shape manually by dragging it around its reference point with the rotation pointer.

Distortion Shortcuts

From the Image menu, choose Transform Shape > Free Transform Shape; then use the following shortcuts while dragging the shape handles in the image window:

To Distort: Ctrl/Command

To Skew: Ctrl+Alt/Command-Option

To create Perspective: Ctrl+Alt+Shift/Command-Option-Shift

To distort a shape:

1. Select the Shape Selection tool from the Tools pane.
2. In the image window, select the shape with the Shape Selection tool.
3. From the Image menu, choose Transform Shape; then choose Skew, Distort, or Perspective **G**.
4. In the Tool Options bar, check that the reference point location is set to the center.

   The reference point can, of course, be set to any location, but the center seems to work best when applying any of the three distortions.
5. Drag any of the shape's control handles to distort the shape.

   Dragging the control handles yields different results depending on the distort option you choose **H**.
6. Click the Commit Transform button, or press Enter.

TIP To rotate your shape in 90- or 180-degree increments or to flip it horizontally or vertically, choose Image > Rotate; then choose from the list of five menu commands below the Free Rotate Layer command.

TIP You can rotate a shape manually by selecting it with the Shape Selection tool and then moving the pointer outside of the selection border until it becomes a rotation cursor I. Drag around the outside of the selection border to rotate the shape. In addition, you can constrain the rotation to 15-degree increments by holding down the Shift key while dragging the rotation cursor.

Creating Custom Shapes

Once you've gained a basic understanding of working with Elements' geometric shapes, you can begin combining those shapes together to create even more interesting and intricate shapes. Shape option buttons allow you to perform a little vector path magic by creating brand-new shapes out of the intersections and overlapping portions of the rectangle, ellipse, and polygon shapes.

The Custom Shape tool is in a world unto itself, working from a library of nearly 400 complex vector graphics grouped into categories as diverse as ornaments, music, fruit, symbols, and nature—far beyond the relatively simple icons and graphics you can build with the basic geometric shape tools.

To add a shape to an existing shape:

1. Follow steps 1 through 5 in the task "To draw a shape," earlier in this chapter.

   Make sure that this first shape's path remains selected **A**. This technique will only work when both shapes are being drawn to the same layer.

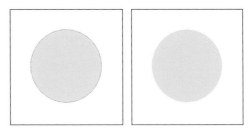

2. With the Shape tool selected, choose a specific shape you want to add from the Tool Options bar.

   Of course, you can use the same shape more than once, if you wish.

3. In the Tool Options bar, set color, value, and geometry options as desired.

4. Still in the Tool Options bar, click to select one of the shape area options **B**.

5. In the image window, click and drag to draw the new shape **C**.

6. To deselect the shapes and hide their path outlines, press Enter.

A When a shape is selected, its path outline is visible (left). The path disappears when the shape is deselected (right).

B The shape area options define how one shape reacts with another.

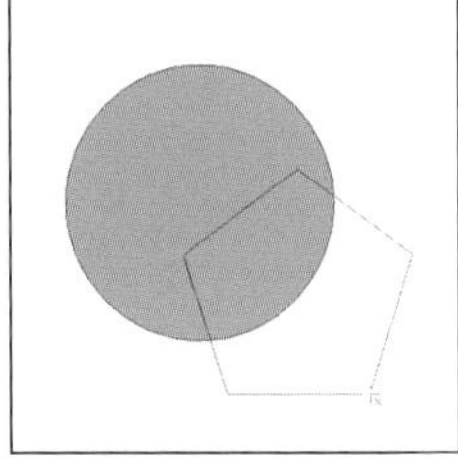
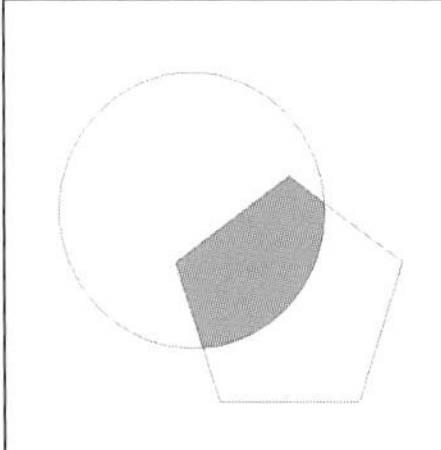

C As the new shape is drawn, only its outline is visible (left). When the new shape is completed, it's filled according to the preset shape area option (right). In this case, the option was set to Intersect Shape.

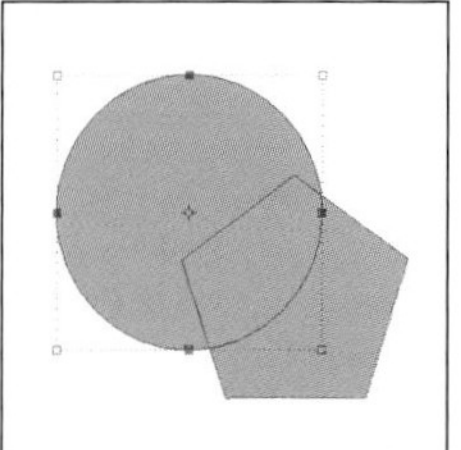
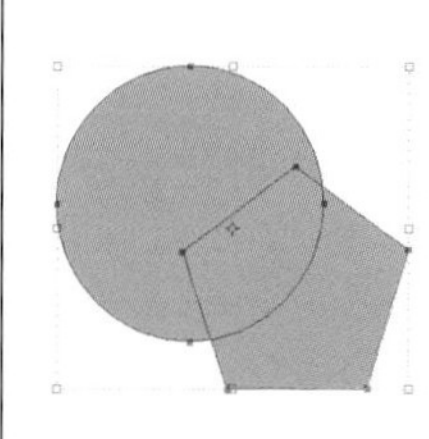

D Shift-click to select the shapes you want to combine.

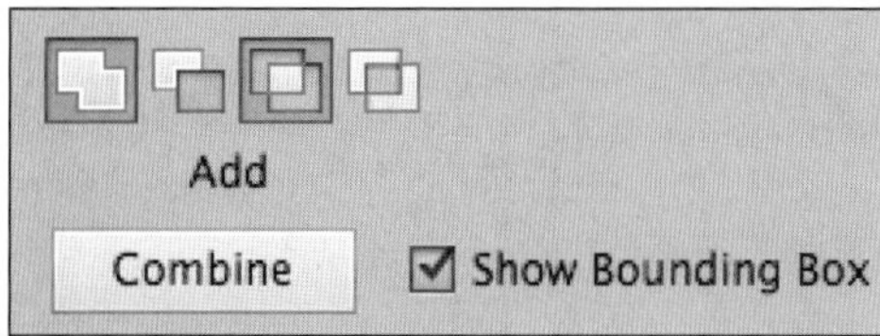

E The Combine button groups multiple shapes.

To combine multiple shapes:

1. Select the Shape Selection tool from the Tools pane.
2. In the image window, click to select the first shape; then Shift-click to select the additional shapes you want to group **D**.
3. In the Tool Options bar, click the Combine button **E**. The shapes become one complex shape.

TIP The Layers panel can be a useful tool when working with the shape tools. Its layer thumbnails provide good visual feedback, particularly when you're building complex shapes and want to verify that the new shapes you create are being placed on the correct layers.

continues on next page

About the Shape Geometry Options Panels

Each shape tool (with the exception of the Shape Selection tool) has its own unique geometry options. The two rectangle tools and the Ellipse and Custom Shape tools all offer similar options for defining size, proportions, and constraint properties; and the Polygon and Line tools each have their own unique sets of options **F**. The Polygon tool's most distinctive option is the Star checkbox. When Star is selected, you're presented with a couple of indent properties that fold the polygon in on itself, so that the points of its angles become the tips of a star shape **G**. When the Line tool is selected, you can choose from a small set of Arrowheads options based on the pixel weight of the line.

TIP To constrain the proportions of any shape (to make a rectangle a perfect square or an ellipse a perfect circle, for example) without the aid of the Geometry Options panel, hold down the Shift key as you drag.

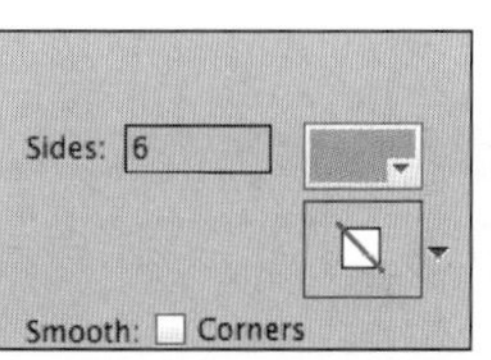

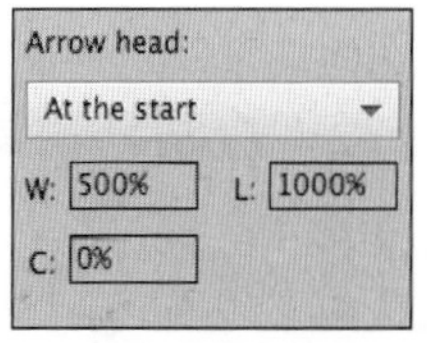

F The Polygon tool's geometry options and the Line tool's arrowhead options.

G Using the Polygon tool's Star option, a six-sided polygon (left) can be changed into a six-point star (right).

TIP You can only combine shapes that appear on the same layer on the Layers panel, like those I created in the previous procedure. However, if you've created shapes on separate layers and then decide you want to combine them, all is not lost. With the Shape Selection tool, select one of the shapes. Then from the Edit menu, choose Cut (Ctrl+X/Command-X). In the Layers panel, click to select the shape layer you want to combine the "cut" shape with, and then from the Edit menu, choose Paste (Ctrl+V/Command-V). The shape will be pasted into the selected layer along with the other shape. From there, follow the steps to combine multiple shapes.

TIP When selecting multiple shapes, work from the inside out. In other words, if you have a large shape with a smaller cutout or intersecting shape inside it, select the smaller, inside shape first. Photoshop Elements doesn't assign any stacking order per se to multiple shapes on a layer, but if a larger, outside shape is selected first, the selection sort of covers up any smaller shapes inside, making them next to impossible to select.

TIP Up until the moment multiple shapes are grouped together with the Combine button, they can be selected individually and then scaled, rotated, distorted, and even duplicated with the Copy and Paste commands.

About the Shape Area Options Buttons

Photoshop Elements gives you five options to choose from when creating a new shape or modifying an existing one **H**.

Create New Shape Layer does just that; it draws a new shape on its own, separate layer.

Add to Shape Area draws a new shape on the same layer as the existing shape.

Subtract from Shape Area adds a shape to the same layer as the existing shape, creating a cutout or hole.

Intersect Shape Areas adds a shape to the same layer as the existing shape and causes only those areas where the two shapes overlap to be visible.

Exclude Overlapping Shape Areas does just the opposite of Intersect Shape Areas, creating a cutout or hole where the two shapes overlap.

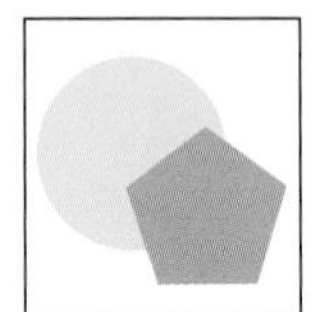

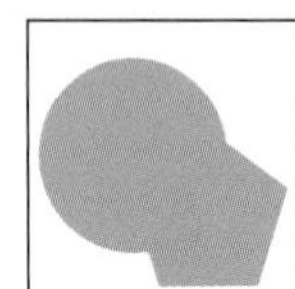

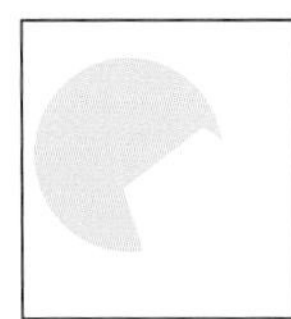

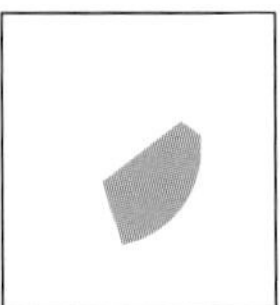

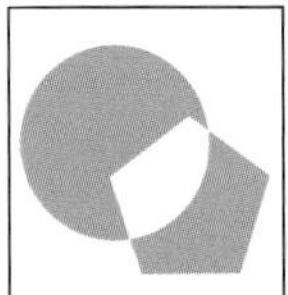

H In the Tool Options bar, click to select one of five shape area options.

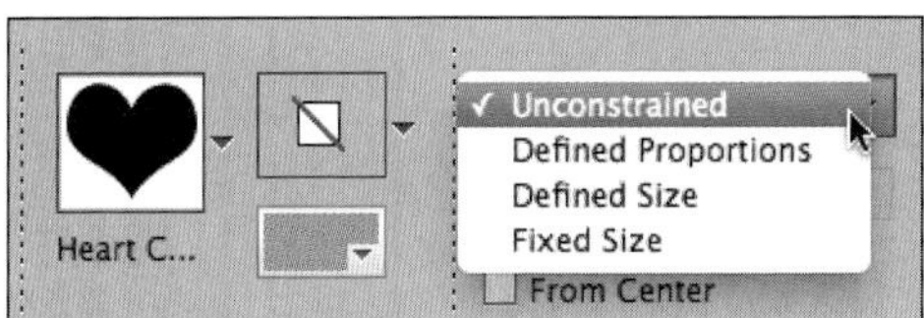

I The Custom Shape tool offers geometry options similar to those for the Ellipse and Rectangle tools.

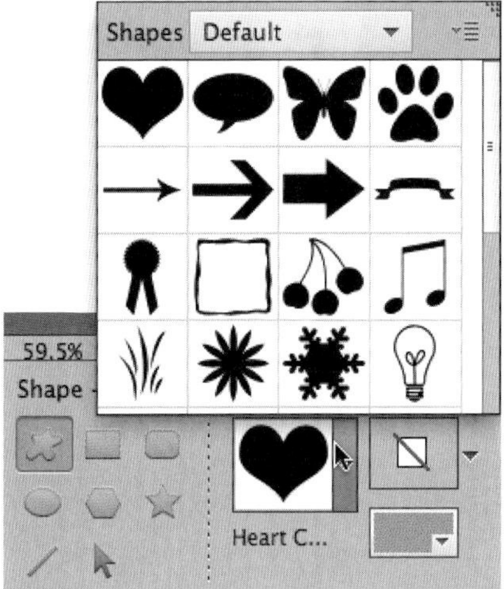

J Open the custom shape picker to select from sets of complex shape thumbnails.

K You draw a custom shape just as you would any other shape: simply by clicking and dragging. Here, I clicked to apply the butterfly shape (left) and then dragged with the mouse to enlarge it (right).

To draw a custom shape:

1. Select the Custom Shape tool by doing one of the following:
   - Select the Shape tool in the Tools pane, and then click the Custom Shape button in the Tool Options bar.
   - Press U to toggle between the shape tools until the Custom Shape tool is selected.
2. To select a shape color, do one of the following:
   - Click the current foreground color swatch at the bottom of the Tools pane, or click the color box in the Tool Options bar to open the Color Picker.
   - Choose a color from the Color Swatches panel.
3. In the Tool Options bar, select from the available options or leave the options set to Unconstrained **I**.
4. Still in the Tool Options bar, click to open the custom shape picker **J**.
5. Click to choose from the list of default shapes, or select a different shape set from the Shapes drop-down menu.
6. In the image window, click and drag to draw the selected shape **K**.
7. Press Enter to deselect the shape.

TIP Custom shapes can be used in combination with other shapes and with the shape area options just like any of the basic geometric shapes.

If you ever want to paint on a shape or apply any filter effects to it, you'll first need to convert the shape from a vector path to a bitmap.

To convert a vector shape to a bitmap:

1. To open the Layers panel, do one of the following:
   - Click the the Layers button on the Task bar.
   - From the Window menu, choose Layers.
2. On the Layers panel, click to select the layer containing the shape (or shapes) you want to convert to bitmaps **L**.
3. From the Panel Options menu on the Layers panel, select Simplify Layer **M**.

   The vector shape is converted to a bitmap, and instead of showing the shape's path, the layer thumbnail displays the shape's image on a transparent background **N**.

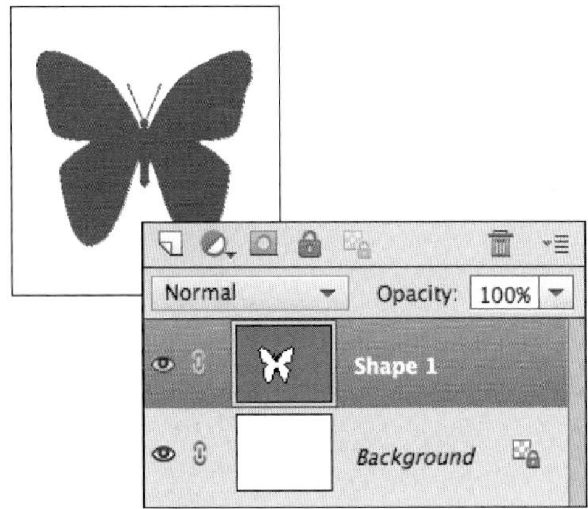

L Use the Layers panel to select a custom shape's layer.

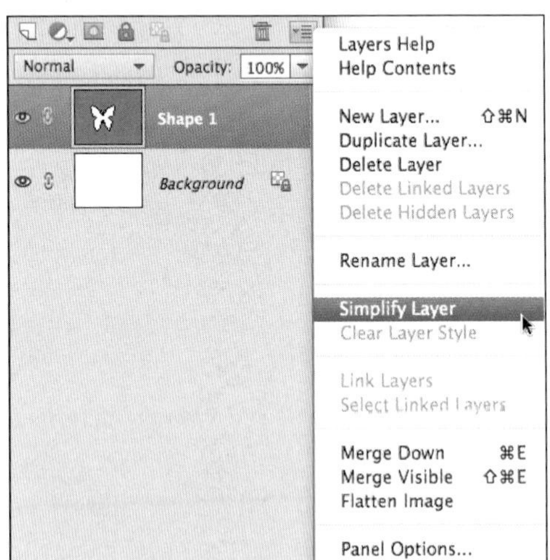

M The Simplify Layer command converts a custom shape's vector path to a bitmap graphic.

N The vector path layer thumbnail (left) and the converted bitmap thumbnail (right).

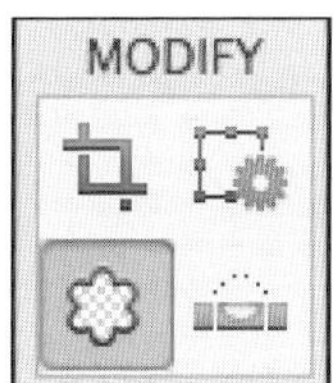

Ⓐ The Cookie Cutter tool.

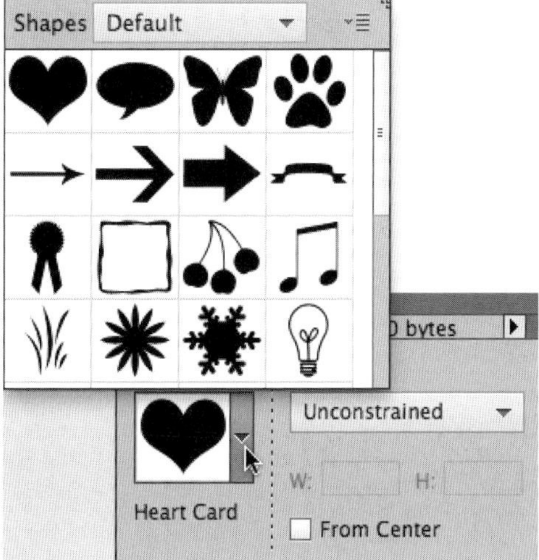

Ⓑ The Cookie Cutter tool uses the same shape libraries as the Custom Shape tool.

Using the Cookie Cutter Tool

The Cookie Cutter tool isn't exactly a painting or drawing tool, although right up to the moment you click the Commit Transform button, it behaves in exactly the same way as the Custom Shape tool. The Cookie Cutter tool uses the Custom Shape tool's libraries of shapes to create distinctive masked versions of image layers. The difference between the two (and it's a biggie) is that the Custom Shape tool creates vector shapes, whereas the Cookie Cutter tool creates a raster image. So, although you can initially scale, rotate, and otherwise distort a Cookie Cutter shape just like a vector graphic, once you commit the shape to your image, the final result is still a raster (or bitmap) image layer. Once you understand the Cookie Cutter's limitations, it can still be a fun and useful tool.

To mask an image with the Cookie Cutter tool:

1. From the Tools pane, click to select the Cookie Cutter tool (or press Q) Ⓐ.
2. In the Tool Options bar, choose how to size the cutter in the drop-down menu, or leave the option set to Unconstrained.
3. Click to open the Cookie Cutter shape picker Ⓑ.
4. Choose from the list of default shapes, or select a different shape set from the Custom Shapes drop-down menu.

continues on next page

5. In the image window, click and drag over an image layer to draw the selected shape.

   The image now appears only within the Cookie Cutter shape, leaving the rest of the layer transparent **C**.

   If you apply the Cookie Cutter tool to a flattened, background layer, it automatically converts the layer to a working layer with transparency.

6. To reposition the shape in the image window, place the cursor anywhere inside the shape bounding box, and then click and drag.

   Notice that as you drag the shape, different areas of the original image are revealed, as if you were moving a window around on a solid wall **D**.

7. To scale, rotate, or otherwise transform the shape, refer to the section "Transforming Shapes," earlier in this chapter.

8. When you're satisfied with the size and position of your masked shape, click the Commit Transform button, or press Enter.

   Once you commit the shape to the image layer, you can apply blending modes, opacity changes, and filters just as you would on any other raster image layer.

TIP For a similar effect that affords you more flexibility (namely, the ability to transform your layer mask indefinitely), create a shape with the Custom Shape tool, and then follow the steps in the section "Creating Clipping Masks," in Chapter 7.

C When you draw a shape with the Cookie Cutter tool, any underlying images are visible only within the shape.

D Moving the shape changes which portion of the image shows through.

Working with Text

When you think about all of the sophisticated photo retouching, painting, and drawing you can do in Photoshop Elements, manipulating type may not be a priority on your to-do list. However, you can create some amazing projects with the type tools, including greeting cards, posters, announcements, and invitations—and you don't have to fire up another software application.

This chapter covers the text formatting options and special type effects you can create with Photoshop Elements. If you've had any experience with word processing programs, the basic text formatting options will be familiar to you. But unlike a word processor, Photoshop Elements lets you create myriad special effects, using the type warping and masking tools and layer styles.

In This Chapter

Creating and Editing Text

When you use the type tools, your text is automatically placed on a new, unique layer. Since the text exists on its own layer, you can modify your text every way layers allow, including moving, applying blending modes, and changing the opacity. Also, having text on its own layer allows you to go back and edit it whenever you want.

You'll likely want to adjust the position of your text, and this is done just as easily as moving an object on any other layer. If you want to paint on your text or apply filters or effects to it, you'll need to simplify the layer by converting it to a standard bitmap. But remember: After a type layer has been simplified, it becomes part of the image, which means you can no longer edit the text. Fortunately, as long as you don't close the file, the Undo History panel will let you go back to the state your type was in before it was simplified. And you can always save a separate version of your file prior to simplifying the type layer.

To add text to an image:

1. Click to select the Type tool on the Tools pane (or press T) **A**. By default, the Horizontal Type Tool is selected **B**.

   Your pointer changes to an I-beam, as in many other text-editing programs **C**.

2. In the image window, move the pointer to the area where you want to insert your text, and then do one of the following:

   - Click to create a text insertion point. This method is perfect if you're setting just a single line of text, or a simple two- or three-line title or heading.

A The Type tool.

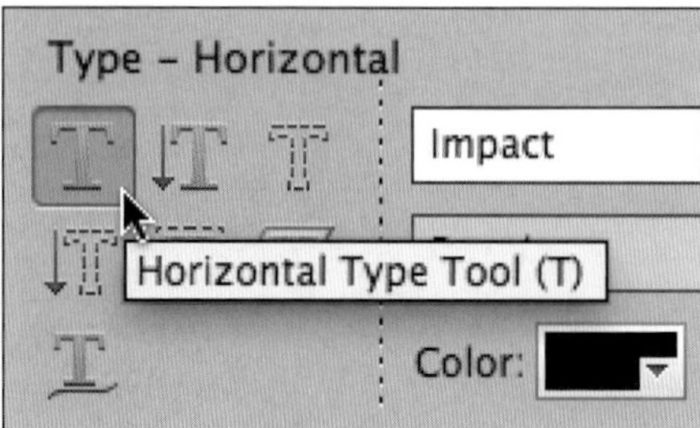

B Choose one of the Type tools from the Tool Options bar.

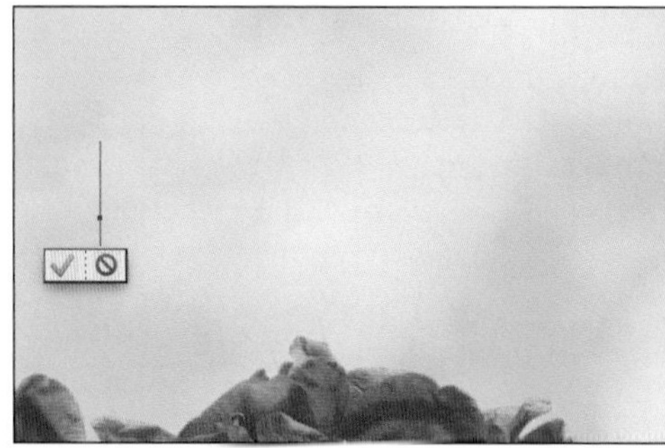

C When using one of the type tools, your pointer changes appearance to look like an I-beam. The text entry point is indicated by a vertical line whose height is based on the type size.

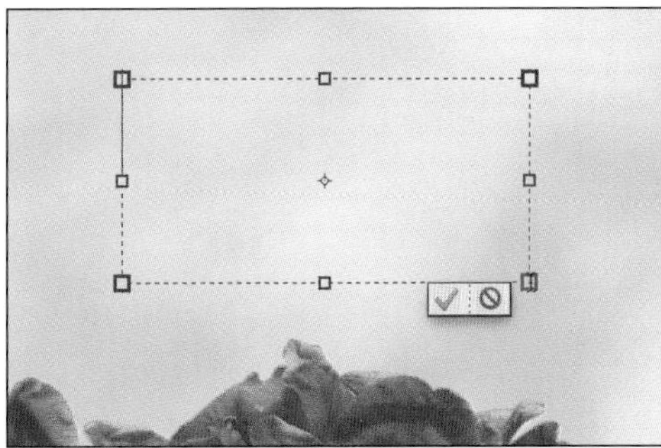

D Alternatively, drag the I-beam to create a paragraph text box.

E After you click once to establish the insertion point of your type, just start entering text. Press the Enter key to move to a new line.

F To make changes to existing text, click the appropriate layer on the Layers panel.

- If you want to set a long text paragraph, click and drag to create a paragraph text box **D**.

3. Type your text **E**. If you want to start a new line, press Enter.

   If you've created a paragraph text box, the text automatically flows to a new line when it bumps up against the border of the text box.

4. To confirm the text you've entered, do one of the following:

   - Press the Enter key on the numeric keypad (or the equivalent on laptops).
   - Click anywhere in your image, click a panel, or click a tool on the Tools pane.

   A new type layer is created and is visible on the Layers panel. The layer name is the text you entered.

To edit text:

1. Click a type layer on the Layers panel to make it active **F**.
2. In the image window, click in the text and edit as you would in any basic word processor.
3. Confirm your edits by clicking anywhere in your image.

TIP Consider changing the font size before you begin typing (which I describe shortly); 12-point text is easily lost in a high-resolution photo.

TIP If you want to add more text to a different part of your image, simply click elsewhere in the image and start typing. The new text is added to its own separate layer.

TIP Your image must be in grayscale or RGB mode if you want to add type to it. Elements' two other image modes, bitmap and indexed, don't support type layers.

To move text:

1. On the Layers panel, click the type layer you want to move.
2. Click the Move tool on the Tools pane.

   When you click the Move tool, your type is surrounded by a selection bounding box, allowing you to move the type as a single object anywhere on your image.
3. In the image window, drag your text to a new location **G**.

To simplify a type layer:

1. Choose a type layer on the Layers panel by clicking on it.
2. From the Layer menu or from the Layers panel menu, choose Simplify Layer.

   The layer ceases to be a type layer and the text is treated as pixels instead.

TIP You can also move a type layer while the Type tool is selected: Hold Ctrl/Command and click the layer; then drag it into position.

TIP When you simplify a type layer, does its icon in the Layers panel look empty? The tiny thumbnail may not appear to display your text if the type is small in relation to the full image size. Try this: Click the More drop-down menu and choose Panel Options. In the dialog that appears, click Layer Bounds in the Thumbnail Contents section, and then click OK. The layer's thumbnail icon displays only the text, not the entire image.

G Because text exists on its own separate layer, you can move it to different areas in the image by using the Move tool.

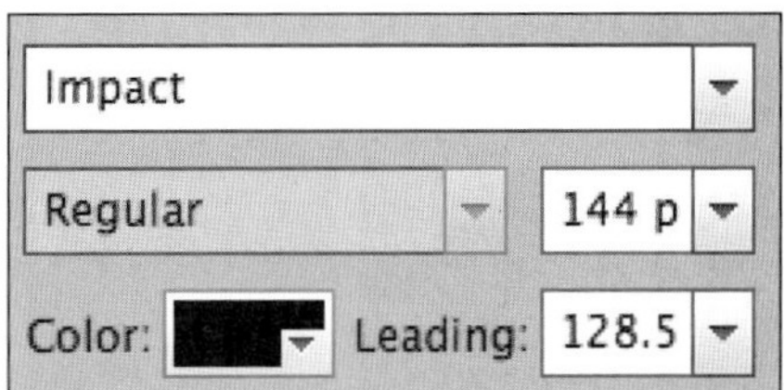

A The type formatting tools are all available on the text Tool Options bar.

B Drag across text with the text pointer.

C Double-click within a word to select it.

D Triple-click anywhere in a line of type to select the entire line.

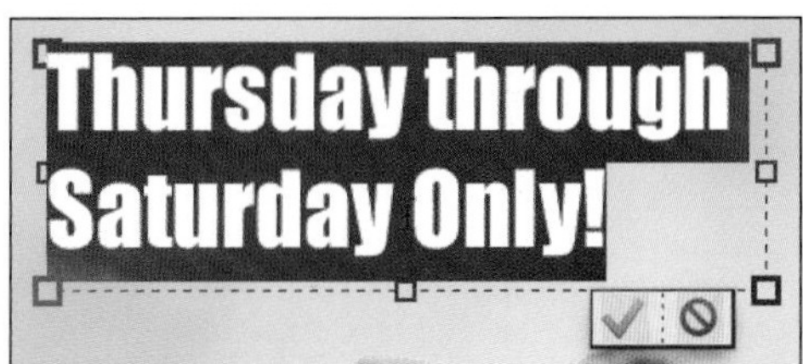

E Quadruple-click anywhere in a paragraph to select the entire paragraph.

Changing the Look of Your Text

You should be comfortable using the type formatting tools—font family, font style, and font size—because they're very similar to those found in most word processing programs. You can also change the text alignment and text color. All of these options are available on the Tool Options bar **A**.

To change any of these attributes, you first need to select the text characters you want to change. Most of the time, you'll want to select and apply changes to an entire line of text, but you can also select individual words or even individual characters.

To select text:

1. Click the type layer you want to edit on the Layers panel, or click on the type itself with the Move tool.
2. Select a type tool.
3. To select the text, drag across the characters to highlight them **B**, or do one of the following:
   - Double-click within a word to select the whole word **C**.
   - Triple-click to select an entire line of text **D**.
   - Quadruple-click to select an entire paragraph of text **E**.

TIP **You can select all the text on a layer without even touching the text with your pointer. Just select the type layer on the Layers panel and double-click the T icon.**

To choose the font family and style:

1. Select the text you want to change.
2. From the Tool Options bar, choose a font from the font family menu **F**.
3. Still in the Tool Options bar, choose a style from the font style menu **G**.

   If the font family you selected doesn't include a particular style, you can click the Faux Bold or Faux Italic button to change the look of your text **H**.

TIP If you haven't memorized the look of each and every font on your computer (and who has?), Photoshop Elements' font family menu displays an example of each font next to its font name. You can change the size of font samples or turn the display of the samples off by choosing Edit > Preferences > Type and then using the drop-down menu in the Type Options section of the Type Preferences dialog I.

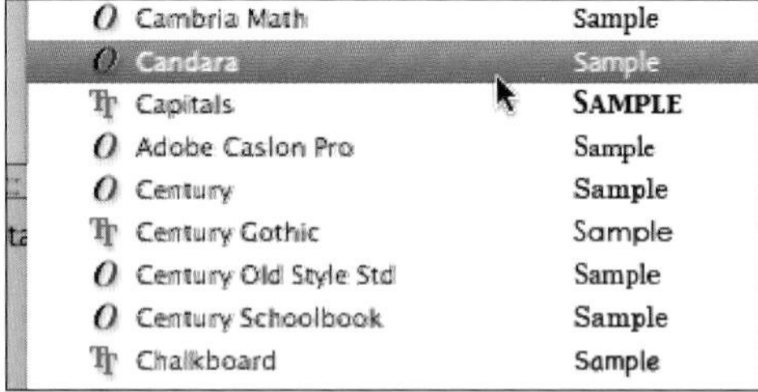

F All available fonts are listed on the font family menu.

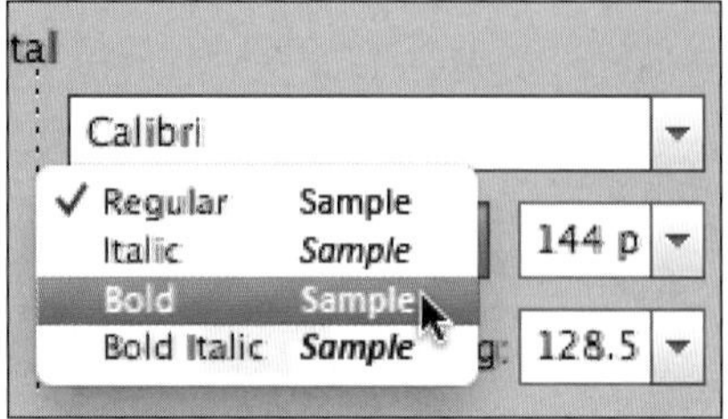

G Many fonts allow you to select a style from the font style menu.

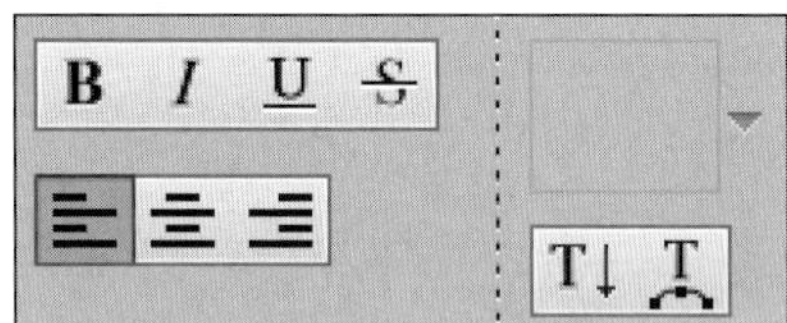

H If a font doesn't include style options, you can apply a bold or italic format with the icons in the Tool Options bar.

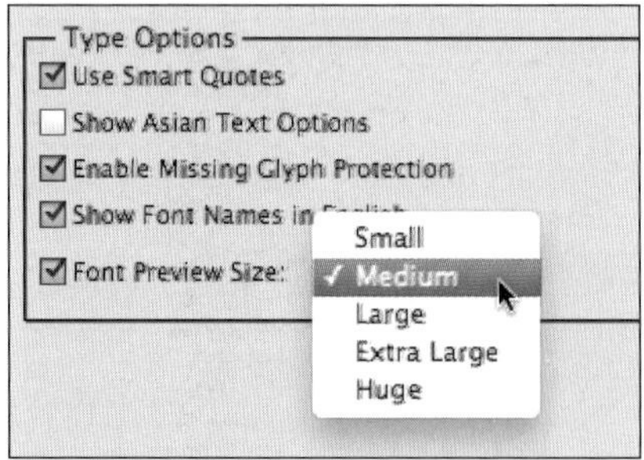

I Options in the Type Preferences dialog let you control the display of font previews in the font family menu.

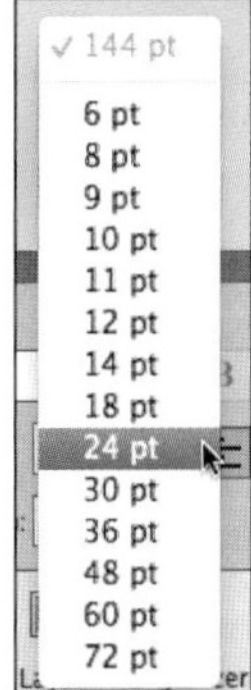

Ⓙ Use the type size menu to adjust the size of your type. To use a size not listed, just enter it in the text field.

Type size

Ⓚ Hold down the Shift key to quickly increase your type size in 10-point increments.

To change the font size:

1. Select the text you want to change.
2. Choose a size from the type size menu in the Tool Options bar Ⓙ.

   To change to a type size not listed on the menu, just enter a new value in the type size text field.

TIP Quickly adjust the type size up and down using keyboard shortcuts. Just select your text and then press Ctrl+Shift+. (period)/Command-Shift-. (period) to increase the size in 2-point increments. To reduce the size of the text, press Ctrl+Shift+, (comma)/Command-Shift-, (comma).

TIP You can also adjust the type size up and down in 1- or 10-point increments. Select your text and then select the type size in the type size menu in the Tool Options bar. Next, use the up and down keys on your keypad to size the type up and down in 1-point increments. If you hold down the Shift key while pressing the up or down keys, the type will adjust in 10-point increments Ⓚ.

TIP To change the default measurement unit for type, go to the Photoshop Elements Preferences and choose Units and Rulers. Here you can select among pixels, points, and millimeters (mm).

To change the line spacing:

1. Select the lines of text you want to change.
2. Choose a value from the line space menu in the Tool Options bar Ⓛ.

   To change to a line spacing value not listed on the menu, enter a new value in the line space text field.

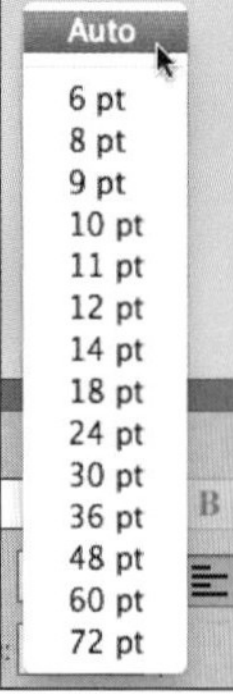

Ⓛ Use the line space menu to select line spacing for your type. You can also enter a line spacing value in the menu text field.

To apply underline or strikethrough:

1. Select the text you want to change.
2. Click either the Underline or Strikethrough icon in the Tool Options bar to apply that style to your text Ⓜ.

TIP The default line spacing value for any type size (Auto) serves as a good starting point, but it's surprising that something as simple as increasing or decreasing line spacing can have a dramatic visual impact Ⓝ.

TIP If your type layer is set to a vertical orientation, the underline appears on the left side of the type.

Ⓜ Apply underline and strikethrough from the Tool Options bar.

Big Bloomin'
Flower Show

Big Bloomin'
Flower Show

Ⓝ Default line spacing (top), and the same type size but with smaller line spacing (bottom).

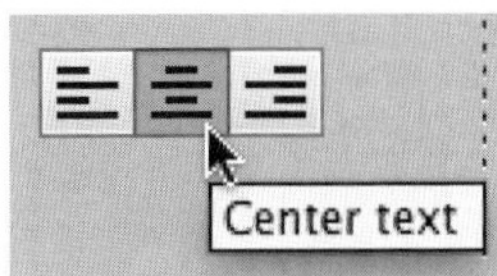

Ⓞ Aligning text within a paragraph box: Left Align (top); Center (middle); Right Align (bottom).

Ⓟ Change the text color by clicking the color selection drop-down menu.

To change the alignment:

1. Select the text you want to change.
2. From the Tool Options bar, choose an alignment option Ⓞ.

   The type shifts in relation to the origin of the line of text, or in the case of paragraph text, in relation to one side of the text box or the other. For point and click type, the origin is the place in your image where you first clicked before entering the type.

   - Left Align positions the left edge of each line of type at the origin, or on the left edge of the paragraph text box.
   - Center positions the center of each line of type at the origin, or in the center of the paragraph text box.
   - Right Align positions the right edge of each line of type at the origin, or on the right edge of the paragraph text box.

To change the text color:

1. Select the text you want to change.
2. Click the Color drop-down menu in the Tool Options bar and choose a color swatch Ⓟ. Or, click the Color Picker button at the lower-right corner to view more color options.
3. Click OK to apply the color to your text.

TIP You can also change the color of all text on a text layer without selecting the text itself. With the Text tool active, click to select a text layer in the Layers panel to make it the active layer, then follow the procedure to change the text color.

Working with Vertical Text

Most of the time, you'll use the standard Horizontal Type tool. But you can also change your type to a vertical orientation whenever you want. One of the reasons Elements includes both horizontal and vertical types is to accommodate the needs of the Asian-language versions of the product, such as Korean, Japanese, and Chinese.

To create vertical text:

1. Click the Type tool on the Tools pane and then choose the Vertical Type tool in the Tool Options bar **A**.

   The pointer changes to an I-beam.

2. Move the pointer to the area where you want to insert your text, and then do one of the following:

   - Click to create a text insertion point.
   - Click and drag to create a paragraph text box.

3. Type your text on the image **B**. The characters appear in descending order on your image.

4. To start a new line that will appear to the left of the first line, press Enter **C**.

   If you've created a paragraph text box, the text automatically flows to a new line when it bumps up against the bottom of the text box.

   To create and control the position of another line of vertical text, reselect the Vertical Type tool and create a separate, independent vertical type layer.

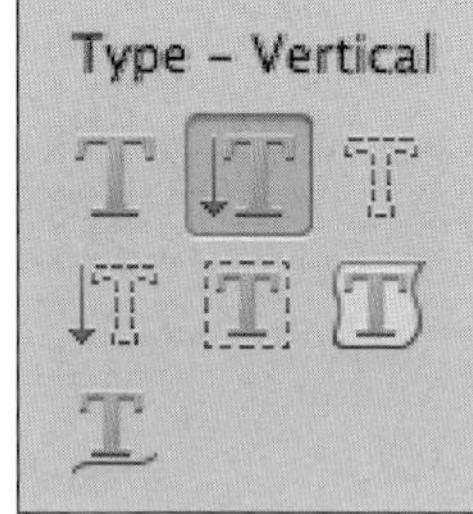

A The Vertical Type tool is located on the Tool Options bar.

B When you use the Vertical Type tool, your text appears in descending order (from the top down) on your image.

C When you press Enter, another line of vertical type is added to the left of the first line.

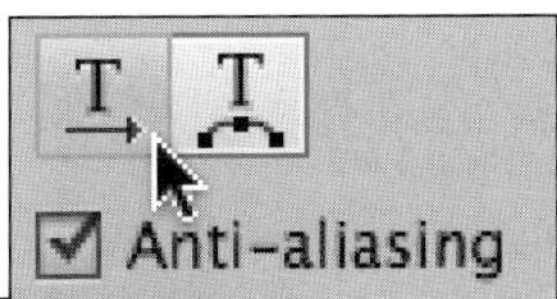

Ⓓ Switch between horizontal and vertical type by clicking the Change text orientation icon in the Tool Options bar.

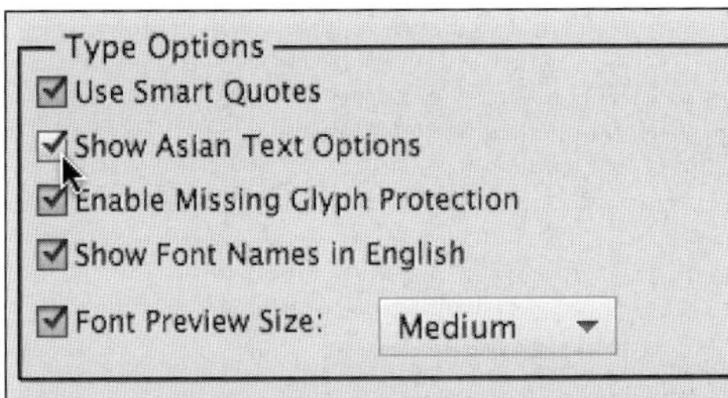

Ⓔ If your system supports Asian text options, you can work with them by selecting this feature in the Preferences > Type dialog.

To change the orientation of the text:

1. Select a type layer on the Layers panel.
2. Select the Type tool on the Tools pane and then click the Change text orientation icon in the Tool Options bar Ⓓ.

   The text changes to the opposite orientation: If your text is horizontal, it flips to vertical orientation—and vice versa.

TIP If you have Asian language fonts installed on your computer and you want to use the Asian type formatting options, choose Edit > Preferences > Type and select Show Asian Text Options Ⓔ.

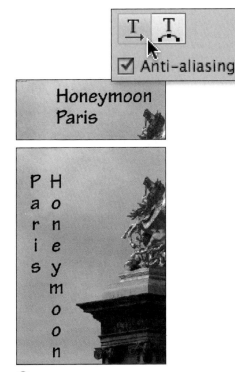

Creating Text on Paths

Text can be much more dynamic when it interacts with the imagery it's built upon. You can add text that follows the edge of a selection, a shape, or a custom path using three text tools. Once the text is created, you can resize, reposition, and restyle it as you wish.

A The text on path tools appear in the Tool Options bar.

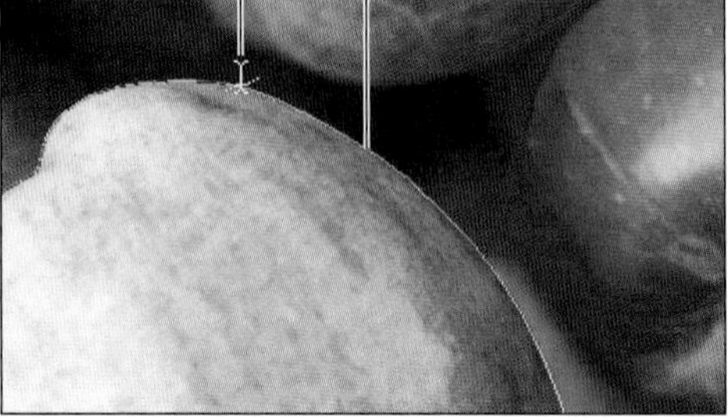

B Click where you want the text to begin.

C Type the text.

To create text on a selection:

1. Select the Text on Selection tool **A**.
2. Define the selected area: the tool acts like the Quick Selection tool, grabbing areas based on color and contrast.

   To change the size of the selection brush, switch to the Quick Selection tool and adjust the size there. Then, choose the Text on Selection tool again.
3. Optionally drag the Offset slider in the Tool Options bar to enlarge or retract the selection.
4. Click the Commit button to complete the selection; the edge becomes the path.
5. Position the mouse pointer over part of the path where you want to start typing; the cursor changes to an I-beam **B**.
6. Type the text, which follows the path **C**.
7. Click the Commit button or press Enter to apply the text.

To create text on a shape:

1. Select the Text on Shape tool.
2. In the Tool Options bar, choose a shape from the first drop-down menu.

   If you want to change the appearance of a shape, you need to specify the settings using the corresponding shape's tool. For example, to change the number of sides of a polygon, select the Polygon

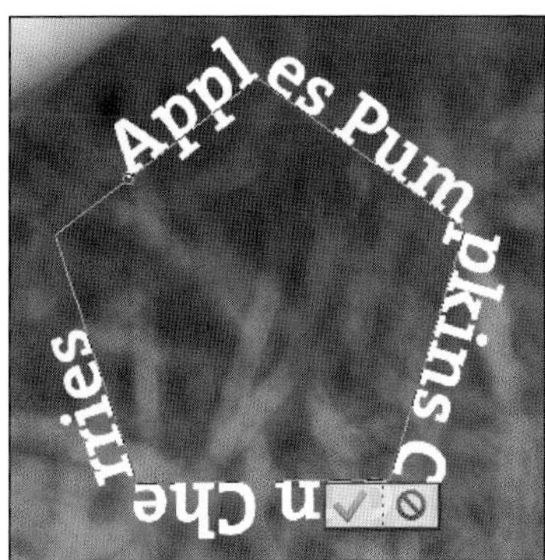

D Text flows around a polygon.

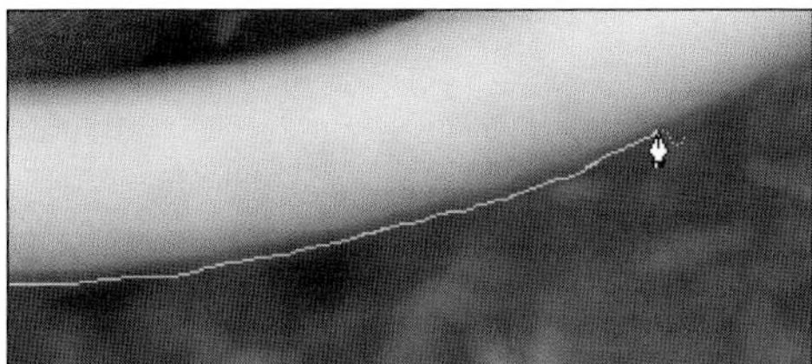

E Draw a freehand path.

F Text on a custom path can be less than smooth.

G Use the Refine Path tool to move control points.

tool (the tool itself, not the option in the Text on Shape tool) and change the value in the Sides field. The same goes for the curves of the Rounded Rectangle.

3. Draw the shape on your image and commit it.
4. Click the path and type your text **D**.
5. Click the Commit button or press Enter to apply the text.

To create text on a custom path:

1. Select the Text on Custom Path tool.
2. Click and drag to draw a line **E**, and commit it when you're done.
3. Click the path and type your text **F**.

   Don't be concerned if the text appears as if it went through an earthquake; Elements is placing the letters over a bumpy path. (The Editor doesn't offer full-blown Beziér curves to smooth the path; Adobe wanted to simplify the path-creation process.) You can modify the path as described below.
4. In the Tool Options bar, click the Modify button). The path's control points appear.
5. Drag the control points to alter the shape of the path **G**.
6. Click the Draw button to stop editing the path.

TIP I won't sugarcoat it. Editing control points on custom paths can be fiddly, time consuming, and frustrating. Depending on the shape you need, you may be better off creating text on a shape or selection instead.

TIP Even if you don't make custom paths, the tool is still useful: You can use the Refine Path mode to adjust control points on paths created using selections or shapes.

continues on next page

To edit the text formatting:

1. In the Layers panel, click the text layer you want to edit.
2. With any of the text on path tools active, click the type to insert your cursor, and then select the text.
3. Use the formatting controls in the Tool Options bar to choose typeface, size, and other formatting **H**.
4. Click the Commit button or press Enter to apply the edits.

H The formatting settings appear in the Tool Options bar when text is selected.

To reposition the text:

1. With any of the text on path tools active, click the type to insert your cursor.
2. Locate the origin point, a small circle where you started to enter your text **I**.
3. Hold Ctrl/Command and drag to slide the text away from the origin point; the cursor appears with an arrow icon.

   The behavior of the text as you drag depends on a couple factors:

   - If you drag above the text baseline, the letters remain on top of the line **J**. Pulling the mouse pointer below the baseline causes the text to flow along the inside of the shape.
   - Dragging behind the origin point makes the text disappear. To position the first letters further left, Ctrl/Command-click the origin point and move it before you slide the letters.

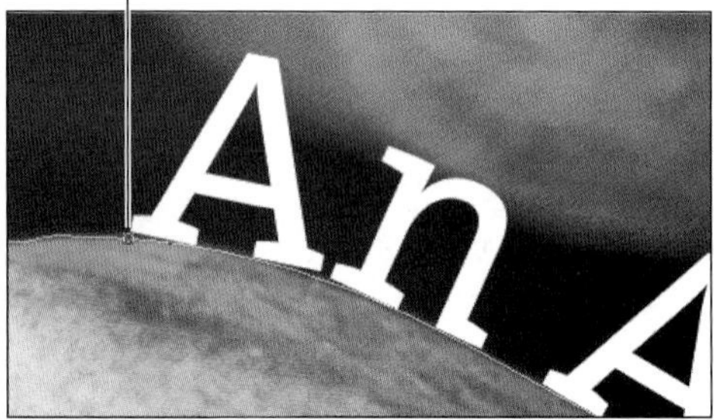

I The origin point can be hard to spot at first.

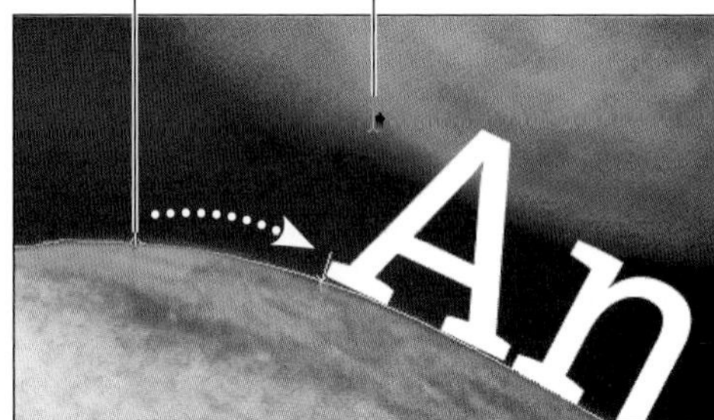

J Drag to reposition the text on the path.

TIP **With no text selected, hold Ctrl/Command and click to move the entire path.**

TIP **Apply modifications such as drop shadows using the options in the Effects panel K. See "Applying Layer Styles to Text," later in this chapter.**

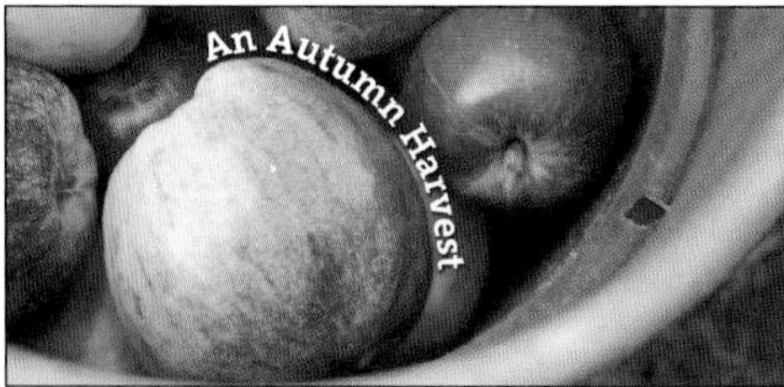

K Apply effects to text on path layers.

Ⓐ You'll usually want to anti-alias your text, especially when using larger type sizes. This example shows 60-point type viewed at 200 percent.

Ⓑ When using type sizes of about 14 points or less, you may want to turn off anti-aliasing so your text doesn't become blurry. This example shows 10-point type viewed at 200 percent.

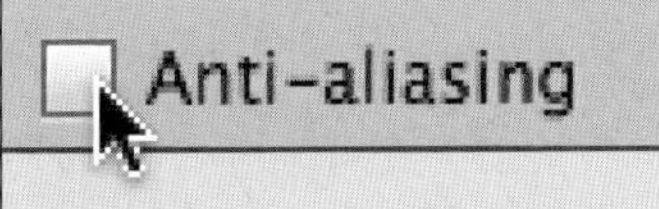

Ⓒ Turn anti-aliasing off and on with this icon in the Tool Options bar.

Anti-aliasing Text

You can choose to smooth the edges of, or anti-alias, your text, just as you can with image selections as discussed in Chapter 6. In most cases, you'll use Photoshop Elements to create fairly large, display-size text. For this reason, you'll normally want to anti-alias your text so it doesn't appear to be jagged Ⓐ.

The exception is when you use smaller font sizes, such as 14 points or less, and are planning to use the image for onscreen viewing on the Web. At smaller sizes, anti-aliasing actually makes your text less readable, and the smoothing effect looks more like blurring Ⓑ. Also, in the process of anti-aliasing, many more colors are generated, and not all Web browsers support all of these colors, so some unwanted color artifacts may appear around the edges of your type. By default, anti-aliasing is turned on.

To turn anti-aliasing off and on:

1. Select a type layer on the Layers panel.
2. Do one of the following:
   - Click the Anti-aliasing icon in the Tool Options bar. To reselect anti-aliasing, click the icon again Ⓒ.
   - From the main menu, choose Layer > Type > Anti-Alias Off, or Layer > Type > Anti-Alias On.

Warping Text

Photoshop Elements lets you distort text easily using the Warp tool. You can choose from 15 different warping options in the Warp Text dialog. In this dialog, you can adjust the amount of the bend in the type, as well as the horizontal and vertical distortion.

Even after you've warped your text, it's still completely editable, and you can make additional formatting changes to it at any time. But because the warp effect is applied to the entire type layer, you can't warp individual characters—it's all or nothing.

To warp text:

1. Select a type layer on the Layers panel.
2. From the Tools pane, select a type tool (so that the type options appear in the Tool Options bar) and click the Create Warped Text icon **A**.

   The Warp Text dialog appears.
3. Choose a warp style from the drop-down menu.
4. Choose either Horizontal or Vertical orientation for the effect **B**.
5. You can also modify the amount of Bend and Horizontal or Vertical distortion using the sliders **C**.
6. Click OK to apply the effect.

A Click the Create Warped Text icon in the Tool Options bar to experiment with distortions.

B The Horizontal and Vertical orientation options create radically different results.

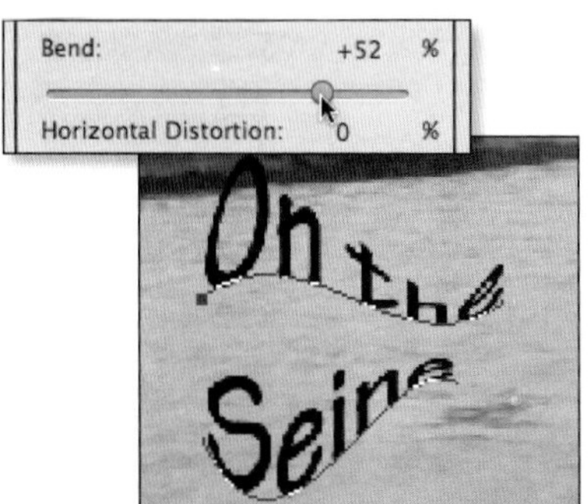

C In this example, the Bend slider helps to dramatically exaggerate the fish shape.

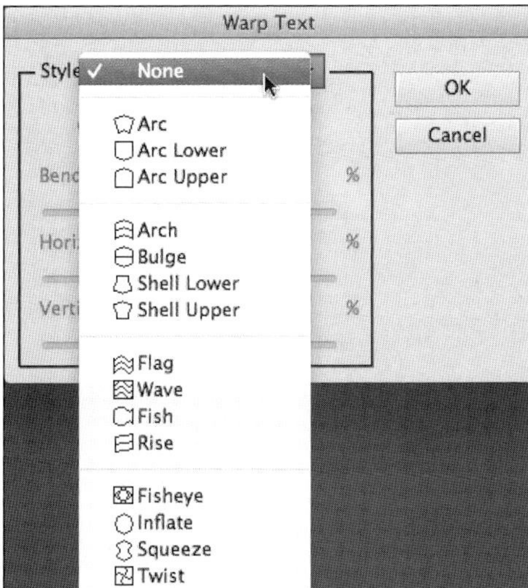

D To remove text warp, select None from the Style drop-down menu.

To remove text warp:

1. On the Layers panel, select a type layer that's been warped.
2. Select a type tool and click the Create Warped Text icon in the Tool Options bar.
3. Choose None from the Style drop-down menu **D**.
4. Click OK to remove the effect.

TIP As you experiment with the various warping options, your text can undergo some pretty dramatic changes. For this reason, you might want to move your text around to see how it looks in different parts of your image. Luckily, you can do this without closing the Warp Text dialog. If you move your pointer into the image area, you'll see that it automatically changes to the Move tool so you can move your text around while adjusting the warping effect.

Creating Text Effects Using Type Masks

Sometimes the text effects you want to create are better done with a type selection, not the actual, editable type. The Horizontal and Vertical Type Mask tools let you enter text, which is automatically converted to a selection in the shape of type. Since it's a selection, you can do everything you can do to any other selection—you can paint or fill the type or transform its geometry by skewing it or applying perspective. Unlike the previous type tools discussed, the type mask tools do not create a unique layer. The type selection appears on whichever layer is active at the time you use the tool. The bottom line: A type selection is just like any other selection, but in the shape of text.

To create a selection with the type mask tools:

1. Make sure your active layer is the one where you want the text selection to appear **A**.
2. Select either the Horizontal or Vertical Type Mask tool **B**.
3. Set the type options (such as font, style, or size) in the Tool Options bar.
4. Enter text on the image by either clicking or clicking and dragging and then typing your text.

   The text appears reversed out of the colored mask overlay **C**.
5. Commit your text selection by clicking outside the selection or pressing Enter.

   Your text area is selected **D**.

   You can now apply additional changes to the selection.

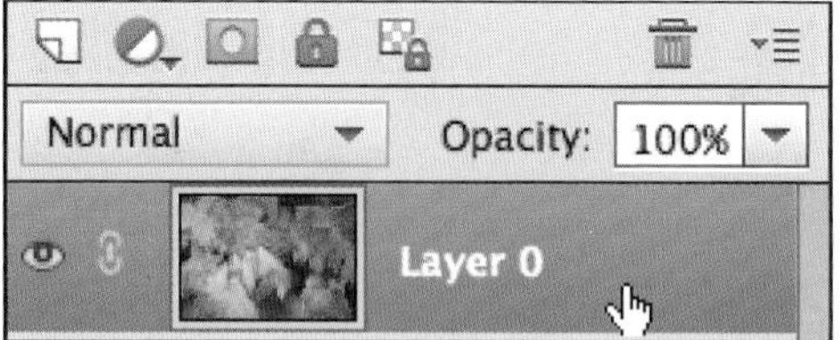

A To create a type mask, first select the layer on which you want it to appear.

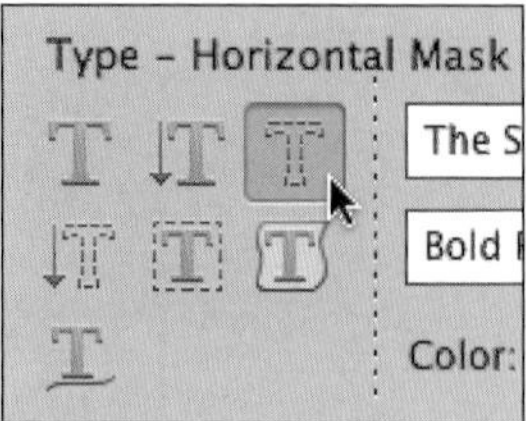

B Choose either the Horizontal or Vertical Type Mask tool.

C Your type appears reversed out of the colored mask.

D After you commit the type, it appears as a selection with the typical selection border.

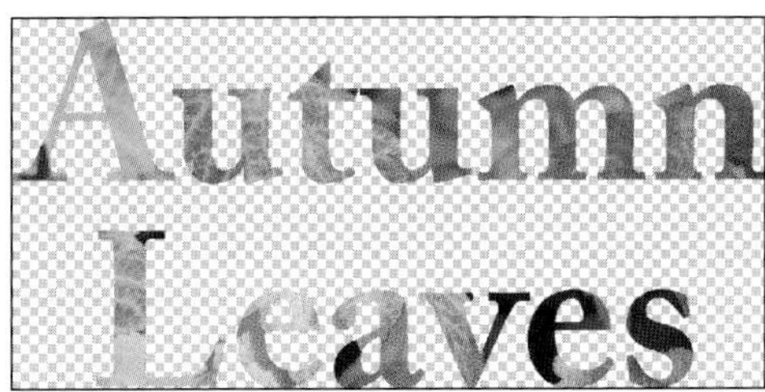

E You can create all sorts of interesting text effects by filling type with images.

F To fill text with a gradient, start by making a type selection.

G Click the Gradient tool on the Tools pane and then choose a gradient.

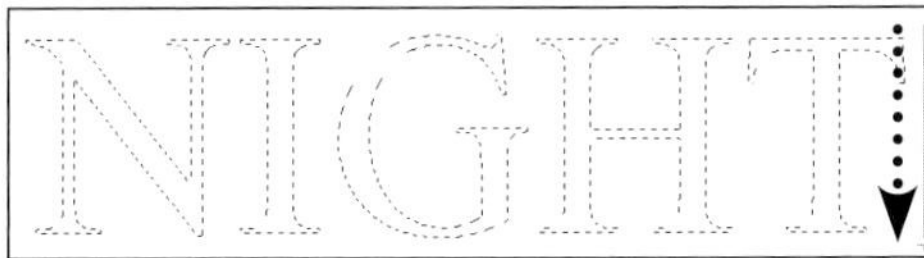

H Drag in the direction you want the gradient to appear inside your type.

I This example uses the Linear gradient.

To fill a text selection with an image:

1. Create a text selection following the steps in the preceding task.

   Be sure to position the selection over the image you want to show through the text.

2. Copy the selection to the clipboard by choosing Copy from the Edit menu, or by pressing Ctrl+C/Command-C.
3. From the File menu, choose New > Image from Clipboard.

   Your text selection appears in its own file, with the image peeking through E.

To apply a gradient to a text selection:

1. Create a text selection following the steps in the task "To create a selection with the type mask tools" F.
2. Click the Gradient tool on the Tools pane and choose any gradient style in the Tool Options bar G.
3. Drag across your text selection to establish the direction of the gradient H.
4. Deselect the text selection.

   Your text appears with the gradient fill I.

TIP Up until the moment you commit the text, you can edit your type masks (change their font, size, line spacing, and alignment) just as you would any other line or paragraph of type.

TIP You can move a text selection around in the image window as if it were any other selection. Once you click the Commit icon, select any of the marquee selection tools from the Tools pane. Move the cursor over your text selection until it becomes the Move Selection icon. Then you can click and drag to reposition your text selection.

Applying Layer Styles to Text

Since the Horizontal and Vertical Type tools create a unique text layer, you can use layer styles to make all sorts of unusual and interesting changes to your type. The significant advantage of using layer styles with your text (as opposed to using type masks) is that your text remains editable.

To apply a layer style to text:

1. Enter text in your image using either the Horizontal or Vertical Type tool **A**.
2. Make sure the appropriate type layer is selected on the Layers panel; then, on the Effects panel, choose a style from the Layer Styles panel list **B**.
3. Click the Apply button to apply the style to your text **C**.

TIP When choosing a font, it's a good idea to go with bolder sans-serif typefaces. This way, your type is more likely to remain readable after you've applied the style.

TIP If you're not quite getting the look you want, remember that you can set lighting angle, shadow distance, and other options by selecting Layer Style > Style Settings from the Layer menu, or by double-clicking the Layer Style icon to the right of the layer name in the Layers panel.

A To use layer styles with your type, first enter text with one of the type tools.

B You can use any of Photoshop Elements' dozens of layer styles on your type.

C Sophisticated effects that would be difficult to create manually are easily applied to text.

Preparing Images for the Web

You may want to post your digital photos to a Web page or a social-networking site. Whether you decide to post a snapshot of an old push mower to eBay or just want to share vacation photos with your Aunt Ruth, the considerations are much the same.

Size and speed influence most decisions regarding image preparation for the Web, and they are the central themes of this chapter. While broadband is now widely available worldwide, it's still a good idea to optimize the size of your digital images: the smaller the image file size, the more quickly it appears, even with the fastest Internet connection.

I'm not abandoning aesthetics—after all, there's little purpose in uploading a photograph that's too fuzzy or distorted to be seen clearly. This chapter's focus is also about creating compact files that look good.

If you're looking to post a gallery of photos instead of optimizing and saving images one at a time, see Chapter 15.

In This Chapter

Understanding Image Requirements for the Web

Preparing images for the Web presents a set of challenges distinct from printing to paper. Even with abundant broadband worldwide, a significant percentage of Web users have dial-up or relatively slow broadband connections. This means your images need to be small enough to download quickly while retaining color and clarity comparable to your original image.

Photoshop Elements offers some digital sleight of hand through a process called optimization. Optimization pares down and streamlines an image's display information based on settings you can choose among and preview to determine the best combination of values.

By limiting the number of colors in an image, or by selectively discarding pixels that are less critical than others, Elements removes information from an image and reduces the associated file size. Once an image has been streamlined in this way, it is *optimized* Ⓐ.

Photoshop Elements offers four file format options for optimizing an image: JPEG, GIF, PNG-8, and PNG-24. Generally speaking, JPEG and PNG-24 are most appropriate for images that contain subtle transitions of tone and color (like photographs), while GIF and PNG-8 are best for graphics or illustrations containing a lot of flat color or typography Ⓑ.

Ⓐ The original illustration (top) contains a great deal of detail and subtle gradations of tone and color. The over-optimized version (bottom) is greatly simplified and contains far less color and image information.

Ⓑ The photograph on the top, with its subtle and varied tones and color, is a good candidate for JPEG optimization, whereas the flat, bold colors and use of typography in the illustration on the bottom make it more appropriate for GIF optimization.

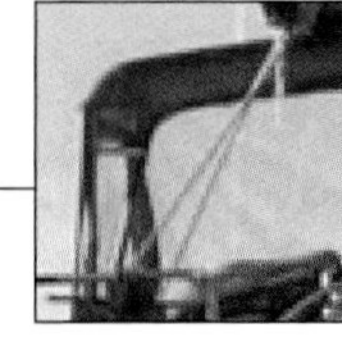

A This image was duplicated (top) and then reduced 50% (bottom). Notice in the zoom views that the reduced image isn't as detailed as the original. That's because, even though both have the same number of pixels per inch, the reduced image contains fewer pixels overall.

Changing Image Size and Resolution

As you'll see in this chapter, the Save for Web dialog can optimize a photo when you want to save a Web-ready copy but keep your original version's resolution. But what if you're editing images that will be used just as Web site navigation elements? Or perhaps you need to resize a logo for a project?

The Image Size dialog adjusts pixel dimensions, image dimensions, and resolution. You will often capture one image and then use it for different purposes, so it's important to understand how these adjustments affect your image file.

For the Web and other onscreen viewing, it's common to adjust the pixel dimensions, or number of pixels, to control the resolution and/or file size of the image. This is known as *resampling*. The Resample Image checkbox is probably the most important feature to understand. When this box is checked, the pixel dimensions change—that is, the pixels will increase or decrease in number as the image is resampled **A**. When the box is *not* checked, the pixel dimensions are locked in, and no resampling can occur.

When preparing an image for print, you can change the *document* size (the size the image will print), but the number of pixels in the image and the size that the image displays onscreen will stay the same. (See Chapter 15 for details on printing.)

To resize an image for screen viewing:

1. From the Image menu, choose Resize > Image Size to open the Image Size dialog.
2. Make sure the Resample Image box is checked, and click the Resample Image drop-down menu **B**.

   When you resample an image, its pixels are transformed using a process known as an *interpolation*. Interpolation is a computer calculation used to estimate unknown values based on existing known values—in this case, pixel color values. So, when you resample an image in Elements, its existing pixels are changed using one of five primary interpolation methods **C**:

   - Bicubic is the default option and generally produces the best results and smoothest gradations.
   - Bilinear produces medium-quality results.
   - Nearest Neighbor is the fastest method, but may produce jagged effects.
   - Bicubic Smoother can be used when you're increasing the size of an image, or *upsampling*. Typically, I strongly advise against upsampling, because there is usually a noticeable loss of image quality and sharpness. But I've seen acceptable results with Bicubic Smoother, as long as I don't resize much above 120 percent.
   - Bicubic Sharper can be used when you're reducing the size of an image, or *downsampling*. Its purpose is to help retain sharpness and detail. My success with this option has been mixed.

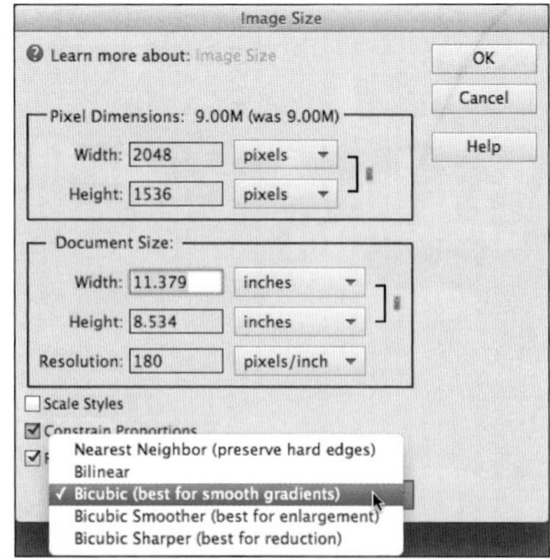

B The Resample Image drop-down menu includes five options for specifying how the resampling occurs.

C You can resample an image using one of three calculation methods: Bicubic (left), Bilinear (center), or Nearest Neighbor (right). Bicubic does the best job at retaining detail and anti-aliasing, whereas Nearest Neighbor creates images with a rougher quality.

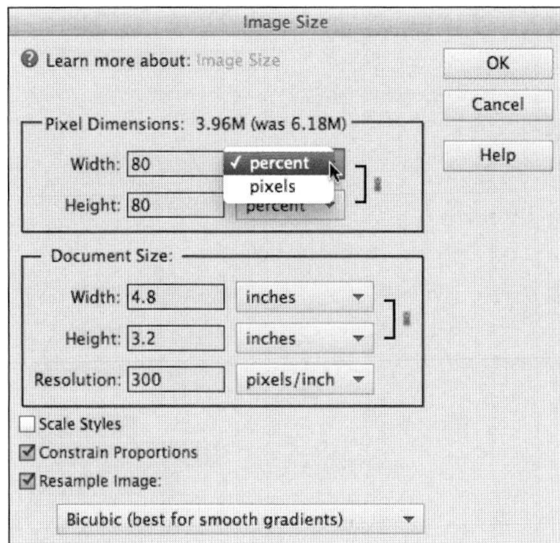

D Pixel dimensions can be entered as pixels or as percentages.

3. To maintain the current width-to-height ratio, make sure Constrain Proportions is checked.
4. Enter new values in the Pixel Dimensions fields. You can enter values in pixels or as percentages **D**.

   If you choose percent, you can enter a percentage amount in either the Height or Width field to automatically scale the image to that percentage. The new file size for the image is displayed at the top of the dialog (along with the old file size in parentheses).
5. Click OK to complete the change. The image is resized larger or smaller, depending on the pixel dimensions or percentage you entered.

TIP When you change an image's size by changing its pixel dimensions, you also change its print size (you'll see the change in the width and height dimensions in the Document Size fields of the Image Size dialog). Although these images are acceptable for onscreen viewing or as quick test prints, you may be disappointed with their printed quality. That's because resampling discards some image information, which reduces sharpness and detail.

About the Save for Web Dialog

The Save for Web dialog might be more appropriately called the "Prepare Web Images" or "Optimization" dialog. Within it, you'll find all the tools, drop-down menus, and text fields necessary to transform any digital photograph, painting, or illustration into a graphic that will work well in a Web browser.

The original and optimized image previews, the heart of this dialog, provide instant visual feedback whenever setting adjustments are made. Information fields below the image previews constantly update to reflect the current optimization format, file size, and download times. And at any time in the optimization process, you can preview and verify exactly how your image will appear in any Web browser loaded on your computer.

Choosing File Formats

- JPEG: JPEG is the most common file format for images on the Web. Because it supports 24-bit color (which translates to over 16 million colors), it's the ideal format for optimizing photos without sacrificing too much image quality. However, because it's a lossy format—meaning that it doesn't provide as much fidelity as the original information by selectively reducing quality to reduce image file size—it's not the best choice for images where detail and sharpness are critical, such as scanned line art, vector graphics, or images containing a lot of type.
- GIF: If you want to keep the detail in your images as sharp as possible, try using the GIF format. The GIF format sacrifices subtle gradations of tone and color, but retains the sharpness and image detail that can be lost with the JPEG format, making it a good choice for animations, images with transparency, vector graphics, and images with type.
- PNG: PNG comes in two main flavors, both supported by Elements: PNG-8, which is similar to GIF, and PNG-24, which is similar to JPEG. PNG is a newer image format than both GIF or JPEG, and it wasn't until 2002 or 2003 that you could rely on browsers to display PNG images correctly.

  Versions of Internet Explorer earlier than IE 7 may have problems with features like transparency. If you're creating images that will mostly be viewed by people who have newer browsers, PNG is a reasonable choice; if your audience is mostly using old computers and browsers, it's not so good.

  Although in some cases PNG-8 images can be slightly smaller than comparable GIF images, PNG formats (particularly PNG-24) tend to produce images markedly larger than their GIF and JPEG counterparts. Keeping with the goal of controlling file size, stick with GIF and JPEG formats for optimizing your images.

Optimizing an Image for the Web

With the Save for Web command, Photoshop Elements provides a simple, automated method that saves an optimized copy of your original image. Feel free to experiment with the custom settings, but the predefined settings should satisfy the requirements of most of your optimization tasks.

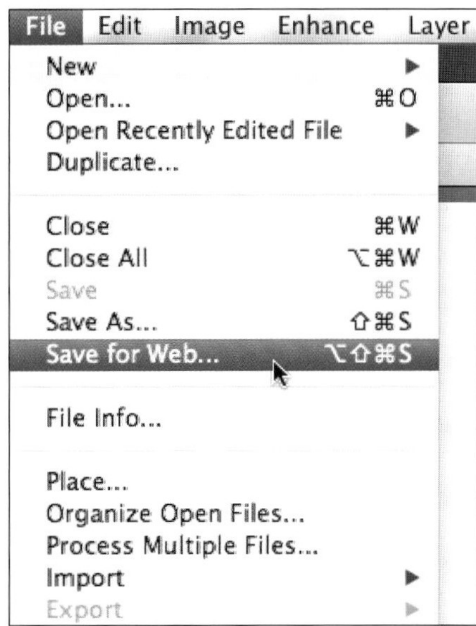

Ⓐ Open the Save for Web dialog from the File menu.

To save an image for the Web:

1. Open the image you want to optimize.
2. From the File menu, choose Save for Web Ⓐ, or press Ctrl+Alt+Shift+S/Command-Option-Shift-S. The Save for Web dialog opens on top of the active image window, displaying the image in side-by-side original and optimized previews Ⓑ.

continues on next page

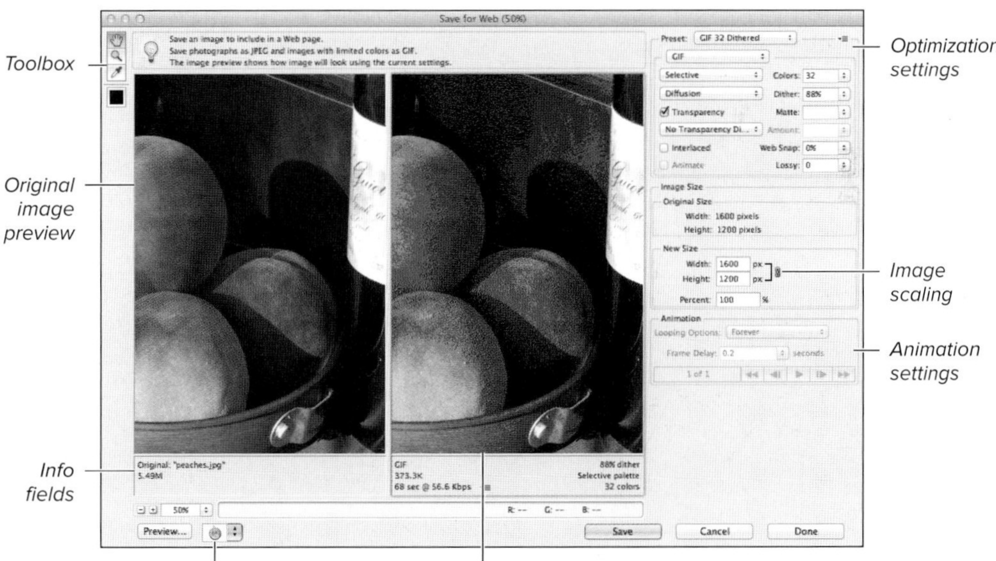

Ⓑ The Save for Web dialog. The image on the left shows the original image. The image on the right shows a preview of what the same image will look like after it's been optimized.

3. From the Preset drop-down menu, choose a predefined optimization setting **C**.

   The various drop-down menus within the Preset portion of the dialog change to reflect the setting you've selected **D**, as does the optimized preview in the center of the dialog.

4. Click the OK button.

5. In the Save Optimized As dialog, type a new name for your file and verify that the file type matches the optimization format you chose in the Save for Web dialog.

6. Choose a location for your file and then click Save.

   The Save Optimized As and Save for Web dialogs automatically close, and your optimized image is saved to the location you specified.

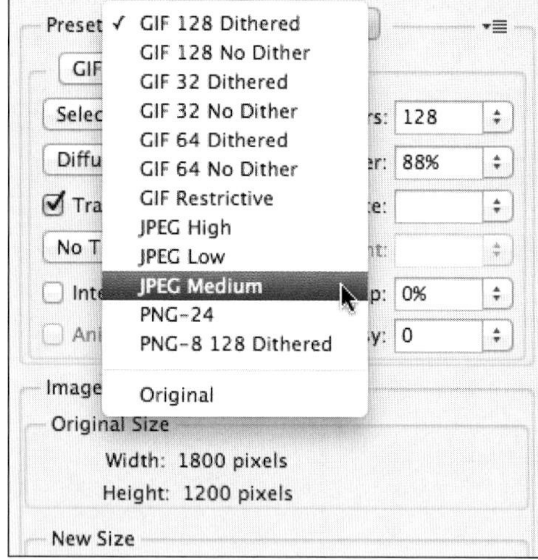

C Choose from the list of predefined settings for JPEG, GIF, or PNG optimization formats.

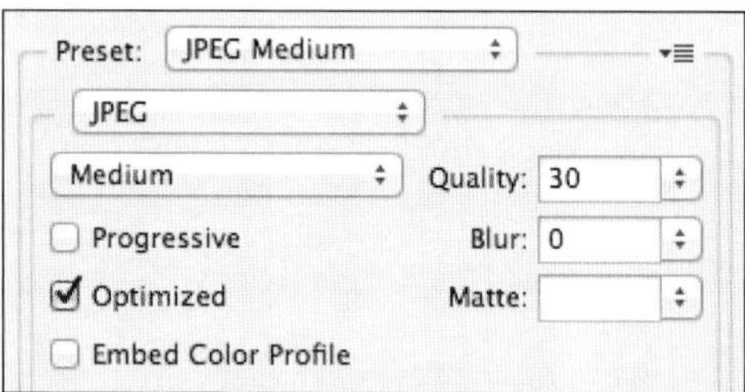

D Once you've chosen a predefined optimization setting, the rest of the options change accordingly. Here, the options have automatically changed to reflect the Medium JPEG optimization format.

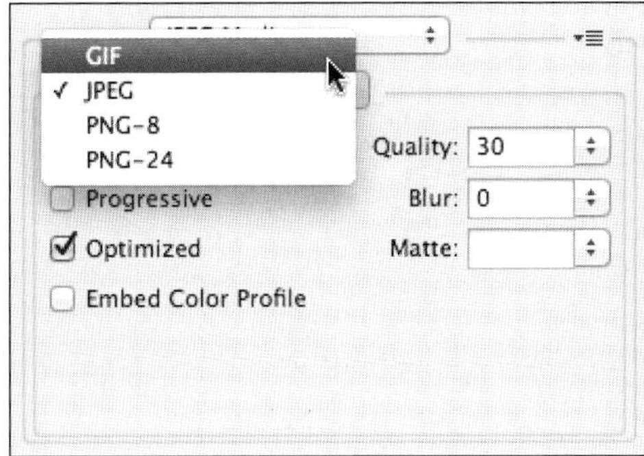

Ⓐ Optimization formats can be changed at any time from the drop-down menu.

Adjusting Optimization Settings

You're not limited to using predefined settings to optimize your images. Fine-tune the settings further by using the collection of drop-down menus, checkboxes, and sliders available in the Settings portion of the Save for Web dialog. For example, if you want your JPEGs to retain a little more image quality, you can change the default quality setting for a Medium JPEG image from 30 to 45, improving its sharpness and detail without increasing its size much. As you make adjustments, refer to the optimized image preview to see how your changes affect the image, as well as view its current potential file size and download time.

To apply custom JPEG optimization settings to an image:

1. Open the image you want to optimize, then choose File > Save for Web to open the Save for Web dialog.
2. From the Preset drop-down menu, choose one of the predefined JPEG settings.

   You don't have to choose one of the presets, but they can serve as a good jumping-off point for building your own settings. For instance, if you decide small file size and quick download time are priorities, you might want to start with the predefined JPEG Low setting and then customize the settings from there.
3. Verify that JPEG is selected from the Optimized file format drop-down menu, or if you've decided to skip step 2, choose JPEG from the Optimized drop-down menu Ⓐ.

continues on next page

4. To set the image quality, do one of the following:

   ▸ From the compression quality drop-down menu, select a quality option **B**.

   ▸ Drag the Quality slider while referring to the optimized preview **C**.

   The Quality slider has a direct impact on the Quality drop-down menu, and vice versa. Remember that a setting in the Very High or Maximum range will create a file six to eight times larger than one saved in the Low range.

5. Select the Progressive checkbox if you want your image to build from a low-resolution version to its final saved version as it downloads in a Web browser **D**.

   This option is more critical for large, high-quality images with download times in the tens of seconds. Rather than leaving a blank space, the low-res image appears almost immediately, giving your Web page visitors something to look at until the complete file is downloaded.

6. Select the Embed Color Profile checkbox if you previously saved a color profile with the image and want that information preserved.

   Unless your photo or art contains some critical color (a logo with a very specific corporate color, for instance), leave this box unchecked. Not all browsers support color profiles, and including this information can increase file size significantly.

7. If your original image contains transparency, see "Making a Web Image Transparent" later in this chapter.

8. Click the OK button to rename and save your optimized image.

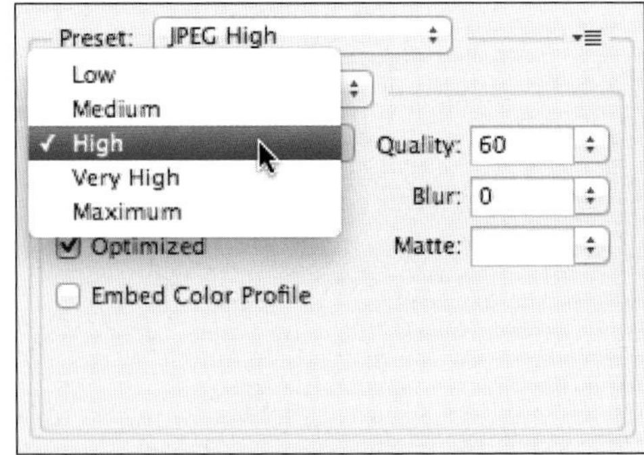

B Choose from five basic quality options for JPEG images.

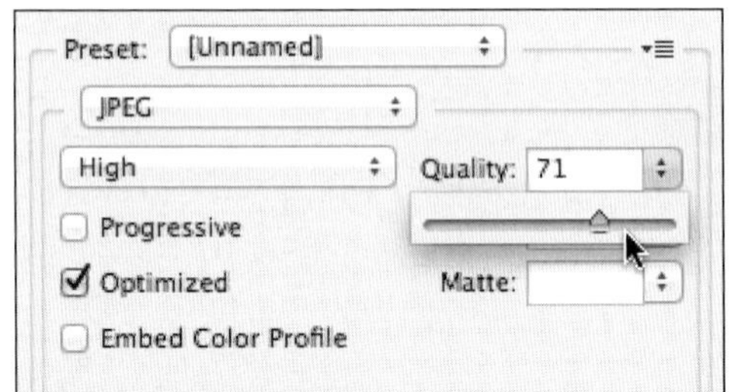

C Once a quality option has been selected, use the slider control to fine-tune it.

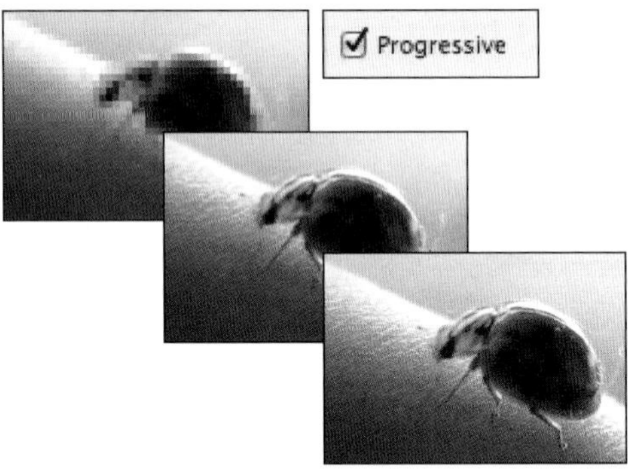

D The Progressive feature draws your JPEG image incrementally on a Web page as it downloads, eventually displaying the image in its final state.

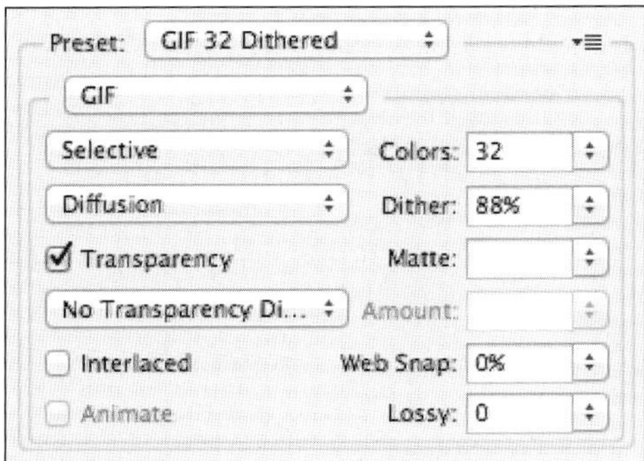

E Choose the GIF setting to optimize illustrations, vector art, or type.

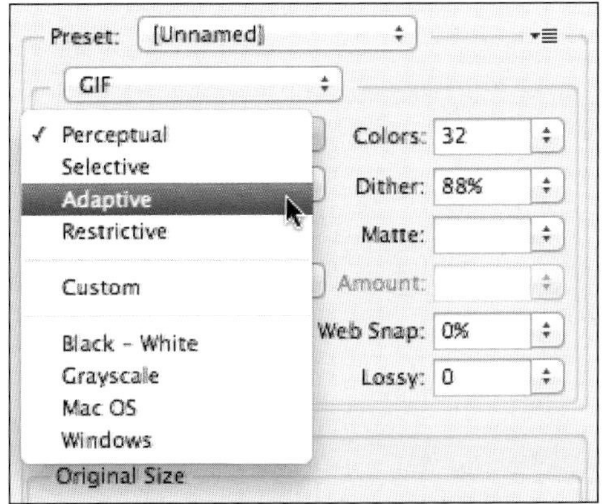

F The GIF format offers several schemes for interpreting and displaying the color in your image.

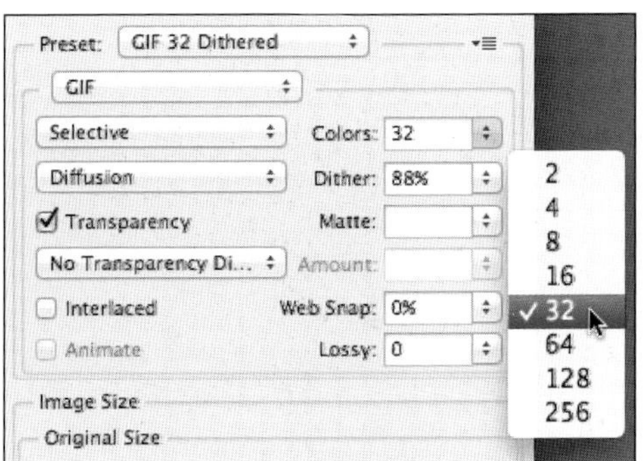

G A GIF image can contain from 2 to 256 colors.

To apply custom GIF optimization settings to an image:

1. Open the image you want to optimize, then choose File > Save for Web to open the Save for Web dialog.
2. From the Preset drop-down menu, choose one of the predefined GIF settings, or choose GIF from the Optimized file format drop-down menu **E**.
3. From the Color Reduction Algorithm drop-down menu, choose a color lookup table to apply to your image **F**. (See the sidebar "About Color Models," later in this chapter.)
4. From the Colors drop-down menu, choose the maximum number of colors that will appear in your image **G**.

   You can choose from the list of eight standard color panel values, use the arrows to the left of the text field to change the values in increments of one, or simply enter a value in the text field and press Enter.

   When formatting GIF images, the number of colors you specify will have a larger impact on final file size and download time than any other attribute you set. Naturally, the fewer colors you select, the smaller the image file size will be, so experiment with different values, gradually reducing the number of colors, until you arrive at a setting you find acceptable.

continues on next page

5. Use the Dither slider to specify a percentage for the dither **H**.

   Higher percentages create finer dither patterns, which tend to preserve more detail in images where limited color panels have been specified.

   Although not accessible from the Save for Web dialog, Photoshop Elements gives you the option to save a GIF image with one of three different Dither options. (For more information, see the sidebar "Choosing Dithering Options.")

6. If you want your image to build from a low-resolution version to its final saved version as it downloads in a browser, select the Interlaced checkbox **I**.

   Interlacing a GIF image works in much the same way as applying the Progressive option to a JPEG image. If you choose not to select the interlace option, your image won't display on a Web page until it's completely downloaded.

7. If your original image contains transparency, see "Making a Web Image Transparent" later in this chapter.

8. Click the OK button to rename and save your optimized image.

TIP If you want to save an image in the PNG-8 format, you'll notice it uses all the same options as for GIF, and the procedures for applying custom PNG-8 settings will be exactly the same as those for GIF. The only options available for PNG-24 are transparency and interlacing.

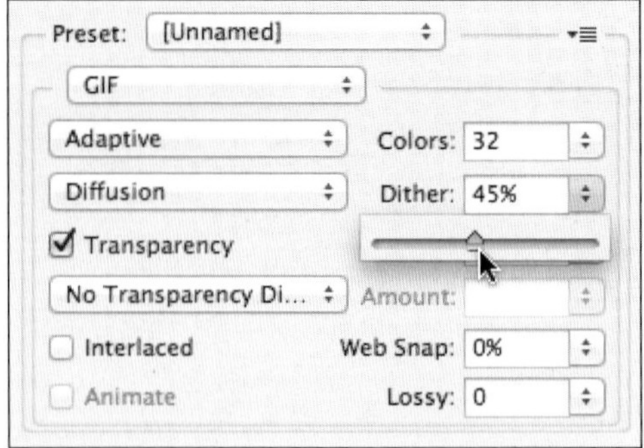

H Since diffusion is the default dither option for any GIF image you create in the Save for Web dialog, you can control the amount of dithering that occurs: from 0 to 100 percent.

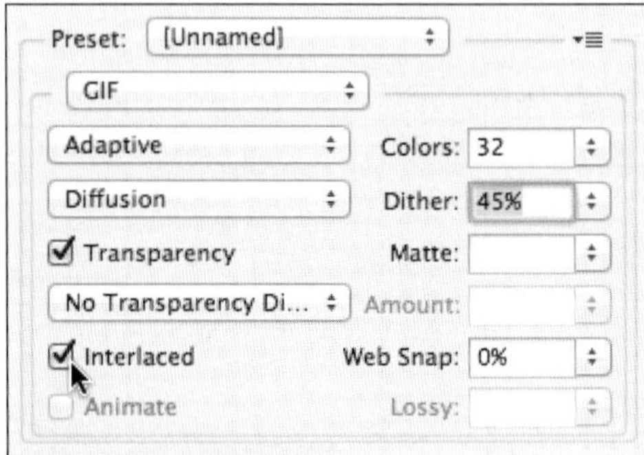

I The Interlaced feature works like JPEG's Progressive option to draw your image incrementally on a Web page as it downloads.

Choosing Dithering Options

Because a GIF image works with a limited color panel, it's impossible to reproduce most of the millions of colors visible to the human eye, much less subtle gradations of tone and color. GIF optimization employs a little visual trick called dithering to fool the eye into perceiving more colors and softer transitions than are actually there. By reorganizing pixels of different hues and values, dithering can do a surprisingly good job of simulating thousands of colors with a panel of a hundred colors or less **J**. Dithering involves placing colors adjacent to one another in a small checkerboard pattern of pixels to create the illusion of another color. Blue and yellow pixels mixed together will blend to create green. Black and white pixels mixed in varying proportions will simulate a graduated fill or soft-edged drop shadow. (Dithering is related to halftoning, which uses dots of different sizes to show varying shades of gray or colors.)

Dithered GIFs created via Save for Web use a diffusion dither. But if you save an image from the Save As dialog (File > Save As) and select CompuServe GIF from the Format drop-down menu, Photoshop Elements offers you a choice of three dithering options.

Diffusion is the default scheme for any of the predefined GIF settings; it creates a random pattern that usually yields the most natural-looking results. Diffusion is the only option that allows you to control the percentage of dither present in your image.

Pattern, as its name implies, lays down pixels in a uniform grid pattern. It can have the effect of a very coarse halftone screen such as you might see in low-resolution newspaper photography.

Noise creates a random pattern similar to Diffusion, but attempts to blend color transitions further by allowing color from one area to spill over slightly into an adjoining area. It occasionally produces an interesting effect, but will rarely be your first choice.

J The original image (left) relies on thousands of subtle tonal and value changes to define shapes, shadows, and highlights. The GIF-optimized version (right) shows the close-up results of dithering. Since GIF optimization uses a limited panel of colors, it gathers together pixels of whatever colors are available to reproduce an approximation of the original image.

Optimizing Images to Specific File Sizes

Photoshop Elements has yet one more little optimizing trick. There may be times when image quality isn't as critical as the data size of your files. Perhaps you want to email a weekend's worth of photos to some friends, but don't want to clog up their mailboxes with megabytes of image files. You can send a batch of mediocre-quality images, and then let them pick out the ones they'd like you to create high-resolution copies or prints of.

On the right side of the Save for Web dialog, just next to the main optimization settings drop-down menu, is the Optimize to File Size arrow button. Click the button, and then select Optimize to File Size **K**.

In the Optimize to File Size dialog, type in the size you want your file to be **L**. In the Start With area of the dialog, you can also choose from Current Settings, which tells Elements to do its best with your Save for Web settings; or Auto Select, which allows Elements to choose the format that will work best for your image, given the file size constraints.

K Choose Optimize to File Size for additional optimization control.

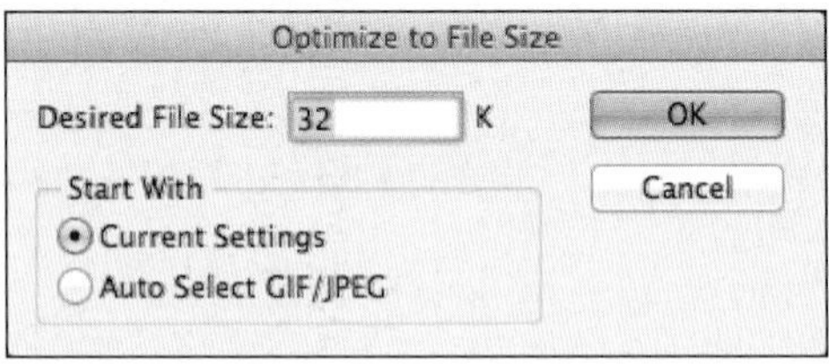

L In the Optimize to File Size dialog, you can choose to have file size take priority over image quality.

About Color Models

Although you certainly don't have to be proficient in Web color theory to save images for the Web that look good, a little background information on the different color models will help you make more informed decisions as you choose colors for your Web images. When you optimize an image using the GIF format, Photoshop Elements asks you to pick a color model from the Color Reduction Algorithm drop-down menu. Since GIF images are limited to just 256 colors, color models help to define which colors—from the vast spectrum of millions of colors—will be used in any individual optimized image. Sets of colors are given priority over others depending on the color model chosen, as follows:

- Perceptual color leans toward colors to which the human eye is most sensitive.
- Selective color draws from the largest possible range of colors, incorporating colors from the Web-safe panel as much as possible. Selective is the default option.
- Adaptive color favors those colors that appear most often in a particular image. For instance, a seascape may contain colors primarily from the blue spectrum.
- Restrictive (Web) is limited to the standard 216 Web colors and typically produces color the least true to the original image. Virtually all browsers and personal computer monitors are capable of displaying in thousands and millions of colors; Web colors are an artifact of a time in which 8-bit (256-color) video cards were common, nearly a decade ago.

Making a Web Image Transparent

In just a few simple steps, you can preserve the transparency of any image using options available in the GIF formatting settings. Once transparency has been set, an image of any shape (even one with a transparent cutout) can be placed on a Web page and made to blend seamlessly—matted—with its background.

Ⓐ The Background layer is created by default when an image is opened, but it doesn't allow transparency.

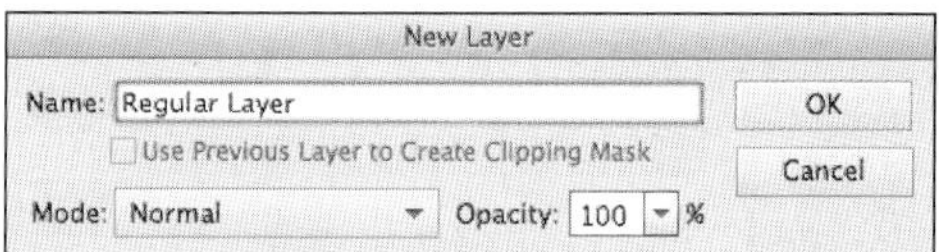

Ⓑ Rename the background layer so you can create transparency in the image.

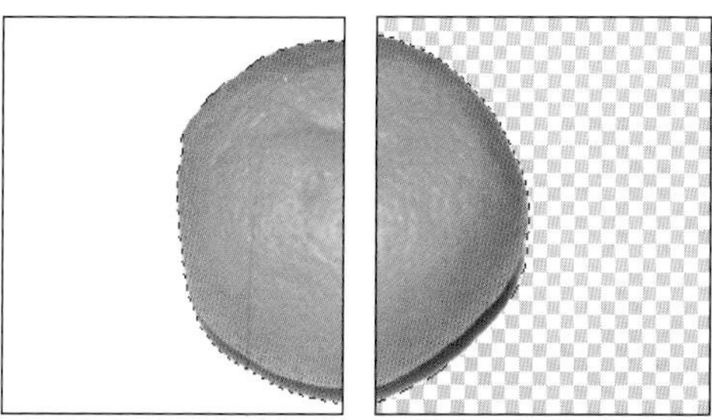

Ⓒ Select the parts of the image to remove, and use Delete to create a transparent background.

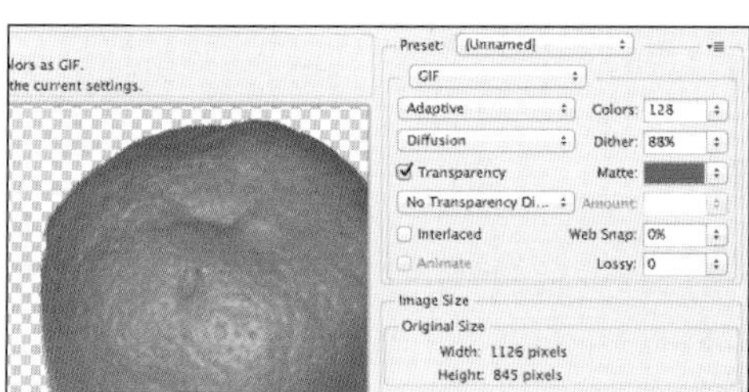

Ⓓ GIF optimization offers the added bonus of preserving transparency in your Web-bound images.

To apply transparency to an image:

1. Open the image you want to make transparent.
2. By default, Elements creates a single layer for an image called Background Ⓐ. In the Layers panel, double-click the Background layer, change its name in the Name field to something like "Regular Layer" Ⓑ, and then click OK.
3. Using any combination of selection tools you choose, select the part of the image that you want to be transparent. (See Chapter 6.)
4. Choose Edit > Delete to remove those selected parts of the image. A checkerboard pattern fills those areas, indicating they're now transparent Ⓒ.
5. Choose File > Save for Web to open the Save for Web dialog.
6. Select any one of the GIF formats from the Preset drop-down menu.
7. If it's not already selected, click to select the Transparency checkbox.

   The image in the optimized preview area will be displayed against a transparency grid pattern Ⓓ.

continues on next page

8. To select the color that will be used to blend, or matte, your image with the Web page background color, choose one of these two options:
   - Click the Matte color box to open the Color Picker; then select a color from the main color window or enter color values in either the HSB, RGB, or Web color space text fields **E**.
   - From the Matte drop-down menu, choose a color option **F**.

   Only the semitransparent pixels around the edges of the image are filled with the matte color. If the matte color matches the color of the Web page background, the transition between the transparent image and its background will be seamless **G**.

TIP **JPEG doesn't support true transparency, but you can set transparent areas in your source image with the background of the Web page for which the JPEG image is intended. Follow the steps in the earlier task, "To apply custom JPEG optimization settings to an image," and then click the Matte color box to open the Color Picker. Select a color; then click OK. The transparent areas fill with the matte color.**

TIP **If your Web page will use a patterned background, set the matte color to None; otherwise, you'll get a distracting halo of color around the image.**

TIP **The Eyedropper Color option is helpful only if the color of your Web page background also happens to be present in your image. The Other option simply opens the Color Picker. You're better off using the Matte drop-down menu only when selecting the White, Black, or None options.**

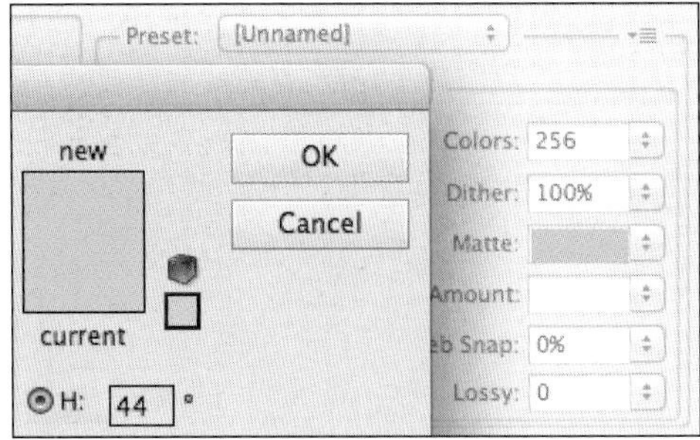

E Choose a matte color from the Color Picker to match your intended Web page background.

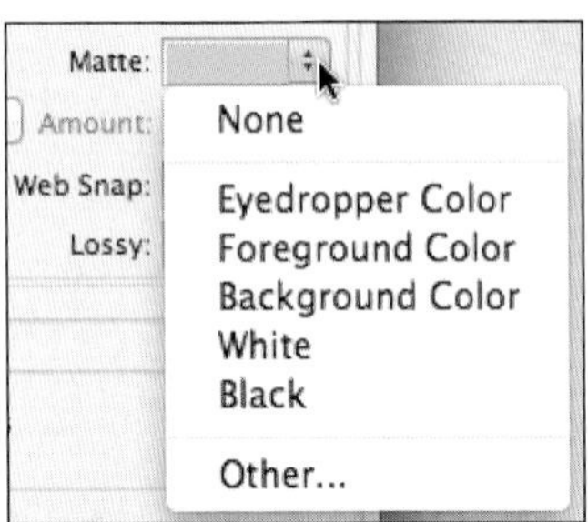

F Choose an option from the Matte menu to use a preset color.

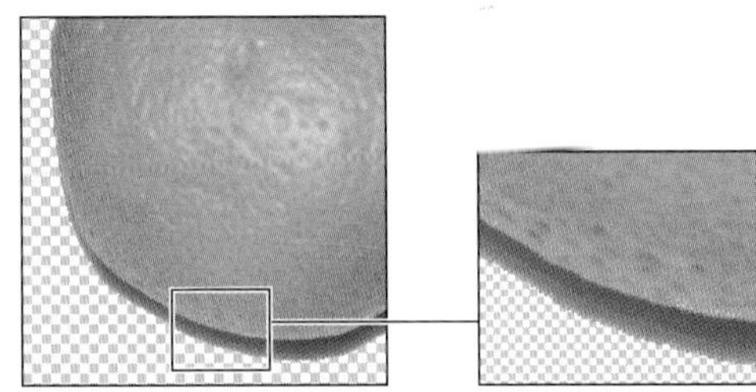

G The color you select from the Matte drop-down menu or color box fills in the semitransparent pixels around your image, helping to maintain a smooth edge and creating a seamless transition when the image is placed on a Web page of the same color.

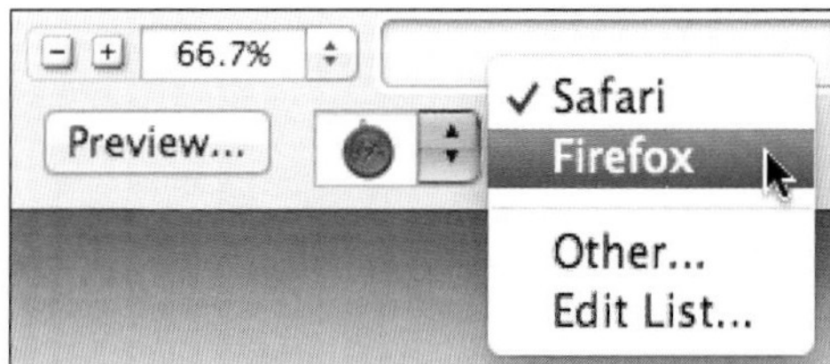

Ⓐ You can open your optimized image directly in a browser for previewing.

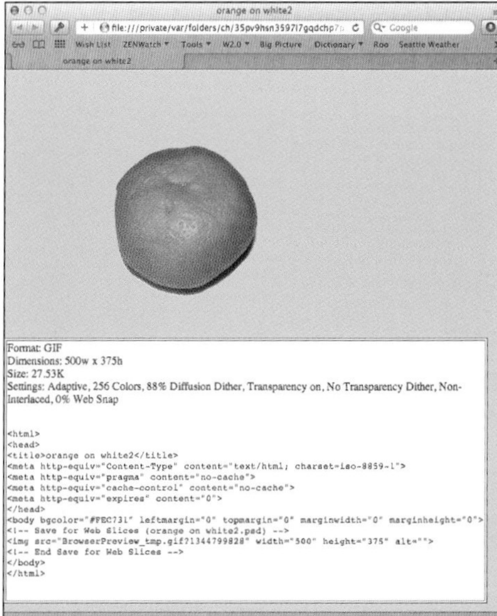

Ⓑ When your image opens in a browser, it's accompanied by all of the settings you specified in the Save for Web dialog.

Previewing an Image

Before you commit to saving your optimized image, you should see exactly how it will appear in a Web browser window. Although the Save for Web optimized preview gives you a good approximation of how the final image will look, there's no substitute for seeing the image displayed in its natural environment.

To preview an image in a Web browser:

1. At the bottom of the Save for Web dialog, click the Preview button or click the current browser icon.

   Or, choose a different Web browser from the Preview drop-down menu Ⓐ.

   The browser opens displaying the optimized image plus its dimensions and the settings you specified Ⓑ.

2. Close the browser window to return to the Save for Web dialog. The optimized version hasn't yet been saved; that was just a temporary preview file.

Saving and Printing Images

For most of the book so far, we've stuck to working with photos in the Editor and the Organizer, with a brief foray into creating Web-friendly versions of images. But there are times when you want to save images in other file formats or prepare them for printing.

In this chapter, I'll begin with a discussion of formatting options and then move on to other considerations for saving your image files and outputting them to paper.

I'll look at how to format and save multiple images (known as *batch processing*) and then look at tools you can use to lay out, organize, and catalog your image files. In addition, I'll look closely at the steps necessary to get the best prints from your digital images, whether you're printing them at home or uploading your files to an online photo service.

In This Chapter

Saving Files

As you work on an image in the Editor, it's good practice to save the file to your hard drive regularly. When you save a file, you can choose from a number of file formats.

If you're interested in posting images to the Web, you can choose the Save for Web option. Saving your images for the Web involves its own set of unique operations; these are covered in detail in Chapter 14.

To save a file:

From the File menu, choose Save, or press Ctrl+S/Command-S.

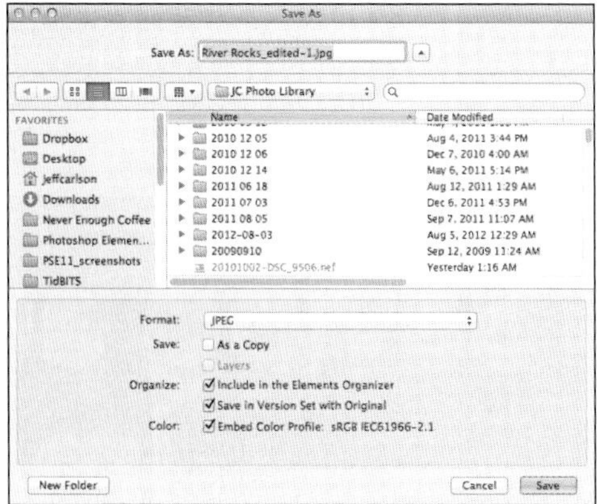

A The Save As dialog includes several options beyond just naming the new file.

To save a file in a new format or to a specific location:

1. From the File menu, choose Save As, or press Ctrl+Shift+S/Command-Shift-S. The Save As dialog appears **A**.
2. Choose a destination for the file by browsing to a location.
3. In the Save As field, type a name for the file.
4. Click the box for Include in Elements Organizer to make sure the version shows up in your library.
5. If you want to save the file in a different format, choose one from the Format drop-down menu.

   If you're not sure which format to use, choose either the native Photoshop format (PSD), which is the best all-purpose format, or the JPEG format, which works especially well with digital photos. When saving an image as a JPEG file, choose the highest quality setting possible. (Also see "Understanding File Formats" a couple pages ahead.)

Working with Version Sets

In the digital photography realm, the "negative" is the original image file captured by your camera. On the computer, you're working with those original files. So, for example, if you were to change a photo from color to grayscale and save it, then you've lost the color version forever.

To guard against that, Elements offers the ability to save the file in a version set when you perform a Save As operation. You're saving a new copy, but it's linked to the original image in the Organizer as a revision **B**; otherwise, the edited version would appear as a completely separate image. Click the expansion arrow icon to the right of the image to view or hide the version set.

B A version set tracks image edits.

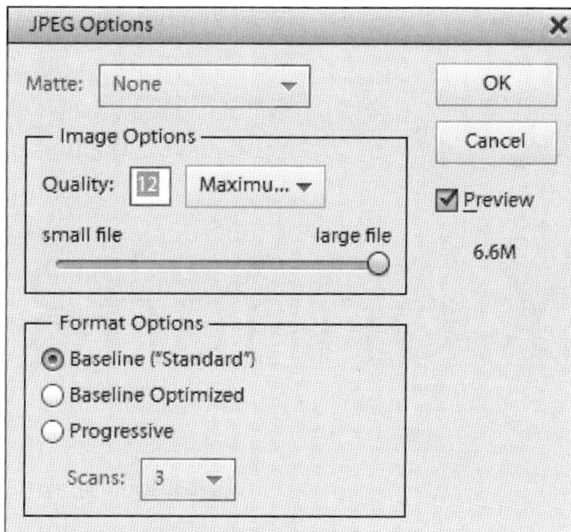

C Each image format has its own specific settings, such as those shown in this dialog for saving a JPEG file.

6. If you want to be sure not to alter your original file, select the As a Copy option to save a duplicate. This selection protects your original file from changes as you edit the duplicate.
7. To include color profile information, make sure the Embed Color Profile box is selected. For more information on managing color in your images, see Chapter 8.
8. When you've finished entering your settings, click Save.

   Depending on the format you chose, you may be prompted to set other options, such as with JPEG files **C**.

TIP Saving using the As a Copy option is a good idea if you're experimenting with various changes and want to ensure that you keep your original version intact. It's also handy if you want to save an image in more than one file format, which is useful if you want to save a high-quality copy for printing and keep a smaller-sized file to email to friends.

TIP Photoshop Elements allows you to customize how files are saved. From the Edit menu, choose Preferences > Saving Files. See "Setting Preferences for Saving Files," later in this chapter.

Understanding File Formats

Photoshop Elements lets you save an image in many different file formats, from the native, information-rich Photoshop format to optimized formats for the Web, such as GIF and JPEG. Among these is an extremely specialized collection of formats (PCX, PICT Resource, Pixar, PNG, Raw, Scitex CT, and Targa) you'll rarely need to use and won't be discussed here. What follows are descriptions of the most common file formats.

Photoshop

Photoshop (PSD) is the native file format of Photoshop Elements, meaning that the saved file will include information for any and all of Elements' features, including layers, styles, effects, typography, and filters. As its name implies, any file saved in the PSD format can be opened not only in Photoshop Elements, but also in Adobe Photoshop. Conversely, any Photoshop file saved in its native format can be opened in Photoshop Elements. However, Photoshop Elements doesn't support all the features available in Photoshop, so although you can open any file saved in the PSD format, some of Photoshop's more advanced features (such as layer sets) won't be accessible to you within Photoshop Elements.

A good approach is to save every photo you're working on in the native Photoshop format and then, when you've finished editing, save a copy in whatever format is appropriate for that image's intended use or destination. That way, you always have the original, full-featured image file to return to if you want to make changes or just save in a different format.

Choosing Compression Options

As you save images in the various formats available, you're presented with a variety of format-specific dialogs, each containing its own set of options. One of those options is a choice of compression settings. Compression (or optimization) makes an image's file size smaller; the file downloads faster when you post it to a Web page, for example. Following is a brief rundown of the compression schemes:

JPEG: JPEG works best with continuous-tone images like photographs. It compresses by throwing away image information and slightly degrading the image, and is therefore a lossy compression.

LZW: This is the standard compression format for most TIFF images. Although it works best on images with large areas of a single color, LZW helps reduce file sizes at least a little for nearly any image to which it's applied. Since it works behind the scenes, throwing out code rather than image information (and so doesn't degrade the image), LZW is a lossless compression.

RLE: This is a lossless compression similar to LZW, but it's specific (in Elements) to BMP compressed files. It's particularly effective at compressing images containing transparency.

ZIP: This compression scheme is also similar to LZW, but it has the advantage of adding a layer of protection to files that makes them less susceptible to corruption if they're copied between systems or sent via e-mail. Zip files are common on the Windows platform, and Mac OS X can open them.

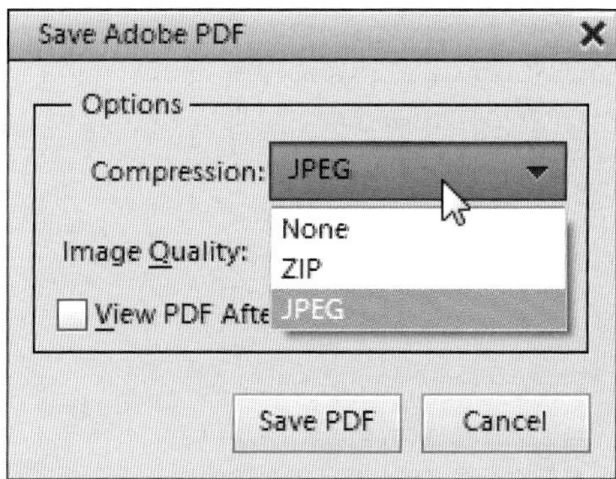

Ⓐ When you save your work as a PDF file, you can apply JPEG or ZIP compression.

Photoshop EPS

Photoshop EPS is actually a format you don't want to use. Although EPS (Encapsulated PostScript) files are compatible with a host of graphics and page layout programs, they're not the best choice for saving bitmap images, which are what Photoshop Elements creates.

The EPS format adds layers of PostScript code to describe everything from the way an image appears in preview to the way it is color managed, which translates into overhead in the form of bloated file size and slower display time. Any advantage this format holds for displaying and printing vector art and typography is lost on Photoshop Elements' raster art.

JPEG and GIF

The two major Web file formats (JPEG and GIF) are covered in detail in Chapter 14, so I'll look at them just briefly here. Of particular note is the fact that you can use the Save As command to save an image as a GIF or JPEG file, with virtually all of the same file options as in the Save for Web dialog—so the obvious question is: Why use one saving method over the other when saving for the Web?

The Save for Web dialog offers several features the individual GIF and JPEG Save As command dialogs don't. For one, Save for Web provides a wonderful before-and-after preview area.

No less valuable is the flexibility you have to change and view different optimization formats on the fly. An image just doesn't appear the way you expected in GIF? Try JPEG. Additionally, with the click of a button, you can open and preview your optimized image in any browser present on your system.

Photoshop PDF

Portable Document Format (PDF) is the perfect vehicle for sharing images across platforms or for importing them into a variety of graphics and page layout programs. PDF is also one of only three file formats (native Photoshop and TIFF are the other two) that support an image file's layers; layer qualities (like transparency) are preserved when you place a PDF into another application like Adobe Illustrator or InDesign. The real beauty of this format is that a PDF file can be opened and viewed by anyone using Adobe's free Acrobat Reader software. PDF offers two compression schemes for controlling file size: ZIP and JPEG Ⓐ.

TIFF

Tagged Image File Format (TIFF) is a workhorse among the file formats. The format was designed to be platform independent, so TIFF files display and print equally well from both Windows and Macintosh machines. Additionally, any TIFF file created on one platform can be transferred to the other and placed in almost any graphics or page layout program.

You can optimize TIFF files to save room on your hard drive using one of three compression schemes, or you can save them with no compression at all B. Of the three compression options, LZW is the one supported by the largest number of applications and programs.

The Pixel Order option should be left at the default of Interleaved. The Byte Order option encodes information in the file to determine whether it will be used on a Windows or Macintosh platform. On rare occasions, TIFF files saved with the Macintosh option don't transfer cleanly to Windows machines. But since the Mac has no problem with files saved with the IBM PC byte order, I recommend you stick with this option.

Checking the Save Image Pyramid checkbox saves your image in different tiers of resolution, but since not many applications support the Image Pyramid format, leave this box unchecked.

Checking the Save Transparency checkbox ensures transparency will be maintained if you place your image into another application like Illustrator or InDesign.

If your image contains layers, choose from two Layer Compression schemes, or choose to discard the layers altogether and save a copy of your image file.

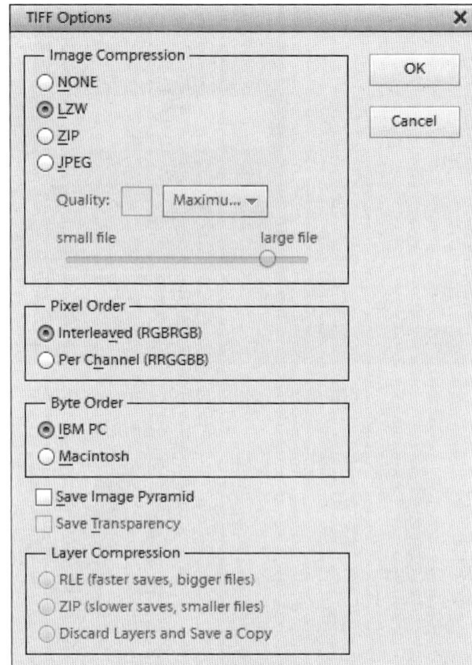

B Although the TIFF format offers several compression schemes, LZW is usually the most reliable.

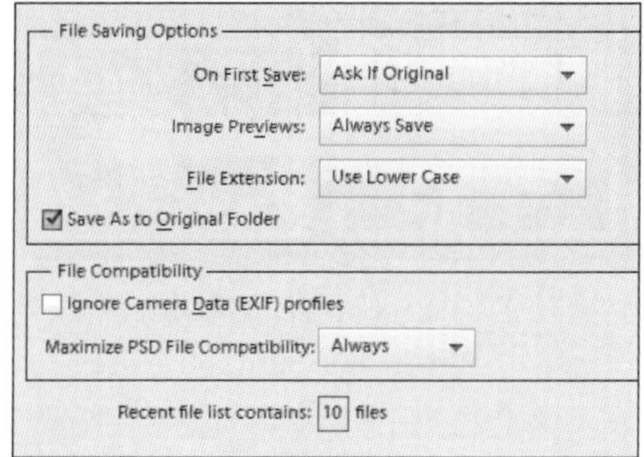

Ⓐ The Saving Files pane of the Preferences dialog.

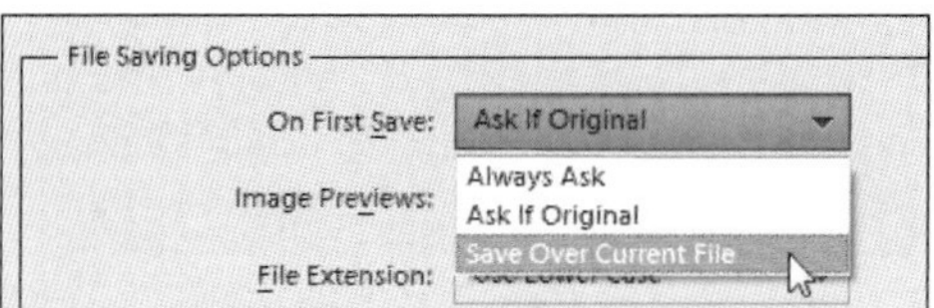

Ⓑ The On First Save drop-down menu lets you control when the Save As dialog appears.

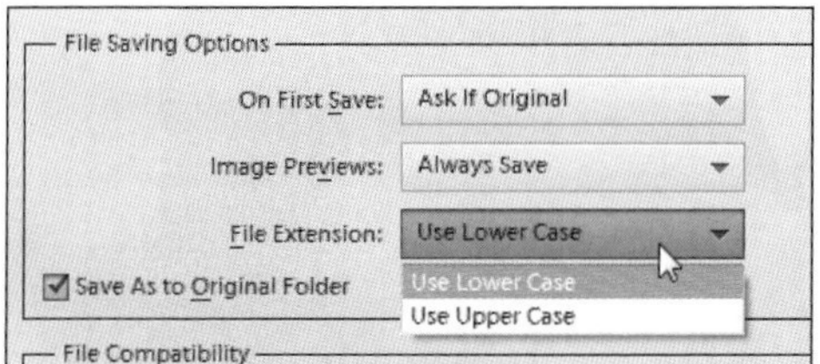

Ⓒ Use the File Extension drop-down menu to determine how you want filename extensions displayed.

Setting Preferences for Saving Files

The Saving Files portion of the Preferences dialog provides a number of ways to control how Elements manages your saved files.

To set the Saving Files preferences:

1. From the Edit menu, choose Preferences > Saving Files. The Preferences dialog opens with the Saving Files window active Ⓐ.
2. From the On First Save drop-down menu, you can choose when you want to be prompted with the Save As dialog Ⓑ.
3. From the Image Previews drop-down menu, choose an option to either save or not save a preview with the file.
4. From the File Extension drop-down menu, choose whether file extensions should be upper or lower case Ⓒ.
5. In the File Compatibility portion of the dialog, set the Maximize PSD File Compatibility drop-down menu to Always. This gives you the maximum number of compatibility options.
6. If you're pre-processing Raw files in another program, deselect the Prefer Adobe Camera Raw for Supported Raw Files option.
7. To assign your own color profile to images, select the Ignore Camera Data (EXIF) profiles checkbox.
8. In the text field labeled Recent file list contains, enter a number from 1 to 30.
9. Click OK to close the dialog and apply your preferences settings.

Adding Personalized File Information in the Editor

With any Photoshop Elements file open, choose File Info from the File menu to open the File Info dialog **D**. Within this dialog, you can add personalized information specific to any file, including title, author, description, and copyright information. Although most of the information entered here is accessible only by opening the dialog from within Photoshop Elements, some of it does have practical uses both inside and outside the application. Entries from the Document Title, Author, Description, and Copyright Notice text fields can be included when you create a Picture Package discussed later in this chapter.

Also, the Description field can be included with any saved image (see "Setting more printing options" later in this chapter). And if you select Copyrighted from the Copyright Status drop-down menu, a copyright symbol appears in the Image Window title bar, alerting anyone who receives a copy of your file that it's copyright protected **E**.

The File Info dialog is useful for retrieving information, too. Many digital cameras include EXIF annotations (such as date and time, resolution, exposure time, and f-stop settings) for each digital photo. To access this information, click the Camera Data tab. Any EXIF information imported with the photo from your digital camera is displayed **F**. You can use this information to note settings from your more successful photos—a handy reference for future outings. You can also view EXIF annotations in the Information panel in the Organizer.

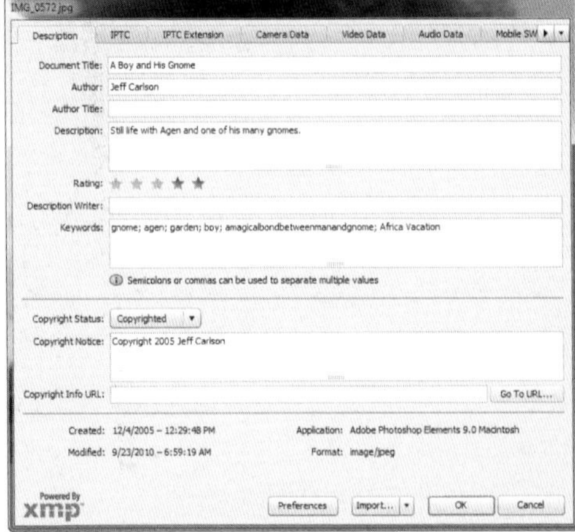

D Use the File Info dialog to add title, copyright, and other information to any specific file.

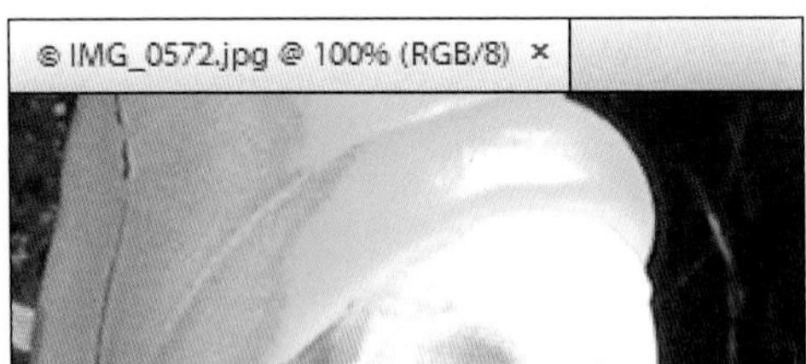

E When a file is assigned copyright status in the File Info dialog, a copyright symbol appears next to the filename at the top of the image window.

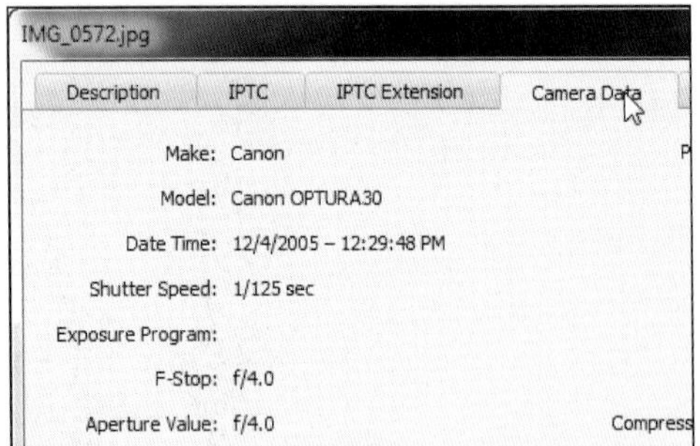

F The File Info dialog displays EXIF information included with photos imported from digital cameras.

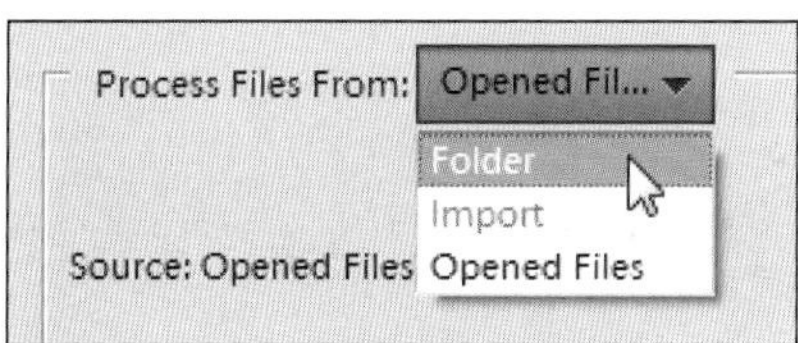

Ⓐ You can save groups of files from a number of different sources.

Ⓑ Select a folder containing all the images you want to convert at one time.

Formatting and Saving Multiple Images

You've just finished a prolific day of shooting pictures, and as a first step to sorting through all those images, you'd like to convert them to Elements' native Photoshop format and then change their resolution to 150 dpi. You could, of course, convert them individually, but the Process Multiple Files command can do all that tedious, repetitive work for you.

To batch process multiple files:

1. From the File menu, choose Process Multiple Files to open the dialog of the same name.
2. From the Process Files From drop-down menu Ⓐ, do one of the following:
   - To select images within a folder on your hard drive, choose Folder, click the Browse button, and then locate and select the folder containing the images you want to convert Ⓑ. If you spot folders within the folder you select that also contain files you want to convert, click the Include All Subfolders checkbox in the Process Multiple Files dialog.
   - To select images stored in a digital camera, scanner, or PDF, choose Import; then select the appropriate source from the From drop-down menu. The choices in the From drop-down menu will vary depending on the hardware connected to your computer.
   - To select files that are currently open within Photoshop Elements, choose Opened Files.

continues on next page

3. Click the Destination Browse button; then locate and select a folder to save your converted files.

   In the Browse for Folder dialog that appears, you're also offered the option of creating a new folder for your converted files.

4. If you want to add a file-naming structure to your collection of converted images, select the Rename Files checkbox; then select naming options from the two drop-down menus **C**.

   Refer to the Example text (located below the Rename Files checkbox) to see how the renaming changes will affect your filenames.

5. Select the Compatibility checkboxes for whichever platforms you want your filenames to be compatible with.

   A good approach is to select all three of these, just to be on the safe side.

6. If you want to change either the physical dimensions of your image or its resolution, click the Resize Images checkbox, then do one or both of the following:

   - To convert all of your images to a specific size, first select a unit of measure from the units drop-down menu, then enter the width or height in the appropriate text field, making sure that the Constrain Proportions checkbox is selected **D**.
   - From the Resolution drop-down menu, choose a resolution in dots per inch (dpi) to change the resolution of all your images **E**.

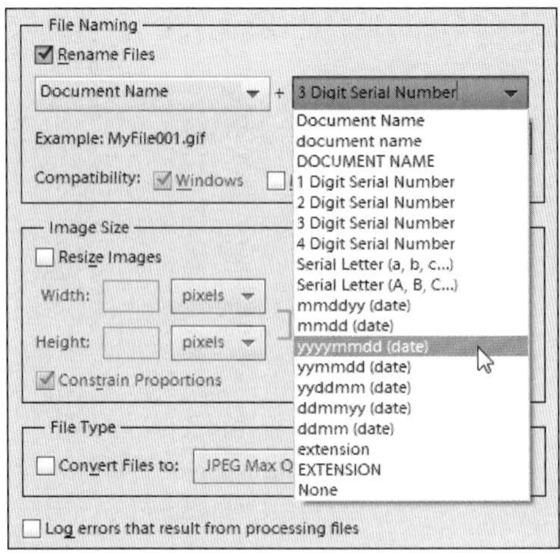

C Choose from a number of file-naming options to arrange your images in consecutive order.

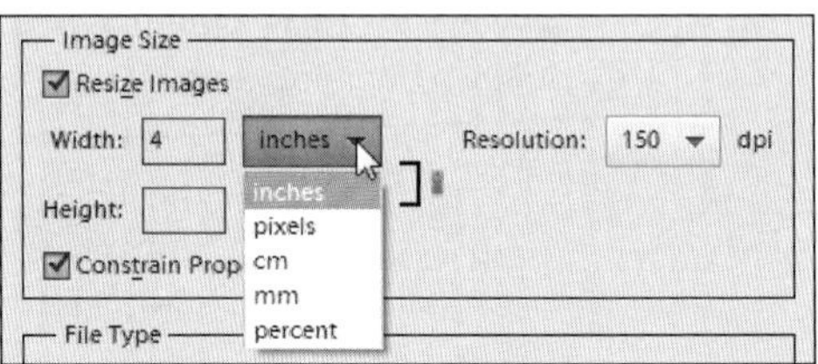

D You can resize entire groups of images to the same width or height dimensions.

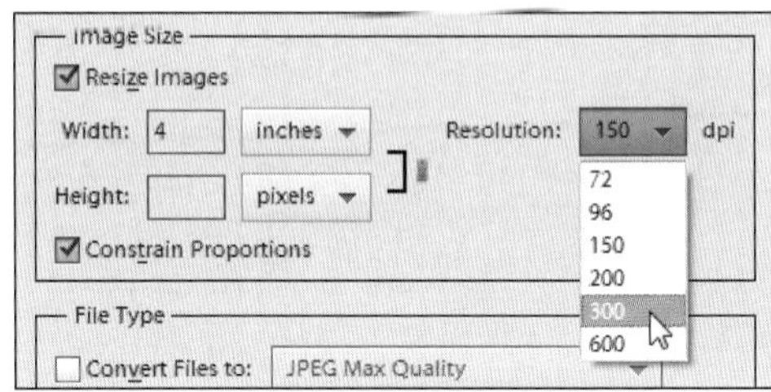

E Choose a resolution to apply to all of the files in your selected group.

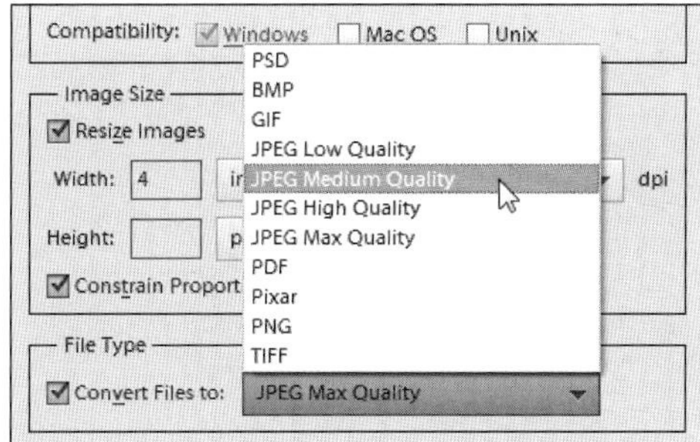

F Choose a formatting option to apply to all the files in your selected group.

The resolution setting in this dialog is in dots per inch (print resolution) rather than pixels per inch (screen resolution), so changing just the resolution here will do nothing to alter your image, or change its file size. It changes only the dimensions of the final printed image and has no effect on the size it displays onscreen.

7. From the Convert Files to drop-down menu, choose the desired format type **F**.
8. Click OK to close the dialog and start the batch process. The selected files are opened, converted in turn, and then saved to the folder you've chosen.

   If you've chosen one of the import options, an additional series of dialogs appears, guiding you through the selection of images to import.

TIP Using a little simple math can help you convert pixel dimensions to inches. Multiply the resolution you've selected by the number of inches (of either height or width) that you want your final image to be. For example, if you've selected a resolution of 72 dpi, and you want the width of your images to be 4 inches; simply multiply 72 by 4, then enter the total (288) in the width text field.

Displaying and Printing Images

When it comes to printing and resolution, it helps to keep a few basic details in mind to avoid confusion.

You know that image resolution is described in *pixels per inch*, or *ppi*. Print resolution, however, is usually described by the number of *dots per inch*, or *dpi,* a printer is capable of printing. If you want to print a high-quality flyer or photo, you may want to use an image resolution as high as 300 pixels per inch, so that a maximum amount of image information is sent to the printer.

(For more details on adjusting image size, see "Changing Image Size and Resolution" in Chapter 14.)

To resize an image for printing:

1. From the Image menu, choose Resize > Image Size.
2. To maintain the current width-to-height ratio, check that the Constrain Proportions option is selected.
3. Uncheck the Resample Image box.
4. Choose a unit of measure (or a percentage) and then enter new values for the width or height in the Document Size portion of the dialog **A**.

   In the Document Size portion of the dialog, the resolution value changes accordingly. For instance, if you enter width and height values of half the original image size, the resolution value will double, and the image will print clearer and sharper. That's because you're compressing the same number of pixels into a smaller space. So, when scaled at 50 percent, an image 4 inches wide

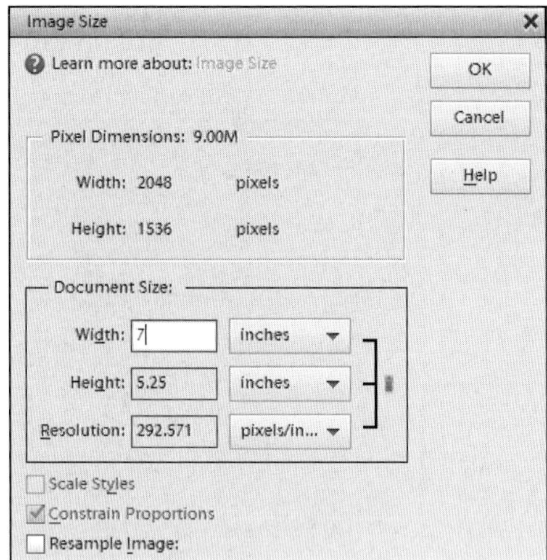

A Enter new width and height values to change an image's print size.

Recommended Resolutions

There are no absolute rules for the best resolution to use when working with images for printing. The best approach is to try a few settings and see what works well for your specific situation. Here are a couple of typical situations:

- For color images printed on color ink-jet printers, a range of up to 150 ppi is often ideal. The exact resolution will depend on your printer and the type of paper on which you are printing.
- For color or high-resolution black and white images printed on photo printers, you'll want a resolution between 150 and 300 ppi.

If you want to create higher-quality professional projects, such as magazine or print design work, be aware that Photoshop Elements is not capable of producing CMYK files (the color-separated files used for high-end printing). If you need to handle these kinds of jobs, consider buying the full Photoshop CS software.

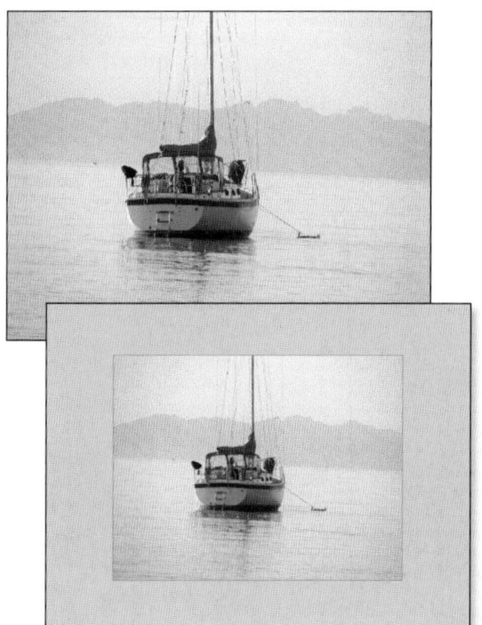

Ⓑ An image can be viewed at an approximation of its final print size, even when its resolution differs from the computer's display.

with a resolution of 150 pixels per inch (ppi) will print at 2 inches wide and at a resolution of 300 ppi.

5. Click OK to complete the change.

   The image's print size will be changed, but since it still contains the same number of pixels, it will appear to be unchanged on your screen. You can, however, view a preview of the final print size onscreen:

   - From the View menu, choose Print Size. The image is resized on your screen to approximate its final, printed size Ⓑ.
   - From the View menu, choose Actual Pixels, or press Ctrl+1/Command-1 to return the display size to 100 percent.

TIP To return the dialog to its original settings, press Alt/Option to change the Cancel button to Reset, then click Reset.

Downsampling vs. Upsampling

Downsampling, which is the term for decreasing resolution by *removing* pixels from your photo, is one of the easiest and most common ways to make your files smaller. If you take an 8 x 10 photograph of your grandmother and shrink it to a 4 x 5 image by reducing its pixel count, you've just downsampled it. Elements "throws away" unneeded pixels intelligently, with little visible impact on the quality of your image.

But *upsampling*, which is the term for increasing resolution by *adding* new pixels to your photo, should be avoided whenever possible. If you take a 4 x 5 photograph and try to enlarge it to 8 x 10, Elements must manufacture those pixels out of thin air. They tend to add a ghosted, fuzzy appearance to any hard edge—the overall effect is that your image can look out of focus.

Because downsampling rarely detracts from the quality of your images, you should capture all your original files at the highest resolution possible, whether you're scanning an image or snapping a digital photo.

Printing an Image

Whether you're printing final photos for clients or just some snapshots for family, you can print to a local printer from within Photoshop Elements.

To print an image:

1. Do one of the following:
   - In the Organizer, select the photos you would like to print.
   - In the Editor, open the files you want, or select them in the Photo Bin.
2. Click the Create drop-down menu in the upper-right corner of the window.
3. Choose Photo Prints.
4. From the options that appear, click the Local Printer button. The Print dialog opens **A**.
5. Select a printer and optionally adjust settings specific to it from the Select Printer and Select Paper Size options.
6. Click the Select Print Size drop-down menu and choose the size at which the image will print **B**. The page preview reflects the page size in proportion to the image you want to print.

   Choosing Custom opens the More Options dialog (see the opposite page).
7. Specify the number of copies of each page to print.
8. Click the Print button to send the job to the printer.

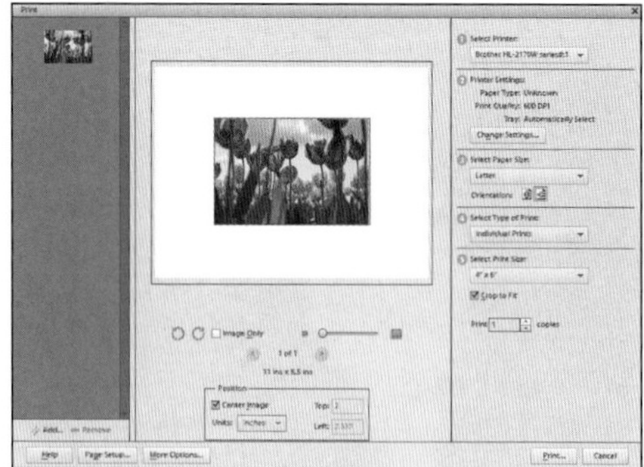

A The Photoshop Elements Print dialog.

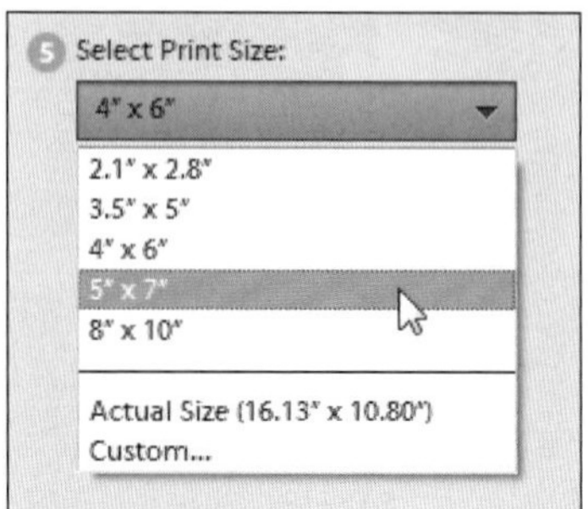

B Choose the size the photo will be on the printed page.

Cropping in the Print Dialog

One frustration with printing photos is that the standard aspect ratios of photo prints are different than the ratio used by most cameras. You can pre-crop the image in Elements, but that involves creating a duplicate and cropping the duplicate. Blech.

Instead, after selecting a print size, apply the cropping in the Print dialog. Click the Crop to Fit checkbox to let Elements frame the new size. If that's not quite what you're looking for, drag the image in the preview to move it within the frame (indicated by a blue box). You can also drag the size slider below the preview to further adjust how the image is framed.

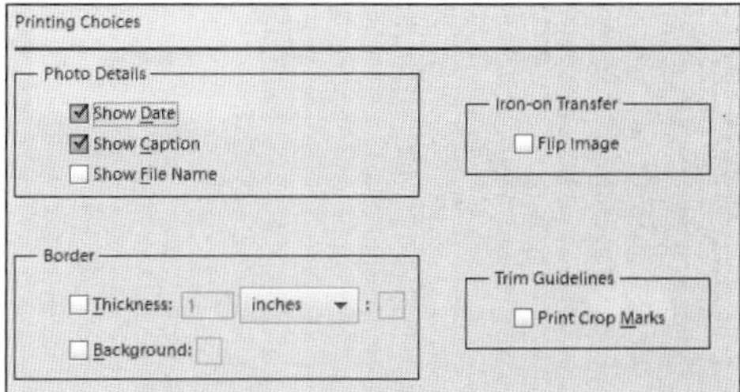

C The More Options print dialog.

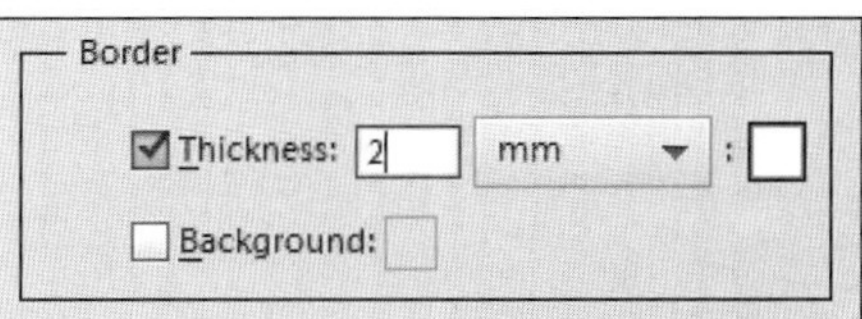

D Select a measurement unit and size for your border.

E Crop marks positioned at the corners.

Setting more printing options

Elements offers optional print settings for adding more information to your prints. They can be helpful when printing drafts or outputting images for other projects.

To set more printing options:

1. Before you print, click the More Options button and, in the dialog that appears **C**, do one of the following:
   - In the Photo Details area, click the checkboxes to display an image's date, caption, or file name. If a document title or description has been entered for the image in the File Info dialog, it will be represented in the page preview as gray bars. (See the sidebar "Adding Personalized File Information in the Editor" earlier in this chapter.)
   - In the Border area, click the Thickness checkbox and specify a width for a line if you want one **D**. Click the small color swatch to the right to select the border's color. You can also set a background color for the page.
   - If you're making transfers for t-shirts, click the Flip Image checkbox under Iron-on Transfer to invert the image horizontally. (If your printer's driver has an invert image option, make sure that's not selected—otherwise, the image will flip back to its original orientation when printed.)
   - Under Trim Guidelines, click the Print Crop Marks button if you want to include crop marks **E**.
2. Click the Apply button to view the changes in the preview without leaving the More Options dialog. Or, click OK to return to the Print dialog.

Creating a Contact Sheet

You may have lots of photos downloaded from your digital camera, but with unhelpful filenames like 102-0246_IMG.JPG, organizing and sorting them can be a difficult task. And although the Organizer lets you view and sort through your images, sometimes it's nice to have a printed hard copy to study and mark up. In traditional photography, contact sheets are created from film negatives and provide a photographer or designer with a collection of convenient thumbnail images organized neatly on a single sheet of film or paper.

The steps for creating a contact sheet are slightly different depending on whether you're using Elements under Windows or Mac OS X, so I'm covering them separately.

A The option to create a contact sheet is found within the Photo Prints category.

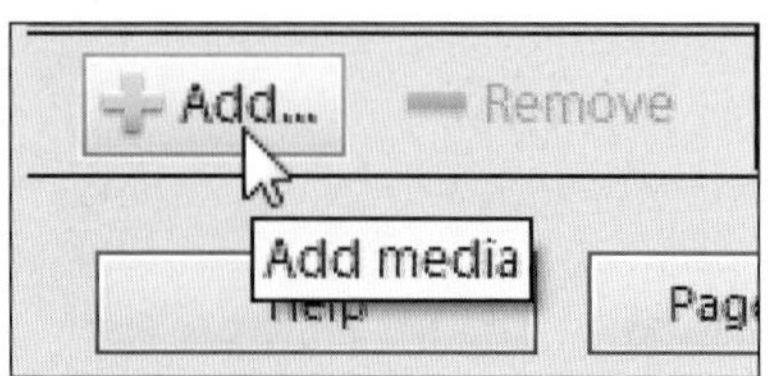

B Add more photos to the contact sheet.

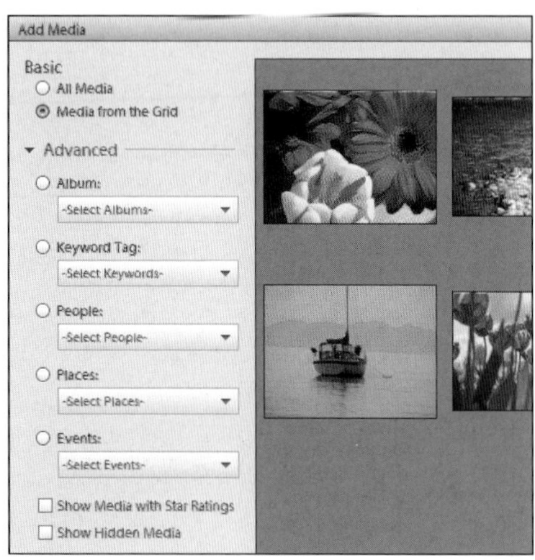

C The Add Media dialog lets you bring in photos you hadn't previously included.

To make a contact sheet (Windows):

1. Do one of the following:
   - In the Organizer, select the photos you would like to include.
   - In the Editor, open the files you want, or select them in the Photo Bin.
2. Click the Create drop-down menu in the upper-right corner of the window and choose Photo Prints.
3. Choose Contact Sheet **A**. The Prints dialog opens.
4. Specify the printer, and optionally select printer settings and paper size.
5. If you want to add more images to the contact sheet, click the Add button in the lower-left corner of the Print Photos dialog **B**. Otherwise skip to Step 10.

   The Add Media dialog opens **C**.

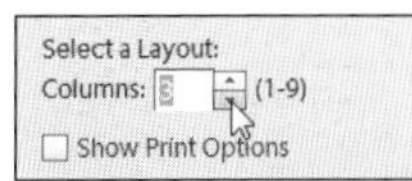

D Control the number of thumbnails that appear on each page of your contact sheet.

Choosing Paper

A wide range of paper is available for your inkjet printer. For most photos, you'll want to print on either photo paper or glossy photo paper (glossy photo paper is thicker, and a little more durable). Quality matte paper is often preferred for high-resolution photographs, and you can even find archival-quality paper that won't fade for 100 years. If you just want to print a quick proof, your regular inkjet printer paper will do in a pinch.

Before you start buying paper, it's a good idea to review the documentation that came with your printer (or check out your printer manufacturer's Web site) to see a list of recommended paper choices.

6. Select from one of the following options (in both the Basic and Advanced areas); note that you can restrict the search using just one criterion:
   - All Media displays every photo you've imported into the Organizer.
   - Media from the Grid displays all of the photos currently visible in the Organizer's Browser window.
   - Album displays photos that you've organized into a single photo album.
   - Keyword Tag displays photos to which you've assigned one specific attribute tag.
   - The People, Places, and Events drop-down menus let you choose these specific criteria.
7. If you choose any of the Advanced options, choose an item from the respective drop-down menu.

   The Add Media dialog updates to display all photos from the option you selected in the Add Media From area.
8. Click to select the photos you want to include on your contact sheet, and then click Done.

   The preview window in the center of the Print Photos dialog now includes all the photos you have selected.
9. Click the arrows to the right of the Columns text field to designate the number of columns per page your photo thumbnails will occupy **D**.
10. Click More Options to select the type of text information you would like to have appear below each photo thumbnail.
11. Click Print to send the completed contact sheet to your printer.

To make a contact sheet (Mac):

1. Do one of the following:
   - In the Organizer, select the photos you would like to include.
   - In the Editor, open the files you want, or select them in the Photo Bin.
2. Click the Create drop-down menu in the upper-right corner of the window and choose Photo Prints.
3. From the options that appear, click the Contact Sheet button **E**.

   If you're in the Organizer, the software alerts you that the feature is handled by the Editor; click Yes to continue and open the files there.

   Otherwise, the Contact Sheet dialog opens **F**.
4. From the drop-down menu in the Source Images area, choose Current open documents. (You can alternately choose Folder and specify a folder of images on your hard disk.)
5. Specify the paper size, printing resolution, and color mode of the printer you're using.
6. In the Thumbnails pane, choose how the photos will be arranged on the page by specifying the number of columns and rows, and choosing a sort order. You can also control the spacing between images or leave it set to Auto-Spacing.

E Create a contact sheet from within the Photo Prints category.

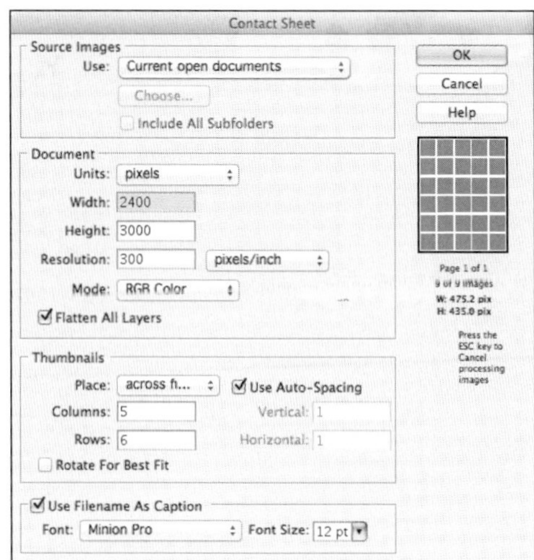

F Set up printing options in the Contact Sheet dialog.

Ⓖ The contact sheet is assembled and ready for printing.

7. If you want each image to be labeled with its filename, mark the Use Filename As Caption checkbox and specify a font and size for the text.

8. Click OK.

   Elements builds the contact sheet before your eyes (it actually runs a script that opens each image, resizes it, and places it in a new document). After a short time, the contact sheet is assembled and ready for printing Ⓖ.

Creating a Picture Package

Photoshop Elements' Picture Package creates a page with multiple copies of the same image, just like the kind you'd receive from a professional photographer's studio.

The steps to make a picture package differ slightly under Windows and Mac OS X, so I'm listing them separately.

To create a picture package (Windows):

1. Do one of the following:
   - In the Organizer, select the photo you would like to print.
   - In the Editor, open the file you want, or select it in the Photo Bin.
2. Click the Create drop-down menu in the upper-right corner of the window and choose Photo Prints.
3. From the options that appear, click the Picture Package button. The Picture Package dialog opens **A**.
4. From the Select a Layout drop-down menu, choose the layout and dimensions for your picture package.
5. Click the Fill Page With First Photo checkbox to include as many copies of the image as will fit **B**.
6. Click Print to send your completed picture package to the printer.

A A picture package creates pages that you can print and cut out for framing.

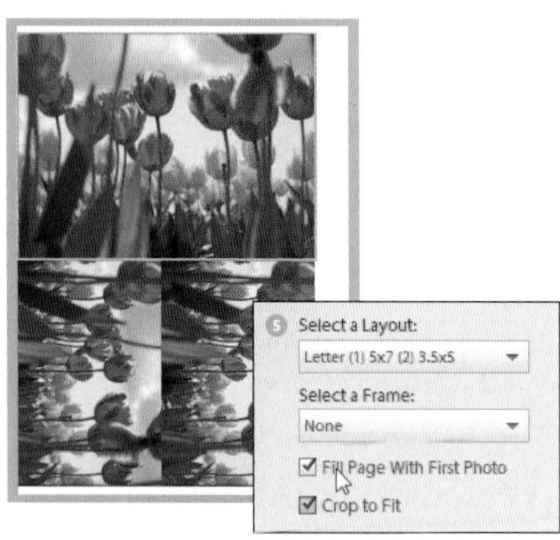

B Mark the Fill Page With First Photo option to group the prints onto the page.

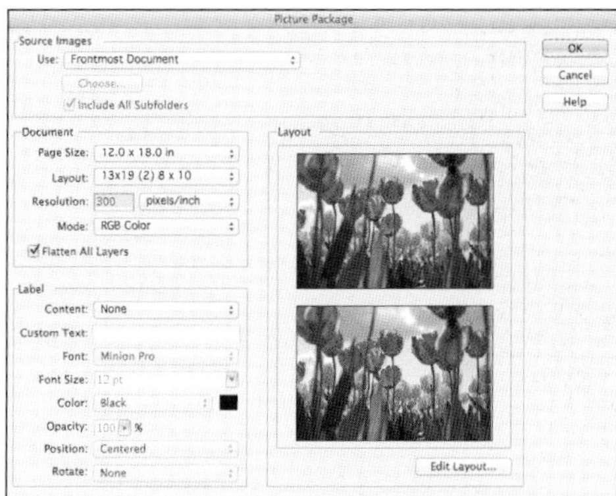

C The Mac interface for creating a picture package.

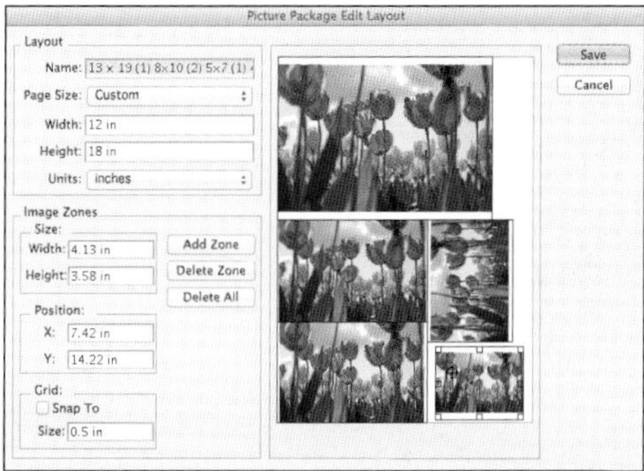

D Edit the layout of the picture package page.

E The finished picture package.

To create a picture package (Mac):

1. Do one of the following:
   - In the Organizer, select the photo you would like to print.
   - In the Editor, open the file you want, or select it in the Photo Bin.
2. Click the Create drop-down menu in the upper-right corner of the window and choose Photo Prints.
3. From the options that appear, click the Picture Package button.

   If you're in the Organizer, the software alerts you that the feature is handled by the Editor; click Yes to continue and open the files there.

   Otherwise, the Picture Package dialog opens **C**.
4. From the drop-down menu in the Source Images area, choose Frontmost Document if it's not already selected. (You can alternately specify a file or folder on your hard disk.)
5. In the Document pane, use the Layout drop-down menu to determine how the images are arranged, which you can preview in the Layout pane.
6. To customize the layout, click the Edit Layout button and fine-tune the appearance of the page **D**. Click Save to apply the changes.
7. Click OK. Elements builds the picture package in a new file **E**.

Ordering Prints

In the past, you'd shoot a roll of film, take it to a photo developer, and after a few days (or a few hours) you'd have prints of all your images. Now, you can order prints directly from within Photoshop Elements—and order just the images you want, rather than everything shot on the roll.

To order prints:

1. In the Organizer, select one or more photos to print. Or, in the Editor, choose open image files in the Photo Bin.
2. Click the Create drop-down menu in the upper-right corner of the window and choose Photo Prints.
3. Click the Order Prints from Shutterfly button **A**. Elements prepares the images and then brings up an order dialog.
4. Enter your login information if you already have an account with the vendor; otherwise, you can sign up for a new account within the order screen.
5. A single 4 x 6 print is selected for each image. Change quantities for any of your photos by editing the number fields **B**.
6. Click Next to specify recipients for the order.
7. Click Next to review the order.
8. Click Next to enter your credit card information and billing address, and then click the service's Place Order button.

   The images are uploaded, printed on photo paper, and mailed in a few days.

A Create a photo prints order.

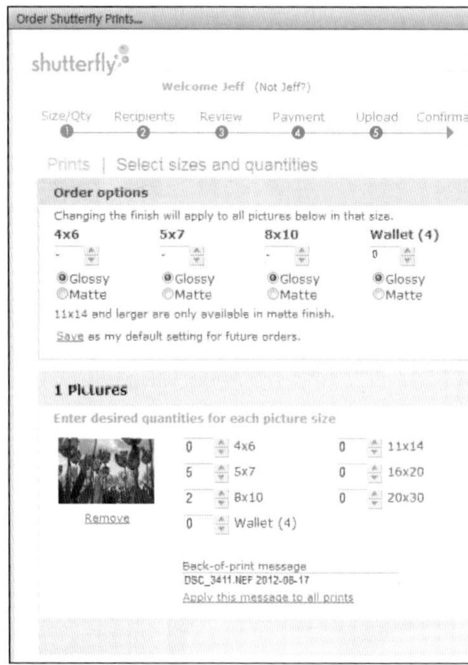

B The Review Order screen lists the photos you've chosen along with other ordering options.

Sharing Your Images

If you're shooting photos and making compositions within Photoshop Elements, it's a safe bet that you want to share them with others. In the past, you'd make prints and either carry them everywhere or send them through the mail. Now, you can upload photos to social media sites like Flickr and Facebook, email photos directly, make your own slide show (without the cumbersome projector), and more.

In Photoshop Elements 11, Adobe also introduces support for Revel, its service for sharing photos among computers and devices. When you export photos to Revel, other people who have access to your images can view, rate, and edit them.

In This Chapter

Uploading to a Photo Sharing Service

Uploading photos to a social networking service such as Flickr or Facebook is often the easiest way to share your photos to a wide audience. Elements supports many services directly. I'll use Flickr in my example below.

To upload to a photo sharing service:

1. In the Organizer, select one or more photos you wish to upload.
2. Click the Share drop-down menu in the upper-right corner of the window and choose Flickr **A**.

   The first time you do so, you'll need to authorize Elements as a legitimate sharing service within Flickr. Click the Authorize button in the Share to Flickr dialog, which takes you to Flickr's site on the Web. Return to the Share to Flickr dialog and click the Complete Authorization button. The Upload to Flickr interface appears **B**.
3. The photos you selected appear in the Items field; click the Add (+) or Remove (–) buttons if you want to change which images are uploaded.
4. If you wish to include the photos in a set, click the Upload as a set checkbox and specify a photoset you've previously set up at Flickr or create a new one by typing its title in the Set Name field.
5. Specify the photos' privacy settings under the heading Who can see these photos?
6. Type keyword tags in the Tags field, separated by spaces.
7. Click the Upload button to publish the photos.

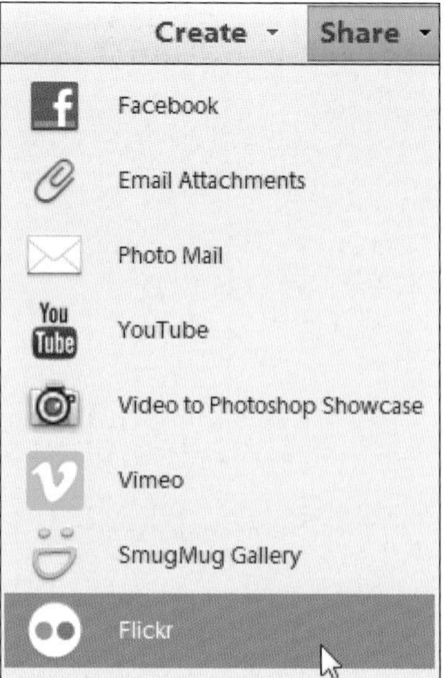

A Share to many popular social media sites and galleries.

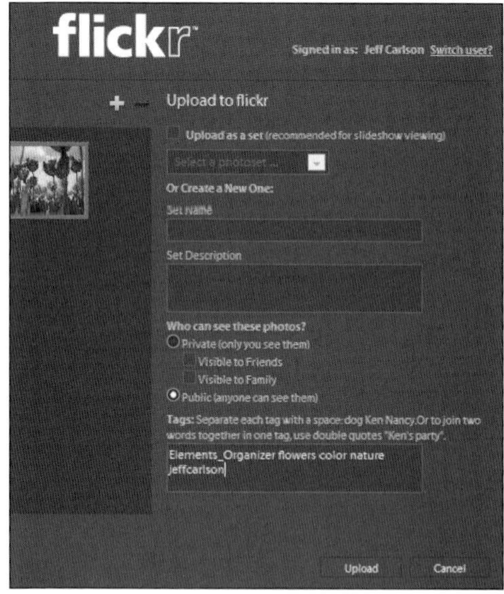

B Upload directly to Flickr from the Organizer.

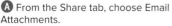

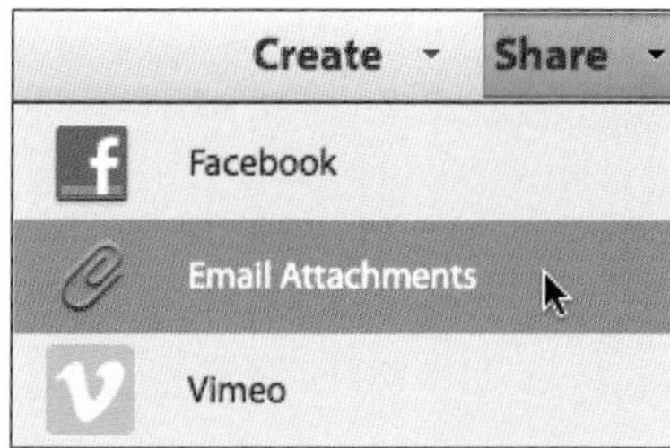

Ⓐ From the Share tab, choose Email Attachments.

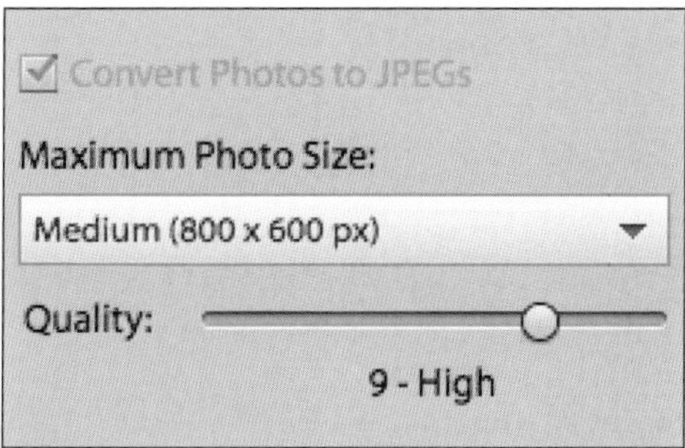

Ⓑ The Quality slider allows you to make size and quality adjustments to your image, just as you can in the Save for Web dialog.

Sending Images by Email

Elements can streamline the process of sending digital photos to family and friends. If your photo is too large or is in the wrong file format, Elements can automatically resize your image, if you prefer.

To attach a simple photo to email:

1. In the Organizer, select the photo or image you want to send.
2. Click the Share drop-down menu and click the Email Attachments button Ⓐ.
3. From the Maximum Photo Size drop-down menu, you can choose to change the size of your attachment or leave it unchanged.

   If you choose an option other than Use Original Size, use the Quality slider to control the size and download speed of your attachment Ⓑ.

   If the source image is not a JPEG file, you also have the option of converting the outgoing file by selecting the Convert Photos to JPEGs checkbox.
4. Click Next. Elements converts the images and attaches them to an outgoing message in your default email program.

Making Your Own Slide Show (Windows)

With the Windows version of Photoshop Elements, you can create a self-contained, portable slide show—a useful and elegant way to share your photos and images with friends and family.

Although Elements can output a slide show as a movie (.wmv) or even burn it to a DVD, in this exercise I'll focus on creating a slide show as an Adobe Acrobat PDF (Portable Document Format) file. The operative word here is portable. You can view a PDF file on nearly any Windows or Macintosh computer, as long as Adobe's Acrobat Reader is installed.

When you open the PDF file in Acrobat Reader, the slide show automatically opens in full-screen mode. Slides can change with a transition you select when creating the PDF Ⓐ. In an automatic slide show, the slides change at preset intervals you set when you generate the file. Alternatively, if you prefer to advance each slide manually, you can create a slide show that changes slides with keyboard commands.

Ⓐ When you create a slide show, you can specify how your slide show transitions from one image to the next. This slide show displays the Wipe Down transition, where a new image rolls down over the previous image's slide.

To create a PDF slide show:

1. In the Organizer, select one or more photos that will appear in the slide show.
2. Click the Create drop-down menu and select the Slide Show button Ⓑ.

   Click Slide Show. The Slide Show Preferences dialog opens, where you select the different options for your slide show. Here you can apply transition effects, change the background color, crop photos to fit a landscape or portrait format, and set quality options Ⓒ.

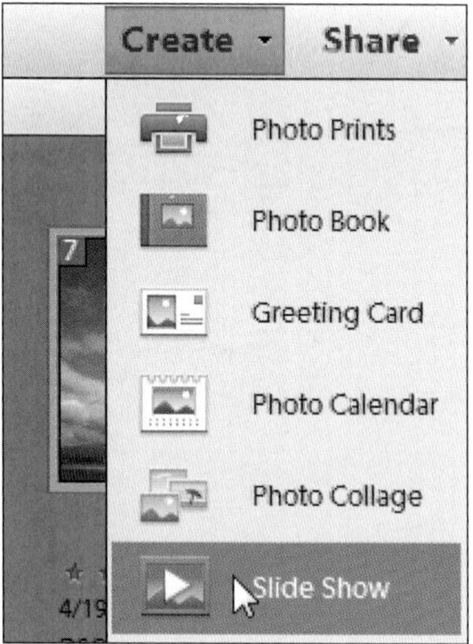

Ⓑ The Create button leads to a variety of creations.

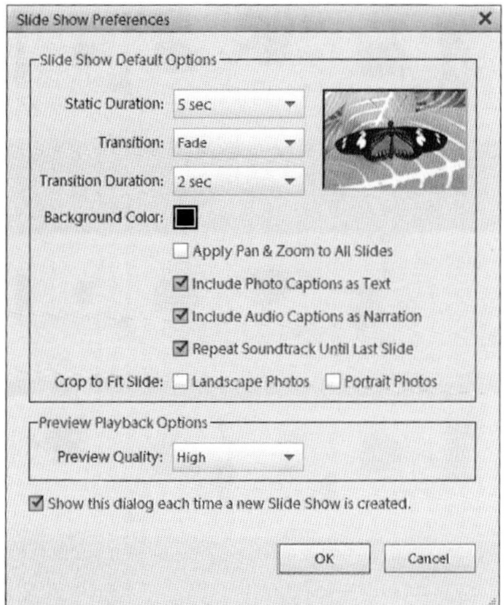

C Set options before you create your slide show in the Slide Show Preferences dialog.

D The Slide Show Editor.

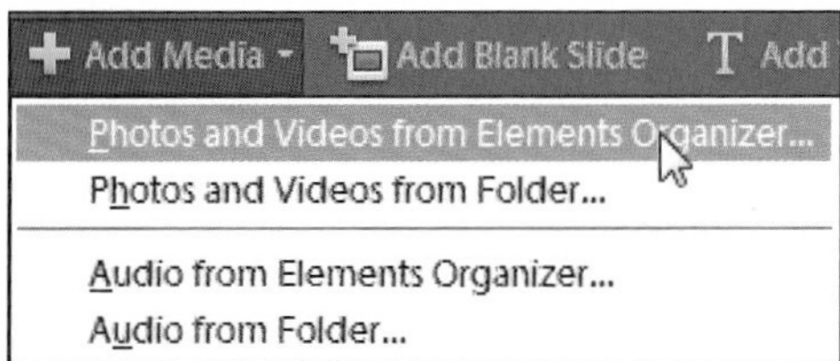

E Add photos, video, and even audio to a slide show from the Organizer or from a folder.

3. Select the options you would like to apply to your slide show, then click OK to close the dialog. The Slide Show Editor window opens **D**.
4. To preview your slide show, first click the Rewind and then the Play button below the Slide Show preview.

To add photos to the slide show:

1. Click the Add Media button above the preview window, and then choose a source for your photos from the menu **E**.

   Note that you can also add video and audio files to a slide show.
2. Click to select the photos you want to include in your slide show, and then click Done (or click Open, if your source was a folder). The Slide Show Bin at the bottom of the Slide Show Editor is populated with all of the photos and video you selected, complete with the transitions you chose from the Slide Show Preferences dialog.

TIP You can return to the Slide Show Preferences dialog at any time during the creation of your slide show by choosing Slide Show Preferences from the Edit menu.

TIP A variation of a slide show is a flipbook, which creates a movie out of images; click the Create tab and choose Flipbook from the More Options menu.

To reorder slides:

1. In the Slide Show Bin, click to select the slide you want to move **F**.
2. Hold down the mouse button and drag the slide to a different location in the Slide Show Bin.

   When you release the mouse button, the slide and its transition snap into place in the new location **G**.

   Alternately, you can click the Quick Reorder button above the Slide Show Bin so that you can see all of the slides in your slide show at once. Click and drag to move slides in the Quick Reorder window just as you do in the Slide Show Bin.

F Select a slides in the Slide Show Bin.

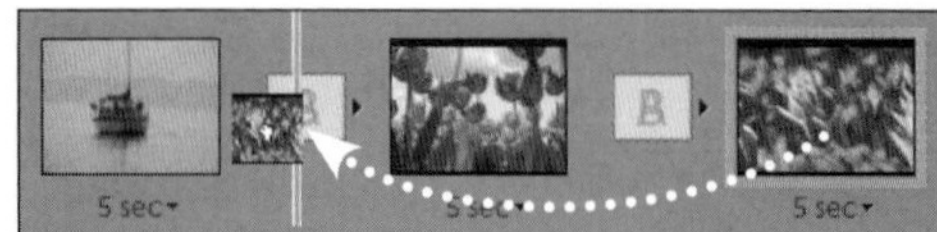

G Click and drag a slide in the Slide Show Bin to move it to a different spot in your slide show (top). When you release the mouse button, the slide and its transition snap into place.

To edit slide transitions:

1. In the Slide Show Bin, click the transition between the two slides you would like to change **H**.
2. From the Transition drop-down menu, select a new transition **I**.

   If you'd like, you can also change the duration of the transition—the amount of time it takes to transition from one slide to the next.

3. From the Duration drop-down menu, select a time, in seconds.

TIP You can apply new transition effects to more than one slide at a time by selecting multiple transitions at once. Click to select the first transition you want to change, and then Ctrl-click to select subsequent transitions. Alternately, if you want to select every transition in your slide show, choose Select All Transitions from the Slide Show Editor Edit menu.

H Click any transition to edit its properties.

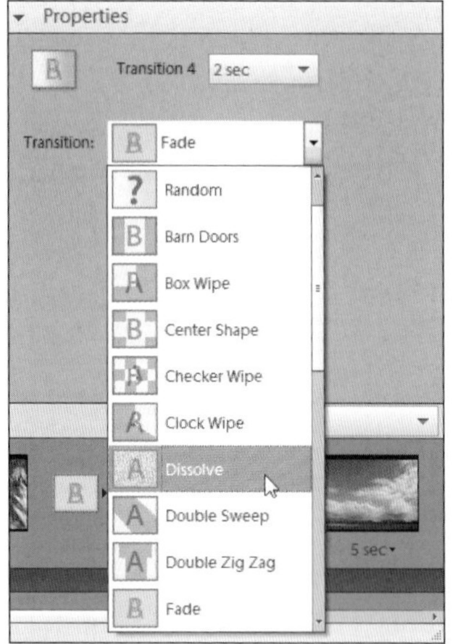

I The Slide Show Editor offers a myriad of transitions.

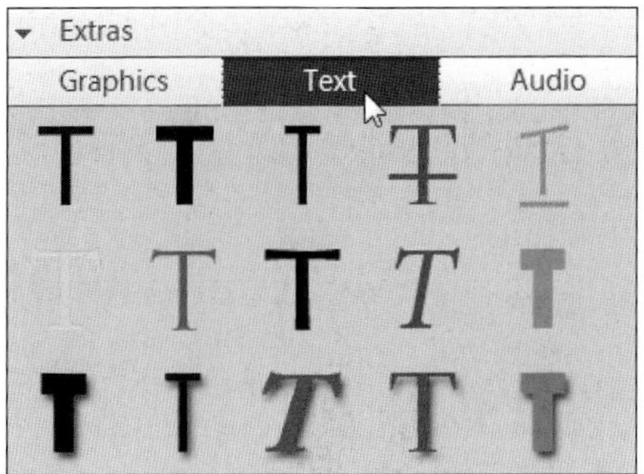

Ⓙ The Slide Show Editor offers a collection of type styles from which to choose.

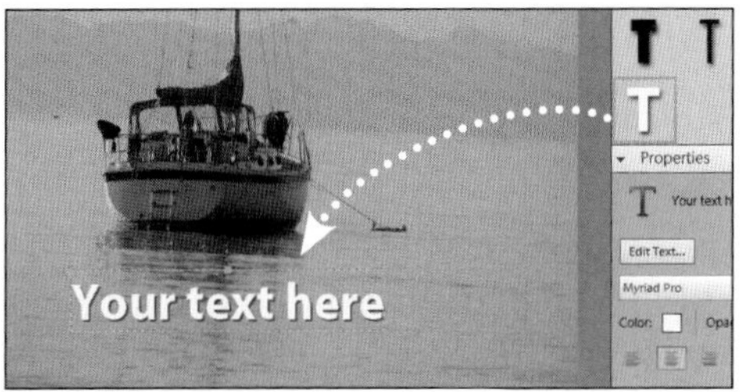

Ⓚ Drag to add a text placeholder to a slide.

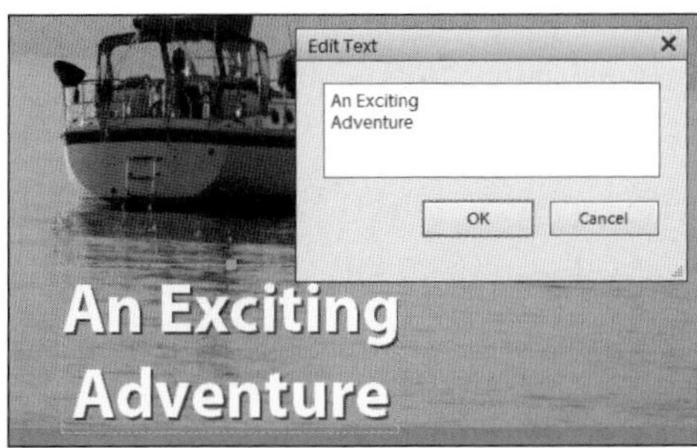

Ⓛ As you type, the text appears immediately in the Preview.

To add text to a slide:

1. In the Slide Show Bin, click to select the slide onto which you want to apply text.

   The slide appears in the Slide Preview.

2. Click the Text button in the Extras pane to open the default text collection Ⓙ; then scroll to find the text style you would like to use.
3. Drag the selected text icon directly onto the slide in the Slide Preview Ⓚ.
4. Double-click the default text in the Slide Preview to open the Edit Text box.
5. Type the text you would like to appear on your slide and then click OK Ⓛ.
6. Use the controls in the Properties area of the Slide Show Editor to change the font, size, color, and orientation of the text.
7. You can reposition the type by clicking anywhere within its bounding box and dragging it to a new location.

TIP If you want to add some whimsy to your slides, feel free to drag elements from the Graphics section of the Extras pane to the slide preview area.

TIP The Narration button in the Extras pane enables you to record audio narration that will accompany the currently selected slide.

To save a slide show:

1. Click the Save Project button (you can also choose Save Slide Show Project from the File menu, or press Ctrl+S).
2. In the Save dialog, type a name for your slide show and click Save **M**.

   Your slide show is saved to the Organizer's Photo Browser.
3. To close the Slide Show Editor, do one of the following:
   - From the File menu, choose Exit Slide Editor, or press Ctrl+Q.
   - Click the close button in the Slide Show Editor window.
   - If you want to output a slide show right away, leave the Slide Show Editor open and proceed to the next task.

To output a slide show:

1. Click the Output button near the top of the Slide Show Editor.

   The Slide Show Output window opens.
2. To output the slide show, first check that Save As a File is selected in the options column on the left side of the window **N**.
3. Choose the Movie File (.wmv) radio button to create a movie slide show; this option retains transitions, videos, and any Pan & Zoom settings.

   Or, click the PDF File radio button in the center of the window.
4. Choose the image size and other settings you would like to apply to your slide show **O**.

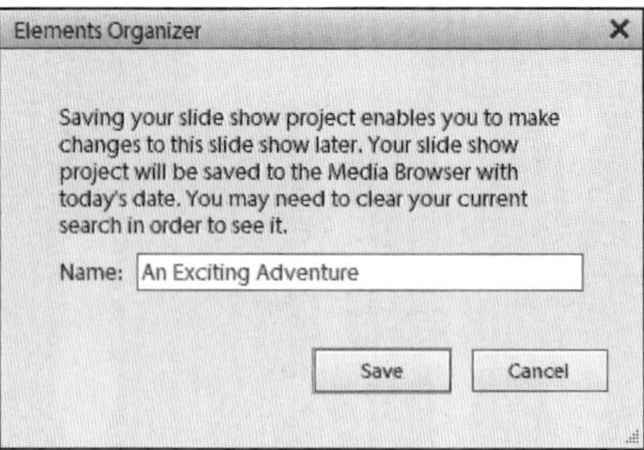

M The Slide Show Editor has its own unique Save dialog.

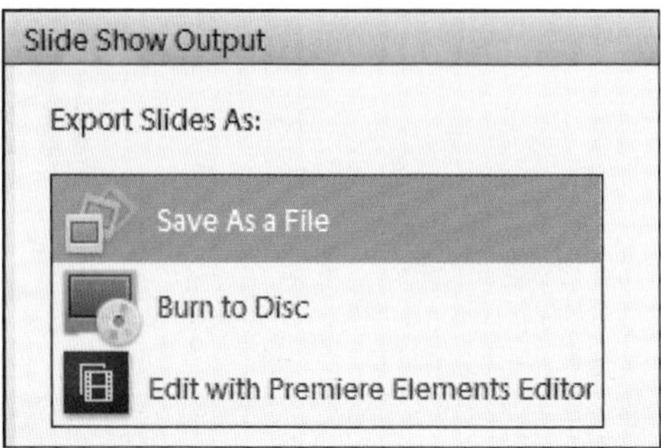

N The Slide Show Output window offers several different ways to export your slide show.

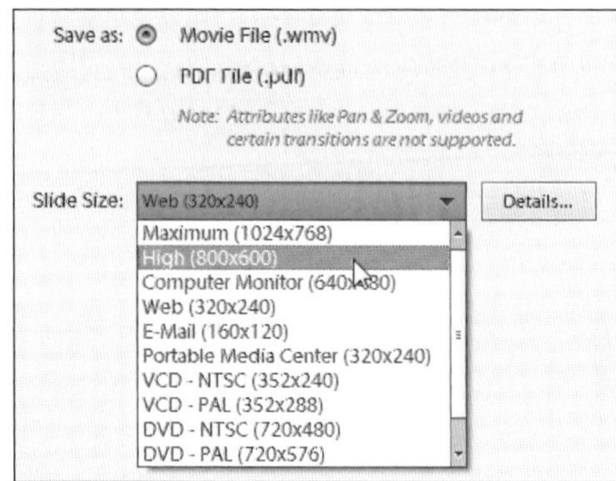

O You can export a slide show as either a movie file or a PDF.

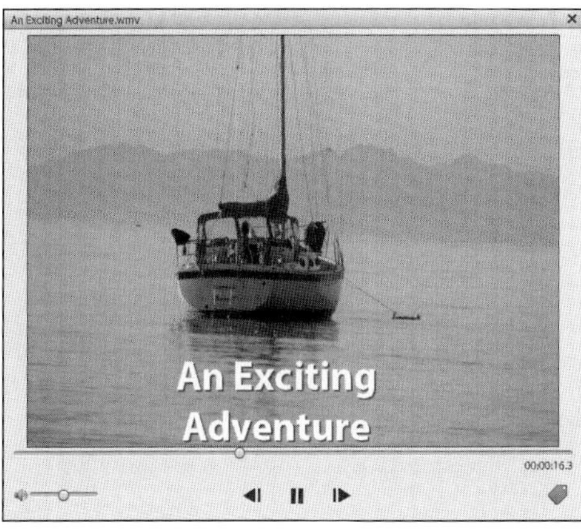

P Play a movie slide show from the Organizer.

Slide Show Options on the Mac

I wasn't entirely honest when I said the slide show feature was available only under Windows. On the Mac, you can go to the Organizer's Create pane, click More Options, and choose PDF Slide Show. But what you get is a very basic PDF file that simply displays one photo at a time if you view it in Acrobat Reader or Adobe Acrobat Pro. That's not nearly as compelling or fun to create.

Instead, I recommend saving the images you want to the hard disk, then using them to build a slide show in iPhoto or a dedicated application such as Boinx's wonderful FotoMagico (boinx.com/fotomagico/).

5. Click OK. Then, in the Save As dialog, navigate to the location where you would like to save your slide show, rename it if you would like, and click Save.
6. After creating the output file, you're asked if you would like to import the file into your catalog; click Yes or No.

To view a movie slide show:

To view a movie slide show, double-click it in the Organizer (if you opted to import it there; otherwise, open the file in Windows Explorer). The file opens, where you can play it and apply keyword tags **P**.

To view a PDF slide show:

1. Make sure Adobe Acrobat Reader is installed on your computer. If it's not, install it from the Photoshop Elements installation disc, or download it free from www.adobe.com.
2. In Acrobat Reader, open the PDF slide show you created.

   The slide show appears, taking up the full screen. If the slide show is set to run automatically, each image will be displayed for the time you set in the Slide Show dialog.
3. To navigate through your slide show, use the following keyboard commands:
   - Move forward one slide by pressing Enter or the right arrow key.
   - Move back one slide by pressing Shift+Enter or the left arrow key.
   - Exit Full Screen view and access Acrobat Reader's interface by pressing Ctrl+L.

Share with Adobe Revel

Elements ties directly into Adobe Revel, the company's product for sharing photos between applications and mobile devices. (Currently Revel is on the Mac and iOS devices, with apps for Windows and Android devices in development.)

What I like about Revel is that it's designed to let people interact with photos. You can export images from the Organizer and watch them almost immediately show up in Revel. Then a friend with access to your collection (called a "carousel" in Revel) can review, rate, and make basic edits on your photos. Those changes appear on your devices, where you can edit them or revert back to the original versions without losing any data.

Currently, Revel integration in Elements is pretty basic—you can share photos from the Organizer to a Revel carousel, and you can import photos from Revel into the Organizer. However, I'm optimistic that more capabilities will arrive in the future.

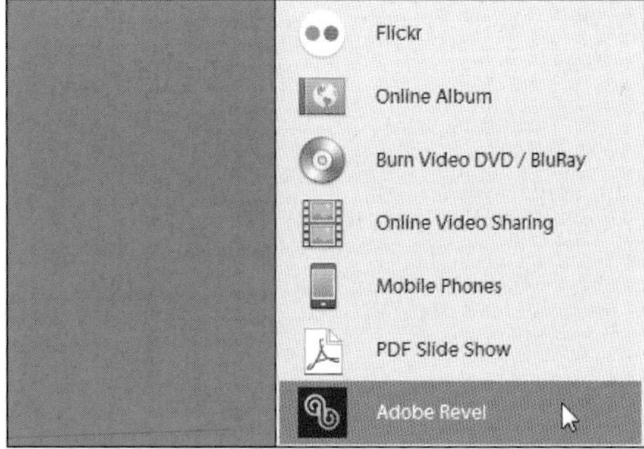

Ⓐ Share photos to Adobe Revel from within the Organizer.

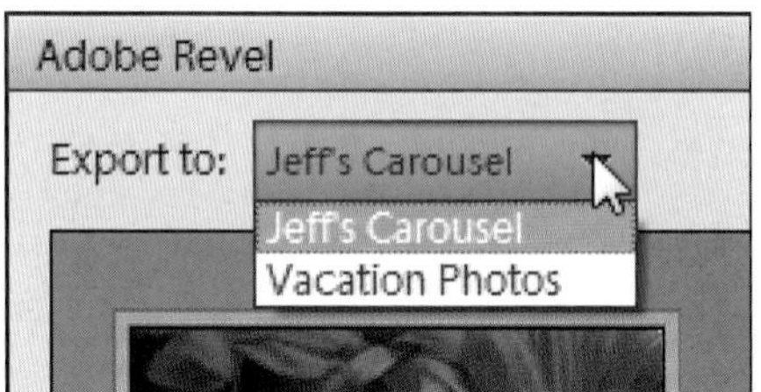

Ⓑ If you have multiple carousels, choose one.

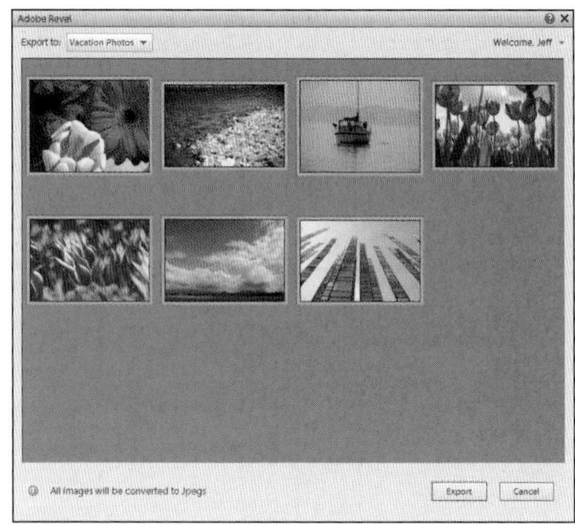

Ⓒ Upload the selected photos to Revel.

To share photos to Revel:

1. In the Organizer, select the photos you wish to export to Revel.
2. Click the Share drop-down menu and choose Adobe Revel Ⓐ.
3. If this is your first time connecting with Revel from Elements, enter your Revel login information.
4. In the Adobe Revel dialog, click the Export To drop-down menu to choose which carousel to use Ⓑ. (That might just be your default carousel. To create new ones, you need to do it in the Revel app on the computer or device.)

D Bring photos from Revel into your Elements library.

E Choose which photos to import into the Organizer.

5. If you decide you want to exclude any of the photos you initially selected, deselect it in the dialog.
6. Click Export to upload the photos **C**.

To import photos from Revel to the Organizer:

1. Click the Import drop-down menu and choose From Adobe Revel **D**.
2. In the Adobe Revel dialog that appears, choose a carousel from the Import From drop-down menu.
3. Select the photos you want to import **E**.
4. Click the Browse button to specify where the files should be saved. By default, Elements creates a new Revel folder in your computer's default pictures location.
5. Click the Import button to download the files.

TIP Revel works only with JPEG images, so any raw photos you upload are converted to JPEG format.

To edit photos in Revel:

1. On your computer or mobile device, open the Revel app.

   (For ease of description here, I'm going to refer to the iOS version. If you're viewing on a computer, substitute "click" for "tap" below.)

2. If you need to switch to a different carousel, tap the Settings button in the lower-right corner and then tap the carousel name **F**.

3. Tap an image to open it.

4. To mark the photo with a star (since Revel doesn't have a multi-star rating system), tap the star button in the lower-left corner of the screen.

5. Tap the Develop button to edit the image.

6. Using the editing controls at the bottom of the screen, do any of the following:

   - Tap the Auto button to let Revel figure out its best guess for adjustments.
   - Tap the Looks button and select an effect from the filmstrip **G**.
   - Tap the Adjustments button to expose sliders for White Balance, Exposure, and Contrast settings **H**. You can also tap the double-arrow icon in each control to reveal further adjustments. For example, the Exposure slider affects the image's overall exposure level. But tapping the arrows expands to show separate sliders for Exposure, Highlights, and Shadows.

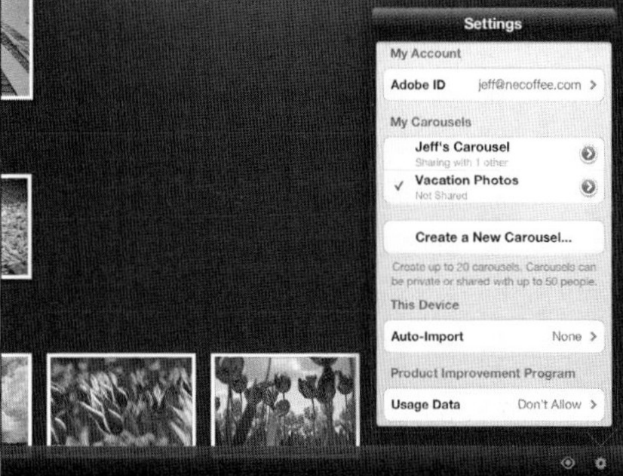

F Choose a carousel in Revel's settings.

G Apply preset looks.

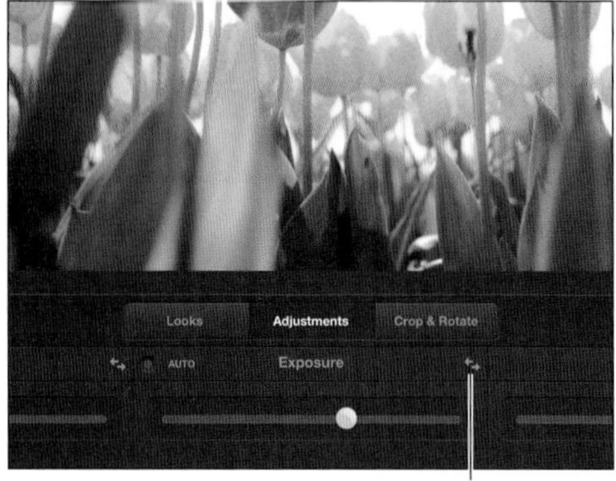

H Apply preset looks.

Ⓘ In all Revel clients, the edited version of the image appears.

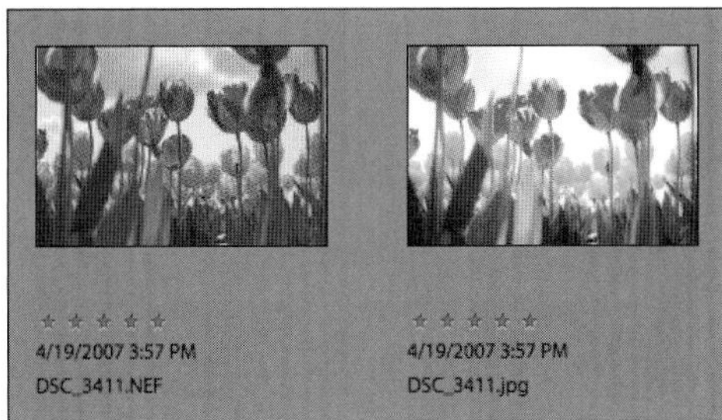

Ⓙ After re-importing the edited image into the Organizer, it shows up next to the original as a separate file.

Ⓚ Share a carousel with others.

- Tap the Crop & Rotate button to change the visible portion of the photo, rotate it in 90-degree increments, straighten it, or flip the image horizontally or vertically.
- At any time, tap the Compare button to temporarily view the original image.

7. Tap the Apply button when you're happy with the adjustments.

   The edited version is saved, and all of your Revel clients (but not Elements) appear with the updated image Ⓘ.

8. To bring the edited version into Elements, follow the instructions on the previous pages for importing images from Revel. The photo is added as a new file Ⓙ.

To revert to the original image:

1. In the Revel app on the computer, choose Edit > Revert to Original.
2. Click the Apply button.

To share carousels with friends:

1. In the Revel app, tap the Settings button.
2. Tap the details button to the right of the carousel name you want to share.
3. Tap the Add user button Ⓚ.
4. Enter your friend's email address and then tap Done.
5. Tap Done to send an invitation to join the carousel.

TIP You can delete photos and carousels, but when you do, they're removed from all devices (but not Elements) that share them.

Troubleshoot at Startup

It takes a lot of code to run an application capable of complex image manipulation, so there are bound to be some rough areas. If Elements seems just a little off to you, there are several key combinations you can press while starting the program to weed out data corruption or possible troublesome plug-ins.

From the Photoshop Elements welcome screen, do any of the following:

- Hold the Shift key and click the Photo Editor button. A dialog appears asking if you'd like to skip loading optional and third-party plug-ins. Click Yes to start the Editor with just the Elements default plug-ins enabled. This technique can help you determine if a third-party plug-in might be interfering with the Editor.
- Hold Shift and click the Organizer button to bring up the Catalog Manager dialog for managing catalogs (see Chapter 3).
- Hold Ctrl+Shift/Command-Shift and click the Photo Editor button to specify a folder to load new third-party plug-ins.
- Hold Ctrl+Alt+Shift/Command-Option-Shift and click either the Organizer or the Photo Editor button to be asked if you want to delete the program's settings file. If a preference becomes corrupted, this combination starts the application from a blank slate.
- Hold Ctrl+Alt/Command-Option and click the Photo Editor button to specify which drives to use for scratch disks (temporary storage for data that Elements uses while processing images).

Editor Keyboard Shortcuts (Windows)

TO CHOOSE A TOOL

Tools	
Move	V
Zoom	Z
Hand	H
Eyedropper	I
Marquee	M
Lasso	L
Recompose	W
Quick Selection Brush	A
Type	T
Crop	C
Cookie Cutter	Q
Straighten	P
Red Eye Removal	Y
Spot Healing Brush	J
Clone Stamp	S
Eraser	E
Brush	B
Smart Brush	F
Pencil	N

TO CHOOSE A TOOL

Tools *(continued)*	
Paint Bucket	K
Gradient	G
Shape	U
Blur	R
Sponge	O

TO CYCLE THROUGH TOOLS

Marquee tools	M
Lasso tools	L
Type tools	T
Healing Brush tools	J
Clone Stamp tools	S
Eraser tools	E
Brush tools	B
Smart Brush tools	F
Shape tools	U
Blur & Sharpen tools	R
Sponge, Dodge & Burn	O

WORKING WITH TOOLS

Marquee Tool	
Draw marquee from center	Alt-drag
Constrain to square or circle	Shift-drag
Draw from center and constrain to...	Alt+Shift-drag

Move Tool	
Constrain move to 45°	Shift-drag
Copy selection or layer	Alt-drag
Nudge selection or layer 1 pixel	Arrow key
Nudge selection or layer 10 pixels	Shift+arrow

Lasso Tool	
Add to selection	Shift-click, then draw
Delete from selection	Alt-click, then draw
Intersect with selection	Alt+Shift-click, then draw
Change to Polygonal Lasso	Click, then Alt-drag

Polygonal Lasso Tool	
Add to selection	Shift-click, then draw
Delete from selection	Alt-click, then draw
Intersect with selection	Alt+Shift-click, then draw
Draw using Lasso	Alt-drag
Constrain to 45° while drawing	Shift-drag

Magnetic Lasso Tool	
Add to selection	Shift-click, then draw
Delete from selection	Alt-click, then draw
Intersect with selection	Alt+Shift-click, then draw
Add point	Single-click
Remove last point	Backspace or Delete
Close path	Double-click or Enter

WORKING WITH TOOLS

Magnetic Lasso Tool *(continued)*	
Close path over start point	Click on start point
Close path using straight line segment	Alt-double-click
Switch to Lasso	Alt-drag
Switch to Polygonal Lasso	Alt-click

Crop Tool	
Rotate crop marquee	Drag outside crop marquee
Move crop marquee	Drag inside crop marquee
Resize crop marquee	Drag crop handles
Resize crop box while maintaining its aspect ratio	Shift-drag corner handles

Shape Tools	
Constrain to square or circle	Shift-drag
Constrain Line tool to 45°	Shift-drag
Transform shape	Ctrl+T
Distort	Ctrl-drag
Skew	Ctrl+Alt-drag
Create Perspective	Ctrl+Alt+Shift-drag

Type Tool	
Select a word	Double-click in text
Select a line	Triple-click in text
Select a paragraph	Quadruple-click in text
Select all characters	Ctrl+A
Left-align text	Ctrl+Shift+L
Center text	Ctrl+Shift+C
Right-align text	Ctrl+Shift+R
Increase by 2 points	Ctrl+Shift+ . (period)
Decrease by 2 points	Ctrl+Shift+ , (comma)
Scroll through fonts	Select font in menu+up/down arrow

WORKING WITH TOOLS

Paint Bucket Tool

Change color of area	Shift-click outside canvas

Brush and Pencil Tool

Decrease or increase size by 10 pixels	[or] (bracket keys) (or by 1 pixel when size is less than 10 pixels)

Smudge Tool

Smudge using Foreground color	Alt-drag

Eyedropper Tool

Choose Background color	Alt-click

DISPLAY SHORTCUTS

Change View

Zoom In	Ctrl+Spacebar-click/ drag or Ctrl++ (plus)
Zoom out	Alt+Spacebar-click/ drag or Ctrl+– (minus)
Zoom to 100% / Actual pixels	Double-click Zoom tool or Ctrl+Alt+0 (zero)
Zoom to fit window / Fit on screen	Double-click Hand tool or Ctrl+0 (zero)
Show/hide edges of selection	Ctrl+H
Show/hide ruler	Ctrl+Shift+R

Hand Tool

Toggle to zoom in	Ctrl
Toggle to zoom out	Alt
Fit image on screen	Double-click tool

DISPLAY SHORTCUTS

Zoom Tool

Zoom out	Alt-click
Actual size	Double-click tool

Move Image in Window

Scroll up one screen	Page Up
Scroll down one screen	Page Down
Scroll left one screen	Ctrl+page up
Scroll right one screen	Ctrl+page down
Scroll up 10 pixels	Shift+page up
Scroll down 10 pixels	Shift+page down
Scroll left 10 pixels	Ctrl+Shift+page up
Scroll right 10 pixels	Ctrl+Shift+page down
Move view to upper left	Home key
Move view to lower right	End key

MENU SHORTCUTS

File Menu

New	Ctrl+N
Open	Ctrl+O
Open As	Ctrl+Alt+O
Close	Ctrl+W
Close All	Ctrl+Alt+W
Save	Ctrl+S
Save As	Ctrl+Shift+S
Save for Web	Ctrl+Alt+Shift+S
Print	Ctrl+P
Exit	Ctrl+Q

Edit Menu

Undo	Ctrl+Z
Redo	Ctrl+Y
Cut	Ctrl+X
Copy	Ctrl+C
Copy Merged	Ctrl+Shift+C
Paste	Ctrl+V
Paste Into Selection	Ctrl+Shift+V
Color Settings	Ctrl+Shift+K
Preferences > General	Ctrl+K

Image Menu

Free Transform	Ctrl+T
Image Size	Ctrl+Alt+I
Canvas Size	Ctrl+Alt+C

Enhance Menu

Auto Smart Fix	Ctrl+Alt+M
Auto Levels	Ctrl+Shift+L
Auto Contrast	Ctrl+Alt+Shift+L
Auto Color Correction	Ctrl+Shift+B
Auto Red Eye Fix	Ctrl+R
Adjust Smart Fix	Ctrl+Shift+M
Adjust Lighting > Levels	Ctrl+L
Convert to Black and White	Ctrl+Alt+B

MENU SHORTCUTS

Enhance Menu *(continued)*

Adjust Color > Adjust Hue/ Saturation	Ctrl+U
Adjust Color > Remove Color	Ctrl+Shift+U

Layer Menu

New > Layer	Ctrl+Shift+N
New > Layer via Copy	Ctrl+J
New > Layer via Cut	Ctrl+Shift+J
Create Clipping Mask	Ctrl+G
Arrange > Bring to Front	Ctrl+Shift+]
Arrange > Bring Forward	Ctrl+]
Arrange > Send Backward	Ctrl+[
Arrange > Send to Back	Ctrl+Shift+[
Merge Down	Ctrl+E
Merge Visible	Ctrl+Shift+E

Select Menu

All	Ctrl+A
Deselect	Ctrl+D
Reselect	Ctrl+Shift+D
Inverse	Ctrl+Shift+I
Feather	Ctrl+Alt+D
Nudge selection marquee 1 pixel	Arrow key
Nudge selection marquee 10 pixels	Shift+Arrow key

Filter Menu

Last Filter	Ctrl+F
Adjustments > Invert	Ctrl+I

Organizer Keyboard Shortcuts (Windows)

MENU SHORTCUTS

File Menu

Get Photos and Videos > From Camera or Card Reader	Ctrl+G
Get Photos and Videos > From Scanner	Ctrl+U
Get Photos and Videos > From Files and Folders	Ctrl+Shift+G
Catalog	Ctrl+Shift+C
Make a CD/DVD	Ctrl+Alt+C
Copy/Move to Removable Drive	Ctrl+Shift+O
Backup Catalog	Ctrl+B
Duplicate	Ctrl+Shift+D
Rename	Ctrl+Shift+N
Move	Ctrl+Shift+V
Export As New File(s)	Ctrl+E
Set as Desktop Wallpaper	Ctrl+Shift+W
Save Metadata to Files	Ctrl+W
Print	Ctrl+P
Exit	Ctrl+Q

MENU SHORTCUTS

Edit Menu

Undo	Ctrl+Z
Redo	Ctrl+Y
Copy	Ctrl+C
Select All	Ctrl+A
Deselect	Ctrl+Shift+A
Delete from Catalog	Delete key
Rotate 90° Left	Ctrl+Left
Rotate 90° Right	Ctrl+Right
Edit with Photoshop Elements Editor	Ctrl+I
Edit with Premiere Elements Editor	Ctrl+M
Adjust Date and Time	Ctrl+J
Add Caption	Ctrl+Shift+T
Update Thumbnail	Ctrl+Shift+U
Visibility > Mark as Hidden	Alt+F2
Stack > Automatically Suggest Photo Stacks	Ctrl+Alt+K
Stack > Stack Selected Photos	Ctrl+Alt+S

MENU SHORTCUTS

Edit Menu *(continued)*

Stack > Expand Photos in a Stack	Ctrl+Alt+R
Stack > Collapse Photos in Stack	Ctrl+Alt+Shift+R
Color Settings	Ctrl+Alt+G
Preferences > General	Ctrl+K

Find Menu

By Filename	Ctrl+Shift+K
All Version Sets	Ctrl+Alt+V
All Stacks	Ctrl+Alt+Shift+S
By Media Type > Photos	Alt+1
By Media Type > Video	Alt+2
By Media Type > Audio	Alt+3
By Media Type > Projects	Alt+4
By Media Type > PDF	Alt+5
By Media Type > Items with Audio Captions	Alt+6
Items with Unknown Date or Time	Ctrl+Shift+X
Untagged Items	Ctrl+Shift+Q
Unanalyzed Content	Ctrl+Shift+Y

View Menu

Refresh	F5
Media Types > Photos	Ctrl+1
Media Types > Video	Ctrl+2
Media Types > Audio	Ctrl+3
Media Types > Projects	Ctrl+4
Media Types > PDF	Ctrl+5
Full Screen	F11
Timeline	Ctrl+L
Set Date Range	Ctrl+Alt+F
Clear Date Range	Ctrl+Shift+F
Details	Ctrl+D

MENU SHORTCUTS

Help Menu

Photoshop Elements Help	F1

NAVIGATING IN THE PHOTO BROWSER

Move Selection up/down/left/right	Up/Down/Left/Right
Show full-size thumbnail of selected photo	Enter

VIEWING PHOTOS IN FULL SCREEN MODE

Start slide show	Spacebar
Show next slide	Right/Down
Show previous slide	Left/Up
Pause slide show	Spacebar
End slide show	Esc

Editor Keyboard Shortcuts (Mac OS X)

TO CHOOSE A TOOL

Tools	
Move	V
Zoom	Z
Hand	H
Eyedropper	I
Marquee	M
Lasso	L
Recompose	W
Quick Selection Brush	A
Type	T
Crop	C
Cookie Cutter	Q
Straighten	P
Red Eye Removal	Y
Healing Brush	J
Clone Stamp	S
Eraser	E
Brush	B
Smart Brush	F
Pencil	N

TO CHOOSE A TOOL

Tools *(continued)*	
Paint Bucket	K
Gradient	G
Shape	U
Blur	R
Sponge	O

TO CYCLE THROUGH TOOLS

Marquee tools	M
Lasso tools	L
Type tools	T
Healing Brush tools	J
Clone Stamp tools	S
Eraser tools	E
Brush tools	B
Smart Brush tools	F
Shape tools	U
Blur & Sharpen tools	R
Sponge, Dodge & Burn	O

WORKING WITH TOOLS

Marquee Tool	
Draw marquee from center	Option-drag
Constrain to square or circle	Shift-drag
Draw from center and constrain to...	Option-Shift-drag

Move Tool	
Constrain move to 45°	Shift-drag
Copy selection or layer	Option-drag
Nudge selection or layer 1 pixel	Arrow key
Nudge selection or layer 10 pixels	Shift-arrow

Lasso Tool	
Add to selection	Shift-click, then draw
Delete from selection	Option-click, then draw
Intersect with selection	Option-Shift-click, then draw
Change to Polygonal Lasso	Click, then Option-drag

Polygonal Lasso Tool	
Add to selection	Shift-click, then draw
Delete from selection	Option-click, then draw
Intersect with selection	Option-Shift-click, then draw
Draw using Lasso	Option-drag
Constrain to 45° while drawing	Shift-drag

Magnetic Lasso Tool	
Add to selection	Shift-click, then draw
Delete from selection	Option-click, then draw
Intersect with selection	Option-Shift-click, then draw
Add point	Single-click
Remove last point	Backspace or Delete
Close path	Double-click or Return

WORKING WITH TOOLS

Magnetic Lasso Tool *(continued)*	
Close path over start point	Click on start point
Close path using straight line segment	Option-double-click
Switch to Lasso	Option-drag
Switch to Polygonal Lasso	Option-click

Crop Tool	
Rotate crop marquee	Drag outside crop marquee
Move crop marquee	Drag inside crop marquee
Resize crop marquee	Drag crop handles
Resize crop box while maintaining its aspect ratio	Shift-drag corner handles

Shape Tools	
Constrain to square or circle	Shift-drag
Constrain Line tool to 45°	Shift-drag
Transform shape	Command-T
Distort	Command-drag
Skew	Command-Option-drag
Create Perspective	Command-Option-Shift-drag

Type Tool	
Select a word	Double-click in text
Select a line	Triple-click in text
Select a paragraph	Quadruple-click in text
Select all characters	Command-A
Left-align text	Command-Shift-L
Center text	Command-Shift-C
Right-align text	Command-Shift-R
Increase by 2 points	Command-Shift- . (period)
Decrease by 2 points	Command-Shift- , (comma)
Scroll through fonts	Select font in menu+up/down arrow

WORKING WITH TOOLS

Paint Bucket Tool	
Change color of area	Shift-click outside canvas
Brush and Pencil Tool	
Decrease or increase size by 10 pixels	[or] (bracket keys) (or by 1 pixel when size is less than 10 pixels)
Smudge Tool	
Smudge using Foreground color	Option-drag
Eyedropper Tool	
Choose Background color	Option-click

DISPLAY SHORTCUTS

Change View	
Zoom In	Command-Spacebar-click/drag or Command-+ (plus)
Zoom out	Option-Spacebar-click/drag or Command-– (minus)
Zoom to 100% / Actual pixels	Double-click Zoom tool or Command-Option-0 (zero)
Zoom to fit window / Fit on screen	Double-click Hand tool or Command-0 (zero)
Show/hide edges of selection	Command-H
Show/hide ruler	Command-Shift-R
Hand Tool	
Toggle to zoom in	Command
Toggle to zoom out	Option
Fit image on screen	Double-click tool

DISPLAY SHORTCUTS

Zoom Tool	
Zoom out	Option-click
Actual size	Double-click tool
Move Image in Window	
Scroll up one screen	Page Up
Scroll down one screen	Page Down
Scroll left one screen	Command-page up
Scroll right one screen	Command-page down
Scroll up 10 pixels	Shift-page up
Scroll down 10 pixels	Shift-page down
Scroll left 10 pixels	Command-Shift-page up
Scroll right 10 pixels	Command-Shift-page down
Move view to upper left	Home key
Move view to lower right	End key

MENU SHORTCUTS

File Menu

New	Command-N
Open	Command-O
Open As	Command-Option-O
Close	Command-W
Close All	Command-Option-W
Save	Command-S
Save As	Command-Shift-S
Save for Web	Command-Option-Shift-S
Print	Command-P
Exit	Command-Q

Edit Menu

Undo	Command-Z
Redo	Command-Y
Cut	Command-X
Copy	Command-C
Copy Merged	Command-Shift-C
Paste	Command-V
Paste Into Selection	Command-Shift-V
Color Settings	Command-Shift-K
Preferences > General	Command-K

Image Menu

Free Transform	Command-T
Image Size	Command-Option-I
Canvas Size	Command-Option-C

Enhance Menu

Auto Smart Fix	Command-Option-M
Auto Levels	Command-Shift-L
Auto Contrast	Command-Option-Shift-L
Auto Color Correction	Command-Shift-B
Auto Red Eye Fix	Command-R
Adjust Smart Fix	Command-Shift-M
Adjust Lighting > Levels	Command-L
Convert to Black and White	Command-Option-B

MENU SHORTCUTS

Enhance Menu *(continued)*

Adjust Color > Adjust Hue/ Saturation	Command-U
Adjust Color > Remove Color	Command-Shift-U

Layer Menu

New > Layer	Command-Shift-N
New > Layer via Copy	Command-J
New > Layer via Cut	Command-Shift-J
Create Clipping Mask	Command-G
Arrange > Bring to Front	Command-Shift-]
Arrange > Bring Forward	Command-]
Arrange > Send Backward	Command-[
Arrange > Send to Back	Command-Shift-[
Merge Down	Command-E
Merge Visible	Command-Shift-E

Select Menu

All	Command-A
Deselect	Command-D
Reselect	Command-Shift-D
Inverse	Command-Shift-I
Feather	Command-Option-D
Nudge selection marquee 1 pixel	Arrow key
Nudge selection marquee 10 pixels	Shift-Arrow key

Filter Menu

Last Filter	Command-F
Adjustments > Invert	Command-I

Organizer Keyboard Shortcuts (Mac OS X)

MENU SHORTCUTS

File Menu

Get Photos and Videos > From Camera or Card Reader	Command-G
Get Photos and Videos > From Scanner	Command-U
Get Photos and Videos > From Files and Folders	Command-Shift-G
Catalog	Command-Shift-C
Make a CD/DVD	Command-Option-C
Copy/Move to Removable Drive	Command-Shift-O
Backup Catalog	Command-B
Duplicate	Command-Shift-D
Rename	Command-Shift-N
Move	Command-Shift-V
Export As New File(s)	Command-E
Save Metadata to Files	Command-W
Print	Command-P
Quit	Command-Q

MENU SHORTCUTS

Edit Menu

Undo	Command-Z
Redo	Command-Y
Copy	Command-C
Select All	Command-A
Deselect	Command-Shift-A
Delete from Catalog	Delete key
Rotate 90° Left	Command-Left
Rotate 90° Right	Command-Right
Edit with Photoshop Elements Editor	Command-I
Edit with Premiere Elements Editor	Command-M
Adjust Date and Time	Command-J
Add Caption	Command-Shift-T
Update Thumbnail	Command-Shift-U
Visibility > Mark as Hidden	Option-F2
Stack > Automatically Suggest Stacks	Command-Option-K
Stack > Stack Selected Photos	Command-Option-S

MENU SHORTCUTS

Edit Menu *(continued)*	
Stack > Expand Photos in a Stack	Command-Option-R
Stack > Collapse Photos in Stack	Command-Option-Shift-R
Color Settings	Command-Option-G
Preferences > General	Command-K
Find Menu	
By Filename	Command-Shift-K
All Version Sets	Command-Option-V
All Stacks	Command-Option-Shift-S
By Media Type > Photos	Option-1
By Media Type > Video	Option-2
By Media Type > Audio	Option-3
By Media Type > Projects	Option-4
By Media Type > PDF	Option-5
By Media Type > Items with Audio Captions	Option-6
Items with Unknown Date or Time	Command-Shift-X
Untagged Items	Command-Shift-Q
Unanalyzed Content	Command-Shift-Y

View Menu	
Refresh	F5
Media Types > Photos	Command-1
Media Types > Video	Command-2
Media Types > Audio	Command-3
Media Types > Projects	Command-4
Media Types > PDF	Command-5
Details	Command-D
Full Screen	F11
Timeline	Command-L
Set Date Range	Command-Option-F
Clear Date Range	Command-Shift-F

MENU SHORTCUTS

Help Menu	
Photoshop Elements Help	F1

NAVIGATING IN THE PHOTO BROWSER

Move Selection up/down/left/right	Up/Down/Left/Right
Show full-size thumbnail of selected photo	Return

VIEWING PHOTOS IN FULL SCREEN MODE

Start slide show	Spacebar
Show next slide	Right/Down
Show previous slide	Left/Up
Pause slide show	Spacebar
End slide show	Esc

Index

A

B

D

E

F

G

H

I

J

K

L

M

P

Q

R

S

T

U

V

W

X, Y, Z